Origen's Doctrine of Subordination

European University Studies

Europäische Hochschulschriften
Publications Universitaires Européennes

Series XXIII
Theology

Reihe XXIII   Série XXIII
Theologie
Théologie

Vol./Band 272

PETER LANG
Berne · Frankfurt am Main · New York · Paris

J. Nigel Rowe

Origen's Doctrine of Subordination

A Study in Origen's Christology

PETER LANG
Berne · Frankfurt am Main · New York · Paris

CIP-Kurztitelaufnahme der Deutschen Bibliothek

Rowe, J. Nigel:
Origen's doctrine of subordination: a study in
Origen's christology / J. Nigel Rowe. - Berne;
Frankfurt am Main; New York; Paris: Lang,
1987.
 (European university studies: Ser. 23,
 Theology; Vol. 272)
 ISBN 3-261-03537-4

NE: Europäische Hochschulschriften / 23

©Peter Lang Publishers, Inc., Berne 1987
Successors of Herbert Lang & Co. Inc., Berne.
All rights reserved.
Reprint or reproduction, even partially, in all forms such sas
microfilm, xerography, microfiche, microcard, offset strictly prohibited.
Printed by Weihert-Druck GmbH, Darmstadt (West Germany)

ACKNOWLEDGEMENTS

The author desires to express his gratitude to the University of Leeds for accepting him as an external student for the purpose of preparing the thesis now published in book form; to Dr. L.W. Barnard, formerly Senior Lecturer in Theology at the University, for the regular and painstaking help which he gave to the author as supervisor; to Dr. R.P.C. Hanson, former Professor of Theology at Manchester University, for the encouragement previously given to the author in his attempts to unravel the thought of Origen; and to Dr. Barnard and the other two examiners, Professor D.E. Jenkins and the Revd. B. Drewery, who adjudged the thesis worthy of the degree of Doctor of Philosophy.

He also wishes to thank the firm of Hodder and Stoughton Ltd. for permission to quote *in extenso* from the work of Dr. C.J. Cadoux, *The Case for Evangelical Modernism*, on p.241.

EDITIONS OF ORIGEN'S WORKS REFERRED TO

GCS (Die griecishen Christlichen Schriftsteller der ersten Jahrhunderte), Vols. 1 to 12 (Leipzig – Berlin, 1899-1959).

PG (Patrologia Graeca, J.P. Migne), Vols. XII to XIV (Paris, 1857).

The Philocalia of Origen, ed. J.A. Robinson, Cambridge, 1893.

Fragments of the Commentary on Ephesians, JTS 3 (1901-2), pp. 233-244, 398-420, 554-576.

Fragments of the Commentary on I Corinthians, JTS 9 (1907-8), pp. 231-247, 353-372, 500-514 and 10 (1908-9), pp.29-51.

Fragments of the Commentary on Romans, JTS 13 (1912), pp. 209-244 and 357-368, and 14 (1913), pp.10-22.

Conversations with Heraclides, ed. J. Scherer, Sources Chrétiennes 67, Paris 1960.

Commentaires inédits des Psaumes, ed. R. Cadiou, Paris, 1936.

A.S. (Analecta Sacra), ed. J.B. Pitra, Vol. II (1884), pp.349-483, and Vol. III (1883), pp. 1-527, 538-550.

BOOKS REFERRED TO

Bertrand F.	Mystique de Jésus chez Origène. *Paris 1951.*
Beskow P.	Rex gloriae: the kingship of Christ in the early Church. *Stockholm, 1962.*
Cadiou R.	Introduction au systeme d'Origène. *Paris 1932.*
Crouzel H.	Origène et la connaissance mystique. *Paris 1961.* Théologie de l'image de Dieu chez Origène. *Paris, 1956.*
Dupuis J.	L'Esprit et l'homme: étude sur l'anthropologie religieuse d'Origène. *Bruges, 1967.*
Eichinger M.	Die Verklärung Christi bei Origenes. *Vienna, 1969.*
Faye E. de	Origène, sa vie, son oeuvre, sa pensée, 3 vols. *Paris, 1923-1928.*
Grillmeier A.	Christ in Christian Tradition. *Tr. John Bowden, 2nd ed. London, 1975.*
Grillmeier A.	Das Konzil von Chalkedon, 3 Vols., *Wurzburg, 1951, 1953, 1954.*
Gronau K.	Das Theodizeeproblem in der altchristlichen Auffassung. *Tubingen, 1922.*
Gross J.	La divinisation du chrétien d'après les Pères grecs. *Paris 1938.*
Gruber G.	ZΩH: Wesen, Stufen und Mitteilung des wahren Lebens bei Origenes. *Munich, 1962.*

Hanson R.P.C.   Allegory and Event. *London, 1959.*

Harl M.   Origène et la fonction révélatrice du Verbe Incarné. *Paris, 1958.*

Kelber W.   Die Logoslehre von Heraclit bis Origenes. *Stuttgart, 1958.*

Koch H.   Pronoia and Paideusis. *Berlin – Leipzig, 1932.*

Lieske A.   Die Theologie der Logos-Mystik bei Origenes. *Munster, 1938.*

Marcus W.   Der Subordinatianismus als historiologisches Phänomenon. *Munich, 1963.*

Mersch E.   Le Corps Mystique de Christ. *Louvain, 1933.*

Miura-Strange A.   Celsus und Origenes: das Gemeinsame ihrer Weltanschauung. *Giessen, 1926.*

Molland E.   The conception of the Gospel in the Alexandrian Theology. *Oslo, 1938.*

Nemeshegyi P.   La Paternité de Dieu chez Origène. *Tournai, 1960.*

Nygren A.   Agape and Eros. *Tr. by P.S. Watson, London, 1953.*

Pannenberg W.   Basic Questions in Theology Vol. II. *London, 1971.*

Prat F.   Origène. *Paris, 1907.*

Rüsche F.   Blut, Leben und Seele. *Paderborn, 1930.*

Rüsche F.   Das Seelenpneuma: Seine Entwicklung von der Hauchseele zur Geistseele. *Paderborn, 1933.*

Schendel E.	Herrschaft und Unterwerfung Christi. *Tubingen, 1971.*
Temple W.	Christus Veritas. *London, 1925.*
Verbeke G.	L'Évolution de la doctrine du Pneuma du Stoïcisme à saint Augustin. *Paris – Louvain, 1945.*
Völker W.	Das Vollkommenheitsideal des Origenes. *Tubingen, 1931.*
Wintersig A.	Die Heilsbedeutung der Menschheit Jesu in der vornizänischen Theologie. *Tubingen, 1932.*

ABBREVIATIONS OF PERIODICALS

BLE	Bulletin de littérature ecclésiastique
CH	Church History
EB	Estudios biblicos
EJ	Eranos Jahrbuch
JLW	Jahrbuch für Liturgiewissenschaft
JTS	Journal of Theological Studies
M	Typescript read at Montserrat Conference
NTT	Nederlands Theologisch tijdschrift
OCP	Orientalia Christiana Periodica
RchSR	Recherches de science religieuse
RET	Revista Espanola de Theologia
RHPR	Revue d'histoire et de philosophie religieuse
RHR	Revue de l'histoire des religions
RSPT	Revue des sciences philosophiques et théologiques
RvSR	Revue des sciences religieuses
SC	La Scuola Cattolica
SJT	Scottish Journal of Theology
TQ	Theologische Quartalschrift
TSK	Theologische Studien und Kritiken
TU	Texte und Untersuchungen zur Geschichte der altchristlichen Literatur
VC	Vetera Christianorum
VS	La vie spirituelle
ZKT	Zeitschrift für Katholische Theologie

ARTICLES REFERRED TO

Aeby G.	"Les missions divines de saint Justin à Origène." *Paradosis 12, 1958, pp. 146-102.*
Armantage J.	"Origen's defence of the resurrection of the body." *M, 1973.*
Balas D.	"The idea of Participation in the structure of Origen's thought." *M, 1973.*
Balthasar H. Von.	"Le Mysterion d'Origène." *RchSR 26, 1936, pp. 513-562, and 27, 1937, pp. 38-64.*
Bardy G.	"La spiritualité d'Origène." *VS, 31 suppl., 1932, pp. 80-106.*
Boon R.	"De spiritualiteit van Origenes." *NTT 14, 1959-1960, pp. 24-56.*
Bürke G.	"Des Origenes Lehre vom Urstand des Menschen." *ZKT 72, 1950, pp. 1-39.*
Cadiou R.	"Le développement d'une théologie: pression et aspiration." *RchSR 23, 1933, pp. 411-429.*
Casel O.	"Glaube, Gnosis, und Mysterium." *JLW 15, 1941, pp. 169-195.*
Cornelis H.	"Les fondements cosmologiques de l'eschatologie d'Origène." *RSPT 43, 1959, pp. 32-80, 201-247.*
Crouzel H.	"Origène devant l'Incarnation et devant l'histoire." *BLE 61, 1960, pp. 81-110.*

D'Alès A.	"La doctrine d'Origene d'apres un livre recent." *RchSR 20, 1930, pp. 224-268.*
Daniélou J.	"L'unité des deux Testaments." *RvSR 22, 1948, pp.27-56.*
D'Hotel J.C.	"La sanctification du Christ d'après Heb. ii.11." *RchSR 47, 1958, pp. 518-525.*
Gögler R.	"Die christologische und heilstheologische Grundlage der Bibelexegese des Origenes." *TQ 136, 1956, pp. 1-13.*
Javierre A.	"Hacia una definicion plena del 'soma' origenista." *RET 9, 1949, pp. 359-411.*
Lebreton J.	"Les degrés de la connaissance religieuse d'après Origène." *RchSR 12, 1922, pp. 265-296.*
Lomiento G.	"Christo didaskalos di pochi e la comunicazione ai molti secondo Origene." *VC 9, 1972, pp. 25-54.*
Loofs F.	"Das altchristliche Zeugnis gegen die herrschende Auffassung der Kenosisstelle Phil. ii. 5-11." *TSK 100, 1927-28, pp. 1-102.*
Lot-Borodine M.	"La doctrine de la 'déification' dans l'Eglise grecque jusqu'au XIe siecle." *RHR 105, 1932, pp. 5-43, 106, 1932, pp. 525-574, and 107, 1933, pp. 8-55.*
Lowry C.W.	"Origen as Trinitarian." *JTS 37, 1936, pp. 225-240.*
Lubac H. de	"Sens spirituel." *RchSR 29, 1949, pp. 542-576.*
Macaulay W.	"The nature of Christ in Origen's Commentary on John." *SJT 19, 1966, pp. 176-187.*

Maydieu J.	"La procession du Logos d'après le Commentaire sur Jean." *BLE 35, 1934, pp. 3-16, 49-70.*
Orbe A.	"La excelencia de los profetas segun Origenes." *EB 7, 1955, pp. 191-221.*
Pollard T.E.	"Logos and Son in Origen, Arius and Athanasius." *TU 64, 1957, pp. 282-287.*
Puech H.	"Un livre recent sur la mystique d'Origène." *RHPR 13, 1933, pp. 508-536.*
Rahner H.	"Das Menschenbild des Origenes." *EJ 15, 1947, pp. 197-248.*
Rahner H.	"Die Gottesgeburt: Die Lehre der Kirchenväter von der Geburt Christi in Herzen der Glaubigen." *ZKT 59, 1935, pp. 333-418.*
Refoulé F.	"La christologie d'Evagre et l'origénisme." *OCP 27, 1961, pp. 221-266.*
Rivière J.	"Théologie du sacrifice rédempteur." *BLE 45, 1944, pp. 3-12.*
Rossi G.	"La dottrina delle creazione in Origene." *SC 20, 1921, pp. 339-357, 427-435.*
Rius-Camps J.	"Comunicabilidad de la naturaleza de Dios segun Origenes." *OCP 34, 1968, pp. 5-37, 36, 1970, pp. 201-247, and 38, 1972, pp. 430-453.*
Rius-Camps J.	"Origenes y Marcion." *M, 1973.*
Vagaggini C.	"La natura della sintesi origeniana e l'ortodossia e l'eterodossia della dogmatica di Origene." *SC 82, 1954, pp. 169-200.*
Wiles M.	"Eternal generation." *JTS 12 (New Series), 1961, pp. 284-291.*

Wilken R.L. "Tradition, Exegesis and the Christological Controversies." *CH 34, 1965, pp. 123-145.*

THESES REFERRED TO

Fitzgerald E.   Christ and the Prophets:
A study on Origen's teaching on the economy of the O.T. Dissertatio ad lauream, Pontificia Universitas Gregoriana 1956.

Extract printed under the same title, Rome 1961.

Franco R.   El final del reino de Cristo en algunos autores antenicenos:
Dissertatio ad lauream, Pontificia Universitas Gregoriana 1954.

Hirschberg M.   Studien zur Geschichte der simplices in der alten Kirche:
Ein Beitrag zum Problem der Schichtungen in der menschlichen Erkenntnis. Inaugural dissertation zur Erlangung der Doktorwürde einer hochwürdigen theologischen Fakultät der Universität zu Heidelberg 1944.

Laeuchli S.   Probleme des Geschichtlichen bei Origenes:
Thesis Union Theol. Sem., New York 1950.

Mumm H.J.   A critical appreciation of Origen as an exegete of the Fourth Gospel:
Thesis Hartford Seminary 1952.

Primmer A.   'Απάθεια und 'Έλεος im Gottesbegriff des Origenes:
Dissertation sur Erlangung des Doktorgrades an der philosophischen Fakultät der Universitat Wien 1955.

Teichtweier G. Das Sein des Menschen: Ein Beitrag zur Anthropologie des Origenes. Inauguraldissertation zur Erlangung des Doktorgrades einer Hohen Kath-Theol. Fakultät der Eberhard-Karl-Universität in Tübingen 1953.

PREFACE

This thesis is an attempt to examine and evaluate the Christology of Origen. It should not be imagined that his views are of no relevance today; on the contrary, he develops to their logical conclusions various lines of thought deriving from the traditional view of Jesus Christ as both Divine and human, and thus shows that those conclusions cannot be reconciled with each other. Perhaps he himself was unaware of this incompatibility; such is the fate of those who are the objects of adulation in their own lifetime, and against whom, therefore, no one ventures to make damaging criticisms.

The present writer has endeavoured to approach the writings of Origen with a completely open mind, so that he may assess the evidence without partiality; but in so doing he has tried to take account of the views of others who have treated of this subject. He has found the study of their writings most stimulating, and would in particular acknowledge that in one instance his attention has been drawn to an important passage regarding possible limitations in Christ's knowledge which he might otherwise have overlooked.

There is one observation which the writer specially wishes to make, and that is that it appears ludicrous to regard Origen as a devotee of Scripture. His knowledge of the Bible may well have been unrivalled, but in all honesty let us admit that he simply uses it as a peg on which to hang his own preconceived ideas. This becomes clear from the way in which he arbitrarily attaches his own meaning to many Sciptural passages which he quotes, without bothering to ascertan the meaning which the original authors attached to them.

On the other hand, let us not criticise him unduly for this seemingly cavalier attitude: after all, Scripture itself is a heterogeneous collection of books which bear abundant signs of the limited character of the outlook of their authors, and therefore we cannot construct a theology on the basis of Scripture alone. We need rather to use our minds to estimate the extent to which the witness of Scripture to theological truth is reliable. Admittedly, we, like Origen, can be regarded as under the influence of our own preconceived ideas, but this in itself is no criticism: it all depends on whether they are harmonious with one another and with the facts of which they claim to be the explanation.

LIFE OF ORIGEN

Origen was born about 185 A.D. in Alexandria, a city of Egypt, the eldest son of Christian parents. In his youth he became well versed in Scripture and in Greek philosphy. He was a great admirer of his father Leonidas, in fact so much so that his theology was influenced in the sense that he tended to think of God the Father as existing in splendid isolation from the universe. Leonidas suffered martyrdom in the persecution of the Emperor Severus, and Origen was only prevented from sharing his fate because his mother hid his clothes. At the age of 18, he started a catechetical school, that is, a centre for giving instruction to enquirers about the Christian faith. He was thus launched on his meteoric career as a lecturer and writer. He took a step, however, which he seems afterwards to have regretted, that of self-castration, partly no doubt in order to escape the sexual temptations arising from being surrounded by admiring females, partly as a result of an unfortunately worded injunction in the Gospels which would appear to recommend the adoption of celibacy from necessity rather than from choice, and partly, perhaps, in order to undergo in part the martyrdom which had been denied to him in full. This again had a profound effect on his theology, as I shall suggest at the end of my book. The bishop of Alexandria refused to ordain him to the priesthood on account of his disability, but the bishop of Caesarea in Palestine did not object to doing so, and so Origen migrated to Caesarea where he continued to write and lecture. He was cruelly tortured during the persecution of Christians by the Emperor Decius round about 250 A.D., and died a few years later at Tyre, where his splendid tomb was on view for centuries, though it has now disappeared.

GENERAL CONTENTS

Acknowledgements

Editions of Origen's works referred to — v

Books referred to — vii

Abbreviations of Periodicals — xi

Articles referred to — xiii

Theses referred to — xvii

Preface — xix

Life of Origen — xxi

Chap. I
The Relation of the Word to the Father in the process of creation — 3
APPENDIX — 17
NOTES — 19

Chap. II
The Role of the Word of God as the Agent by Whom the knowledge of God is conveyed to human beings — 37
NOTES — 53

Chap. III
The gifts which the Son receives from the Father – light, glory, wisdom, judgement — 69
NOTES — 79

Chap. IV
The gifts which the Son receives to bestow on human beings – reason, sanctification and wisdom — 87
NOTES — 95

Chap. V
  The self-humiliation of the Divine Word   105
  APPENDIX   157
  NOTES   159

Chap. VI
  The human and Divine aspects of Christ's personality   199
  NOTES   221

Chap. VII
  The eventual reconciling of human beings to the Father by
  Christ, and His consequent subjugation to the Father   233
  NOTES   267

Conclusion   287

Index of passages referred to in Origen's works   295

Index of Authors referred to   313

CHAPTER I

CONTENTS

THE RELATION OF THE WORD TO THE FATHER IN THE PROCESS OF CREATION

The knowledge we can acquire about the relation of the Son to the Father is due to the bounty of the Father alone	3
Only God Himself possesses underived existence	3
The Word acts as the Father's Agent in creation	4
Divinity is arranged in four-fold hierarchy – the Father the Son angels men	7
Christ as the Father of creation	8
Christ imposes form upon chaotic matter – cf. Plato's Demiurge	9
The Son and the Spirit are called κτίσματα and ministering creatures (λειτουργικὰ ζῷα)	10
The Word is immanent in the created universe	11
The Son is μονογενής because derived directly from the Father's being; created things derive their being from the Father through the Son	12
Suggestion that the Father created the universe directly, whereas the Son merely imparts reason to beings possessing it	14
The Son is begotten, according to Origen, in the way in which an act of will proceeds from the mind	14

2.

APPENDIX to Chapter I — 17

NOTES on Chapter I — 19

CHAPTER I

THE RELATION OF THE WORD TO THE FATHER IN THE PROCESS OF CREATION

According to Origen, such knowledge as we can acquire about the way the Son is related to God the Father, whether in His own being or in the process of creation, is due to the bounty of the Father alone. Such is the inference we draw from various passages. For instance, Origen prays the God may send to him and his readers the Divine Word, so that by the bounty of the Father they may become spectators of the depths of the being of that same Word of God.[1] In other words, the Divine Word is only able to act as a purveyor of knowledge about the nature of God because the Father has granted this power to Him.[2] In the same way, only God through His Son can explain the meaning and purpose of the created universe. In a passage in which there is clearly a play on the word λόγος, it is stated that an exact account (λόγος) of the wisdom of God displayed in creation can only be bestowed through the will of the Father of the Word (θέλοντος τοῦ Πατρὸς τοῦ Λόγου) on a ψυχή which is cleansed and aware of its own inadequacy.[3] Origen says, in fact, that the Father knows what each soul is capable of receiving, and thus understands when it is appropriate for a soul to receive the enlightenment which the Divine Word provides.[4]

It would first seem appropriate to discuss Origen's view of Jesus Christ as the Father's Agent in the creative process. Origen makes it clear in a number of passages that only God himself possesses absolute existence. The scriptural statement "There is none beside Thee" (I Sam. ii.2) is explained as meaning that no existent thing possesses existence as something natural to it. God alone possesses existence granted by no-one else; all created things possess existence by the will of their Creator. Hence because at one time we did not exist, it is not strictly true to say that we exist, so far as the time is concerned when we did not exist.[5] So also in *De Princ.* Origen affirms that "all things which exist derive their share of being from Him Who truly is, and who said through Moses "I am Who I am." [6]

It is important to recognise that "existence" means more to Origen than merely "subsisting" in the ordinary sense; it means sharing in the

Divine life in a way only possible for rational beings. In several passages Origen makes it clear that real existence is only derived from participating in the life of God.[7] There is a remarkable fragment [8] where, with reference to the verse "O let my soul live, and it shall praise Thee", Origen says that the implication is that it does not yet live, because as St. Paul says "our life is hidden with Christ in God", in the sense that in so far as we do not yet follow the guidance of the Word of God, our $\psi\upsilon\chi\acute{\eta}$ does not yet live.

And what applies to us applies also to Jesus Christ, in the sense that He derives both existence and "life" in the fullest sense from the Father alone. Thus Origen says [9] that it is no matter for wonder if the ordinary person does not know where Jesus Christ comes from; for he does not see that the Father is His root and source ($\tau\grave{\eta}\nu$ $\dot{\rho}\acute{\iota}\zeta\alpha\nu$ $\kappa\alpha\grave{\iota}$ $\tau\grave{\eta}\nu$ $\pi\eta\gamma\grave{\eta}\nu$ $\alpha\dot{\upsilon}\tau o\hat{\upsilon}$). In another passage [10] Origen says that the Father of the universe gave a share of Himself and of His greatness to His Only-begotten Son, so that He might act as the Image of the Father in His greatness as well as in other respects. Yet again, Origen says [11] that even though Christ is the equal of the Father, both the term $\gamma\acute{\epsilon}\nu\epsilon\sigma\iota\varsigma$ ("bringing into being") and the term $\gamma\acute{\epsilon}\nu\nu\eta\sigma\iota\varsigma$ ("begetting") can still be applied to Him without irreverence, because "begetting" is a special kind of "bringing into being."

But although the existence of the Son is derived from the Father, the Son is also the Father's Agent in imparting existence to all other existing beings. Thus the Word of God is spoken of as the Agent by Whom ($\dot{\upsilon}\phi$' $o\hat{\upsilon}$) all things were made. [12] It is said elsewhere [13] that though the devil may have obtained power over those whom he has not brought into being, they will eventually leave him and become followers of Jesus Christ, their Lord and Creator Who has brought them into being (*qui eos genuit*). On the other hand Origen corrects any misunderstanding of this statement by saying elsewhere [14] that strictly speaking, all things came into being $\delta\iota\acute{\alpha}$ (by means of) the Word of God, and not $\dot{\upsilon}\pi\acute{o}$ (by the agency of) the Word of God, because the ultimate Agent is a Being superior to the Word – none other, in fact, than God the Father Himself. He likewise says that even though all souls and rational beings are incorporeal so far as their own nature is concerned, they were none the less made by God through Christ. [15] (It is noteworthy that there are several passages where, in spite of what Origen says in other places, he implies that the Word of God took human nature directly upon Himself. Thus it is said that Jesus Christ "ministered to the Father in the foundation of all things" before he took human nature upon Himself.[16] In one passage [17] Origen says (with reference to John i. 15) that John the Baptist recognised that Jesus, although conceived six months after himself, was higher in rank because He was his God and δημιουργός (Creator!). In another place, [18] with reference to the devil's offer of the kingdoms of the world (Matt. iv. 10), the devil is said to be rebuked for presuming to give what the Word Himself had brought into being; in yet another, [19] with reference to the passage in Romans (viii. 32) where the Son is said to have been given up by the Father for all human beings, Origen says that if the Creator Himself is bestowed on us, surely the entire creation will be granted to us also.)

Origen makes it clear that it was by virtue of His wisdom that the Word of God created all things.[20] This wisdom was shown not just in bringing them into being, but in doing what was necessary for their welfare. In that sense the wisdom of God is shown in contriving their full development or entelechy.[21] On the other hand, there are several passages where the Father Himself is referred to as Δημιουργός.[22] The solution of the difficulty is hinted at in another passage,[23] where it is made clear that the Son of God is not the Father's servant, but His Coadjutor. If it be pointed out that the Word of God is elsewhere stated to be the ὑπηρέτης of the Supreme God,[24] the apparent contradiction is resolved by saying that the Son bears the same relation to the Father as the disciples are said by Christ to bear to Himself when He calls them not servants but friends, because He has made known to them the inner counsels of the Father.[25] Origen puts the matter in his own way when he says that although St. Paul declares the Father to be the Origin of all things and Christ to be the instrumental Cause of all things,[26] that does not mean that Christ is not on an equality with the Father, even though the Son derives His Divinity from the Father. The matter is summed up very neatly by saying that "Christ is not subordinate to the Father, even though He derives His being from the Father" (*non enim post Patrem est ipse, sed de Patre*).[27]

In fact it is true to say that in Origen's view the Son's relation to the Father is that of "right-hand man", the officer entrusted with all the plans of the director of an enterprise and given authority to carry them out, as Joseph was in Egypt as the Pharaoh's vicegerent.[28] There are various references to the Son as the Father's "right hand".[29] He acts in this capacity not only as Creator of the universe, but also as Governor and Controller of it. Thus it is said [30] that just as the Father is said to have made all things διὰ τοῦ υἱοῦ, so, although He has handed over all things to the Son, He Himself rules over all things δι' αὐτοῦ in virtue of His union with the Son. There is a striking passage [31] where the rebuke addressed to the disciples after the stilling of the storm (Matt. viii. 25) "Why are ye fearful, O ye of little faith?" is interpreted as meaning "If you have accepted Me as the God and Creator of all things, why do you not believe that I have in my power those things which I have made?" There is also a curious passage [32] where the function of feeding young birds is attributed to the Father and the Son at the same time. Origen says that if the Son is Almighty, that is, all-powerful, that is only because He shares the all-mightiness of the Father.[33]

Origen actually suggests that there are some who regard the Word of God as occupying the place of the Father Himself as the Being upon Whom the universe depends.[34] On the other hand, he himself is not always guiltless of confusing the Father with the Son, as when he says[35] that "He" (referring to Christ) gave us heaven, earth and sea for our own use, together with sun and stars, but in the fullness of time gave Himself (*semet ipsum dedit*), seeing that "God so loved the world, that He gave His Only-begotten Son" for the life of the world. He likewise says elsewhere [36] that when the Saviour says "When I receive the congregation, I will recount all Thy marvellous works", He may be teaching us about His own activities (τὰς οἰκείας ἐνέργειας) in describing the Father's nature and purpose. In another very curious passage,[37] it is suggested that when it is said that God alone made great wonders, this is said not so as to disparage the Son but to contrast Him with the demons. The implication seems to be that He and He alone gives the demons power to perform "lying wonders" (τέρασιν ψεύδους II. Thess. ii. 9), so that all that they achieve is ultimately due to Him.

There is one passage where Origen throws into sharp relief the problem of all the evil in the world.[38] He is discussing the insolence of Shimei and his hurling stones at King David. It is agreed, says Origen, that this was not the work of God. Origen considers that this is made clear by the words of David himself "Let him curse, because the Lord has spoken to him, so that He may see my humiliation, and requite me good things for his present cursing." It is thus clear, says Origen, that Shimei's behaviour did not please God; and what did not please Him, He would not have ordered anyone to do. If David said that God ordered Shimei to do these things, that simply means that He allowed him to do them. But this seems too facile a solution of the problem if we remember that according to Origen's own principles, the Word of God exercises complete control over all things, so that nothing happens without His overruling direction. It would seem better to say that everything that happens is in accordance with God's will, but that in the long run certain things which happen now will no longer happen, because God's purpose will have been fulfilled.

It ought to be pointed out that although in Origen's view the Son is the only being who shares the Father's Divinity in it's fullness, there are other beings—angels and men—who possess that Divinity in part.[39] Divinity is thus arranged in a fourfold hierarchy, in which the higher of the inferior types is surpassed by the Word of God, and the Word in turn is surpassed by the God of the universe.[40] In fact certain beings (ie. the angels) are explicitly stated to have been honoured by God with the title of "god" in so far as they partake of His Divinity.[41] In one place Origen points out that St. John inserts the definite article before the word $\theta\epsilon\delta\varsigma$ when that term refers to the $\dot{\alpha}\gamma\acute{\epsilon}\nu\eta\tau o\varsigma$ Cause of all things, but omits it when the word is applied to the $\Lambda o\gamma o\varsigma$.[42] It can scarcely be said that Origen is himself meticulous in this matter; there is a passage in *Convs. with Her.*[43] in which it is said that the offering of prayer should always be made to the Almighty God through Jesus Christ, as being related to the Father through His Divinity, and thus to God through God ($\Theta\epsilon\hat{\omega}$ $\delta\iota\grave{\alpha}$ $\Theta\epsilon o\hat{v}$). Of course this implies that the Son stands in a special relationship to the Father, and on this relationship Origen enlarges in the same treatise. He says[44] that this relationship cannot be expressed by the use of the phrase $\mu i \alpha$ $\sigma \acute{\alpha} \rho \xi$ or $\ddot{\epsilon}\nu$ $\pi\nu\epsilon\hat{v}\mu\alpha$ but in a much higher way as $\epsilon\grave{\iota}\varsigma$ $\Theta\epsilon\acute{o}\varsigma$. We must therefore safeguard both the unity and duality; the unity, in so far as we affirm the full Divinity of Christ, and the duality, in so far as we regard the Son as being distinct from the Father. (This attitude seems in contrast to that of Bishop Heraclides,[45] who affirmed that the Son of God was Divine so far as His spirit was concerned ($\theta\epsilon\grave{o}\nu$ $\mu\grave{\epsilon}\nu$ $\kappa\alpha\tau\grave{\alpha}$ $\pi\nu\epsilon\hat{v}\mu\alpha$). Such an attitude seems to imply that Jesus Christ was simply an inspired man who allowed himself to be indwelt by the Spirit of God, as indeed Origen himself tended at times to suppose in so far as he distinguished the human Jesus from the Divine Word). Origen makes an impressive statement of his doctrine of the unique Sonship of Christ when he says[46] that if God is perfect and thus always has the power of being a Father, His Fatherhood is perpetual. The Sonship of Christ however overflows to other beings, inasmuch as partial rays of the entire brightness of God's glory are bestowed on other rational creatures.[47] And so the term "gods" is applied in Scripture to other beings than the Father and the Son and in particular to the angels and to those to whom the Word of God comes, even though it is strictly speaking a misuse of the term "God" to apply it to anyone other than the Supreme Being. But the only really false use of the term is its application to the gods worshipped by the heathen.[48]

Origen regards the command referred to in Ps. cxlviii. 5 which resulted in the creation of the universe, both visible and invisible, as addressed by the Father to His Only-begotten Son.[49] (Origen here speaks of the Ultimate God as $ἀγένητος$, but this does not imply that the Son was created, because the word does not appear to have meant in Origen's time "uncreated" as distinct from "unbegotten", but simply "underived", "not brought into being."[50] Indeed, Origen insists elsewhere that the Father begets the Son and brings forth the Holy Spirit, not as beings Who did not previously exist, but simply as beings of whom the Father is the origin and source.)[51] It is worth observing that in several places Origen refers to Christ Himself as the Father of creation, in so far as He is the immediate Agent by Whom the creative activity of God is exercised. For instance, in discussing the text "He is my God, and I will honour Him: He is the God of my father, and I will exalt Him",[52] Origen declares that "our Father, Who has created us and brought us into being, is Christ,[53] the Christ Who said "I am going to my Father and your Father, to my God and your God."[54] Origen then points out that it requires a special degree of insight to understand how Christ, in order to preserve the truth that there is one fount of Deity, addresses as His God Him Whom He describes as His Father by nature.[55] Elsewhere, Christ is described not as the Father but as the Husband of the souls who have been created in His image,[56] and who can so easily go astray after false gods.[57] In yet another place He is described as the Master Whose service those created by Him forsake when they sell themselves to the devil by sinning, and Who has bought them back from that service with his own blood.[58] It is also worth observing that Christ is also called "Father", not primarily in the sense of Creator, but in the sense of Redeemer. Thus in one place [59] the apostles are compared to children in so far as they are converted by the agency of the Holy Spirit; they are in fact said to be the children whom God gave to the Saviour in accordance with the words of the prophet Isaiah.[60] Elsewhere [61]Christ is described as "the Father of the world to come"[62] in so far as He guides souls on their journey to the Father. We shall see this conception of Christ's Fatherhood more fully expressed in a later chapter.[63]

When Origen describes the method of creation, he seems to regard the Son of God as performing the role of the Demiurge or Craftsman described in Plato's *Timaeus*, in so far as He implants form upon chaotic matter in accordance with the achetypes residing in Him as the Wisdom of God.[64] Likewise in *De Princ.* Origen says that the Wisdom Who is the Son of God forms within Himself beforehand and contains the types and causes of all created nature.[65] The world is constructed in accordance with the principles (λόγους) prefigured in the Son Who is the Wisdom of God, just as a house and ship have as their source (ἀρχή) the plans and principles of the architect.[66] Origen stresses that the Wisdom of God is a separate being (ὑπόστασιν) Who contains the various conceptions (θεωρημάτων) which embrace the principles (λόγους) of all things. This is what is implied in the statement in Scripture that "God established me (ie. wisdom) as the beginning of His ways with a view to His work."[67] The created universe exists because it partakes of Divine Wisdom. Some of its components understand the wisdom which created them, but a far greater number do not.[68] Elsewhere the Word of God is said to be Himself a universe (κόσμος), in so far as the principles (λόγους) of all things reside in Him; in fact He is a more complex (ποιλικώτερος) universe than that which is apprehended by the senses, presumably inasmuch as the principles underlying the sensible universe only reveal themselves gradually.[69] In a curious interpretation of the word καταβολή as used in John xvii. 24, Origen regards the creation of the material universe as a result of the fall of immaterial spirits from a state of perfection.[70]

There is one passage in which Origen says that God the Father exercises His almighty power by means of the creative activity of the Son.[71] In another striking passage, with reference to the Gospel statement that Christ "arose and rebuked the winds and the sea" (Matt. viii.26), Origen says that it was He Who in the beginning "imposed bars and gates" and said "To this point shall you come no further, and your waves shall be broken in yourself" (Job xxxviii. 10, 11).[72] It is in this way that Origen solves the conundrum of how God could be almighty before the universe came into being; for in the Son Who is the Wisdom of God the creation was always present in form and outline.[73] This reasoning seems to us to be mere word-play; but Origen was driven to this course by an exaggerated emphasis on the changelessness of God so natural to one who had inherited the Platonic way of thinking.[74]

Origen is said by Justinian to have called both the Son and the Holy Spirit created beings (κτίσματα), and to have numbered them with other creatures, and in fact to have called them "ministering creatures" (λειτουργικὰ ζῷα). [75] We have already pointed out [76] that all that Origen need be supposed to have meant was that the being of the Son and the Holy Spirit is derived from God the Father; but Origen may also have had in mind the description of the angels as "ministering spirits" in Heb. i. 14. The angels minister to those who are destined to inherit salvation; the Son and the Holy Spirit minister to the Father in the creation of the world. Origen considers that the operation of the Son and the Spirit in the creation of the universe was indicated by the Psalmist when he declared that "by the word of the Lord the heavens were established, and all their power by the spirit of His mouth." [77] Elsewhere, with reference to the changing of the water into wine at Cana of Galilee, Origen says that Christ manifested His glory in this way, in so far as it belonged to the Creator (κτίστης) and not to a created being (κτίσμα), such as the disciples, to change the substance of the water into wine (τὸ οὐσίαν μεταβαλεῖν). [78] In yet another passage Origen says [79] that whereas heretics either deny that the Father and the Son are of one nature, or else confuse the three Divine Persons in such a way as to suggest that one God can be referred to in three ways, those who have grasped the truth on the one hand assign their respective qualities to the Father, the Son and the Holy Spirit, but at the same time declare that their substantial nature is the same; in other words, even though the Son and the Spirit act as the Father's delegates in creating and sustaining and redeeming the universe, they are not essentially inferior to Him. Such also appears to be the meaning of the curious passage [80] where Origen, in commenting on the answer given in Matt. xx. 23 to the request of James and John, says that when different levels (βαθμούς) are spoken of as existing in the Trinity, this must be understood of our own condition. For instance, if the Father is said to be greater than the Son, this statement does not apply to their own nature and substance, but to our own condition. The suggestion seems to be that though the Son and the Holy Spirit are equal to the Father in essence, they carry out His commands so far as the requirements of the created universe are concerned, whatever apparent lowering of their status this may involve, and can thus be thought of from this point of view as inferior to the Father. [81]

So far as the actual process of creation is concerned, Origen uses the passage "He spake and they were made; He commanded and they were created" (Ps. cxlviii. 5) as a means of distinguishing the creation of material substance *ex nihilo* from the imposition of the qualities whereby the original substance became differentiated into individual creatures. [82] Origen could have gone on to suggest that it was within the province of the Father alone to perform the initial act of creation, but within that of the Son to perform the second act whereby formless matter was moulded into form; but he does not in fact do this, even though such a conception would be more in keeping with his idea of the immanence of the Word of God in the universe as a privilege granted to Him by God the Father.[83]

It is by invoking this idea of the immanence of the Divine Word that Origen explains the answer addressed by John the Baptist; "There standeth one among you whom you know not", etc. (John i. 26).[84] In the same way, Origen suggests that although the prophets foretold that an "effulgence and image of the Divine nature" would enter human life together with the incarnate soul of Jesus, it would not be the case that the Word of God from Whom the Divine rays proceed existed nowhere outside the human Jesus. [85] Elsewhere, Origen describes the Divine Word as not being allotted one place like other gods in human form, but as extending over all the world ($\delta\iota\hat{\eta}\kappa o\nu$ $\dot{\epsilon}\pi\grave{\iota}$ $\pi\hat{a}\sigma a\nu$ $\tau\grave{\eta}\nu$ $o\dot{\iota}\kappa o\upsilon\mu\dot{\epsilon}\nu\eta\nu$) so as to attract to the good life by His Divinity those whom He finds inclined thereto. [86] Indeed, because the Word of God pervades the whole of creation, the creative process never ceases ($\ddot{\iota}\nu a$ $\dot{a}\epsilon\grave{\iota}$ $\tau\grave{a}$ $\gamma\iota\nu\acute{o}\mu\epsilon\nu a$ $\delta\iota$' $a\dot{\upsilon}\tau o\hat{\upsilon}$ $\gamma\dot{\epsilon}\nu\eta\tau a\iota$). [87] It is on these lines that Origen interprets the statement "He, Christ, shall be great" [88] in the angel's message to the Virgin Mary; for he explains it as meaning not only that Christ is Lord and Craftsman ($\delta\eta\mu\iota o\upsilon\rho\gamma\acute{o}\varsigma$) of all things, but also that He pervades the universe ($\dot{\omega}\varsigma$ $\delta\iota\acute{\eta}\kappa\omega\nu$ $\pi a\nu\tau a\chi o\hat{\upsilon}$).[89] There is a passage in *Comm. in Rom.* [90] where Origen makes a distinction between two different modes of the immanence of the Divine Word. With reference to the passage "There stands in the midst of you one whom you know not", he says that this is true only potentially (*possibilitate*), and not actually (*efficacia*), because those addressed are capable of apprehending Him (*possunt eum capere*), but do not apprehend Him in fact; whereas He is actually present among those of whom He said "Where two or three are gathered in My Name . . ." It must be acknowledged, however, that Origen is here faced with a dilemma, because it is doubtful whether the distinction which he makes is ultimately valid. Either the Divine Word is present or He is not. It would be better to say that while He is universally present, His presence manifests itself more clearly in some individuals and some actions than in other individuals and other actions. (The dilemma is even more apparent in another passage, [91] where Origen says that just as the animating principle of our being (ψυχή) pervades the whole extent of our body, even so nothing is empty of God. Nevertheless God does not fill the sinner, because the sinner is filled with unclean spirits, and these must be removed before God can take their place. This appears to introduce a very rigid distinction between good and evil, whereas in fact what appears to be evil may well be an essential ingredient in the production of what is supremely good).

But even though Origen is insistent on the all-pervasiveness of the Divine Word, he also insists that it is still true that it is the Father Who principally indwells the created universe, and that it is only because the Son resides in Him that the Son is allowed to permeate the whole of Creation (δι' ὅλης ἐφθακέναι τῆς κτίσεως) as a secondary Divinity (ὡς μετ' αὐτὸν δευτέρῳ καὶ θεῷ λόγῳ τυγχάνοντι). [92] This is also the implication of Origen's statement that it is "the Word of God Who embraces all things" (*sermo Dei universa complectens*) Who condemns and forbids the making of likenesses of things in heaven and on earth prohibited in the second commandment. [93]

Elsewhere, Origen points out that the Word of God fashioned the world in a different capacity from that in which He redeemed the world. He considers that St. John indicates this fact when he subjoins to the statement "In the beginning was the Word" the statement that "the Word was with God." When He came into the world at the time of the Virgin Birth, He was sent by the Father; [94] but He did not bring the universe into being as one sent by the Father; He did so rather because He shared in the Father's Divinity and acted as His Co-adjutor. [95]

Origen points out that when the Son is described as Only-begotten (μονογενής), what is meant is that the Son is derived from the Father's being; whereas created things do not derive their being directly from the Father (παρὰ πατρός), but from the Father through the Word (διὰ τοῦ λόγου). For if other things received their beginning from the Father (παρὰ πατρός), the Son could hardly be called Only-begotten, because many other beings would derive their being from the Father. Whereas the Only-begotten Son is said to be full of grace and truth (John i. 14), because He is identifiable with the things of which He is said to be full. [96] Thus Origen says that the Only-begotten Son of God, Who is His Word and Wisdom, has access to all the varied power of

God, because He is implanted in God (*pertingit et pervenit ad omnem virtutem Dei, insertus ei*). [97] Elsewhere Origen makes the same point by saying that the Only-begotten Son is Son by nature, and therefore His Sonship is eternal and unalterable; whereas others only become "sons of God" in so far as the Son of God has given them power to do so. Origen says that other sons derive their birth (ie. spiritual birth) from God, but are not born with the same birth as that with which the Only-begotten Son is born. There is as much difference between the true Son and those to whom it is said "You are sons of the Most High" as there is between the true God and those to whom it is said "I have said: you are gods." [98] Origen seems to be suggesting that it was not appropriate for the Father to perform the act of creation directly, but only by means of One Who shared His own being. At any rate, in one place [99] he says that the phrase "the firstborn of all creation" ($\pi\rho\omega\tau\acute{o}\tau\sigma\kappa\sigma\varsigma$ $\pi\acute{\alpha}\sigma\eta\varsigma$ $\kappa\tau\acute{\iota}\sigma\epsilon\omega\varsigma$) [100] is applied by St. Paul to Christ because He is the earliest of the things which God has made ($\tau\hat{\omega}\nu$ $\delta\eta\mu\iota\sigma\upsilon\rho\gamma\eta\mu\acute{\alpha}\tau\omega\nu$), and that it was to Him that God said with reference to the fashioning ($\delta\eta\mu\iota\sigma\upsilon\rho\gamma\acute{\iota}\alpha\varsigma$) of man: "Let us make man in our image and likeness." [101]

It is not however clear that even if we were to regard the Father alone as exercising creative activity, the Son would thereby be deprived of His unique relationship to the Father, in so far as the Son would be the only product of God's activity Who would be derived from His very being and so be "of one substance" with Him, to use the Nicene terminology. In fact, to insist on the creative activity of the Son makes it very difficult to separate creation from redemption, inasmuch as creation itself is a continuous process, as Origen himself admits, [102] whereby the universe is brought into the state in which the Father intends it to be. If the Son of God is thought of as active in the world only from the time of the incarnation, the process of redemption is more easily seen as supplementing and completing the process of creation. In fact in one passage [103] Origen seems to suggest that the gift of life is derived directly from the Father, because the Father imparts to others the life which is His eternal possession, with the result that they receive life as participating in it ($\mu\epsilon\tau\sigma\upsilon\sigma\acute{\iota}\alpha\varsigma$ $\tau\rho\acute{o}\pi\omega$). [104]

In a recently published book [105] it is stated that "redemption is a part of creation – it is the task of 'winning back' which is ever-present in the risk of creativity: and the Word of God by Whom the heavens were made is that same Word of God Who 'suffered to redeem our loss'." The author is driven to make redemption into one aspect of creation by identifying Jesus of Nazareth with the eternal Word of God Who is eternally active in the world of His making. It will be contended in a later chapter that in making this identification no allowance is made for the true humanity of Jesus Christ;[106] but in any case, if the Word of God is equally occupied in both creation and redemption, it becomes very difficult to think of each as a process separate from the other, because creation inevitably means "bringing new situations into being", and that is also how redemption can be described, at any rate from one point of view.

There are however certain passages where it seems to be suggested that the Son of God is not responsible for creation as such, but is simply the Giver of reason to those who are endowed with it. Thus in *De Princ.* Origen suggests that the Father is the direct Creator of the universe in so far as He "imparts to each being its existence from His own substance" (ἀπὸ τοῦ ἰδίου), whereas "the Son, being less than the Father, is concerned with rational beings alone" (φθάνων ἐπὶ μόνα τὰ λογικά).[107] But even that limitation does not altogether remove the difficulty of separating creation from redemption. A little later it is stated that "all rational creatures are partakers of the Divine Word, ie. of reason, and thus have in undeveloped form the qualities of wisdom and righteousness which are the essence of Christ",[108] and a little later still it is stated that Christ is the Word or Reason by sharing in which human beings are entitled to be called "rational."[109] In another passage it almost seems to be suggested that the real function of the Word of God is to unfold the rationality existing in undeveloped form in each human being: at any rate it is stated that the Primal Λόγος bears the same relationship to rational beings (λογικά) as the Father does to the Son Who is His Image and to the images of His Son, because the Father is the Source of Divinity and the Son of reason.[110] Elsewhere Origen says that ever since the human race began, Christ the Word or Reason of God has spoken to everyone in their hearts, and has taught them about all the virtues, and has thus proved His words "My sheep hear my voice" to be true.[111]

Perhaps the difficulty of separating creation from redemption may be to some extent solved by referring to the statement of Origen that the Father does not beget the Son by an act of separation, as the upholders of the Valentinian heresy suppose.[112] If that were so, the Son would not share the entire nature of the Father. No, the Word Who is the Wisdom of God is begotten in the way in which an act of will proceeds from the mind:[113] thus it is that the will of the Son is perfectly harmonious with that of the Father.[114] But it could surely be maintained that the method by which the Father creates other beings is analogous to the method of human pro-creation in so far as other beings display only certain aspects of the Divine Nature, and not that Nature in its entirety.[115] Even if the function of creation is reserved to the Father, none the less by asserting that the Father brings the Son into existence in a manner different from that in which He brings other beings into existence, the consubstantiality of the Son with the Father is surely safeguarded.[116] The difference between the Divine generation of the Son and human pro-creation is well brought out by a story told in the biography of Archbishop William Temple[117] of how at a conference one speaker referred to what the Bishop's "revered father" had said, and the Bishop replied that if his revered father had said it, he himself entirely disagreed with it. A human father does not transmit his entire nature to his son; both simply manifest certain aspects of human nature as such. Whereas between the Divine Father and the Divine Son there is complete identity of nature and therefore complete harmony.

APPENDIX TO CHAPTER I

ORIGEN'S VIEW OF THE INTERPRETATION OF SCRIPTURE

It is worth observing that Origen takes the same view of the way in which we can acquire a true understanding of the written Word of God as of the way in which we can understand the relationship between the Son and the Father, namely that it is only possible when God sends His Word to enable us to do this. [118] The mystical meaning hidden in the words of Scripture can only be revealed through Christ (διὰ Χριστοῦ) in the Holy Spirit. [119] The puzzling passages of Scripture can only be explained as a result of praying to God that His Word may come to us and enlighten us as to the inner meaning of the events there narrated. [120]

NOTES ON CHAPTER I

1. *Comm. in Joh.* XX.1 (GCS 4.327.9-11). Cf. *Contra Cels.* V.1 (GCS 2.2.10,11), and Crouzel, *Origène et la connaissance mystique* (Paris, 1961) p.113.
2. Cf. *Frag. in Luc.* 163.9-12 (GCS 9.293), where it is said that only God Himself can teach human beings the truth about Himself, and then only when there is worthy desire to receive it. Cf. also *Matt. Comm. Series* 28 (GCS 11.54.27-29).
3. *Hom. in Jer.* XXXIX (Philocal. JAR.33,12-17).
4. *Comm. in Cant.* I (GCS 8.92.8-13). Cf. Nemeshegyi, *La Paternité de Dieu Chez Origène*, (Tournai, 1960) p.155 and note 7 thereon. See also appendix to this chapter.
5. *Hom I in I Reg.* (GCS 8.20.16-25). Cf. Nemeshegyi, op. cit., p. 118, n.6, and Crouzel, *Théologie de L'image de Dieu chez Origène* (Paris, 1956) p.162. Cf. also *Hom. in Ps.* XXXVIII.I.10 (PG XII.1399D), and *Sel. in Ps.* XXIX.6 (PG XII.1293C).
6. I.3.6. (GCS 5.57.1-3).
7. *Contra Cels.* VI.64 (GCS 2.134.24,25); *Hom. in Ps.* XXXVI.V.5 (PG XII.1363D); *Frag. in Rom.* XXV.56-58 (*JTS* 13.361); *Comm. in Rom.* IX.2 (PG XIV.1208AB); *Frag. in Eph.* II.2-7 (*JTS* 3.235); Pitra A.S.III.34 (Ps.XXXVIII.14).
8. Cadiou, *Frag. in Ps.* CXVIII.175[a](p.119). Cf. *Comm. in Rom.* IV. 5. (PG XIV.978C). Cf. also Crouzel, *La Conn.*, p.518, and Nemeshegyi, op. cit., p.35, where stress is laid on the identity which in Origen's view exists between existence and moral goodness. God exists fully in so far as He is fully and perfectly good, and other beings only possess existence in proportion to their goodness (see p.130, op. cit). Cf. also Rius-Camps, "Comunicabilidad de la natureza de Dios segun Origenes," *OCP* 36, 1970, pp 215 and 233, and Gruber, ZΩH: *Wesen, Stufen, und Mitteilung des wahren Lebens bei Origenes* (Munich, 1962), p.38.
9. *Frag. in Joh.* LXIX (GCS 4.538.7-9).
10. *Contra Cels.* VI.69 (GCS 2.139.3-9).
11. *Frag. in Matt.* 12.1-11 (GCS 12.20).
12. *Comm. in Joh.* 1.19 (GCS 4.23.16).
13. *Hom. in Exod.* I.5 (GCS 6.153.17-21). Cf. *Hom. in Num.* XII.4 (GCS 7.104.18-22).
14. *Comm. in Joh.* II.10 (GCS 4.64.29-31). Cf. also *Contra Cels.* VI. 60 (GCS 2.130.19-25), and *Frag. in Eph.* I.2-14 (*JTS* 3.235). Cf.

also *Frag. in Luc.* 43 (GCS 9.244), where it is said (with ref. to Luke i.51) that the Son is the Arm of the Father (though the reference here is primarily to redemption, not creation). Cf. also *Comm. in Joh.* I.19 (GCS 4.23.15-18), and I.35 (4.45.11-13); *Frag. in Joh.* I (GCS 4.485.2-4); *Hom. in Gen.* I.11 (GCS 6.13. 18-19); *Hom. in Matt.* IV (GCS 12.268.31-33); Pitra A.S.III.167 (Ps.LXXXIX.4); *Hom. in Num.* XII.2 (GCS 7.98.4).

[15] *De Princ.* I.7.1. (GCS 5.86.5-9).
[16] Ibid.I.Pref.4 (GCS 5.10.6-9).
[17] *Frag. in Joh.* X (GCS 4.492.7-9).
[18] *Frag. in Matt.* 67.2,3 (GCS 12.42).
[19] *Comm. in Rom.* VII.9 (PG XIV.1129C).
[20] *Comm. in Matt.* XVII.14 (GCS 10.623.10-14).
[21] *Frag. in Joh.* I (GCS 4.485.8-12). In the Sources Chrétiennes ed. of *Comm. in Joh.* (Vol.I, p.121, cont. of n.2 on p.120) it is said that according to this passage the Wisdom of God was originally only related to God; but since that Wisdom resolved on the existence of creatures, it took on a relationship to creatures also, as is made clear in the passage in Proverbs (viii.22) where it is said that "the Lord has established wisdom as the beginning of His ways with a view to His works."
[22] *Comm. in Joh.* I.6 (GCS 4.11.18); *Frag. in Joh.* CXXVII (GCS 4.570.24,25); *Matt. Comm. Series* 45 (GCS 11.92.22-27).
[23] *Frag. in Joh.* CXI (GCS 4.564.14-16).
[24] *Comm. in Joh.* II.14 (GCS 4.71.2-11).
[25] John xv.15.
[26] I Cor. viii.6.
[27] *Comm. in Rom.* VII.13 (PG XIV.1140 C-1141A).
[28] Genesis xii.40-44.
[29] *Frag. in Lam.* XLVI (GCS 3.256.1); *Frag. in Matt.* 413.1,2 (GCS 12.172); *Sel. in Ps.* XVI.8 (PG XII.1220A); XVII.36 (1237B); XLIII.3 (1423A); XLIV.5 (1429BC); XLVII.11 (1440D); LXX. 18 (1521B); Pitra A.S.III.108 (Ps.LXXVI.16). Cf. also Pitra A.S.II.354, where with ref. to Exod.xv.6, it is said that the Son is the δεξιά χείρ of the Father Who dashed in pieces the enemy. Cf also ibid.III.99 (LXXIII.11); but it is there said that Christ is described as the χείρ of God when He takes action against the enemies of God's people, but the δεξιά of God when He confers benefits on God's people. Cf. also ibid.134 (Ps.LXXIX.18).
[30] *Frag. in Matt.* 242.2-5 (GCS 12.113). Cf. also ibid.396 1,2 (12.

168).
31 *Hom. in Matt.* III (GCS 12.258.32-259.2).
32 Pitra A.S.II.384 (in Job.xxxviii.41).
33 *De Princ.* I.2.10 (GCS 5.43.14-22). Cf. *Sel. in Ps.* XXIII.10 (PG XII.1269B); XLIX.2 (1449A); Pitra A.S.II.482 (Ps.XXIII.10).
34 *Comm. in Joh.* II.3 (GCS 4.56.7-9). Cf. also *Contra Cels.* VIII.14 (GCS 2.232.3-6), and Nemeshegyi, op. cit., p.63, n.2.
35 *Hom. in Num.* XXIV.2 (GCS 7.229.28-230.4).
36 *Sel. in Ps.* LXXIV.3 (PG XII.1533C).
37 *Sel. in Ps.* CXXXV.4 (PG XII.1656B).
38 *Frag. in II Sam. XVII* (GCS 3.300.8-16).
39 This subject is further discussed in Chapter II pp. 45-47.
40 *Comm. in Joh.* II.3 (GCS 4.57.10-12).
41 *Contra Cels.* VII.65 (GCS 2.215.13-15). Cf. *Sel. in Ps.* LXXVI.14 (PG XII.1540C). In *Comm. III in Gen.* (Philocal. JAR 210) the angels are on the contrary described as θεῖοι.
42 *Comm. in Joh.* II.2 (GCS 4.54.12-17).
43 4.24-27 (Scherer's ed., p.62).
44 Ibid.3.12-4.9. (Scherer's ed., pp.58,60,62).
45 Ibid.2.11-13. (Scherer's ed., p.56).
46 *Comm. in Gen. Tom. I. Frag.* (PG XII.45C).
47 *Comm. in Joh.* XXXII.28 (GCS 4.474.7-12).
48 *Prol. to Cant.* (GCS 8.71.4-13).
49 *Comm. in Joh.* II.14 (GCS 4.71.5-11).
50 The Son is however referred to as ἀγένητος in *Contra Cels.* VI.17 (GCS 2.88.21). On the other hand, in *Sel. in Ps.* I.2, (PG XII.1080B) He is described as γενητοῦ Θεοῦ.
51 *De Princ.* II.2.1. (GCS 5.111.28-31). Lowry on p.238 of his article "Origen as Trinitarian" (*JTS* 37(1936)) says that "in attempting to give a rational account of the pluralistic side of Christianity, and in reaching out accordingly to his native Hellenism . . . . . Origen is led unwittingly into the betrayal of the doctrine of a one only personal God." But he seems to be making an unwarrantable accusation, because orthodox doctrine does not state that God is a Person, but rather that there is one God in Three Persons.
The same criticism can be made of Vagaggini's view of Origen's subordinationism as stated on p.186 of his article "La Natura della sintesi origeniana" (*SC* 82(1954)).
Cf. Mme.Harl, *Origène et la fonction révélatrice du Verbe Incarné*

(Paris, 1958) p.354, where she says that "the subordinationism of Origen is a subordination in the hierarchical sense, not one which implies a difference of nature." In *Comm. in Joh.* II.2 (GCS 4.54.16) and *Comm. III in Gen.* (Philocal.JAR.208.32, 209.1) the Father alone is referred to as ἀγένητος.

[52] Exod.xv.2.
[53] *Pater noster, qui nos fecit et genuit, Christus est.*
[54] John xx.17.
[55] *Deum suum dicit, quem natura patrem vocat. Hom. in Exod.* VI. 2 (GCS 6.193.20-194.1).
Cf. Mme. Harl, op. cit., pp.369,370. "It is not only in relation to the Father that the notion of Fatherhood is valid. In so far as the First-born of the Father is the source of life to others, He too is Father, Father of all those to whom He imparts life, intelligence, and the other Divine attributes." See also p.370, n.112.
Cf. also Maydieu, "La procession du Logos d'après le Commentaire sur Jean" (*BLE* 35 (1934)) p.10, where it is pointed out that the Father does not create by Himself, but it is rather the Son Who is in immediate contact with the matter which has the potentiality of existing.
Christ is also referred to as the Father of created beings in *De Princ.* IV.3.7. (GCS 5.333.21-24); *Sel. in Ps.* III.2,3 (PG XII. 1120D-1121A); Pitra A.S.III.199 (Ps.CII.13).
[56] *Christum, qui eam ex initio ad imaginem suam creavit.*
[57] *Hom. in Exod.* VIII.4 (GCS 6.225.12-17); cf. also ibid. VIII.5 (228.4-11), and X.4 (250.10-14).
[58] *Hom. in Exod.* VI.9 (GCS 6.200.16-24). *Ita videtur tanquam suos quidem recepisse quos creaverat, tanquam alienos autem acquisisse, quia alienum sibi dominum .... quaesiverant.*
[59] *Comm. in Matt.* XIII.18 (GCS 10.227.2-11); cf. ibid.XIV.13 (310. 12-14).
[60] viii.18.
[61] *Hom. in Num.* XXVII.2 (GCS 7.259.1-8).
[62] Isaiah ix.6.
[63] Ch.VII, pp. 260 and 261.
[64] *Comm. in Joh.* I.19 (GCS 4.24.7-10).
[65] 1.2.3 (GCS 5.30.9-11). Cf. Maydieu, op. cit., pp.11 and 12, where it is pointed out that according to Origen, the Son of God is Wisdom in so far as He contains within Himself the archetypal

pattern of the universe, and the Logos in so far as He brings that pattern to light in the created world. Cf. Nemeshegyi, op. cit., pp.119 and 126, where the intelligible world contained in God the Son is described, and Teichtweier's thesis, *Das Sein des Menschen*, p.257.

66 *Comm. in Joh.* I.19 (GCS 4.24, 3-7). So in *Sel. in Ps.* XXIX.8 (PG XII.1296C) it is said that the causes (λόγοι) of things on the earth express the nature of the Word (λόγον) Who fashioned them.

Origen likewise states elsewhere that although human craftsmen (δημιουργοί) share the creative activity of the Divine Son, He alone can be called λόγος, because He implants in matter the principles on which the τέχνη of human craftsmen is based (*Frag. in Joh.* I (GCS 4.483.4-8)).

67 Proverbs viii.22.
68 *Comm. in Joh.* I.34 (GCS 4.43.16-30).
69 Ibid.XIX.22 (GCS 4.324.4-11).
70 Ibid. (GCS 4.324.16-25); *De Princ.* III.5.4 (GCS 5.273.17-275. 14).
71 *Per Filium etenim omnipotens est Pater* (*De Princ.* I.2.10 (GCS 5.43.4)).
72 *Frag. in Matt.* 163.1-3 (GCS 12.80).
73 *De Princ.* I.2.10 (GCS 5.42.1-4) and I.4.3-5 (65.12-68.3). To quote his exact words, *cum sapientia semper fuerit, secundum praefigurationem semper erant "in sapientia" ea, quae protinus etiam substantialiter facta sunt* (1.4.5 (68.1-3)).
It is true that Origen also considers the possibility that rational beings have existed from all eternity (*De Princ.* I.4.3 (GCS 5.66. 8-14) and I.4.5 (68.10-12)): but it seems likely that he preferred the other solution to the problem as making clearer the distinction between the Divine Word and other beings possessing reason. For a different view, see Lowry, Op. cit., pp.233,234; cf. also Cornelis, "Les fondements cosmologiques de l'eschatologie d' Origène" (*RSPT* 43,1959), p.37. Nemeshegyi in pp.113-124 of op. cit. inclines to our own view; so do Crouzel in L'Image.p.124, n.251, Dupuis in *L'Esprit de l'Homme* (Bruges, 1967) p.30, n.14, Balas in "The Idea of Participation in the Structure of Origen's Thought" (*M*, 1973) pp.6 and 7, and Bürke in "Des Origenes Lehre vom Urstand", p.6.
Lieske on p. 176 of *Die Theologie der Logos-Mystik bei Ori-*

genes (Munster, 1938), says that according to Origen, "the everlasting begetting and existence of the Son is not demanded because the Son is required as the Instrument or Workman of an everlasting creation of the world. His theological argument", says Lieske, "is quite different; Fatherhood requires Sonship, and Sonship requires the essential co-existence of the Father, without the necessity of an everlasting creation of the world being demanded as an additional presupposition of Fatherhood." (Cf. R.Boon, "De Spiritualiteit van Origenes", (*NTT* 14 (1959-1960)) p.25.) On the other hand, Lieske implies on pp.182 and 183 that Origen believed in the eternity of the world itself. So do Wintersig in *Die Heilsbedeutung der Menschheit Jesu in der vornizänischen Theologie* (Tubingen, 1932), p.74, H.Rahner in "Das Menschenbild des Origenes" (*EJ* 15 (1947)), p.204, and Hal Koch on pp.24 and 25 of *Pronoia und Paideusis* (Berlin – Leipzig, 1932), where he wrongly, in the present writer's opinion, identifies the "intelligible world" with the world of rational beings instead of with the world of concepts or archetypes existing in the Divine Mind.

Maydieu on pp.64 and 65 of op. cit. says (wrongly, in my opinion) that the Son only receives the Father's wisdom in order to bring into existence the beings whom the Father desires to create, the implication being that the Son only receives such knowledge as is essential for His creative function. But such a limited view of the Son's knowledge seems out of harmony with the main tendency of Origen's thought, which is to suppose that as the Son is of one nature with the Father, the Son receives all the knowledge possessed by the Father. On p.70, Maydieu appears to suggest that the Father would not have brought forth the Divine Word from all eternity if He had not created the world from all eternity, because the Son is merely the Father's Agent in the creation of the world (contrast Cornelis, op. cit., pp.37,38). Aeby in "Les missions divines de Saint Justin à Origène" (Paradosis 12 (1958)) pp.155 and 156, appears to take the same view. He points out on p.186 that this subordinationism goes back to the Apologist Justin, in so far as the Son is thought of as begotten by the Father for the sake of His external operations. Vagaggini on p.185 of op. cit. agrees with Aeby and Maydieu.

M.F. Wiles in his article "Eternal Generation" (*JTS* New Series 12 (1961), p.288) considers that Origen believed in the eternal

generation of the Logos and also the eternity of all spiritual beings, and goes on to say that "the idea of eternal generation as it stands in Origen's scheme of thought does not really have any effective anti-subordinationist significance at all." But surely it does, even if we suppose (wrongly, in my view) Origen believed in the eternity of created spirits. The Logos is the personification of God's wisdom, and no created spirit occupies this role.
Later on (p.291) Wiles suggests that Origen need not have felt obliged to believe in the eternal generation of the Son by a consideration of the Son in Himself, because (according to Origen) "the Son is not the truth when compared to the Father, but only a shadow and semblance of it on our behalf" (Jerome, Ep.ad Avit. 2 (GCS 5.36, lines 3-6 of notes). (Cf. Ch.III, n.47). But surely Origen is referring to the *Incarnate* Son, Who conveys the truth to human beings as fully as is possible in their state of weakness. This does not alter the fact that the Son possesses all the qualities of the Father, one of which is that of being the Truth.
Rossi, in his article "La dottrina delle creazione in Origene" (*SC* 20 (1921)), ignores the passage relating to the prefiguration of the created universe in the Word of God, and attributes to Origen the doctrine of the eternity of the created universe, or rather that of an eternal succession of created universes. He easily demonstrates (p.345 sqq.) that Vicenzi, in championing the orthodoxy of Origen in this matter, is trying to force the language of *De Princ.* to mean something other than what it appears to mean; but it is striking that when Rossi ultimately evaluates the thought of Origen, he comes to the conclusion that Origen *ought* to have held the view which Vicenzi credits him with having held, and indeed which he appears to the present writer to have in fact held, namely that the plan of the created universe existed eternally in the mind of the Creator, and that the will to create is independent of the carrying out of that will, so that the attribute of omnipotence could be safeguarded even if the universe had never been created (p.356). Rossi seems to me to have failed to prove that if Origen's doctrine were what he claims it to have been, Origen could not be called a pantheist, because a universe eternally created is really indistinguishable in thought from one which is uncreated, and in the same way although in theory the universe according to Origen is dependent on God, in fact the universe and God would be necessary to each other and explain each

other (pp.432-434).

[74] Contrast the view of W.B. Taverner as expressed in his article "Unitarian Theology in Mid-Twentieth Century" (*Faith and Freedom*, Spring, 1953), where he says; "There is no knowable God apart from His Will, and God's existence is impossible apart from His creation. He exists by and in His act. He is a Creator or nothing . . . . Man therefore is borne upon the eternal stream of the Divine Will, and since the Divine Will is formatively present everywhere, he also bears the will of God within himself. His duty . . . . is to come to some awareness of the Divine Will within him, and to enact it, as he can, in his life." Cf. also Pannenberg, *Basic Questions in Theology*, Vol.II (London, 1971), p.138, where he says that "(for the Biblical writers) God is never merely the invisible ground of present reality, but the free, creative source of the even new and unforeseen . . . .Because the freedom of God in relation to the world necessarily remains inaccessible to the inferential procedure that is fundamental to philosophical theology, neither could it grasp the fact that a special gift of God to man was necessary for the knowledge of God." On p.139 he says: "From all this it becomes evident that Christian theology can link up with the philosophical idea of God only by breaking through it at the same time"; and on p.158: "Even in early Christian theology, the inferential procedure (from effect to cause) operated as a set of prior decisions about specific essential features of the concept of God, which consequently appeared to be knowable independently of historical revelation and not in need of any critical refraction. It was not seen that a constriction of the Biblical idea of God, an abridgement of His transcendent freedom and omnipotence, would necessarily be involved in the insistent working out of the philosophical formulation of the question about God."

[75] *Ep.ad Mennam* (Mansi IX.528), quoted in GCS 5.52, lines 10-12 of note on line 1. Cf. ibid. IX.489B, quoted in GCS 5.349, lines 2 and 3 of notes, and ibid.IX.525, quoted in GCS 5.349.13, where the word κτίσμα is used of the Son.

[76] See p.

[77] *De Princ.* IV.4.3 (GCS 5.352.11-13). Origen also declares that the grace of God itself is bestowed upon mankind through the mediation of Jesus Christ, Who is described as the "minister" (ὑπηρέτου) of this boundless grace, and of the Holy Spirit (*De*

Orat. Intro. (GCS 2.297.3-6)).
[78] *Frag. in Joh.* XXX (GCS 4.506.13,14). The fact that Origen can use the word κτιστής as well as κτίσμα of the Son shows that it is no contradiction, as Lowry appears to think (op. cit., *JTS* 37, p. 239, n.1) "to attribute, as Origen did, an equal Divine essence to the Son, and, on the other hand, to subordinate Him so decidedly to the Father."
[79] *Comm. in Rom.* VIII.5 (PG XIV.1170C).
[80] *Frag. in Matt.* 404.1-3 (GCS 12.170).
[81] Cf. Ch.V, p.
[82] *De Princ.* II.1.5 (GCS 5.111.21-25).
[83] As Crouzel points out in *L'Image*, p.93, n.92. Cf. Cornelis, p.38, where he says that Origen does not base the distinction between the Persons of the Father and the Son on any difference of action, and refers to *Convs. with Heracl.* 2.26,27 (p.58, Scherer's ed.). On the other hand Cornelis appears to take a different view in op. cit., p.79, n.143. Cf. *Contra Cels.* IV.57 (GCS 1.330.22) where reference is made to the Divine Word Who changes the qualities (ποιότητας) of matter.
[84] *Comm. in Joh.* VI.38 (GCS 4.146.12-18). See Fitzgerald's comments on this passage on p.229 of his typescript thesis, *Christ and the Prophets.* Cf. also *Comm. in Joh.* VI.30 (GCS 4.140.9-13); *Contra Cels.* II.9 (GCS 1.136.14-29); ibid.V.12 (GCS 2.13.10-18); *De Orat.* X.2 (GCS 2.320.16-20). On the other hand, in *Hom. in Num.* III.2 (GCS 7.15.12-24) Origen interprets John i. 26 differently, as referring to the fact that the human Jesus always took the right course, turning neither to the right hand nor to the left, whereas His disciples, liable as they are to sin, cannot be said to "stand in the midst", but only to "have their dwelling in the midst of the people" (cf.II Kings iv.13).
[85] *Contra Cels.* VII.17 (GCS 2.168.14-23). Cf. Wm. Temple, *Christus Veritas*, (London, 1925) pp. 139-143.
[86] Ibid.VII.35 (GCS 2.186.8-11). Cf. ibid.VI.78 (2.149.35-150.6), where it is said that God has always been doing good to mankind, since nothing good has happened among men apart from the Divine Word Who has visited the souls of those who are able, if only briefly, to admit into themselves His operations. Cf. also *De Princ.* IV.4.1. (GCS 5.350.26-351.6) and *Comm. in Matt.* XIV.11 (GCS 10.302.20-24).
Cf. Nygren, *Eros and Agape*, (tr. P.S. Watson, London, 1953) p.

384, where he says that "to this end (ie. the return of all things to God) the Logos has been throughout the ages immanently active in man; to this end He has come to us in the fullness of time and become flesh."
De Faye (*Origène, sa vie, son oeuvre, sa pensée*, Paris, 1923-1928) seems to suggest (Vol.III, p.144) that it is only since the Incarnation that the Divine Word has been the Instructor and Guide of Mankind. Whereas surely according to Origen the purpose of the Incarnation was simply to enable Him to do this work more effectively. In fact, later (pp.217 and 218) de Faye quotes a passage in *Contra Cels.* (IV.3 (GCS 1.275.26-29)) which expressly states that "*at all times* God through His Word has restored to the right path those who have lent their ears to His teachings."

[87] *Comm. in Joh.* VI.38 (GCS 4.146.12-16). Cf. Pitra A.S.III. 336 (Ps.CXXXV.4), and *Comm. in Ps.* I (Philocal.JAR 39.9.16). Cf. also our Lord's statement "My Father works unceasingly, and so do I" with reference to the man healed on the sabbath day (John v.17).

On the other hand, Origen does not regard the Logos as a purely immanent principle which is the cause of all things. As Lieske says on p.214 of op. cit., "our real participation in the Divine Sonship is in no way merely deduced from the idea that we are necessary expressions of the Logos as a mere intermediary of the Father Who necessarily reveals Himself to the world." Likewise de Faye (op. cit., pp.123,124) points out the similarity between Origen's view of the Logos and that of the Stoics, in so far as both regard Him as the Divine power which pervades the universe and maintains it in a kind of tension (τόνος); but de Faye also recognises that the Logos is the Fashioner of the universe under the Father's directions (ibid., p.125).

[88] Luke i.32.

[89] *Frag. in Luc.* 24.1,2 (GCS 9.236). Cf. *Exhort.ad Mart.* 47 (GCS 1.43.12,13), where reference is made to "the all-pervading living Word" (τὸν αὐτὸν ὅλον δι'ὅλων ἔμψυχον λόγον), and *Frag. in Lam.* VIII (GCS 3.237.20-25), where the same phrase, ἔμψυχος λόγος, is used. Cf. also the striking sentence in *Hom. in I Sam.* xxviii.3-25.7 (GCS 3.290.15) "Every place desires Jesus Christ" (πᾶς τόπος χρῄζει Ἰησοῦ Χριστοῦ).

[90] VIII.2 (PG XIV.1163AB). Cf. Cadiou, *Frag. in Ps.* CXXIV.2 (p. 123), where it is said that the Lord encircles His own people, but

does not encircle those who do not know Him, but rather stands in the midst of them. Presumably this means that if they do not recognise Him, they are deprived of His protection.
91 *Frag. in Jer.* 18 (GCS 3.206.26-207.3).
92 *Comm. in Joh.* VI.39 (GCS 4.149.1-4). Cf. *Contra Cels.* V.39 (GCS 2.43.22) where Origen says that "we may call Him a second God."
93 *Hom. in Ex.* VIII.3 (GCS 6.223.2-6). Cf. *Hom. in Num.* XXIII.4 (GCS 7.216.12-30), where Origen points out that we must not take literally the statement that "God rested on the seventh day from all His works" (Gen.ii.2), because God is continually at work providing human beings with the things they need, and smiting and healing as necessary. He goes on to say that it was this activity in which Jesus Christ regarded Himself as sharing, as is clear from John v.17.
94 Cf. *Contra Cels.* II.71 (GCS 1.193.13-21), and Chapter V, p.108.
95 *Frag. in Joh.* I (GCS 4.484.29-485.4). Cf. *Comm. in Joh.* XX.18 (GCS 4.350.26-29), and *Contra Cels.* II.9 (GCS 1.136.5,6), where it is said that when the Word was commanded, He made everything that the Father enjoined upon Him. Cf. also ibid.II.31 (GCS 1.158.27-30).
96 *Frag. in Joh.* IX (GCS 4.490.20-491.1). Cf. *Contra Cels.* III.34 (GCS 1.231.7,8), where the Son is described as midway between the nature of the underived God and that of derived beings (μεταξὺ ὄντος τῆς τοῦ ἀγενήτου καὶ τῆς τῶν γενητῶν πάντων φύσεως). Cf.also Nemeshegyi, op. cit., p.75.
97 *De Princ.* II.8.5 (GCS 5.163,4-6).
98 *Frag. in Joh.* CIX (GCS 4.563.6-13). The Scriptural reference is to Ps. lxxxii.6.
99 *Contra Cels.* V.37 (GCS 2.41.20-25).
100 Col.i.15.
101 Gen.i.26.
102 See p. 11.
103 *Frag. in Joh.* II (GCS 4.486.3-9).
104 W. Marcus in his book *Der Subordinatianiusmus als historiologisches Phänomenon* (Munich, 1963) (pp.157-160) well illustrates, with reference to various passages discussing whether it is lawful to pray to the Son, the difficulty in which Origen involves himself by thinking of the Word of God as both Divine and human. On the one hand, the Word of God cannot be thought of as

essentially subordinate to the Father, because He shares the Father's nature; but on the other hand, as Man, He is obviously subordinate. The question is, is not Origen trying to have it both ways?

The same difficulty is brought to light on p.161 of op. cit., where the author says that in the order of creation, not only the world of rational beings but the entire created universe is subordinated to the Divine Word and governed by Him. On the other hand, in the process of redemption the Word of God has a special relationship to rational beings, a relationship which is much more restricted and abbreviated than His function as Creator, but one which is calculated to bring the entire world process to its fulfilment.

While what the author says may be true, it seems doubtful whether the distinction made between the sphere of activity of the Word as Creator and His sphere of activity as Redeemer can be rigidly maintained without making Him into two Persons instead of one, because it is the same Word of God Who according to Origen performs both functions.

[105] W.H. Vanstone, *Love's Endeavour, Love's Expense* (Darton, Longman & Todd, 1977), p.70.

[106] See Ch.V, pp.154-156.

[107] *De Princ.* I.3.5 (GCS 5.55.4-56.3). Cf. also *Comm. in Joh.* II.35 (GCS 4.94.12-15), and Kelber, *Die Logoslehre von Heraclit bis Origenes*, (Stuttgart, 1958) p.242. (On the other hand there is a passage in *Contra Cels.* (VI.71 (GCS 2.141.22-25)) where it is stated that the Word of God extends not only to human beings but also to the minutest of things made, so that all things may occur by means of the Word (ἵνα πάντα διὰ λόγου γίνηται).

Cf. also Mme. Harl, op. cit., p.371 where she says that the mediation of the Son is *eternal*, seeing that the totality of Divine attributes present in Him is the means of access to the Father; *historic* as the result of His various manifestations, especially the Incarnation; and *individual*, by His presence as intelligence in each human being.

J. Dupuis also discusses *De Princ.* I.3.5 in op. cit., pp.111-116 but tries to protect Origen against the accusation that he is ascribing a greater dignity to the Holy Spirit than to the Father and the Son, in so far as he thinks of the Spirit as conferring holiness, by saying that according to Origen, true existence is only possessed by those who are holy (cf.pp.3 and 4 of the present work),

and true reason only by the person who lays himself open to the action of the Divine Word. Cf. also Balas, op. cit., pp.12-14, and J. Rius-Camps "Comunicabilidad de la natureza de Dios segun Origenes", *OCP* 36 (1970),p.247, where he says that "in contrast to primary being, which is common to all creatures, Divine being does not come to us immediately from God. God, even if He brings into existence all that truly 'is', does so 'by means of' the Word Who is Wisdom 'in' the Holy Spirit."
Cf. also Lieske, op. cit., pp.156 and 157, where he discusses the Son as the Source of reason in created beings. To quote his own words: "Human beings are in possession of their faculty of reason in so far as the absolute Reason (Logos) exists personally within them, and they are thus as it were partial rays of the essential Brightness of the Father which flows through them."
Prat in his work on Origen (Paris, 1907) also discusses (pp.64 sqq.) *De Princ.* I.3.5, and interestingly enough says that "in describing the operation peculiar to each of the three Divine Persons and the kind of inequality which results, Origen speaks as the other Fathers do. But more often than not, he forgets or neglects these subtle distinctions."

108 *De Princ.* I.3.6. (GCS 5.56.20-57.1).
109 Ibid. (5.57.10,11). Cf. also *Comm. in Joh.* I.37 (GCS 4.47.29-48.4).
110 *Comm. in Joh.* II.3 (GCS 4.55.15-21). Cf. also ibid.II.2 (54.18-22), where it is pointed out that the Divine λόγος is the Source of λόγος (reason) in all rational beings. Cornelis, op. cit., p.62, n.9, refers to the second passage, but also points out that the image of God present in all rational beings is only operative in those who also participate in the Holy Spirit.
111 *Comm. in Rom.* VIII.5 (PG XIV.1167B).
112 *De Princ.* IV.4.1 (GCS 5.348.7,8): υἱοῦ γίνεται πατήρ, οὐ προβαλὼν αὐτόν, ὡς οἴονταί τινες.
113 Ibid. (5.349,7-9): *velut si voluntas procedat e mente*, and ibid. (349.11): οὗτος δὴ ὁ υἱὸς ἐκ θελήματος τοῦ πατρὸς ἐγενήθη. Cf. also *Frag. in Joh.* CVIII (GCS 4.562.16-25).
114 Cf. Nemeshegyi, op. cit., pp.84-91.
115 Cf. the observation of Eusebius in *De eccl. theol.* (GCS Euseb.4. 174.21-23), where he says that God will be all in all at the final consummation in so far as He will make Himself available to all to the extent that the ability (δύναμις) of each can partake of His

Divinity; and again (175.30-34) that God will be all in all inasmuch as He will supply to all, in accordance with the ability of each to receive them, the different aspects (ἐπινοίας) of His Divinity, even though He will reserve for His Only-begotten Son the distinctive and paternal glory and honour and kingship which are incommunicable to the rest.

116 Cf. *Frag. in Heb.* (PG XIV.1307C), where Origen refers to the passage in Wisdom (vii.25) where Wisdom is described as "a most pure effluence" *(aporrhaea)* of the glory of the Almighty, and says that an *aporrhaea* appears to be ὁμοούσιος with that body from which it proceeds, from which it follows that there is one substance common to the Father and the Son. It is interesting to observe that the same word ὁμοούσιος is used by Origen in his account of Heracleon's interpretation of the sentence "You are of your father, the devil" (John viii.44), in so far as according to Heracleon the men addressed are of another nature (οὐσία) than those called ψυχικοί or πνευματικοί (*Comm. in Joh.* XX.20 (GCS 4.352.29-35)). It is worth pointing out that Heracleon would be able to defend his assertion by quoting the words of Christ which follow: "It is your will (θέλετε) to carry out the desires of your father", just as Origen himself regards the uniqueness of the generation of the Son of God as proved by the identity of His will with that of the Father.

Cf. also *Sel. in Ps.* XXXIII.2 (PG XII.1308A), where Christ is described as ἀμετάπτωτος, "unchangeable."

Cf. also Crouzel, *L'Image*, p.105, n.164: Mme. Harl, op. cit., p. 370, n.113; Rius-Camps, Comunicabilidad, *OCP* 34, 1968, pp.10, 11.

117 p.325 of F.A. Iremonger's biography of William Temple.
118 *Hom. in Jos.* VIII.2 (GCS 7.337.6-11). Cf. *Comm. in Cant.* III (GCS 8.208.1,2), where he says: "Let us call upon God, the Father of the Word, that He may reveal to us the secrets of His Word." Cf. also *Hom. in Jos.* XVII.3 (GCS 7.405.19-22), where Origen prays that God may give us His Word as a lamp to our feet and a light for our path, that Word being Jesus Christ, the Light of the world.

Cf. also the statement of Gregory Thaumaturgus that "the same grace is necessary to him who prophesies and to him who hears the prophet, and no-one can understand the prophet if the Spirit Who prophesied does not impart this understanding" (*In Ori-*

genem orat. paneg. 15 (PG X.1093)).
Likewise in treating of prayer, Origen says that one needs the Father to enlighten, the Son to teach, and the Spirit to work within us in order to enable us to understand this subject (*De Orat.* II.6 (GCS 2.303.17-20)).

[119] *Comm. in Joh.* I.15 (GCS 4.19.32-34).
[120] *Frag. in Lam.* CXXV. (GCS 3.278.4-9).

CHAPTER II

CONTENTS

THE ROLE OF THE DIVINE WORD AS THE AGENT BY WHOM THE KNOWLEDGE OF GOD IS CONVEYED TO HUMAN BEINGS

The Father alone makes plans; the Son announces them	37
The Word of God is unique among all words as being self-subsistent	44
The Son reveals the Father by creating the universe in the Father's likeness	45
The Son imparts Divinity to other beings after receiving it Himself	45
The Son is the Archetype from Whom the likeness of other beings to God is derived	47
The goodness of the Father is merely imparted to the Son	50
The vision of God gained through the incarnate Christ is only partial	51
NOTES on Chapter II	53

CHAPTER II

THE ROLE OF THE WORD OF GOD AS THE AGENT BY WHOM THE KNOWLEDGE OF GOD IS CONVEYED TO HUMAN BEINGS

Origen regards the Son not only as operating in the creation of the universe, but also as announcing God's plan in creating the universe. The visions of truth which are contained in the Father's mind are conveyed to the Word of God, Who in turn passes them on to those to whom the Father deigns to grant them. [1] There is, however, an important difference between the Father's mode of communicating His thoughts to the Son and the Son's mode of passing them on to others. The Son possesses all the knowledge which the Father possesses because of His unique status as the Word Who was always with God, whereas the Word only communicates that knowledge piece-meal to the prophets and others as occasion requires. [2] There is a striking passage [3] in which Origen says that only Jesus Christ, on whom the Spirit of wisdom rested, could show forth the mighty acts of the Lord, and only the Word Himself can make audible the praises of God, by transforming those praises, which were formerly merely intelligible, into words and the things signified by words. Some of those praises have already been heard, but others may remain to be heard.

Origen lays great stress on the fact that God's message is mediated to the prophets through Christ. [4] There is one passage where it is suggested that the Mediator of that message is not the Word of God, but the human soul which was inseparably united to Him. [5] Fitzgerald makes much of Origen's insistence in this passage that when the Divine Word visited the prophets, He was already united to a human soul and therefore acted by means of that soul; [6] but this suggestion on Origen's premises is unnecessary, because if that soul itself did not need any intermediary between itself and the Divine Word, it would seem to follow that the prophets did not need one either. When Fitzgerald tries to solve the problem of the "apparent fluctuation in Origen's doctrine concerning the source of the prophets' illumination and sanctification" (ie. between attributing them to the Word alone and to the Word united to a human soul) by invoking the principle of the *communicatio idiomatum*, [7] so that operations referred to the Word of

God can by implication be understood of His human soul also, he seems open to the charge of special pleading. It is more natural to suppose that Origen did not really know his own mind on this matter, as on others.

There is a passage which puts forward a doctrine which we shall discuss more fully later, [8] namely that although the prophets themselves understood what the Word of God revealed to them, they did not impart that knowledge in such a way as to be fully understood by their contemporaries and those who followed them. Such is the implication of the passage [9] where it is said that "even though the Saviour came after the law and the prophets, He took precedence of them in so far as He fulfilled them by revealing the Divine element within them, and also in so far as He was revealed as the cause of the divinely inspired writings of the Old Testament." The same implication seems to be contained in another passage [10] where, with reference to Matthew ix.37,38, Origen says that in calling His Apostles reapers, Christ showed that what the prophets brought about (ie. the preparation of the chosen people for His coming) came about through His own power and assistance, because He, as Lord of prophets and apostles alike, had sown the seeds of which the disciples were to reap the harvest.

There are also two passages where Origen appears to interpret the words in John i.16 "Of His fullness have we all received, and grace for grace" ($\chi \acute{\alpha} \rho \iota \nu$ $\mathring{\alpha} \nu \tau \acute{\iota}$ $\chi \acute{\alpha} \rho \iota \tau o \varsigma$) as meaning that the prophets received an initial revelation from the Divine Word because they were predisposed to do so, and a second and clearer one as a consequence of the former by God's free gift. In one passage, [11] after saying that Abraham saw "the day of Christ" even in his own lifetime (cf. John viii.56), Origen says that the prophets first obtained an introduction through symbols ($\mathring{\epsilon} \nu$ $\tau o \hat{\iota} \varsigma$ $\tau \acute{\upsilon} \pi o \iota \varsigma$) to the truth residing in Jesus, and then obtained a full vision of it through the guidance of God's Spirit. [12] In another passage [13] where the virtue of faith is discussed, it is said that a person first possesses faith as a result of free choice ($\pi \rho o \alpha \iota \rho \epsilon \tau \iota \kappa \hat{\omega} \varsigma$) and then obtains a greater measure as a result of asking God for it as the Apostles did.

But quite apart from the revelation of God which the Word gave to the prophets, that same Word of God acted in other ways so as to guide the nation of Israel to its appointed destiny. There is a memorable passage [14] in which Origen says that if the Lord had done nothing before His incarnation for the salvation of Israel, He would scarcely have said "How often would I have gathered thy children" (Matthew xxiii.37). He goes on to say that this text must be employed against those who would separate the Divinity (τὴν θεότητα) from the flesh of Christ and separate the Old from the New Covenant. Reference is made in various passages to specific visits by the Word of God to Old Testament personages: to Abraham and Sarah to give them a son;[15] to Jacob at Peniel when He wrestled with him; [16] to Moses when he was bidden to flee from Egypt; [17] to Moses directing him to instruct the Israelites to sacrifice the Passover Lamb as a foreshadowing of His own sufferings; [18] to Elisha in order to enable him to cure Naaman the Syrian of his leprosy. [19] With specific reference to the salvation of the Israelites from Egypt, it is stated that it was the Divine Word Who said to the Hebrews when they were terrified of the advancing Egyptians: "The Lord will fight for you, and you will keep silence" (Exod.xiv.14). [20] H. de Lubac is simply reproducing the thought of Origen when he says [21] that "there is an internal continuity and a genuine bond between the Old and the New Covenants, because of the same Divine Will which is at work in both, pursuing stage by stage the same design. If, recalling the events of the desert and the 'spiritual rock' from which the Israelites drank, St. Paul could say, 'That rock was Christ', that is because the event of the desert already proceeded under a supra-temporal impulse towards the event of Easter, and would only find its true meaning in that event." In fact de Lubac observes [22] that we here join the thought of Origen, who saw the prefiguring of the New Covenant in the very means of preparing for it.

Origen seems on the whole to regard the Jewish prophets as gifted with a special degree of insight in so far as they were granted a full awareness of the New Covenant, even though they lived under the Old Covenant. [23] Thus in one place [24] he says that even though the Father can only be satisfactorily approached through Christ, none the less even before the Incarnation the prophets worshipped God in an acceptable manner because they apprehended the as yet unseen Christ. [25] Origen likewise says [26] that it was through the Divine Word Who came to them that they were able to utter the heavenly truths which they saw and heard with the eye and ear of the inward man. Origen in fact considers that there was a mystical union between the prophets and the Christ Whom they foretold. He considered that even the saints who lived before the Incarnation could speak of themselves as being "crucified with Christ", and could say that their life was the life of Christ in them, seeing that they had been spiritually buried with Christ and raised up with Him.[27] They were thus enabled to understand the mysteries of the Godhead, because the Word of God taught them these mysteries even before His Incarnation. Inasmuch as they saw the Son, Who is the image of the invisible God, they are recorded as having seen and heard God Himself.[28]

Mrs. Williamina Macaulay poses the question [29] why according to Origen there should have been an Incarnation, seeing that the pre-Christian saints were taught by the Word of God in His pre-incarnate state, and answers it by saying that the Incarnation was needed by the state of the world, sunk as it was in sin. But the reply could be made that even in the Christian era there are many unbelievers, and many Christians who do not according to Origen pass beyond the stage of apprehending Christ as a man rather than as the Divine Word.[30]

Fitzgerald makes a similar point in suggesting [31] that "this very distinction between the two economies of Christ (ie. His activity in His pre-incarnate state and His activity in His incarnate state) tends inevitably to lessen Origen's emphasis on the Incarnation; Christ's 'economy in the flesh' is no longer for him, as it is for Irenaeus, the sole economy of the God-Man."

On the other hand, Origen at times betrays an uneasy awareness that he may be making too sharp a distinction between the prophets and other Jews by assuming that the prophets had a clearer insight into what they were foretelling than we have any right to assume. In one place, indeed, he says that the prophets anticipated the Christian dispensation in so far as they lived not under law, but under faith, and had thus escaped from the state of transgression in which all lay who lived under the law.[32] But elsewhere he says that if those who lived before Christ's coming were partakers of the Holy Spirit, they did not partake as believers ($\dot{\omega}\varsigma$ $\pi\iota\sigma\tau o\acute{\iota}$), because they were not raised to the rank of adopted sons and thus still had the "spirit of slavery" (Rom. viii.15).[33] In another passage [34] Origen expounds this point of view more fully by saying that it was indeed true that God entered into a special relationship with Abraham, Isaac and Jacob, and also with prophets such as Elijah, but it was also true that until the Resurrection He was not their Father as well as their God.[35]

On the whole, however, Origen takes the view that Abraham and the prophets anticipated the Incarnation. He thus interprets the passage "Many prophets and kings have desired to see the things which you (the apostles) see" (Luke x.24) by saying that there were some righteous men and prophets who like Abraham "saw the day of Christ and rejoiced" (John viii.56) and thus anticipated the disciples, whereas others who were of inferior insight and perception did not attain to this state of bliss.[36] Elsewhere he says that we must not deduce from the statement that "no one knows the Father except the Son and him to whom the Son chooses to reveal Him" that the Father was unknown to the Old Testament saints, because the statement can refer to the past as well as to the future. Moreover, when Christ said "Before Abraham was, I am", He made it clear that when He said "Your father Abraham saw my day and rejoiced", His meaning was that that He revealed Himself to Abraham during Abraham's earthly life.[37] In a rather odd passage, Origen points out that when God promised Abraham that He would give the Promised Land to him and to his seed (Gen.xiii.15), Abraham himself understood "his seed" to refer to Christ, and is therefore said by St. Paul to have "given glory to God" (Rom.iv.20), not so much for the birth of Isaac as because he realised that the Christ was going to be born out of his purified and sin-free body.[38] Origen likewise says that when Abraham was ordered to offer up Isaac, he not only believed that God would raise him from the dead, but also saw in this event a foreshadowing of the Resurrection. That is one way of interpreting the text "Your father Abraham saw my day and rejoiced." Abraham's faith in fact anticipated the Resurrection of Christ, whereas the faith of believers is posterior to it *(quod ille futurum credidit, a nobis creditur factum)*.[39]

There are two very puzzling passages in *Comm. in Joh.* where the uncertainty of Origen's thought becomes very apparent in the matter of the degree of spiritual discernment in Abraham and the prophets. In the first,[40] with reference to the Psalmist's statement "Be still, and know that I am God" (Ps.xlv.11), Origen says that this was addressed to a people (ie. the Jews) who believed in God as Creator ($\delta\eta\mu\iota\text{ου}\rho\gamma\acute{o}\nu$), and that it is not possible to progress from faith to knowledge without inward purification. At the same time, it is made clear in Scripture that no one knows the Father except the Son, whereas it is also stated that it was Abraham's *belief* in God which was reckoned to him for righteousness. The suggestion seems to be that full knowledge of God had to wait for the revelation given in the incarnate life of Christ.[41] In the second passage,[42] Origen refers to the two Scriptural passages "The harvest is plenteous, but the labourers are few" (Matt.ix.37) and "He that reapeth receiveth wages, and gathereth fruit unto life eternal, that both he that soweth and he that reapeth may rejoice together" (John iv.36). He suggests that the sowing and reaping – which of course he interprets as the preaching of the Word and the conversion of those to whom it is preached — were not confined to the Christian era, but went on in Old Testament times, because it would be absurd to suggest that such people as Abraham and Moses and the prophets did not hear the Word of God and impart it to others; and so, says Origen, the incarnate life of Christ simply continued a process which had already been going on beforehand. Likewise in a *Frag. in Luc.*, [43] where Origen makes a distinction between "knowing God" and "believing in God", he asserts that it is heretical to assert that Abraham believed in God without knowing Him as Father. [44]

But even if Abraham and the prophets anticipated the Incarnation, their message was not so clearly proclaimed that others were able to receive the knowledge which they possessed. To such lengths must Origen go in order to assert the continuity between the Old and the New dispensations! There is a passage in which he says that though Moses and the prophets sowed the Word of God (cf. John iv.36), they wrote what they did write, not for the benefit of their contemporaries, but for our benefit, because their message, described by Origen in St. Paul's words as the mystery which in other generations was not made known to the sons of men but has now been revealed to God's holy apostles and prophets (cf. Ephes.iii.5), had to await the bodily appearance of Jesus Christ in order to be fully understood. [45] In a striking metaphor, Origen says that in Christ the true light shone upon the field where the prophetic seeds had been sown, and thus made the fields "white to harvest" (John iv.35). Again, Origen says [46] that Moses had a spiritual perception of the truth underlying the Jewish law and of the allegorical meaning of the historical events he recorded, and that Joshua was better able than we are to understand the truths which his achievements foreshadowed. In other words, the fully mature men of earlier generations received from Christ the same instruction in "the ineffable mysteries of religion" (τὰ ἀπόρρητα τῆς θεοσεβείας μυστήρια) as the Apostles did. Origen goes on to say quite roundly [47] with reference to Rom.xvi.25,26 that if the mystery originally hidden was revealed to the Apostles through the prophetic writings, it follows that though the prophets understood what they were saying, their contemporaries did not. [48]

In another passage [49] Origen seems to suggest that although it might appear that Moses and the prophets did not know God as Father, it may be that even though, left to themselves, they would not have known God as Father but simply as Master (δεσπότου), none the less, because they were acquainted with Christ, they were acquainted with the Father also.[50] He goes on to suggest that even though the prayers recorded in the Old Testament writings are not directed to God the Father,[51] that does not prove decisively that they had to wait till the Incarnation for the spirit of adoption; it may rather have been the case that they experienced the intelligible coming (ἡ νοητὴ ἐπιδημία) of Christ and thus received the spirit of adoption, but none the less did not through their writings allow others to become aware of this, because otherwise the incarnate Christ would not have had the opportunity to pour out His grace upon the whole world.[52]

In one place [53] Origen explains the appearance of Moses and Elijah with the transfigured Christ as indicating that the glory of the Law and the Prophets only appeared with the glorification of Christ, because only as the result of the removal of the veil of the letter could the Law and the Prophets be understood in a spiritual fashion. This seems to mean that the visible glorification of Christ was a parable of the spiritual glorification which results from His being recognised as no mere man, but as the Word of God. Elsewhere[54] Origen interprets the Transfiguration (with reference to John iv.36) as a kind of harvest in which the sowers who were Moses and Elijah, and the reapers who were the Apostles, rejoiced together in so far as both sowers and reapers rejoiced at seeing the glory of the Son of God. It might appear that this passage contradicts the former in so far as it implies that Moses and Elijah themselves had not previously seen the glory of the Son of God: but it may simply mean that only at the time of the Transfiguration did they behold the outward glory which was symbolic of the invisible glory of the Word of God. In a difficult passage in *Frag. in Lam.*,[55] where Lam.iv.20, "Under His shadow we shall live among the nations", is quoted, it is stated that "the breath of our countenance" (πνεῦμα τοῦ προσώπου ἡμῶν) referred to in the first part of the verse is none other than Christ, in so far as Christ bestows the grace (χάρισμα) which makes prophecy possible, the "shadow" being the Law which dimly adumbrates the mysteries expounded in prophecy. He then says that Christ is not only the Inspirer of the prophets but also the Goal of prophecy.[56]

There is however one passage[57] in which Origen finally succumbs to the recognition that the prophets cannot really be assumed to have been on an intrinsically higher spiritual level than their contemporaries, but like them had to wait till the Incarnation for a full and final revelation of the Divine nature.[58] Once more he refers to John iv.36, and points out that it would be unfair if only the reaper received the wages of the harvest and the fruits thereof, so that it must be assumed that in order that both sower and reaper may rejoice, the sower must share in both these things. If the sowers are Moses and the prophets, and the reapers are the Apostles, the message of Moses and the prophets was the seed sown, that message being necessarily somewhat enigmatic, and requiring to be understood in a spiritual manner. But the Apostles did more than understand this message; through the help of the incarnate Christ, they were introduced by the message of the prophets to still more profound and varied truths, and these truths were the harvest which they reaped. But it was also the case that Moses and the prophets reaped the same harvest, because they too benefited from the special (ἐξαιρέτου) coming of Christ into the world in the form of a servant in order to reveal things hitherto unknown. [59] Another passage [60] underlines this attitude, inasmuch as Origen there says that the ancients who lived under the Law possessed only a partial knowledge of the Trinity, because the Incarnation had not occurred in their time. Granted, they believed in the Incarnation and believed in and proclaimed the gifts which it was intended to bestow, but they could not see and obtain the things in which they believed, as is clear from Luke x.24, because their faith had not been brought to perfection by the Incarnation. [61]

From what has been said about God's self-disclosure through the Son in various ways, it is evident that we speak of "the Word of God", we have in mind something different from the words we speak to convey our thoughts to others. We have in mind One through Whom God's wisdom is displayed, just as when we speak of "the powers of God", we have in mind those beings, of whom the Saviour is the chief, through whom the power of God is exercised. [62] Origen likewise says elsewhere that the Word of God has characteristics which distinguish Him from all other words, namely that of being Divine, that of being alive and subsistent, and that of ministering to the Father. [63] Again, Origen says that the true followers of Christ do not include those who suggest that the Father and the Son are one person (τῇ ὑποστάσει ἕνα) and only distinguish the one underlying reality (τὸ ἓν ὑποκείμενον) in respect of aspects (ἐπινοίᾳ) and names. [64] Again, he says that the Word of God in His entirety (ὁ πᾶς δὴ τοῦ θεοῦ λόγος), Who was in the beginning with God, is not a multitude of words (οὐ πολυλογία ἐστίν); for He consists, not of words, but of concepts (θεωρημάτων), each of which is part of the total Word of God. [65] In fact, since all concepts are contained in the Saviour, it may be that certain concepts cannot be comprehended by beings brought into existence other than Himself (τῇ λοιπῇ παρ' αὐτὸν γεννητῇ φύσει), and that He keeps the knowledge of these to Himself.[66] The suggestion seems to be that as He is of one substance with the Father, beings inferior to Him are incapable of receiving all the knowledge which He shares with the Father; indeed for one brief moment Origen doubts whether even the Son Himself is completely conversant with the thoughts of the Father.[67]

But it is also true that the universe itself bears, however imperfectly, the impress of the Father, in so far as created things are fashioned in His likeness, not directly, but through the agency of the Son, Who is *par excellence* the Image of the Father.[68] It is said in one place that God is seen in bodily substances by means of the Word (διὰ τοῦ Λόγου) if from the beauty of created things their Originator is discerned.[69] But more often it is rational beings who are said to be made in the Divine image, [70] as in the passage where Christ is said to have been brought into being in the image of God and then rational beings are said to have been brought into being in that image, and Christ is said to have left for their sakes the Father with Whom He was when He was in the form of God, so that He might be joined to those who had fallen to the material level of existence.[71] Origen explains his meaning in more detail in another passage, [72] where he takes account of the danger apprehended by some of so magnifying the Son as inadvertently to assert the existence of two Gods. The result is that these people are guilty either of denying the separate existence of the Son (this is Sabellianism) or else of denying His full Divinity (this is Arianism). [73] Whereas Origen claims that a distinction can be made between the underived Divinity of God the Father (Who can thus alone be called ὁ θεός) and the divinity of other beings, including God the Son Himself, to whom, strictly speaking, only the word θεός can be applied, inasmuch as their divinity is something imparted to them.[74] The Son, Who is termed by St. Paul "the First-born of all creation"[75] (Col.i.15), was the first to receive the Father's Divinity, and then imparted it to others to whom the word θεός is applied. This statement might appear to be inconsistent with another passage [76] in which it is stated that those who are called "gods" in heaven and on earth are so called because of their participation in Divinity (μετουσίᾳ θεότητος), whereas the Saviour is God not by participation, but in His own nature (οὐ κατὰ μετουσίαν ἀλλὰ κατ' οὐσίαν); but H. Crouzel seems right in pointing out [77] that the inconsistency is more apparent than real, because the manner in which the Son receives the Father's Divinity may not be the same as that in which created beings receive it. This thought is more explicitly expressed by D. Balas [78] when he distinguishes between what he terms "horizontal" and "vertical" participation. The same thought seems to be expressed in another passage of Origen, [79] where it is said that no human being, even if he speaks the words of God, possesses the Spirit of God otherwise than in part; whereas the Saviour, Who Himself speaks the words of God on earth, does not receive the Spirit Himself in order to impart it to others, but imparts it rather as One Who is Himself the fount ($\pi\eta\gamma\eta$) of the Spirit. This presumably means that Christ, in so far as He possesses the nature of the Father, also possesses the Spirit as an inherent endowment, not a transitory gift.

Thus there are many beings deserving of greater honour than men, and these beings can be called "gods", though they are not the gods worshipped by the heathen. Human beings should try to attain to the likeness of these beings, in so far as they manifest the goodness which is characteristic of God Himself. [80] In fact Origen even asserts that Jewish legislators were called "gods" because of the purity of their character. [81] The angels themselves are called "gods", though not in the sense that they deserve our worship, even though they convey to us the benefits which God wishes to bestow upon us. [82] Again, Origen refers to beings who by the agency of the Divine Word have been granted the privilege of sharing in the Divine nature and are thus granted the name of "gods." [83] Similarly, in discussing the sentence in Exodus "Who is like unto Thee, O Lord, among the gods?" (xv.11), he says that reference is here made to those who are called "gods" by virtue of their participation in Divine grace, [84] as is also done in Ps.1xxxii. 1,6. But, he says, though they are capable of receiving the grace of God, [85] none of them resembles God in essence or in power. In fact he compares the relation between them and God to the relation between a picture and the living being whose characteristics it reproduces. [86] Likewise, in discussing the commandment "Thou shalt have none other gods but me", Origen explains [87] that, as St. Paul says, there are those who are called "gods" (I Cor.viii.5,6), but are only allowed that name because the supreme God has appointed them as governors of peoples other than His chosen people. They have in fact been created by the supreme God, and this name "gods" comes to them, not by nature, but by grace. [88] Indeed, in *Hom. in Jos.* Origen speaks of Jesus Christ, "the captain of the Lord's host" (cf.Josh.v.14), as having brought into being all heavenly and earthly potentates and as having invested them with their spheres of government.[89]

There is a notable passage in *Comm. in Joh.* [90] in which we are reminded that on one occasion Moses was called by God to stand "on the rock" (Exod.xxxiii.21). Origen identifies the rock with Christ, and therefore with the truth, seeing that Christ is Truth. [91] But he points out that many people are prisoners of false doctrines, so that they cannot easily stand in the truth. However, once they attain to this state, they have outgrown human status, and they are thus addressed as "gods" by the supreme God. Elsewhere, [92] Origen says that the human state is the result of a declension from an original state of divinity, and then says that when God says "You shall die as men" *(ut homines)* (Ps.lxxxii.7), He means that those addressed will be destroyed so far as they are men, inasmuch as their sins will be blotted out, and they will thus be made once more divine. (Incidentally, those human beings who receive Divine grace can be called not only "gods", but "Christs", in so far as this grace is imparted through Christ, [93] and also "sons of God", in so far as they come to have Christ's sonship. [94] In one place Origen even says that those who set their hope on the Word of God and the words of God can themselves become "words (λόγοι) of God.") [95]

None the less, the ultimate Divinity of the Father is safeguarded inasmuch as it is from the Father that the Son receives the power of imparting divinity to others. It follows that though there are many beings who bear a likeness to the one true God, the Archetype or Model from Whom this likeness is derived is the Word of God, Who was "with God" in the beginning, and by continuing to gaze steadfastly into the depths of the Father's being remains Divine in the full sense. [96] A. Lieske asks [97] whether this passage implies a subordinationist definition of the being of the Divine Word as the top of the pyramid of created λόγοι. Is it simply because He contemplates the Father that He is Son? Or is the union of a deeper kind, that which springs from the begetting of the Son by the Father? This is the answer which Lieske himself gives. [98] J. Maydieu charges Origen with inconsistency [99] in his account of the way in which the Word of God retains His Divinity, but ignores the fact that contemplation is not a mere matter of the exercise of the Son's will (a Pelagian attitude), but springs from the very nature of the Son Himself. In *De Princ.* Origen likewise says that we have been made in accordance with the Image of God Who is the Son, and have Him as the Archetype and truth of the good qualities which we possess. Our relation to the Son is thus the same as the relation of the Son to the Father, Who is the Truth *par excellence*.[100] Thus Origen can say that he who has the virtues is a son of Christ, and therefore also a son of God the Father, because Christ and the Father are one in nature.[101] Elsewhere, varying the metaphor, Origen says that by having the Divine virtues we become the brothers of Christ (cf. Ps.xxii.23 and John xx.17).[102] Yet again elsewhere Origen employs the analogy of husband and wife by saying that the individual soul *(anima)* is united to the Word of God in a union resembling marriage, but can be led astray by her Husband's adversary. If, however, the soul conceives by her Husband, she brings forth the fruit which consists in the virtues of justice, self-control, patience, and so on.[103] Again, with reference to the prince of Tyre, described by Ezekiel as being "the seal of the likeness of God" *(signum similitudinis)*, Origen says that those who have made real progress in virtue receive the stamp of the Divine likeness bestowed by Christ, but only because Christ Himself is sealed with the Divine seal.[104] Again, with reference to the coming of the Word of God to Ezekiel, Origen says that the Word Who was in the beginning with God "makes believers into gods" *(credentes efficit deos)*. If it is said that "they shall die like men" (Ps.lxxxii.7), that is not the fault of Him Who invites us to share in His Divinity and so become the adopted children of God: it is due to our own sins.[105]

Elsewhere, Origen also points out the necessity of human co-operation in the process of being transformed into the Divine likeness; for he says that although Christ is Wisdom, He can only impart His wisdom to those who are anxious to receive it.[106] Again, Origen says that if a person follows the sayings of Christ, he ceases to be human and becomes divine. Christ the Firstfruits of the dead is also the Firstfruits of those who have been transformed by Him into the Divine nature.[107] Again, Origen points out that the "inward man" is said to have God for his Father if he lives and acts in accordance with God's will, and that the Divine seed is said to remain in us when we preserve within ourselves the Word of God and so do not sin (cf.I John iii.9).[108]

Origen in fact says that at the beginning, before the material world came into being, the Only-begotten Son granted invisibly to each rational creature a degree of participation in His own Divinity corresponding to the loving affection with which it had clung to Him.[109] This statement is amplified elsewhere,[110] when Origen says that when God made man in the beginning, He made him in His own image and likeness, in the sense that man's resemblance to God was not only latent, but manifest. But gradually alien elements crept into human nature, with the result that the likeness was lost and only the unseen image remained. Not until the defilement existing in human nature has been removed by the Word of God can the heavenly image become resplendent again. In brief, the Divine image can be obscured by neglect, but not destroyed by sin.[111] On the other hand, a difficulty arises here, in so far as Origen claims that since all things were made through the Divine Word,[112] there was nothing unrighteous in the things which were made, and that all that was made can be demonstrated to be in accordance with the principles of equity and righteousness.[113] But as things are, there is from the superficial point of view great diversity and variety amongst rational natures.[114] How is it possible to reconcile this state of affairs with the perfect wisdom and righteousness of God? The answer lies, says Origen, in the freedom of the human will, which is itself a Divine endowment. This freedom enables rational creatures to turn aside from the highest good and so be involved in evil. The resulting declensions from the highest good are the hidden causes from which all the inequalities of human conditions proceed.[115] To quote his own words, "These were the reasons which gave rise to the diversity existing in the world, because Divine providence arranges each creature in accordance with the varied character of the movements of its mind."[116] Thus it is that the Last Judgement, which will assign to each soul its deserts, will already have been anticipated at previous stages of the history of the universe; "for we must believe that God organises the universe by judgement *at all times.*"[117]

But this does not answer the question how it can be regarded as in accordance with the Divine goodness that rational beings should have been created with the propensity to go astray from what is good. If these beings had possessed this goodness in its perfection *ab initio*, there would have been no possibility of their sinking to a lower level. Origen does not in fact reconcile his doctrine of human freewill with his doctrine of the omnipotence of God. H. Koch takes the same view when he says [118] that whereas Origen's insistence on human freewill is in one way a strength, as upholding the oneness of God and yet maintaining the reality of evil, in another way it is a weakness, because it implies that the creature is so made as to be self-supporting over against God.[119] It seems more in accordance with the facts to say that the very possibility of developing from near-animality to the full stature of human beings is a greater good than an originally perfect creation could ever have been. Thus Dr. E.W. Barnes can say that "man's creation was not a quite incomprehensible and wholly improbable consequence of the properties of electrons and protons . . .; it was the result of some cosmic purpose. And the end towards which that Purpose acted must be found in man's distinctive qualities and powers. In fact, man's moral and spiritual capacities, at their highest, show the nature of the Cosmic Purpose which is the source of his being." [120]

But whatever the defects of Origen's doctrine of creation, it at any rate enables him to uphold the statement of the Saviour that "the Father Who sent me is greater than I", and His refusal to allow Himself to be called "good" in the absolute sense, on the ground that this epithet is reserved for the Father, Whose goodness is merely communicated to the Son. [121] In the same way, Origen says elsewhere that although the Son is good, He is not good purely and simply (οὐχ ὡς ἁπλῶς ἀγαθός) as the Father is, because just as He is the Image of the Father, so His goodness is merely the image of the Father's goodness. [122]There are two passages in which Origen seems to put forward contradictory views as to how the superiority of the Father to the Son is related to the superiority of the Son to other beings. In one place [123] Origen first points out that since the Son is the image of the Father's goodness, the word "good" as applied to the Son is different in meaning from the same word as applied to any inferior being, because the goodness of the Father has more in common with the goodness of the Son than the Son's goodness has with the goodness of a man or an action or a tree. In fact it is true to say that in view of His unique relationship to the Father, the superiority of the Son to other good beings is greater than the superiority of the God Who is supremely good to the Saviour Himself. Whereas in another passage [124] Origen says that although the Son and the Holy Spirit are immeasurably superior to all created beings, they are themselves surpassed to an equal or even greater extent by the Father; for the Son is no more than the image of the Father's goodness and the effulgence of the Father's glory and the unspotted mirror of the Father's energy. He is thus the means whereby, as He Himself pointed out, the Apostles were able to gain a vision of God Himself. The former passage stresses the extent to which an image resembles its original, whereas the latter stresses the difference between the image and its original. It is no matter for surprise if the Arians thought that Origen had prepared the way for them, if one judges by this passage alone. It would be possible to contend that the former passage referred to the Son in His Divine nature and the latter to the Son in His human nature, were it not for the fact that in the second passage the Holy Spirit is coupled with the Son.

Origen has stated that since the Son is the Image of the Father, He was the means whereby the Apostles could gain a vision of God Himself. On the other hand the vision gained was not complete, but only partial. This was made clear to Moses, when he was told by God that he would be set in a "hole of the rock" and thus see the back of God, but not His face (Exod.xxxiii.21-23).[125] The rock is said to be Christ, and the hole in the rock is said to be the Incarnation; hence by seeing the Incarnate Christ one sees the back of God, ie. obtains an incomplete vision of Him.[126] In the same way, Isaiah in his vision only saw the back of God, because His face was veiled by the wings of the seraphim.[127] The same interpretation is put forward elsewhere,[128] inasmuch as it seems to be suggested that the rock is the pre-existent Christ, and the hole in the rock is the Incarnate Christ as the Revealer of God to man.[129] There are two passages where the words addressed to Moses "No man shall see my face and live" (Exod.xxxiii.20) are ascribed to the Son of God, and the disciples who saw His face shine as the sun at the time of the Transfiguration are therefore said to have fallen on their faces because they could not bear the rays of the Divine Word.[130] On the other hand, Origen says with reference to the scarlet cord let down through Rahab's window that the Incarnation of the Saviour does not provide us with the complete and entire vision of God, but allows us to behold the light of Deity as it were by means of a window, which does not permit all the light to shine through.[131]

It seems clear that in these passages Origen is not entirely consistent with the view he expresses elsewhere of the role of Christ as the Revealer of God to man. In an earlier section of this chapter[132] he is shown to have expressly said that it was the pre-existent Word of God with whom the Old Testament saints entered into fellowship, with the result that they thereby entered into fellowship with God the Father Himself; it is not just a matter of obtaining an anticipatory glimpse of the incarnate Christ. In Chapter VII [133] we shall endeavour to show that Origen regards the apprehension of the Word of God as obtained after an initial state in which the incarnate Christ is understood after a human fashion only. Once that stage is left behind, the believer is introduced ever more fully to the Father by the Divine Word, until in the end he obtains the same clear vision of the Father as the Word Himself has.

NOTES ON CHAPTER II

1 *Comm. in Joh.* I.38 (GCS 4.49.33-50.9); cf. ibid.(49.3-8), and *Sel. in Ps.* XLIX.1 (PG XII.1448D). Cf. Crouzel, *L'Image,* pp.81, 84,85, and *La Conn.,* p.97; Orbe, "La excelencia de los profetas segun Origenes" (*EB* 7 (1955)), pp.202,203; Fitzgerald, op. cit., pp.228,229.
2 *Comm. in Joh.* II.1 (GCS 4.53,25-54.1); cf. *De Princ.* I.2.3 (GCS 5.30.11-14).
3 Cadiou, *Frag. in Ps.* CV.2 (p.91).
4 *Comm. in Joh.* VI.6 (GCS 4.113.18-22), XXVIII.24 (420.5-10), XX.42 (385.26-31); *Hom. in Jer.* IX.1 (GCS 3.63.23-64.5); *Hom. in Is.* I.5 (GCS 8.247.20-25); *Contra Cels.* V.12 (GCS 2.14.2-4); *Hom. in Exod.* III.1 (GCS 6.161.22-162.9); *Matt. Comm. Series* 28 (GCS 11.53.11-15); *Frag. in Lam.* CXVI (GCS 3.276.17-20 and 276.32-277.4); *De Princ.* IV.2.7 (GCS 5.318.9-11); *Hom. in Ps.* XXXVI.III.3 (PG XII 1338B). Cf. A. Orbe, op. cit., p.219; J. Rius-Camps, "Comunicabilidad," *OCP* 36.1970 p.244; E. Fitzgerald, op. cit., p.228; Mme. Harl, op. cit., pp.209,210,336-338.
5 *Comm. in Joh.* XX.12 (GCS 4.341.23-25). This also seems to be the implication of the curious passage in which Origen says that even though the Son teaches human beings what He has seen and heard, it is not appropriate to understand these things as pertaining to His Divinity (*Frag. in Joh.* XLVI (GCS 4.521.30-522.2)). E. Fitzgerald, op. cit., pp.102-108, refers to the passage in *Hom. in Jer.* IX mentioned in note 4, but reads more into it than seems implied, in so far as he thinks that the human soul of Christ came to the prophet along with the Divine Word. On the other hand he has a more plausible reason for reading this idea into the quotation from *Hom. in Is.* I.5 also mentioned in note 4, where "my Lord Jesus Christ" is referred to as coming to the prophets (pp. 119-120).
6 Op. cit., pp.84-87.
7 Op. cit., pp.113,114.
8 On pp.
9 *Frag. in Joh.* XII (GCS 4.494.18-22).
10 *Frag. in Matt.* 191.6-10 (GCS 12.92). Cf. ibid. 230,3-5 (12.109); *Comm. in Matt.* XVII.32 (10.684.1-5); *Frag. in Col.* (PG XIV. 1298). Cf. Mme. Harl, op. cit., pp.330,331, note 91, where she points out that according to Origen, Christ was the Servant and

Distributor of the Word of God.

[11] *Comm. in Joh.* VI.3 (GCS 4.109.15-25).

[12] Cf. the discussion of this passage in Crouzel, *La Conn.*, pp.305-306; Gruber, op. cit., p.55; Orbe, op. cit., pp.193.194, and also p.196, where the author says that "the unique privilege of the Apostles (ie. that of beholding the incarnate Lord) did not in any way affect the perfection of the cognitive act (of the prophets in apprehending the mysteries to be later revealed to the outer senses)."
Cf. *Frag. in Rom.* XI.1-8 (*JTS* 13.218), where it is said that "to be entrusted with the oracles of God (Rom.iii.2) does not consist in being entrusted with text itself, but in knowing the underlying mysteries contained in it . . . .. This was the case with Moses and the prophets."

[13] *Frag. in Joh.* XI (GCS 4.493.19-494.3), and *Comm. in Joh.* VI.6 (GCS 4.114.5-9). Cf. on these passages von Balthasar, "Le Mysterion d'Origène" (*RchSR* 27 (1937)), p.42, n.9 (continued on p. 43), where he refers to Origen's "semi-pelagianism", and says that according to Origen, to every virtue of the natural (psychique) man corresponds a spiritual (pneumatique) or charismatic virtue which is a special gift of God." Later, he says that according to Origen, "the effort of man and the effect of grace are included in a more general grace which makes them converge in the way in which Providence makes the efforts of the labourer and the effects of the climate converge." Cf. also Orbe, op. cit., p. 193, n.6.

[14] *Frag. in Matt.* 460 (GCS 12.190); Cf. ibid.461.1-3 (191). Cf. Mme. Harl, op. cit., pp.209,210 (especially note 90).

[15] *Hom. in Matt.* II (GCS 12.251.29-31).

[16] *Sel. in Gen.* XXXII.24,28,30 (PG XII.128BC).

[17] *De Princ.* I Pref.1 (GCS 5.8.2-5).

[18] *Frag. in Matt.* 526,3-6 (GCS 12.215).

[19] *Hom. in Matt.* II (GCS 12.247.31,32); cf. ibid.14-16, Cf. also *Frag. in Eph.* I.12-18 (*JTS* 3.235), where the θέλημα θεοῦ is said to be personified in Christ.

[20] *Contra Cels.* VIII.69 (GCS 2.286.18-20); cf. *Frag. in Lam.* CI (GCS 3.271.18,19).

[21] In his article "Sens Spirituel" (*RshSR* 29 (1949)), p.571.

[22] In note 4 on the same page.

[23] See on this subject J. Rius-Camps, "Origenes y Marcion", (*M*,

1973), pp.21-24.
24 *Comm. in Joh.* II.34 (GCS 4.92.34-93.4); Cf. *Comm. in Rom.* VI 7 (PG XIV.1071B), and *Comm. in Joh.* I.7 (GCS 4.11.26-12.1).
25 Cf. Maydieu, op. cit., p.49, where he says that according to Origen, "the Son was visible with a visibility perceptible to souls before He became visible materially in taking a body." Cf. also Orbe, op. cit., p.204, where after quoting *Comm. in Joh.* I.7, he makes the following comments: — "To the distinguished righteous men of the Old Covenant the opposite occurred to what occurs to the imperfect inheritors of the New Covenant. In spite of Christ's coming in the flesh, there are many today who have not arrived at the fullness of time. The Word of God endowed with Divine glory has not come and disclosed to them the glorious mysteries seen by the righteous men of the Old Covenant through the intelligible coming of Christ. They lack the spiritual maturity which enabled the patriarchs and prophets to contemplate the glorified Son of God." Cf. also de Lubac, op. cit., p.572, and Fitzgerald, op. cit., pp.71-74.
26 *Frag. in Joh.* XLVI (GCS 4.521.22-24); cf. ibid.IX (491.5-9).
27 *Comm. in Joh.* XX.12 (GCS 4.342.11-21). Cf. *Frag. in Rom.* XI 1-6 (*JTS* 13.218).
28 Ibid.VI.4 (GCS 4.110.3-24). Cf. *Frag. in Rom.* XXXI.19-28 (*JTS* 13.366). Cf. Maydieu, op. cit., pp.54,55, where this passage is discussed, and note 8 on p.55, where he says that "for Origen, the Incarnation is an abasement and an inferior knowledge, for it is more valuable to know the intelligible Word of God in an intellectual manner than to know the Word made flesh in the manner employed by the senses." Cf. also J. Rius-Camps, "Comunicabilidad", *OCP* 36, 1976 pp.244,245.
29 On p.185 of her article "The nature of Christ in Origen's Commentary on John" (*SJT* 19 (1966)).
30 This matter is discussed at length in Chapter VI, pp.205-207, 210-216, and also in Ch.VII, pp.236-238.
31 Op. cit., p.139.
32 *Comm. in Rom.* IV.4 (PG XIV.973B).
33 *Frag. in Matt.* 401.1-3 (GCS 12.169), with reference to Matt.xx. 8. Cf. de Lubac, op. cit., p.551, n.3., where he quotes S. Thomas Aquinas as saying that a Scriptural writer is a "defective instrument" in God's hands, and only has an imperfect knowledge of what he speaks about, and also as saying that "even the true pro-

phets do not know everything which the Holy Spirit intends to convey through their visions, words and deeds." On the other hand, in n.4 on p.573 S. Thomas is curiously enough referred to as taking the opposite view.

[34] *Comm. in Matt.* XVII.36 (GCS 10.702.19-703.6); cf. *Frag. in Eph.* XVII.5,6 (*JTS* 3.413).

[35] Mme. Harl, op. cit., p.273, seems to have misunderstood this passage; for she says that "for those who were mature the coming of Christ had already occurred spiritually, and God was already 'God the Father' for Abraham, Isaac and Jacob, because they were already among the living", and supplies as reference this passage in note 22. Surely the reference should be to *Comm. in Joh.* VI.4 (referred to in note 28 on this chapter).
A. Orbe, op. cit., does not appear to have taken this passage into account when he says (pp.217,218) that "the prophets were able to recognise the personal distinctions in God, even though for His higher purpose the manifestation of them to the mass of people was reserved for the Word made flesh", and (p.221) that according to Origen "our actual knowledge of the Divine Trinity can in no way be superior to that of the prophets." As so often, Origen makes large assumptions which he later feels obliged to qualify as the result of being faced with facts which controvert them. Cf. Mme. Harl, op. cit., p.357, where she says that according to Origen, "God was not really unknown, nor even unrecognised in any of His essential aspects, before the coming of Jesus Christ . . . . Thus the incarnate Word seems, in His earthly work, to have revealed almost nothing new about God . . . . The only exception is the teaching that God is Spirit and that He must be worshipped in spirit." Cf. also Crouzel, *La Conn.* p.109, and Aeby, op cit., pp.169,170.

[36] *Frag. in Luc.* 165,1-16 (GCS 9.294). Cf. Pitra A.S.III.348 (Ps. CXXXIX.13); *Frag. in Matt.* 3.40-44 (GCS 12.15); *Comm. in Joh.* II.34 (GCS 4.92.27-34).

[37] *Frag. in Luc.* 162.6-17 (GCS 9.292). H. Crouzel, *La Conn.*, p. 135, regards the phrase "my day" in Christ's saying concerning Abraham as referring to the Incarnation; but this passage shows that Origen regarded Abraham as receiving a revelation of Christ in his own lifetime. Cf. Molland, *The Conception of the Gospel in the Alexandrian Theology* (Oslo, 1938), p.103.
There is indeed a contradiction in Origen's thought on this

matter, as Crouzel, op. cit., p.296, points out, when he says that according to Origen, "in the Law Christ is simply foretold; whatever the perfection of spiritual discernment which the Patriarchs and Prophets had, they did not possess Christ." Crouzel states later (p.301) that "just as Abraham saw the day of the Lord only in hope and in symbol, so the knowledge of Moses remained imperfect because it was only intuition, not possession or union." But surely Origen was at times inclined to think of spiritual perception as being *in fact* possession (ie. of the truth discerned). The seesaw tendency in Origen's thought on this point is well illustrated by referring on the one hand to A. Lieske, op. cit., p.35, where he points out that in one place (*Comm. in Cant.* II (GCS 8. 157.23-158.8)) Origen states that the relationship of love between the Church (considered as the whole company of saints) and Christ attained its completion only after the Incarnation, and on the other to Molland, op. cit., p.109, where he remarks that "Origen's own attitude implies a conception of history which makes it very difficult to attribute a unique significance to the Incarnation" (see also pp.110,111).

38 *Comm. in Rom.* IV.6 (PG XIV.983BC).
39 Ibid.IV.7 (PG XIV.985AB).
40 XIX.3 (GCS 4.301.15-302.2).
41 Cf. Lebreton. "Les degrés de la connaissance religieuse d'après Origene" (*RchSR* 12 (1922)), p.281, where this passage is quoted, and J. Rius-Camps, "Origenes y Marcion", p.20, where it is referred to.
42 *Comm. in Joh.* XIII.44 (GCS 4.271.1-14).
43 162.17-25 (GCS 9.292).
44 On the other hand J. Dupuis, op. cit., p.244, n.165, interprets this passage as meaning that Abraham merely "believed in" the Father, even though he "knew" God (presumably as Creator).
45 *Comm. in Joh.* XIII.46 (GCS 4.272.34-273.11). Origen does not seem to recognise that the prophets referred to by St. Paul are *Christian* prophets. Cf. *Comm. in Matt.* XVI.10 (GCS 10.505.7-11), *Frag. in I Thess.* (PG XIV 1302CD), and *Matt. Comm. Series* 50 (GCS 11.112.15-18 (Greek text)), where the prophets are compared to the clouds on which the Lord will come in His final manifestation in glory.
46 Ibid.VI.4 (GCS 4.111.6-11, 18-23). Cf. Koch, op. cit., p.59, n.3, where this passage is referred to.

[47] Ibid. (GCS 4.111.24-112.3).
[48] Cf. the discussion of this passage by Crouzel, *La Conn.*, p.307, Rius-Camps, "Origenes y Marcion", pp.23,24 and Orbe, op. cit., pp.210,217,218, and n.101 on p.218. Cf. also *Comm. in Rom.* X.43 (PG XIV.1290C), and *Frag. in Rom.* XXXVI 75-80 (*JTS*, 14.13).
[49] *Comm. in Joh.* XIX.5 (GCS 4.303.20-304.5). Cf. *Comm. in Rom.* X.43 (PG XIV.1291A-1292A).
[50] Such is Huet's interpretation of lines 20-29 in the above passage (see PG XIV.523,533, n.5).
[51] He seems to leave out of account Isaiah lxiii.16. Cf. also *De Orat.* XXII.1 and II.4 (GCS 2 346.12-19 and 302.18-24).
[52] Cf. the discussion of this passage in Nemeshegyi, op. cit., p.162, Rius-Camps, op. cit., pp.17 and 20, and Molland, op cit., p.122. Fitzgerald, op. cit., pp.79-81, discusses this passage, and says in particular (p.80) that "Origen puts this more moderate and safer opinion (ie. that the prophets did not know God as Father) in the first place, as though he had been forced by the evidence of the Scriptures to admit at least this distinction between the just of the Old and the New Dispensation."
[53] *Comm. in Rom.* II.5 (PG XIV.881B).
[54] *Comm. in Joh.* XIII.47 (GCS 4.273.27-274.1); cf. *Comm.in Matt.* XII.42 (GCS 10.166.26-167.2).
[55] CXVI (GCS 3.277.7-14).
[56] Crouzel, *La Conn.*, p.327, comments that "the mysteries which the Incarnation shows to have been foreshadowed in the Law are those of the eternal Gospel, perceived by way of the realities of the temporal Gospel"; but this does not make it clear whether the prophets themselves fully foresaw the Incarnation and experienced the disclosures which it made or not.
[57] *Comm. in Joh.* XIII.48 (GCS 4.275.13-276.2).
[58] Cf. Hebrews xi.39,40.
[59] Cf. Mme. Harl, op. cit., p.163, where it is pointed out that Origen considered that Christ's teaching was superior to that of Solomon, and p.164, n.18, where it is pointed out that Origen also said that the Old Testament worthies had the "key of knowledge."
Crouzel, *La Conn.*, pp.308,309, tries to explain the contradiction between *Comm. in Joh.* XIII.48 (referred to in n.57) and ibid.VI. 4 (referred to in n.46) by saying that "the equality of the pro-

phets and the apostles does not relate to the extent and depth of their knowledge, but to their possibilities of obtaining knowledge by virtue of their holiness." This explanation seems extremely forced, and does not really harmonise with the natural interpretation of *Comm. in Joh.* VI.4.

Rius-Camps, op. cit., p.23, says with reference to this passage that the knowledge of the Apostles was superior in point of quantity to that of the prophets, but not in point of quality. But he does not make it clear what he means by this contrast.

Orbe, op. cit., does not take account of *Comm. in Joh.* XIII.48 at all, and so gives a one-sided description of Origen's attitude to the prophets. See Fitzgerald op. cit., pp.63-66, for a discussion of this passage.

60 *Hom. in Jos.* III.2 (GCS 7.302.10-21).
61 Contrast the interpretation of Luke x.24 given in *Frag. in Luc.* 165 (referred to in n.36). Fitzgerald, *Christ and the Prophets* (Rome, 1961, abridged version), p.33, says that "Origen is forced finally to the admission that the actual realisation of a mystery in time not only brings with it an increase in interior joy, but is also the condition on which a perfect knowledge of that mystery depends."
62 *Comm. in Joh.* I.39 (GCS 4.51.16-27). Cf. Crouzel, *La Conn.*, p. 119, where he says that "the role of the Son does not limit itself to His quality of being the Image of God; He is the Agent Who transmits the knowledge of God." Cf. also Teichtweier, op. cit., pp.256,257, where there is a discussion of the development of the meaning of the word λόγος.
63 *Hom. in Jer.* XIX.1 (GCS 3.176.24-177.2). Cf. Maydieu, op. cit., pp.10 and 11, where he points out that according to Origen, it is in order to emphasise the independence of the Logos that He is spoken of in the Prologue to St. John's Gospel as "the Word" by itself, and not as the Word of God. There is one Logos both for angels and men, just as there is one Truth for God, for angels, and for men.

Cf. *Hom. in Num.* XII.1 (GCS 7.95.10-13), where Origen says that the Son is distinct in personality from the Father, but that one substance is common to both. Later however (GCS 7.97.22-24) Origen (or rather his translator) uses the word *substantia* to mean "individual being," when he says that though the Son originates from the Fountain of Deity together with the Holy Spirit,

He exists in His individual being *(propria quidem substantia subsistentem).*
64 *Comm. in Matt.* XVII.14 (GCS 10.624.8-16).
65 *Comm. in Joh.* V.5 (GCS 4.102.28-31). Cf. Maydieu, op. cit., p. 14, where this passage is quoted.
66 Ibid.II.18 (GCS 4.75.19-21) also referred to in Ch.III, n.58. Cf. Völker, *Das Vollkommenheitsideal des Origenes* (Tubingen, 1931), p.132, n.3, where this passage is referred to, and Maydieu, op. cit., p.11.
67 See Ch. III, p. 73,74.
68 *Comm. in Joh.* I.17 (GCS 4.22.19-26). Cf. *Frag. in Luc.* 16.4 (GCS 9.233), where Christ is described as τὸν κύριον καὶ θεὸν τῶν ὅλων; *Sel. in Ps.* XVII.32 (PG XII.1236CD), where it is said that the words "Who is God but the Lord?" can only refer to God the Son; *Frag. in Luc.* 175.1-5 (GCS 9.300), where it is said that we must pray that the term "God" will eventually be applied to the Lord alone; *Frag. in Gal.* (PG XIV.1294 and 1295AB). Cf. Crouzel, *L'Image*, pp.265,266, where it is said that according to Origen, the entire universe is an image of heavenly realities. Cf. also *La Conn.*, p.108, where it is said that "in a broad sense, the visible world is an incarnation of the Divine Word, for it reflects in its constitution the intelligible world which is identifiable with the Son, and is linked with the mysteries which the Word contains."
69 *Sel. in Ps.* XVII.12 (PG XII.1229).
70 Cf. *Hom. in I Sam.xxviii.3-25.* 9 (GCS 3.293.27,28) where it is said that Ἰησοῦς (ie. Joshua) was a τύπος τοῦ ἀληθινοῦ θεοῦ.
71 *Comm. in Matt.* XIV.17 (GCS 10.325.27-326.11).
72 *Comm. in Joh.* II.2 (GCS 4.54.23-55.2). Cf. J. Rius-Camps, "Comunicabilidad", *(OCP* 36,1979) pp.203-205.
73 Cf. J. Rius-Camps, "Comunicabilidad", *(OCP* 34,1968), p.13 and n.3 thereon. However, I find Rius-Camps' reasoning difficult to follow.
74 Cf. *Frag. in Luc.* 92 (GCS 9.263), where it is said that Christ baptises with the Holy Spirit inasmuch as He is Divine (ὡς θεός); *Frag. in Matt.* 192.1-3 (GCS 12.92); *Hom. in Jer.* XXXIX (Philocal. JAR,33.18-20); *Hom. in Exod.* VI.2 (GCS 6.193.22-24), where Jesus Christ is spoken of as referring to the Father as "His God" (in John xx.17) in order to safeguard the truth that there is one God alone. There are, however, passages where Christ is spo-

ken of as θεός with the definite article attached, eg. *Frag. in Luc.* 172.5,6 (GCS 9.299), and Cadiou, *Frag. in Ps.* XLIV.7 (p.79). Cf. also Nemeshegyi, op. cit., pp.99 and 100; Lieske, op. cit., pp. 164, 165; Balas, op. cit., p.17.
De Faye (op. cit., pp.121 and 123) says that according to Origen, "the Logos is a god of the second rank, and cannot be compared with the supreme God . . . . The proof that Origen's Logos is that of the philosophers is that even if he makes Him a God, it is a subordinate God that he makes Him." But that is no criticism, because the Logos in any case derives His being from the supreme God. De Faye then says that "when the philosophic sense of the term Logos had been discarded, the Logos could be made the equal of God . . . . The operation from which would ensue the consubstantiality of the Son with the Father would be made easier." (ibid.) But although Origen may not use the term ὁμοούσιος, it would not seem unreasonable to credit him with the belief that the Son is in fact of one nature with the Father in a sense in which no other being is. D'Alès ("La Doctrine d'Origéne d'après un livre recent" (*RchSR* 20,1930), pp.235,236) echoes de Faye's view by saying that "instead of grasping the Johannine notion of the Logos, Origen has too readily submitted to the influence of a Platonic and Stoic environment, and projected on to the Christian datum the shadows of a profane philosophy. Origen's education conceals from his eye the full majesty of a Son Who is consubstantial with His Father." Cf. also pp.241 and 242. But if the term "Logos" denotes "self-expression", why should Origen be regarded as having attenuated Christian truth?

75 The phrase "advanced in days", originally applied by God to Joshua (Josh.xiii.1), is said by Origen to be applicable to Jesus Christ Himself, because, He is "the Firstborn of all creation", Who as the Sun of righteousness created spiritual days which are illuminated by the light of truth and wisdom (*Hom. in Jos.* XVI. 1 and 2 (GCS 7.395.19,20 and 396.5-9)).
76 *Sel. in Ps.* CXXXV.3 (PG XII.1656A); cf. ibid.XLVII.2 (1440A).
77 *L'Image*, p.106.
78 Op. cit., p.24.
79 *Frag. in Joh.* XLVIII (GCS 4.523.3-9).
80 *Contra Cels.* IV.29 (GCS 1.298.4-20). Cf. ibid.VII.65 (GCS 2. 215.14,15).
81 Ibid.IV.31 (GCS 1.301.32-302.3).

[82] Ibid.V.4 (GCS 2.4.12-23).
[83] Ibid.III.37 (GCS 1.234.2-4).
[84] *Deos illos dicit, qui per gratiam et participationem dii appelantur.*
[85] *Quamvis capaces sunt Dei, et hoc nomine donari per gratiam videantur.*
[86] *Hom. in Exod.* VI.5 (GCS 6.196.17-197.10). See Völker, op.cit., p.131, where this passage is discussed. Cf. the simile of a statue used in describing the Incarnation in *De Princ.* I.2.8 (GCS 5.38. 13-39.4). Cf. also Nemeshegyi, op. cit., p.79. Cf. also *Comm. in Joh.* XX.29 (GCS 4.367.1-4); *Frag. in Joh.* II (GCS 4.486.13-16); *Hom. in Jud.* VI.4 (GCS 7.502.19,20); *Comm. in Matt.* XVI.29 (GCS 10.573.29-574.13); *Frag. in Matt.* 218.3-5 (GCS 12.104); *Comm. in Ezek.* I.3 (PG XIII.770BC); *Comm. in Rom.* II.14 (PG XIV.920BC).
[87] *Hom. in Exod.* VIII.2 (GCS 6.219.20-220.25).
[88] *Ceteris vero, qui ab ipso creati sunt, contulit nomen istud non natura, sed gratia.*
[89] VI.2 (GCS 7.324.17-22). Cf. Crouzel, *L'Image,* pp.163-5.
[90] XX.27 (GCS 4.363.25-364.5).
[91] Cf.p.51.
[92] *Comm. in Rom.* III.1 (PG XIV.925B-926A); cf. *Comm. in Matt.* XVII.19 (GCS 10.638.12-639.4) and XVII.32 (GCS 10.679.19-27); *Comm. in Joh.* I.34 (GCS 4.43.30-33), II.3 (GCS 4.56.5-9), and XXXII.18 (GCS 4.457.6-12); *Comm. in Rom.* IV.9 (PG XIV. 997BC); *Sel. in Ps.* IV.3 (PG XII.1137D-1140A), V.7 (1169B), XII.1 (1204A), XXIII.6 (1268B); Pitra A.S.III.140 (Ps.LXXXI.1) and 141 (Ps.LXXXI.6,7); Cadiou, *Frag. in Ps.* XLII.2 (p.76). Cf. Koch, op. cit., p.73, and Crouzel, *L'Image,* p.163, n.108, where other passages are referred to.
[93] *Contra Cels.* VI.79 (GCS 2.150.21-24); *Comm. in Joh.* VI.6 (GCS 4.115.15-19); *Sel. in Num.* XXIV.8 (PG XII.584A); *Sel. in Ps.* CIV.15 (PG XII.1564C). Cf. J. Rius-Camps, "Comunicabilidad" (*OCP* 38,1972), p.451.
[94] *Matt. Comm. Series* 111(GCS 11.231.23-232.1); *Frag. in Matt.* 5 (GCS 12.13,14); ibid.243.2-4 (GCS 12.113); *Comm. in Rom.* VII.1 (PG XIV.1103C); *Sel. in I Reg.* (PG XII.996). Cf. Nemeshegyi, op. cit., p.228, where he says that the righteous man will become a son of God in the full sense when he entirely resembles and is united to the Only-begotten Son, when long custom has removed from him the very possibility of sinning. Cf. also

Lieske, op. cit., p.15, where he says that the pattern of all conformity to the Logos, the pattern which consists in the union of knowledge and love between the Father and the Son, is not a bare metaphysical projection of the union between created beings and God, but is based rather on Origen's Trinitarian theology of begetting. Lieske criticises Völker for ignoring this; but in fact Völker himself (op. cit., p.131, n.1) stresses the difference between the Sonship which is derived from being Divinely begotten and the sonship derived from Divine grace.

[95] Cadiou, *Frag. in Ps.* CXVIII.74 (p.111).
[96] *Comm. in Joh.* II.2 (GCS 4.55.5-8). Cf. *Hom. in Luc.* VIII (GCS 9.48.2-14,23-49.1 (Greek text)), where it is said that the task of the believer is to transform his soul into the likeness of Christ, Who is Himself the Image of the Father. Cf. Crouzel, *L'Image*, pp.85 and 86, and *La Conn.*, pp.86,87.
[97] Op. cit., p.150.
[98] Op. cit., pp.170-173, Cf. Aeby, op. cit., p.181, n.5, where he says that "the Word is the Image of God not only by virtue of His nature, but also by virtue of His activity."
[99] Op. cit., pp.66,67. Vagaggini, op. cit., pp.185,186, takes the same view.
[100] I.2.6 (GCS 5.36.10-13). Cf. *Comm. in Joh.* I.17 (GCS 4.22.19-22). Cf. Nemeshegyi, op. cit., p.54, n.3, and Bürke, op. cit., pp. 7 and 8.
[101] *Hom. in Ezek.* IV.5 (GCS 8.366.28-367.1). Cf. *Frag. in II Reg. XXI* (GCS 3.302.20-303.2). In fact Origen says that "children" in the true sense, as distinct from "seed" (ie. physical offspring) are those who act as their Begetter acts (*Exh.ad Mart.* 38 (GCS 1.35.30-36.4)). Our Lord's own authority is said to be obtainable for this statement, reference being made to John viii.37 and 39.
[102] *Hom. in Ezek.* IX.1 (GCS 8.407.6-10). The same metaphor is found in *Exh.ad Mart.* 43 (GCS 1.40.14-16); *De Orat.* XV.4 (GCS 2.335.24-336.4); *Comm. in Joh.* I.35 (GCS 4.45.33-46.4); *Sel. in Ps.* XXIV.16 (PG XII.1272C).
[103] *Hom. in Num.* XX.2 (GCS 7.188.4-27). Origen's actual words are: *per singula quae gerimus, parit anima nostra et generat filios* (lines 26,27).
[104] *Hom. in Ezek.* XIII.2 (GCS 8.445.2-6 and 446.7-14).
[105] Ibid.I.9 (GCS 8.332.28-333.14). Cf. *Comm. in Cant.* III (GCS

[106] 8.180.13-21). and *De Princ.* IV.4.5 (GCS 5.356.6), where the actual words are: *participio Filii Dei quis in filios adoptatur.*
De Princ. II.7.3 (GCS 5.150.1-3). Cf. ibid.IV.4.2 (5.351.22-352. 3.); IV.4.8 (5.359.11-14); IV.4.9 (5.362.12-363.3).
[107] *Hom. in Jer.* XV.6 (GCS 3.130.18-21). Cf. *Hom. in Num.* III.3 (GCS 7.19.12-16), and *Comm. in Rom.* II.5 (PG XIV.881C).
[108] *Hom. in Exod.* VIII.6 (GCS 6.230.24-231.6). Cf. *De Orat.* XXII. 4 (GCS 2.349.6-15); *Comm. in Joh.* VI.6 (GCS 4.115.15-19); *De Princ.* IV.4.4 (GCS 5.354.26-355.5); *Frag. in Luc.* 174.6-8 (GCS 9.299). Cf. Crouzel, *L'Image*, p.227.
[109] *De Princ.* II.6.3 (GCS 5.141.27-142.2).
[110] *Hom. in Gen.* XIII.4 (GCS 6.119.15-27).
[111] Origen goes on to say: *manet enim semper imago Dei in te, licet tu tibi ipse superinducas imaginem terreni.*
[112] Cf. Ch. I, pp. 4 and 5.
[113] *De Princ.* II.9.4 (GCS 5.167.26-31); cf. ibid.6 (5.169.25-28).
[114] Ibid.5 (5.168.23-28).
[115] Ibid.2 (5.165.25-166.10). Cf. ibid.6 (5.169.28-170.5).
[116] Ibid.6 (5.170.10-12).
[117] Ibid.8 (5.171.32-172.4).
[118] Op. cit., p.27, n.3.
[119] This matter is discussed again in Ch.VII. pp.247-249.
[120] Quoted in B. Russell, *Religion and Science* (O.U.P., 1936), pp. 192,193.
[121] *Comm. in Joh.* XIII.25 (GCS 4.249.14-18). Cf. *Comm. in Joh.* I. 10 (GCS 4.15.25-28); ibid.VI.39 (4.148.19-22); *Comm. in Matt.* XV.11 (GCS 10.378.10-13); *Comm. III in Gen.* (Philocal.JAR. 188.12,13); *Hom. in Luc.* XXV (GCS 9.152.2-15), where the love of Christ and the love of the Father are said to be reconciled if one loves the Father in the Son and the Son in the Father.
[122] *De Princ.* I.2.13 (GCS 5.47.2-9). The above is a fragment of the original Greek (Justinian Ep.ad.Menn., Mansi IX.525). According to the Latin version of Rufinus, original goodness *(principalis bonitas)* resides in God the Father, and it is from Him that the Son and the Holy Spirit draw into themselves the nature of that goodness (5.48.1-4). Cf. *Sel. in Ps.* XXIX.5 (PG XII.1293B). Cf. Rius-Camps, "Comunicabilidad", *OCP* 36,1970 pp.205,206).
It would seem unreasonable to deduce from the fact that the Son's goodness is the image of that of the Father that there is no identity of being between the Son and the Father, as Lieske does

in op. cit., pp.173 and 174. After all, a copy can reproduce perfectly the features of the original. Indeed, Lieske appears to contradict his own assertion later on (p.198), where he says that whereas there is no likeness of being between God and created beings, the Son alone exists in the closest unity of being with the Father. Cf. also his brief statement on p.212 that "likeness and participation are inseparable."

[123] *Comm. in Matt.* XV.10 (GCS 10.375.20-376.13).

[124] *Comm. in Joh.* XIII.25 (GCS 4.249.18-250.3).

[125] Cf. p.47.

[126] *Hom. in Jer.* XVI.2 (GCS 3.134.8-20). Cf. *De Princ.* II.4.3 (GCS 5.131.3-7). Mme. Harl, op. cit., p.90, n.79, quotes Philo as saying, with reference to the same text in Exodus, that Moses, like anyone else, could not know the essence (ie. the innermost nature) of God, but only His existence as displayed in the powers He exercises.

[127] *Hom. in Is.* I.5 (GCS 8.247.15-20). In *Hom. in Exod.* XII.3 (GCS 6.265.12-16), Origen interprets "the back of God" as meaning what is going to happen in the last days *(quae in posterioribus et novissimis diebus facta sunt),* and thus takes it as referring to the Transfiguration, where Moses and Elijah appeared with Christ in glory. Cf. the Sources Chrétiennes ed. of *Hom. in Exod.*, p.249, n.1. In *Hom. in Ps.* XXXVI.IV.1 (PG XII.1350C), "the back of God" is interpreted as meaning "the things which in the last times would be accomplished by Christ's assumption of human flesh."

[128] *Comm. in Cant.* III (IV) (GCS 8.231.10-16). Cf. *Hom. in Num.* VII.5 (GCS 7.45.3-6).

[129] There are two other interpretations in Origen's writings of Christ as Rock. In *Hom. in Num.* XX.2 (GCS 7.190.1-14) Christ is said to be the rock against which evil thoughts and desires must be dashed before they have time to grow. In *Hom. in Num.* XIX.3 (GCS 7.182.5-12), it is said that he who places his hope in Christ as in a rock and is not enticed by the wiles of heretics will find salvation.

[130] *Comm. in Matt.* XII.43 (GCS 10.167.21-168.2) and *Frag. in Matt.* 365 (2nd col) 6-27 (GCS 12.156).

[131] *Hom. in Jos.* III.5 (GCS 7.307.11-18). Cf. Lot-Borodine, "La doctrine de la 'déification' dans l'eglise grecque jusqu'au XI siècle" (*RHR* 105 (1932)), p.14, where it is pointed out that

Gregory of Nyssa taught that the Word Himself only revealed part of the hidden Divine power, and did not reveal the Divine Nature at all. In taking this view he was a true disciple of Origen. Mme. Harl, op. cit., p.81, points out that in contrast to Origen, Irenaeus sees the incarnate Christ as directly revealing the Father. In her own words, "the aim of the coming of Christ is to make God live among men so that man may see God." She points out on p.82 that Clement is more in accord with Origen in this matter; in fact Clement is quoted as saying that the flesh of Jesus was "a window through which the Lord revealed Himself." Cf. also op. cit., pp.202,203.

Cf. also Maydieu, op. cit., p.51, n.5, where he says that Origen's view is that although the Son is the image of God, He is not the complete image, because God can never be fully visible. This view was shared by Justin, but not by Irenaeus, who took the view that it was only before the Incarnation that God could not be fully seen, whereas afterwards He could be known as the result of being acquainted with the Son.

[132] See p.39,40.
[133] pp. 236-238, 256-263.

CHAPTER III

CONTENTS

THE GIFTS WHICH THE SON RECEIVES FROM THE FATHER – LIGHT, GLORY, WISDOM, JUDGEMENT

The Son as the Light which shines on in the darkness   69

The Son needs the intellectual nourishment supplied by the Father   73

The glory of the Son consists
  (a) in His being acquainted with the Father   73
  (b) in His being acquainted with the universe itself   74

The right to receive honour from men has been granted to Jesus by God   75

The Father gives the power of judgement to the Son
  (a) in that the Son assigns to each human being his deserts
  (b) in that the Son teaches earthly rulers how to exercise their office   76

The judgement exercised by the Son is ultimately that of the Father Who sent Him   77

NOTES on Chapter III   79

CHAPTER III

THE GIFTS WHICH THE SON RECEIVES FROM THE FATHER — LIGHT, GLORY, WISDOM, JUDGEMENT

There are various passages in which Origen enlarges on the good things which Christ receives from the Father, some for Himself alone, and others for Him to impart to human beings also. [1]

Let us first discuss the benefits which the Son receives for Himself. He is spoken of as "Light" in the Gospels, and also as the light which shines in the darkness and is not taken captive by it; whereas the Father is said to be One in Whom is no darkness (I John i.5). The being of the Father is thus shown to be distinct from that of the Son.[2] Origen appears to mean that God the Father is unaffected by the vicissitudes of the temporal order,[3] whereas the Son, in so far as He became incarnate, allowed Himself to be subjected to these vicissitudes. Archbishop Temple in his *Readings in St. John* [4] regards St. John as referring in i.5 of his Gospel not just to the incarnate life of Christ but to His entire activity as the Enlightener of mankind; but this seems to ignore the fact that (as Origen emphasises elsewhere)[5] the Word of God is all-pervading and therefore ultimately responsible for all that occurs.[6]

The Son is also spoken of as being "the true Light"; but the Father cannot be spoken of in this way, because He surpasses the state of being the true Light in the same way as He is greater than truth and surpasses wisdom.[7] On the other hand, the Son as Light reveals the Father Who is the primal Light. The words "In Thy light shall we see light" (Ps.xxxv.10) are quoted in support of this view.[8] In fact the begetting of the Son by the Father is compared to the way in which brightness proceeds from light. Since God is Light by nature, the begetting is therefore eternal.[9] Elsewhere, Origen says that the Onlybegotten Son is the brightness of the Light which is God Himself (cf. Heb.i.3), proceeding from God without separation, as brightness does from light, and illuminating the whole created universe.[10] The intellectual light of sun, moon and stars has been given to them by participation in the true Light, and they must therefore not be worshipped by anyone who sees the true Light, nor by anyone who sees God, the

Father of the true Light. The light of the sun, moon and stars is in fact like a dim speck compared with God Who is Light of the true Light. [11] It is elsewhere said that although our light can shine before men, it cannot shine before Christ, because just as the light of stars fades at the dawning of the sun, even so the light of the Church, like the light of the moon, grows dim when the light of the Sun of Righteousness arises, even though it is resplendent before men. [12] (On the other hand, there is one passage [13] in which the Divine Word is compared to a candle and the Church to the candlestick on which it is set, so that it may give light to all, and so enable them to conduct themselves in accordance with the demands of reason.)

Elsewhere, [14] Origen points out that the truth which resides in Jesus now shows up the shadows for what they are, the shadows consisting of the Jewish Law and the outward accompaniments of Jewish worship. He quotes the verse of the Psalm which states that "truth has sprung up out of the earth, and righteousness has looked down from heaven" (Ps.lxxxvi.12). He later states [15] that Moses was not a minister of the truth, but of the "shadow and imitation" of the truth (cf. Heb.viii.5). Elsewhere [16] he compares the glory resting on the faces of Moses and the prophets to the lamp which is needed till the rising of the sun. Through that glory we are led to see the surpassing glory of Christ Himself, even though the first glory is destroyed by the second, just as we need the partial knowledge which is destroyed by perfect knowledge (cf. II Cor.iii.10 and I Cor.xiii.9,10). There is a curious fragment [17] in which it is stated, with reference to the statement in Luke viii.16 that a candle is put on a candlestick to give light to those who enter the room in which it is, that the Lord compares Himself to this candle and His $\psi v \chi \eta$ to the wick, in so far as He employed His $\psi v \chi \eta$ as the intermediary by which the light of His presence could be transmitted without restriction and without being overcome by the body in which His $\psi v \chi \eta$ resided. In this passage it seems to be suggested that only the Incarnation can transmit the full Light, in spite of what has been said in Ch. II, p.51.

There are many passages in which the effect of the coming into the world of the Divine Light in the person of Jesus Christ is said to be the creation of spiritual day for those who receive that light. Thus in one passage [18] Origen says that just as there are lights in the firmament of heaven to divide the day from the night (cf. Gen.i.14), even so there can be in us lights to illuminate us, namely Christ and His Church, although it is Christ from Whom the Church derives its own light, just as the moon derives light from the sun, so that those who walk in the night of ignorance can be illuminated. The person who makes such progress as to walk honourably as in the day (Rom.xiii.13) is enlightened by Christ directly as the day is by the sun. The Church seems here to be conceived of in a fashion analogous to the way in which the Jewish Law was conceived of by St. Paul, namely as a preliminary teacher who introduces us to Christ (cf. Gal.iii.24).[19] But there are also degrees in the illumination afforded by Christ, depending on the progress of the human mind in its ascension towards Him, just as the human eye can appropriate the light of the sun more fully from a height.[20] Elsewhere [21] Origen says that the Saviour in His capacity as the Light of the world does not illuminate corporeal things, but rather illuminates the incorporeal νοῦς by His own incorporeal power, so that each of us can thus see things which are apprehensible by the mind (νοητά). Origen also regards the spiritual day brought about by the Light of Christ as coming into being in two ways (the reference being to the words "The night is far spent and the day is at hand" in Rom. xiii.12). This day in the universal sense will only come about in the future age after the darkness of this present world has come to an end; but individuals can anticipate the coming of this day in so far as they receive Him into themselves and are thus enabled to do what is good and honourable.[22]

It is worth mentioning that Origen contradicts himself in two ways in connection with his doctrine of Christ as creating spiritual day. In the first place, he says, with reference to John xi.9, that the number of the Patriarchs and the Apostles symbolises the twelve hours of the day, because they have seen the Divine Christ who is the "intelligible day" (νοητή ἡμέρα) in so far as we obtain an understanding of God's message through Him.[23] The implication is that the Patriarchs had knowledge of Christ before the Incarnation. Elsewhere [24] it is stated that the penitent thief on the Cross was enlightened by the Word of God, as was Paul later on after he had persecuted Him. Whereas in another passage [25] it is said that the Lord pointed out that it was in the night that the disciples were made to stumble (Matt.xxvi.31), because the Resurrection had not yet occurred and the disciples were thus unable to recognise fully Who He was and what He had come to do.[26] Secondly, it is suggested in one passage [27] that the righteous man will be in perfect day all his life, because he will have ascended above this world which was created in six days, and will thus praise God "seven times a day" (Ps.cxix.164). But in another passage [28] it is pointed out that according to Ps.i.2 the man who is going to be blessed by God must meditate on the Divine Law "day and night", whereas in Ps.cxix.97 it is said that "I meditate on Thy law all the day." Origen says that the reference in the second passage is to the future life, when we shall attain to perfect holiness, because man's life here is a mixture of virtue and its opposite, in so far as there are bound to be times when he either performs God's will half-heartedly or else transgresses it. [29]

It would seem that Origen did not always distinguish between the knowledge which the disciples had of the earthly Christ and the knowledge which the Christian believer can gain of the unseen Christ. Thus in one passage [30] it is stated that the disciples enjoyed the brightest day when their feet were being washed by Jesus in the upper room, because the stains in the feet of their souls were being cleansed and removed; but there was night when they forsook Him and fled. Nor was there darkness for Peter when he acknowledged His Master to be the Messiah; but there was night for him when he denied his Master. Likewise, as St. John says (xiii.30), the night supervened for Judas when having received the sop he went out of the upper room, because he had in so doing forsaken the Sun of Righteousness. It seems more in accordance with Origen's teaching to say that in the earlier stages of spiritual growth the Light only fitfully appears, but when it dawns in its full brilliance it can never fade away. To receive the Light momentarily is not really to receive it at all, because it is not merely an object of contemplation, but rather a transforming power. [31] The same confusion between the work of Christ on earth and His unseen influence is shown in another passage, [32] where it is said that when the "intelligible sun" ($\nu o \eta \tau \grave{o} \varsigma$ $\mathring{\eta} \lambda \iota o \varsigma$) appeared in the world, the Divine and inexplicable wonders which flashed forth revealed still more the darkness and blindness which had taken captive the souls of those Jews who remained unbelieving. Surely if the Light had shone forth in the full sense, the Jews would have been converted. Another passage [33] gives an insight into Origen's real doctrine of the Divine Light. He there says that we should try to spend three days being buried with Christ and so receive full knowledge of the Divine Trinity, seeing that the Father is light, and in the light of Him Who is the Son we see the Holy Spirit. This passage is a very striking illustration of Origen's twofold doctrine of the knowledge of Christ, the first being "knowledge after the flesh" (II Cor.v.16), and the second a higher kind of knowledge. The consequences of that knowledge are indicated in another passage,[34] where it is said that now that the Word of God has appeared, each of those who believe in Him kindles in himself from the Word, without its being in any way diminished, the Light which It gives, with the result that from one Light many lamps come into being. Origen goes on to say that having received the Word once for all, we must make use of this Light continually, whether in action, or in word, or in thought.

But it should always be remembered that it is from the Father alone that the Son receives the enlightenment which He then imparts to other beings. This seems implied in the passage [35] where Origen says that the Son of God Himself is in need of the intellectual nourishment supplied by the Father, Who is alone self-sufficient; only after having received such nourishment Himself can the Son then impart it to men and angels. Origen also says elsewhere; [36] "Just as my food is the Word of God Who said 'I am the living Bread Who gives life to the world', so the food of Wisdom is the Father Himself."

Let us now consider the distinctive glory of the Son. Origen suggests that it consists in His being acquainted with the Father, with reference to the passage "Now is the Son of Man glorified, and God is glorified in Him" (John xiii.31). The Father being the highest Good, the Son is glorified by the very fact of knowing Him, and thereby knowing Himself. [37] For although a derived knowledge of the Father is possessed by those whose minds are illuminated by the Divine Word, absolute knowledge and understanding of the Father is possessed by the Word alone in accordance with His merits. [38] Elsewhere, Origen also says that it is the Son alone Who knows the Father, and that the pure in heart will only see Him because Christ reveals Him to them. [39] Again, Origen says that since God is Charity, and "one-one knows the Father except the Son, and him to whom it shall please the Son to reveal him" (Matt.xi.27), it follows that no-one knows Charity except the Son, and no-one knows the Son, since He Himself is also Charity, but the Father. [40] On the other hand the Holy Spirit, Who is also called Charity, continually searches for souls to whom He can reveal the surpassing love which comes from God. [41]

But in so far as the Father is known by the Son, the Father can Himself be said to be glorified in the Son. But, Origen goes on to say, it may be that God is more highly glorified in Himself than He is in the Son, in so far as He knows and contemplates Himself more fully than the Son can contemplate Him. [42] This text is referred to by Maydieu [43] after he has quoted [44] another passage [45] which suggests that the Son, being the Truth, knows all that the Father knows. The only way of reconciling these two passages would seem to be to distinguish between what the Son knows in His Divine Nature and what He knows in His humanity. But that tends to make of the Son two persons. This difficulty is discussed more fully later on. [46] In *De Princ.* [47] it is stated that the Son, although He is the Image of the invisible Father, is not the truth when compared with the Father; but He conveys to us the truth which we are able to receive, seeing that we cannot receive the full truth of God Almighty. Origen can only avoid the charge of Arianism in the passage if it is taken as referring to the Son in His human nature. [48] The same comment can be made on the passage [49] where it is stated that God the Father is known more fully by Himself than by the Son, thus exemplifying the truth of the statement made by the Son that "the Father Who sent me is greater than I" (John xiv.28).[50]

But the glory of the Son has another aspect, in so far as He is fully acquainted with the universe itself (ἡ περὶ τῶν ὅλων γνῶσις συμπληροῖ τὸ μέγεθος τῆς δόξης αὐτοῦ), knowing as He does alike what is open and what is secret. [51] Thus Origen says in one place that the beginning and end of all things can only be understood by Jesus Christ and the Holy Spirit, and that this is why the prophet Isaiah speaks of two seraphim only as standing in the immediate presence of God, veiling His face with two wings and His feet with two other wings (Is.vi.2,3). [52] But the wisdom this displayed by the Son is granted to Him by the Father, from which it follows that His glory is granted to Him by the Father alone.

In several passages the Son's knowledge of the universe is connected with His activity as Creator. Thus in one passage [53] Origen suggests that the devil, when he described the world in the third temptation, thought that he was in some way revealing it to Christ, whereas the truth was that Christ, as Maker of all things, was ignorant of nothing. Elsewhere [54] it is said that if the Father were to announce His deeds to the Son, He would be speaking to One Who was posterior to the deeds, whereas the Son is the Father's Agent and is thus fully aware of the Father's deeds. Origen also says that our Lord's knowledge of human nature is simply part of His universal knowledge,[55] and that the only reason why He asked who had touched His clothes was that the woman who was cured of the issue of blood should make the admission of her cure openly to all.[56]

Elsewhere, Origen makes a distinction between knowledge of actual fact and knowledge of what is possible, when he says that not only is the knowledge possessed by God unattainable by any derived being other than Christ and the Holy Spirit,[57] but the Saviour contains within Himself a complete assemblage of concepts (συστήματος θεωρημάτων), not all of which can be grasped by the things brought into being apart from Himself. [58] On the other hand the Only-begotten Son imparts to other beings such a share in this knowledge as they are worthy to receive. He Himself, as Truth, understands the significance (λόγον) of all things; otherwise He would not be the Truth in its entirety; that is the significance of the statement regarding the heavenly Horseman in the last book of the Bible [59] that "He has a name written which no one knows but He Himself." On the other hand, those who participate in Him as the supreme Reason are admitted to knowledge from which others are shut out. [60]

(It is interesting, however, that Origen in one place observes that God is said in Scripture to be ignorant of what is not worthy of His knowledge. [61] This would seem to mean that in so far as His will is transgressed, His knowledge of such transgression only extends to persuading or compelling the transgressor to mend his ways.)

But the glory of the Son is derived not only from His universal knowledge, but also from His sinlessness. Origen begins by saying that through being without sin the Son gives glory to the Father to a greater extent than any other being does. But being thus glorified, the Father gives back to the Son a glory greater than He receives from the Son; for it is a greater thing for the Son to be glorified in the Father, the lesser in the greater. It befitted Him Who is the greater to return the glory with which the Son glorifies Him by granting to the Son the privilege of being glorified in the Father. [62] Origen also says that the right to receive honour has been granted to Jesus by God "so that all men may honour the Son as He honours the Father" (John v.23). The prophecies which occurred before His birth, and the miracles which He performed, were confirmations of His right to receive honour.[63] It is elsewhere said that our Lord is never found in Scripture to have said "I am Christ." [64] It sufficed for the faith of believers that He should do the works of God and display the power of God. Thus it was that He could pronounce Peter blessed as one who had not heard from Himself, but had learnt from the Father, that He (Christ) was the Son of the living God. [65] In the same way Origen says [66] that though Christ was greater than Abraham and the prophets, He did not elevate Himself to that status, but received it from the Father, so that when the Jews asked Him "Whom makest thou thyself?" (John viii.53), they showed themselves unaware that Jesus did not make Himself what He was. That was why He replied to this question by saying "If I honour myself, my honour is nothing: it is my Father Who honours me" (viii. 54). Elsewhere Origen says [67] that when it is said that it is God's intention that all should honour the Son as they honour the Father (John v.23), this means that prayer must be made to Christ in the same way as to God the Father, Christ must be invoked in the same way as the Father, and requests and thanksgivings must be addressed to the Son in the same way as to the Father. It will be pointed out, however, in a later section [68] that Origen does not always suggest that prayer be made directly to the Son in the same way as to the Father, because this would ignore the fact that the Son is not the ultimate Giver of benefits, but merely transmits them from the Father.

Another of the gifts bestowed by the Father on the Son is that of judgement. Thus with reference to the advice given by Jethro to Moses to appoint subordinate officers to make decisions on minor matters (Exod.xviii.22), Origen declares that "though the Father has given all judgement to the Son" (John v.22), the Son is not the only judge, but has also appointed other superintendents to judge human beings in matters of minor importance, while reserving major matters to Himself. [69] Origen says in fact [70] that the Father has given to the Son the authority to assign to each human being his deserts by virtue of the fact that He (the Son) is the personification of righteousness and judgement. Origen thus reveals the defects of all merely human justice: no other judge than the Son of God, he says, can so impress the marks of righteousness and justice on his soul as not to stand in need of righteousness and justice in their ideal forms, just as a painter cannot reproduce all the features of the thing painted. Elsewhere [71] Origen says that justice in itself ($αὐτοδικαιοσύνη$), justice which is real ($οὐσιώδης$), is Christ, "Who is made for us wisdom from God, and justice, and sanctification, and redemption" (I Cor.i.30); and from that justice the justice in each person is imprinted. [72] This statement is echoed in a passage where Origen says that what St. Paul means by saying that the Son of God "subdues all His enemies under His feet" (I Cor.xv.27) is that "He restores the corrupted laws of ruling and reigning" [73] by teaching earthly rulers how to exercise their office. [74] The opportunity is thus obtained of pointing out that when Jesus stood before Pilate, He Who was appointed Judge of all creatures by the Father, and can thus be called King of kings and Lord of lords, humbled Himself to the extent of standing before the judge of the land of Judaea. [75]

Elsewhere, [76] Origen interprets the words "The Lord brings the counsel of the nations to naught, and frustrates the plans of the peoples" (Ps.xxxiii.10) by saying that the Divine power of Jesus can, when He wishes, quench the anger of His enemies and scatter the counsels of the rebellious by the grace of God ($\theta\epsilon i\alpha\ \chi\acute{\alpha}\rho\iota\tau\iota$). This statement is explained in another passage [77] where Origen says that the Father, having given us the Son, seeks the glory of the Son in each of those who have received Him. That glory will be found in those who attend to themselves and cultivate the rudiments of virtue implanted within them. [78] But in others He will not find it, and will judge them accordingly. But the Father exercises such judgement through the agency of the Son, Who said not only "The Father has committed all judgement to the Son" (John v.22), but also "I can of my own self do nothing: as I hear, I judge; and my judgement is just, because I seek not my own will, but the will of Him Who sent me" (ibid.v.30). This being so, the judgement exercised by the Son is not His in the last resort, but that of the Father Who speaks through Him. [79] The same sentiment is expressed when Origen says [80] that to discern the merits of men and to see who has guile in himself and who has not belongs not to any of the many sons of God, but solely to the Only-begotten, the King of the chosen race, and that Jesus showed that He was Son of God by being able to do this.

On the other hand, it would appear that there is a judgement exercised directly by the Father; for Origen says [81] that it did not befit the Saviour to seek His own glory and thus to pass judgement on those who refused to give it to Him; it was rather a matter for the Father, Who had Himself glorified the Son, to demand the glory due to the Son from human beings, and to judge them if they refused to give it to Him. Likewise, the Son expects those to whom He imparts the knowledge of God the Father to give the Father the glory which is due to Him; and if His expectation is disappointed, He will exercise the authority given to Him to pass judgement upon them. In the same way Origen says [82] that because God is Love *(caritas)*, and the Son, Who derives His being from God, is likewise Love, God requires in us something like Himself. Having shown to us His love in Christ Jesus, He requires that we be united to Himself through this love in a relation of kinship.

NOTES ON CHAPTER III

[1] *Comm. in Joh.* I.10 (GCS 4.15.26-28). Cf. *Matt. Comm. Series* 121 (GCS 11.256.19,21,22 and 12,13). *Ubi autem est Jesus ... ibi sunt omnia simul bona, et innumerabiles divitiae spiritales in manibus eius, et pax.* And above: *Jesus ... quasi Filius Dei, et pax constitutus, et verbum, et sapientia, et omnia bona.* Cf. also *Contra Cels.* III.34 (GCS 1.231.8,9), where it is said that "Christ brings to us the benefits of the Father" (φέροντος ἡμῖν τὰς ἀπὸ τοῦ Πατρὸς εὐεργεσίας).
Cf. also *Hom. in Num.* XII.1 (GCS 7.97.9,10 and 96.9,10 and 94. 22-25); XII.4 (7.104.28-105.1); XX.2 (7.190.22-24 and 191.4,5); XXIII.4 (7.216.5-11).
Cf. also Mme. Harl, op. cit., pp.290-292.

[2] *Comm. in Joh.* II.23 (GCS 4.80.1-6).

[3] Cf. I. Tim.vi.16.

[4] pp. 7 and 8.

[5] See Ch.I, pp.11 and 12.

[6] Crouzel, *L'Image,* p.103, would appear to agree with the present writer; for he suggests that the word οὐσία, as used in the passage referred to in n.2, may either mean "individual existence" or else refer to the entire reality of the Word of God, ie. not only His Divine Nature, but also His position as Mediator between the Father and the world. (Crouzel also points out that the Word in His Divine Nature acted as Mediator even before the Incarnation: but this fact seems irrelevant to his contention.) In *La Conn.*, p. 132, Crouzel explains this passage of Origen by reference to the Incarnation. Cf. also Mme. Harl, op. cit., p.132. See also *Comm. in Joh.* II.26 (GCS 4.83.25-31), where it is said that it is not strictly true to say that there is "no darkness" in the Incarnate Son, because in His benevolent activity towards mankind He took the darkness of our souls upon Himself in so far as He was subject to distress and tribulation (Mark xiv.34).

[7] *Comm. in Joh.* II.23 (GCS 4.80.12-15). See also Balas, op. cit., p.9. On the other hand, Origen in one passage applies to the Father the phrase "the true Light which enlightens every man" (John i.9), when he says that after death the soul traverses the various "resting-places" and is increasingly enlightened until the time when it can endure to behold "the true Light, which enlightens every man" (*Hom. in Num.* XXVII.5 (GCS 7.262.28-

263.4). The same idea is expressed in ibid.XXVII.6 (264.8-12), where the goal of the soul's journey is described as "the Father of lights" (James i.17).
8   *De Princ.* I.1.1 (GCS 5.17.12-14). Cf. J. Rius-Camps, "Comunicabilidad", (*OCP* 38,1972), p.432.
9   *De Princ.* I.2.4 (GCS 5.33.1,2), and *Frag. in Heb.* (PG XIV.1307 BC). Cf. Nemeshegyi, op. cit., pp.70 and 71, and Boon, op. cit., p.29.
10 *De Princ.* I.2.7 (GCS 5.37.7-9). Maydieu, op. cit., p.68, suggests that the metaphor of brightness proceeding from light is avoided by Origen in *Comm. in Joh.* so as to avoid the suggestion of emanationism or modalism. Origen does not restrict himself to this extent in *De Princ.*
11 *Contra Cels.* V.11 (GCS 2.11.19-23 and 12.3-5).
12 *Hom. in Ezek.* IX.3 (GCS 8.411.17-27). Crouzel *L'Image*, p.109, n.186, and *La Conn*, p.134, quotes this passage as referring to the Second Coming; but why should it not refer to the personal knowledge of Christ which the believer gains after initial instruction by the representatives of the Church?
13 *Frag. in Luc.* 123.3-5 (GCS 9.277).
14 *Hom. in Jos.* XVII.1 (GCS 7.400.19-401.5).
15 Ibid.XVII.2 (GCS 7.403.14,15).
16 *Comm. in Matt.* X.9 (GCS 10.10.23-26, 28-30). Cf. *Comm. in Joh.* II.17 (GCS 4.74.11-18); ibid.XXXII.27 (GCS 4.473.3-9); *Frag. in Joh.* VI (GCS 4.488.9-16); ibid.XVII (GCS 4.496.23-25); ibid.CXVII (GCS 4.566.15,16); *Hom. in Lev.* XIII.2 (GCS 6.468.23-469.8); *Comm. in Matt.* XVI.3 (GCS 10.470.21-26); *Frag. in Matt.* 43 (GCS 12.33).
Cf. also de Lubac, op. cit., pp.575, 576, where he says:- "Is it the case that no ray of the light which was going to shine in Jesus filtered through under the Old Law? Indeed not. But these rays, like those of the dawn, proceeded already from the Sun which was to come. One could thus, like Origen, call them a shadow." Cf. also Crouzel, *La Conn.*, (pp.140-142).
17 *Frag. in Luc.* 122.1-4 (GCS 9.276). I adopt Fruchtels's conjecture πῦρ διήκων μὴ τῷ τῆς σαρκὸς ὀστράκῳ κρατούμενος. See Ch.V, pp.128-130.
18 *Hom. in Gen.* I.5 (GCS 6.7.11-21). Cf. *Hom. in Ps.* XXXVI.III.9 (PG XII.1344A-C); *Hom. in Ps.* XXXVIII.I.8 (PG XII.1398D-1399A); *Sel. in Ps.* CI.25 (PG XII.1560A); *Sel. in Ps.* CXVII.24

[19] (PG XII.1584B); Pitra A.S.III.540 (in Jer.xvii.21-26). Cf. Ch.VI, pp.210, 211 and Ch.VII, pp.238,239, where the Christian Gnostic is distinguished from those who simply receive the testimony of others.
[20] *Hom. in Gen.* I.7 (GCS 6.9.10-18).
[21] *Comm. in Joh.* I.25 (GCS 4.31.17-20). Cf. Mme. Harl, op. cit., p. 108, where Origen is quoted as saying that Christ is the Light which at the same time enables the eye to see and the object to be seen. Cf. also Mersch, *Le Corps Mystique du Christ* (Louvain, 1933), p.356.
[22] *Comm. in Rom.* IX.32 (PG XIV.1233AC). Cf. Pitra, A.S.II.382 (in Job xxxv.10). Cf. also *Frag. in Joh.* XXXIV (GCS 4.509.25-510.1); *Hom. in Jud.* I.1 (GCS 7.464.9-16, 465.21,22); *Frag. in Luc.* 100.10-14 (GCS 9.267); *Sel. in Ps.* CXIX.5 (PG XII.1629D, 1632A).
[23] *Frag. in Joh.* CXXXVII (GCS 4.573.6-10).
[24] *Frag. in Joh.* CXII (GCS 4.564.19-565.4).
[25] *Matt. Comm. Series* 87 (GCS 11.201.5-12).
[26] Cf. Ch.II, p.40, where something similar is said of the Old Testament prophets.
[27] *Sel. in Ps.* CXVIII.164 (PG XII.1624C). Cf. Cadiou, *Frag. in Ps.* CXVIII.91[a](1) (p.113), where it is said that for the saints, their sun does not set, since the Lord is to them an everlasting light. Cf. also ibid.c.8, lines 1-6 (p.86), and also *Frag. in Apol. of Pamph.* on Ps.XVIII.6 (PG XII.1241-1244), where it is said that the Church is set in that Sun which brings about eternal day.
[28] *Sel. in Ps.* CXVIII.97 (PG XII.1605BC).
[29] Cf. Ch.VII, pp.236 and 243, where it is pointed out that Origen at times suggests that the full vision of God is only obtainable in the after-life.
[30] *Comm. in Joh.* XXXII.24 (GCS 4.469.1-14).
[31] See Ch.VII, pp.261,262.
[32] *Frag. in Joh.* XCIV (GCS 4.557.31-558.6).
[33] *Comm. in Rom.* V.8 (PG XIV.1040C).
[34] Pitra A.S.III.292 (Ps.CXVIII.105).
[35] *Comm. in Joh.* XIII.34 (GCS 4.259.17-25). Cf. Crouzel, *La Conn.*, p.168.
[36] *Hom. in Is.* III.3 (GCS 8.256.29-257.1).
[37] *Comm. in Joh.* XXXII.28 (GCS 4.473.10-15).
[38] *Contra Cels.* VI.17 (GCS 2.88.16-21). Cf. Matt.xi.27. Cf. also

Crouzel, *La Conn.,* p.513, and Maydieu, op. cit., pp.52,53, where he says: "The procession of the Son is unique because the Son alone sees the Father. It is purely intelligible because the Son is the thought of the Father; by a kind of dynamic current which is effected by a permanent rhythm of coming and going in the sphere of the Divine Life enfolded in itself, the Father apprehends the Son and the Son apprehends the Father." Cf. also *Frag. in Joh.* XIII (GCS 4.495.20-25), and Maydieu, op. cit., pp.51-53, where this passage is discussed.

39 *Comm. in Cant.* III (GCS 8.215.1-3).
40 Cf. *Hom. in Num.* XIV.4 (GCS 7.128.12,13).
41 *Prol. in Cant.* (GCS 8.74.21-30). See Teichtweier, op. cit., p.268, where this passage is quoted.
42 *Comm. in Joh.* XXXII.28 (GCS 4.473.22-31).
43 Op. cit., p.65.
44 On p.64.
45 *Comm. in Joh.* I.27 (GCS 4.34.19-31).
46 See Ch.V, p.113. Cf. also Aeby, op. cit., pp.159-161.
47 *De Princ.* I.2.6 (quotation from Jerom. ad Avitum 2 (GCS 5.36, lines 2-6 of notes)). Cf. Ch.I, n.73.
48 Cf. Aeby, op. cit., pp.159-161.
49 *De Princ.* IV.4.8 (GCS 5.360.2-7).
50 On the other hand Prat, op. cit., p.66, quotes a passage from *Hom. in Reg.* I.13 (PG XII.1009) which suggests that there is no distinction to be made among the three Divine Persons so far as greatness is concerned. He remarks: "We are here far from the language of subordination. It is forgotten when it does not serve to solve exegetical difficulties(!). There is no longer any hierarchy among the Persons . . . they are so united amongst themselves in the same Divine essence that the distinction of Persons seems compromised. But the accusations of Sabellianism and Arianism levelled against Origen cancel each other out. It is simply that having in mind the heresies he had to combat, he emphasised now the union and now the distinction of Persons." I think that Prat is too concerned here to defend Origen; he is not prepared to recognise the inner contradiction in Origen's thought arising from his having made too sweeping assumptions which were afterwards called in question by the facts.
51 *Comm. in Joh.* XXXII.28 (GCS 4.473.17-22). Cf. on this point Nemeshegyi, op. cit., pp.110.111.

52 *De Princ.* IV.3.14 (GCS 5.346.11-17). Cf. *Hom. in Num.* XVIII. 2 (GCS 7.169.4-13), where it is said that only the Son and the Holy Spirit know the plan and purpose of the Father. Cf. also *Sel. in Ps.* IX.2,3 (PG XII.1188A).
53 *Frag. in Luc.* 97.2-4 (GCS 9.266).
54 Cadiou, *Frag. in Ps.* XLIV.2, p.77. Cf. *Frag. in Jer.* 17 (GCS 3. 206. 13,14) and Pitra A.S.II.383 (in Job xxxviii.5).
55 *Comm. in Joh.* X.46 (GCS 4.225.11), with reference to John.ii. 25.
56 *Frag. in Luc.* 127.8-10 (GCS 9.280). Cf. Ch.V,pp. 119,120,where the extent of our Lord's knowledge is also discussed.
57 *Comm. in Joh.* II.28 (GCS 4.85.4-8).
58 Ibid.II.18 (GCS 4.75.19-21) also referred to in Ch.II. n.66. It is to be noted that Origen uses the word γενητοῖς to mean "derived beings" in the previous quotation and γεννητῷ φύσει with the same meaning in the present one, both words being intended to include Christ and the Holy Spirit.
59 Rev.xix.12.
60 *Comm. in Joh.* I.27 (GCS 4.34.19-31) and II.8 (4.62.14-19). Cf. Pitra A.S.III.160 (Ps.LXXXVIII.9).
61 *Hom. in Ps.* XXXVI.III.9 (PG XII.1343D).
62 *Comm. in Joh.* XXXII.29 (GCS 4.475.12-25). Mumm on p.182 of his thesis, *A critical appreciation of Origen as an exegete of the Fourth Gospel*, remarks that "in spite of Origen's emphasis on the equality of the Father and the Son, a decided note of subordinationism appears as he discusses the comparative glory of each." Cf. also *Sel. in Ps.* IV.9,10 (PG XII.1168B).
63 *Contra Cels.* VIII.9 (GCS 2.227.20-26).
64 Origen seems to have overlooked John iv.26.
65 *Matt. Comm. Series* 33 (GCS 11.63.23-64.3).
66 *Comm. in Joh.* XX.44 (GCS 4.388.17-29).
67 *Comm. in Rom.* VIII.5 (PG XIV.1166A).
68 See Ch,V, pp.112,113.
69 *Hom. in Exod.* XI.6 (GCS 6.259.13-16). *Constituit sibi et alios principes, qui judicet populum de minoribus causis, Verbum autem, quod gravius fuerit, referant ad ipsum.* Cf. *Matt. Comm. Series* 62 (GCS 11.143.8-16) and *Frag.in Matt.* 202 (GCS 12.97).
70 *Comm. in Joh.* II.6 (GCS 4.60.24-31). Cf. *Frag. in Rom.* XV.3-5 (*JTS* 13.221).
71 Ibid.VI.6 (GCS 4.114.34-115.5). Cf. also Pitra A.S.III.268 (Ps.

CXVIII.40), and 301,302 (Ps.CXVIII.142).
72 Cf. Nemeshegyi, op. cit., p.76, where he discusses the meanings of αὐτοδικαιοσύνη and other abstract nouns to which αὐτο- is prefixed. Cf. also p.109, and Crouzel, *L'Image*, p.231.
73 *Regendi... regnandique corruptas restitueret leges.*
74 *De Princ.* III.5.6 (GCS 5.277.7-11). Cf. also the words in III.5.7 (278.15,16): *regendi ac regnandi summam, quam in universa emendaverat creatura.* Cf. Pitra, A.S.III.104 (LXXIV.3), and *Frag. in Eph.* IX.90-95 (*JTS* 3.401).
75 *Matt. Comm. Series* 118 (GCS 11.250.15-29).
76 *Comm. in Joh.* X.25 (GCS 4.197.28-34).
77 Ibid.XX.38 (GCS 4.379.7-26).
78 Cf. *Hom. in Jer.* V.8 (GCS 3.38.8-13), where Origen says that if we wish to lay aside the covering which comes from dishonour, we must hasten to perform honourable deeds, in accordance with the Saviour's words "That all may honour the Son as they honour the Father" (John v.23); for the righteous honour the Son as He honours the Father.
79 In *Hom. in Num.* VIII.1 (GCS 7.50.34-51.7), Origen also quotes the text "The Father has committed all judgement to the Son" as indicating that only the Son is aware of the length of the penalties which human sins require, and how far those penalties can be counteracted by the good deeds and sufferings which have been performed and endured on earth by the same individual. In *Hom. in Num.* XXI.1 (GCS.7.199.27-200.5), Origen also says, quoting the same text, that the Son is authorised by the Father to assign to each individual the type of blessedness which he deserves in the future life, whether it be a share in the "land of the living", or simply a share in the wisdom of God. The second class of individuals is said to share the glory conferred on Jesus Christ Himself, reference being made to John xvii.24 (ibid.XXI.3 (7.203.7-20)). Cf. Ch.VI, pp. 214-216 where the same suggestion seems to be made in other language, namely that Christians can be divided into two categories, depending on whether or not they are able to appreciate Divine mysteries.
80 *Frag. in Joh.* XXVI (GCS 4.504.1-4).
81 *Comm. in Joh.* XX.38 (GCS 4.379.33-380.6).
82 *Prol. in Cant.* (GCS 8.70.12-17).

CHAPTER IV.

CONTENTS

THE GIFTS WHICH THE SON RECEIVES TO BESTOW ON
HUMAN BEINGS – REASON, SANCTIFICATION AND WISDOM

The fundamental gift of the Word of God to the
individual soul is reason								87

But the chief gift is sanctification						87

Goodness is not an essential part of the nature of
men and angels; it can be lost, and is only received
from God										88

The Son prepares created beings in various ways –
either by admonition or by chastisement – to receive
sanctification									89

Though Christ as Wisdom pervades the universe, only
through the incarnate Christ is this wisdom fully
appropriated by created beings						92

NOTES on Chapter IV								95

CHAPTER IV

THE GIFTS WHICH THE SON RECEIVES TO BESTOW ON
HUMAN BEINGS – REASON, SANCTIFICATION AND WISDOM

When we turn to consider the gifts bestowed by Christ on human beings, we discover that the fundamental gift is reason. [1] Thus Origen says that natural law and reason and freewill are betrothal gifts of the Word of God to the individual soul, bestowed so that it may later on be more fully enlightened by the Word Himself. [2] Elsewhere, [3] with reference to John the Baptist's statement about Christ "In your midst stands One whom you do not know" (John i.26), Origen says that the Word of God is present to every rational being, in so far as the faculty of thought is in the midst of us; for it is there that the indwelling reason (ὁ ἐνδιάθετος λόγος) is present, this being the faculty which the Word of God Who came to be baptised supervises (ἐπισκοπεῖ). Origen appears to mean that the personal Word of God aims to bring into consciousness and activity that aspect of Himself which lies dormant in individual human beings. [4] The same idea seems expressed in the passage [5] where the statement "If I had not come and spoken to them they would not have had sin" (John xv.22) is interpreted to mean that by virtue of that power by which Christ is said to fill the world (ie. the power of reason), He visits each man and speaks to him inwardly and teaches him to distinguish good from evil. Elsewhere, [6] Origen makes the somewhat cryptic remark that it is possible for one who is a "seed of Abraham" to become his child (τέκνον) through diligence. This would seem to mean that just as Abraham used to the full his inborn ability to become acquainted with Christ, so others can do the same. [7] On the other hand, Origen also says that it is possible through negligence and lack of cultivation to cease even to be Abraham's seed – a suggestion which seems to contradict his doctrine of universal redemption, in so far as it implies that the gift of reason can be so atrophied as to become unusable.

But the chief gift which Christ bestows is sanctification, ie. being made like God so far as holiness is concerned. Thus Origen says,[8] with reference to Hannah's declaration that "there is none holy like the Lord" (I Sam.ii.2: *non est sanctus nisi Dominus*), that however much progress in holiness *(sanctitate)* a man may make, no-one can be holy in the same manner as the Lord, because He is the Giver of holiness, and man is the receiver *(ille sanctitatis largitor est, iste susceptor)*. [9] Elsewhere [10] Origen says that however righteous, however holy a being may be, not only among men but among higher and more distinguished creatures, he cannot be considered righteous when compared with God. Only our Lord and Saviour Jesus Christ is accounted righteous *(justificatur)* in the sight of the Father, because "whatever the Father does, these things the Son also does in like manner" (John v.19). Origen also says [11] that it is through the agency of the Divine Word that human beings become righteous, both before and after the Incarnation. But the power to do what is praiseworthy is only bestowed on those prepared by faith and virtue to receive it.[12]

Elsewhere he points out that it cannot be said of men and angels that goodness resides in them as part of their nature *(non substantiale sit in ipsis bonum)*, because that is only the case with the Father, the Son, and the Holy Spirit, in Whose nature there is nothing compound, so that goodness cannot be said to belong to it as a consequence of anything,[13] nor can it be taken away.[14] Thus it is said elsewhere [15] that God does not love righteousness as man does, so that he may possess it within himself and act in accordance with it. In a curious interpretation of Mark xi.2, where reference is made to an ass "upon which no man has yet sat", Origen declares that this means that those who eventually believed in Jesus never subjected themselves to reason before He came to dwell in them (πρὸ τῆς Ἰησοῦ ἐν αὐτοῖς ἐπιδημίας).[16] Elsewhere, the kingdom of heaven referred to in Matt.iii.2 is said to mean the presence (παρουσία) of Christ, because this grants to us a share in the Holy Spirit and access to the unchangeable goodness in store for the saints in the coming age.[17] Again, Origen says that the righteous are so called after the righteousness of Christ, and the wise after the wisdom of Christ, just as those who are members of Christ are called Christs (χριστοί) after Him.[18]

It follows that all beings other than the Persons of the Divine Trinity only possess goodness accidentally, and they are therefore liable to lose it, because they only receive it as something imparted by the Divine nature.[19] In the same way, Origen elsewhere says that there is no nature which is not capable of receiving both good and evil, with the exception of the nature of God, which is the source of all good things, and the nature of Christ and the Holy Spirit.[20] Other beings only become holy as the result of receiving the Holy Spirit, and thus do not possess it as something natural to them, but as something added, something therefore which can also disappear. [21] Again, he says that no rational being, of whatever kind, possesses by nature (οὐσιωδῶς) blessedness of which it can never be deprived. For if the highest form of life (τὴν προηγουμένην ζωήν), were something of which it could never be deprived, how could it then be true that God alone has immortality (I Tim.vi.16)? [22] (On the other hand Origen confuses "life" in the sense of "spiritual life" and "life" in the sense of "natural life" when he says that whereas God alone possesses the life which is unchangeable and unalterable (τὴν ἄτρεπτον πάντη καὶ ἀναλλοίωτον ζωήν), Christ Himself did not possess the Father's immortality, seeing that He tasted death on behalf of all (Heb.ii.9). [23] Origen has in fact said earlier that no one can be called "living" unless he has holiness together with life.) [24] Again, when our Lord called the disciples "evil" (Matt.vii.9,10), He meant that even if they chose to follow Him, they still possessed the changeability (τὸ τρεπτόν) of the human mind, whereas only the Son of God was unchangeable (ἄτρεπτος) both in His Godhead and in His manhood. [25] Elsewhere, Origen points out that it depends on man's own efforts to imitate God whether he acquires the virtues which exist in God essentially *(per substantiam)*, because whereas in God these virtues exist for ever, in man they are only acquired gradually and individually. [26] In a striking passage, Origen compares the city of Jerusalem to the individual soul (ψυχή), whose magnificence derives from wisdom and the virtues, but whose virtue is changeable, with the result that she can be deserted and widowed. [27]

But just as the Son imparts sanctification and righteousness to human beings, so the Father imparts sanctification and righteousness to the Son. [28] The Son prepares all creatures in one way or another – whether by admonition or by chastisement – to receive the sanctification which the Father desires to bestow; and in particular the Son tasted death apart from the Father (χωρὶς θεοῦ) on behalf of all men. [29] Thus Origen says [30] that when it is stated that "God renders to each man what he deserves", this does not mean that God punishes human beings because he hates them; He is simply applying remedies which, even though their purpose is the improvement of the sinner, none the less cause feelings of pain at the time. Elsewhere [31] it is stated, with reference to the hardening of Pharaoh's heart, that the Word of God, as a physician of the soul, employs remedies of various kinds, depending on the condition of those who are spiritually sick. If the disease has penetrated into the inmost parts, the doctor has to draw it out by administering greater pains and inflammations than were previously experienced, as with those bitten by a mad dog. In another passage [32] it is also stated that God hardened Pharaoh's heart in the sense of refraining from inflicting severe punishment until his wickedness had reached its peak, so as to give him the opportunity of repenting. To quote Origen's own words, "it is not the case that God hardens him whom He wishes to harden, but the person who refuses to submit to God's patience is hardened." (This explanation seems rather far-fetched, and takes inadequate account of God's universal operations, both outside and within human beings.) [33] There are two passages where God is said to be "cruel in order to be kind", as the common phrase has it. There is a mercy which is so overcome by the prospect of the distress which would be caused to the patient that it refrains from taking the measures which would be needed to cure the disease. Such mercy is not characteristic of God. [34]

The wrath of God is in fact not the same as human wrath — an emotion — but rather His reaction to those who do not submit to being guided by His Word. Thus Origen says that though Jesus brings to perfection every rational creature, He does so in different ways. For those who obey reason are perfected by reason alone, whereas those disobedient to reason need hardships ($\pi\acute{o}\nu\omega\nu$), so that after those hardships they may be assisted by reason and so finally attain perfection in this way. [35] Elsewhere, it is said that God's anger ($\theta\upsilon\mu\acute{o}\varsigma$) is a manifestation of His goodness, because it accomplishes a salutary work by chastening the offender. Origen goes on to say that the abundance of God's goodness and kindness is stored up for those who fear Him and for them alone, because if they did not fear Him they would lay up wrath for themselves through despising the riches of His kindness and patience. [36] Origen interprets the words "Our God is a consuming fire" (Heb.xii.29) as meaning that in so far as there exist in us those things which deserve to be consumed, God is a fire which consumes them; but when they have been consumed, God will cease to be a consuming fire and will become, as St. John says, Light. [37]

As has been said, the wrath of God is not a feeling; indeed that is made evident by the fact that He foreknows everything. The same is true of His so-called "repentance", whereby he changes from one course of action to another in His dealings with human beings. There is no question of His having been mistaken, because this change of action is in accordance with His pre-determined plan. God knows whether human beings will show themselves unworthy of His kindness. [38]

It is thus true that even though God is not affected by any emotion, we can none the less lay up wrath for ourselves by our sins (cf. Rom.ii.5). [39] We can therefore say "Lord, do not rebuke me in Thy anger, nor chasten me in Thy wrath" (Ps.vi.1), and "Chasten us, Lord, but with judgement, and not in Thine anger, lest Thou make us few in number" (Jer.x.24), in so far as we are prepared to see the error of our ways. [40] It is also possible to distinguish between the "perfect will of God" (Rom.xii.2) and His will as related to our own condition, even though His will is always good. Origen adduces as an example the will of God that Saul should be made king of Israel. This was not His acceptable and perfect will, but arose from His displeasure with the people of Israel for refusing to have Him as their sole King (I Sam.vii.7 sqq.). The will of God is thus sometimes accomplished in granting our desires, so that we may be punished by reaping the bitter consequences. [41] This is one way in which God acts in a human fashion, bearing with His people's moods as a man bears with the moods of his son (cf. Deut.i.31). [42] In fact, the incarnate Son of God pursued the same course, in so far as He carried out this plan of God in governing human beings, and was thus called the Son of Man (the man standing for God, as is often the case in the parables). [43]

On the other hand, His patience is not inexhaustible. He is liable to act as a rod ($ῥάβδος$) towards those who are selfwilled and thus do not accept the love and gentleness of the Father. [44] But once a person accepts the chastisement inflicted by Christ as Rod, He ceases to be a rod but ascends and becomes a flower, in the sense that He enables the person chastened to bring forth the fruit of good works.[45] Origen likewise says elsewhere [46] that Christ becomes different things to different people according to their spiritual state. A slothful and negligent person needs Him as "rod", because he needs the compulsion of the rod to transfer him to a different state; whereas the person who has made progress in good living displays Christ as "flower." [47]

The curious situation thus arises that sinners are not only doers of wrong but also victims of wrong, inflicted by their own sinful tendencies. Hence those who are punished are avenged at the same time as they are punished. They are punished in so far as they have done wrong, but avenged in so far as they are wronged by their own wickedness. That wickedness is blotted out by the punishment, but those who are wronged are set free from it. [48]

What has so far been said is summed up in the passage which says that although the Word of God bestows the gift of reason on all beings which are rational, there is yet a second gift which He bestows on them, that of righteousness and wisdom, though this is only bestowed on those who have been sanctified by the Holy Spirit. [49] But all this is ultimately ascribable to the Father, Whose work of bringing creatures into existence is perfected when those creatures make the progress they are intended to make by receiving Christ in His characters of wisdom and sanctification. [50] It is worth observing that the wisdom imparted through Christ is said by Origen to have been at work to a lesser extent in notable men of previous generations, eg. Solomon. In other words, although Christ as Wisdom pervades the universe, it is only through the incarnate Christ that this wisdom is fully appropriated by human beings. [51] Elsewhere, Origen says that there is in each of us a well of living water which is equivalent to the hidden image of God, a well which has been filled with earthly thoughts and desires; but now that our Isaac has come, we have the opportunity to dig these wells and remove the earthly element from them so as to find in them living water (the reference is to Gen.xxvi.18). [52] Elsewhere, Origen says that He who said "I am the living Bread which came down from heaven" is the Word of God by which souls are fed and with which the righteous man continually fills his soul. [53] Elsewhere, again, Origen says that the words "Repent, for the kingdom of heaven is near" can be taken to mean that the Christ Who includes all the virtues within Himself has taken up residence among us and speaks to us, and therefore the kingdom of heaven is within (ἐντός) His disciples. [54]

It is passages such as these, and also the one referred to in note 29, which lead one to wonder whether Anders Nygren is liable to be charged with over-simplification when he suggests that the love *(agape)* of God shown in Christ's life and death was intended not for the philosophically minded, because these could ascend to God in spirit without such earthly aids, but for those less intellectually gifted to whom the truth could only be conveyed by means of events discernible by the senses. [55] Granted that Origen did distort the Faith by viewing it through Platonic spectacles, it could still be argued that for both classes of men — intellectuals and others — the saving acts of God in Christ were in Origen's view required for bringing home the real nature of God to them.

On the other hand Koch [56] seems justified in saying that Origen's Christianity was not the kind to which we are accustomed, nor for that matter is it that of St. Paul or of the Gospels. The concepts of love *(agape)* and of the forgiveness of sins, and the eschatology of the Gospels, lay outside Origen's own outlook. Origen was convinced that Christianity was of much greater practical utility than philosophy, but its purpose was merely that of leading souls upward to the knowledge of God. [57]

M. Hirschberg [58] remarks that "Koch has made it clear that the Greek motive of Providence stands out too strongly against the Christian motive of Love" (ie. in God's dealings with men). The two motives are surely not irreconcilable, but at the same time Origen's idea of the purpose of the love of God seems to have been that it was intended to lead to a fuller knowledge of God, whereas the authentic Christian view is that it enables human beings to carry out the purpose of God. Odo Casel [59] brings out the underlying tension in Origen's thought. He first says that for the higher knowledge called "Gnosis", the exercise of the human intellect is insufficient; the decisive factor is Christ, ie. the Divine revelation of the Father through the Incarnate Son, Who now fills the Church with His spiritual presence. But Casel then goes on to say that by "Christ" we must understand not merely the Teacher of the Gospel Who lived in the flesh, but Christ in His entire reality, in His Divine being as the Word of God, in His pre-existence as the Giver of the old Law. Hence when Casel goes on to say that according to Origen "Jesus Christ is the Truth, and men can only participate in the Truth through Him", that statement is ambiguous: Origen in a number of passages declares his belief that the Old Testament prophets themselves attained to the vision of Truth apart from the Incarnate Christ. [60]

NOTES ON CHAPTER IV

1. *Comm. in Joh.* II.3 (GCS 4.55.20,21). Cf. R. Franco's thesis, *El final del reino de Cristo en algunos autores antenicenos*, p.60, where this passage is quoted.
2. *Comm. in Cant.* I (GCS 8.91.4-17).
3. *Frag. in Joh.* CXVIII (GCS 4.566.24-30).
4. Cf. Mme. Harl, op. cit., p.94, where it is said that according to the philosophers of the 2nd century, "man receives the light of reason (logos), but darkened by the descent to a bodily state." Cf. also Kelber, op. cit., pp.243,244, and especially the following passage: "Origen is here (ie. in *Frag. in Joh.* CXVIII) saying that an experience of the Divine Word corresponding to the historical Baptism in Jordan is to be looked for in the principal part (ἡγεμ-ονικόν) of each person. We could express it in modern terms as the breakthrough of the higher self into the self – an experience occurring in the natural process of earthly life. Just as the self of Jesus of Nazareth gave place to the Christ-self in the Jordan Baptism, so each man is confronted with his Christ-self on his way through life, so that in the sphere of his natural gift of reason, his λόγος ἐνδιάθετος, and in his lower self, he may give place to Christ." Cf. also Fitzgerald's typescript thesis, pp.229 and 230, where this passage is quoted, and where the author comments: "Here we find Origen using the common Stoic terminology to explain the presence of Christ in mankind prior to the Incarnation in terms of the universal presence of the Word in mankind as taught by St. John in the prologue of his Gospel, and by the philosophers of the Stoic school."
5. *Comm. in Rom.* III.2 (PG XIV.931C).
6. *Comm. in Joh.* XX.5 (GCS 4.332.19-21).
7. Cf. Ch.VII, p.260, where a similar idea is expressed.
8. *Hom. in I Reg.* I.11 (GCS 8.20.4-13). In *Hom. in Num.* XI.8 (GCS 7.90.10-15) Origen likewise insists that it is only the being *(Substantia)* of the Divine Trinity which is by nature holy and does not receive holiness from any other source.
Cf. the discussion of this passage in D'hôtel's article "La sanctification du Christ d'après Heb.ii.11" (*RchSR* 47 (1958)), pp.518-520. Cf. also Rius-Camps, "Comunicabilidad" *OCP* 34, 1968, pp.7 and 23,24.
9. Cf. Mme. Harl, op. cit., p.136, where she says that "under the

title of logos . . . Origen speaks of the Divine wisdom imparted to man at the time of his creation, placed in him as a source of virtue and knowledge, a germ which can be developed."

10 *Comm. in Rom.* III.2 (PG XIV.932AB).
11 *Contra Cels.* VI.78 (GCS 2.150.1-6). Cf. *Hom. in Ps.* XXXVI.II.4 (PG XII.1333B) and *Comm. in Rom.* III.6 (PG XIV.939C).
12 *Frag. in Joh.* XLIV (GCS 4.519.5-10).
13 *De Princ.* I.5.3 (GCS 5.72.23-73.1). Cf. R. Cadiou, *Introduction au système d'Origène* (Paris, 1932), pp.52,53.
14 Ibid.I.5.5 (GCS 5.77.19-23).
15 *Frag. in Joh.* CXXVII (GCS 4.570.20-22). Cf. ibid.L (524.24-525.1), and *Sel. in Ps.* XVI.1 (PG XII.1217A).
16 *Comm. in Joh.* X.32 (GCS 4.206.11-15). Cf. *Contra Cels.* I.57 (GCS 1.108.8-10); *Sel. in Ps.*IV.2 (PG XII.1136C).
Kelber, op. cit., pp.255,256, quotes *Contra Cels.* 1.57 wrongly (unless the reference is mistaken), and also says, wrongly, that in this passage, as in others, sonship in relation to God the Father is ascribed to the Divine Word and not to Christ, who is distinguished from Him by Origen. Even if in certain passages such a distinction is made, the unique sonship of the Divine Word overflows, as it were, to Christ regarded as the soul perfectly united to the Word.
17 *Frag. in Matt.* 38 II (GCS 12.31). Cf. *Comm. in Joh.* I.10 (GCS 4.16.8-11).
18 *Comm. in Matt.* XII.11 (GCS 10.88.15-31). Cf. *Contra Cels.* VI. 64 (GCS 2.134.25-135.2) and *Sel. in Ps.* III.8 (PG XII.1131A).
19 *De Princ.* I.6.2 (GCS 5.80.10-14). Cf. Rius-Camps "Comunicabilidad", *OCP* 38,1972, p.434, n.3, where a distinction is made between the possession of reason by created incorporeal beings — a possession which is substantial — and the possession of holiness, which is accidental.
20 *De Princ.* I.8.3 (GCS 5.100.11-18).
21 Ibid. (GCS 5.100.18-21). Cf. Balas, op. cit., pp.18,19. Cf. also Rius-Camps, "Comunicabilidad", *OCP* 38,1972, p.443, where he says: "The gratuitous presence of the Spirit of God in 'spiritual' beings and its radical separability from rational beings confirms the unique character of the Divine nature, in so far as it is invisible and incorporeal, immaterial and intelligible."
22 *Comm. in Joh.* II.18 (GCS 4.75.4-11).
23 Ibid.II.17 (74.29-75.3).

[24] Ibid.74.2,3. See Rius-Camps, "Comunicabilidad", *OCP* 36,1970, 36, pp.226,227, where he points out that Gruber, op. cit., p.96, solves the problem by invoking the idea of the interchange of qualities between the incarnate Christ and the Word of God.
[25] *Frag. in Matt.* 141.1-3 (GCS 12.72).
[26] *De Princ.* IV.4.10 (GCS 5.363.20-29). It may be questioned, however, whether it is true that in man the virtues are only acquired separately, if it is true that they are bound up with each other as various aspects of the Divine Nature. See also Völker, op. cit., pp.216,217, and Crouzel, *La Conn.*, P.146.
Cf. also Nemeshegyi, op. cit., p.195, where he says that "though Origen and Plato both employ the words 'assimilation' and 'imitation' to describe their religious ideal, Origen's 'assimilation' is not the same as that of Greek philosophy, because it consists in charity, and in particular the charity which loves its enemies."
Cf. also pp.199 and 200, where it is said that "the spirit who possesses the least degree of goodness is to that extent the object of God's fatherly bounty. On the other hand, *the* Son of God is the Only-begotten Word, who receives that bounty in its fullness. There is an infinite scale between these two extremes. Origen would thus say that the soul, in so far as it bears an indestructible mark of goodness, is already the child of God . . . but one cannot become a 'son' in the full sense except by a kind of 'communication of qualities', through assimilating and uniting oneself perfectly to the Only-begotten Son."
Cf. also Lot-Borodine, op. cit., (*RHR*, 106,1932), p.565, where he describes the "synergism" characteristic of the Eastern outlook, according to which grace re-inforces our human efforts. He says in particular that "each virtue has its interior double, which is a supernatural virtue which increases it and raises it."
[27] *Frag. in Lam.* VIII (GCS 3.237.27-238.11).
[28] *Comm. in Joh.* I.34 (GCS 4.44.1-30).
[29] *Comm. in Joh.* I.35 (GCS 4.45.6-24). Cf. Rius-Camps, "Origenes y Marcion", p.25.
[30] *De Princ.* II.5.3 (GCS 5.135.29-136.12).
[31] *Ex Comm. in Ex.* (PG XII.269A-271C). Cf. Pitra, A.S.II.356 (in Num.xxii.7), and III.38 (Ps.XLI.10,11).
[32] *Comm. in Rom.* VII.16 (PG XIV.1146C-1147A).
[33] Cf. Nemeshegyi, op. cit., p.230, where he says that "Origen lacked the experience of overwhelming conversion, of dazzling grace.

That is why he does not think of God as electing and predestinating man to salvation in the way Augustine does . . . Universal Father and the God Who elects, these two aspects of God's nature must be reconciled to give a correct impression of God's mysterious operations."
Cf. also the discussion of the hardening of Pharaoh's heart in Koch, op. cit., pp.128-131, in Rius-Camps "Origenes y Marcion", pp.8 and 9, and in Gronau, *Das Theodizeeproblem in der altchristlichen Auffassung* (Tubingen, 1922), p.37 and n.1 thereon (though there the hardening of Pharaoh's heart and the consequent punishment are merely represented as being for the warning of others).

34 *Comm. in Ezek.* VII.4 (PG XIII.789C), and VIII.18 (799BC). Cf. Pitra A.S.III.265 (Ps.CXVIII.29) and 274 (Ps.CXVIII.58). Cf. also Cadiou, *Frag. in Ps.* CXVIII.29 (p.106), where it is said that God shows pity in accordance with law (κατὰ νόμον). A person is pitied according to law in so far as he lives according to law after mercy has been shown to him. This is the pity shown by Christ the Word of God. Cf. also Pitra A.S.II.449 (Ps.II.5), where it is said that the anger of God is heavy punishment inflicted for the benefit of the sinner. Cf. also A. Primmer's thesis, 'Απάθεια und Ἔλεος im Gottesbegriff des Origenes, p.56, where he says that "for Origen, law and punishment have no value of their own, but they have as their goal the correction of the sinner. When this has been successful, mercy is in place."

35 *Comm. in Joh.* XIII.37 (GCS 4.263.5-11) (surely οὐ should be supplied before κατὰ τὸν αὐτὸν τρόπον in line 7). Cf. also *Frag. in Jer.* 16 (GCS 3.206.2-4); ibid.52 (224,12-225.7); *Contra Cels.* V.15 (GCS 2.16.22-25); *Sel. in Gen.* XLIX.9 (PG XII.145AB); Cadiou, *Frag. in Ps.* II.12[c] (p.73); CV.4 (p.91); CXVIII.65 (p. 110); Pitra A.S.III.13,14 (Ps.XXXVII.1,2) and 169 (Ps.LXXXIX. 12); *Frag. in I Cor.* X.2-5 (*JTS* 9.239).
Cf. also Koch, op. cit., pp.143 and 144.
I think Hirschberg on pp.203 and 204 of his thesis *Studien zur Geschichte der simplices in der Alten Kirche* goes too far when he says that the fear of God is the only notion whereby the "simple" disciples are influenced. In quoting *Contra Cels.* VI.13 (GCS 2.83.28-84.1), in support of this view, he takes liberties with the text in so far as he imports into it the idea of the "fear of God" which is absent from the original Greek. In other words,

even those believers who are incapable of appreciating the rational grounds of faith need not simply be under the sway of fear of the consequences of disobedience.

[36] *Comm. in Matt.* XV.11 (GCS 10.379.12-380.3). Cf. ibid.XVI.21 (548.22-28).
See Primmer, op. cit., p.60, where he says that according to Origen, "God manifests His goodness precisely in so far as He sometimes withdraws it . . . Origen is not so much concerned to deny the mercy of God as to champion His goodness." The author distinguishes on p.62 between the mercy shown to those worthy of it and the mercy shown to all men. I suppose the former is mercy shown directly, and the latter is mercy shown indirectly (through punishment).

[37] *Comm. in Matt.* XVII.19 (GCS 10.639.23-640.6). Cf. *Comm. in Rom.* VIII.12 (PG XIV.1198A); *Hom. in Jud.* III.2 (GCS 7.482.1-6); Pitra A.S.III.79 (Ps.LXVII.3).
Cf. also Crouzel, *L'Image*, p.258, and Cornelis, op. cit., p.205, where it is said that "God is a fire, but one which acts in the sphere which may properly be called divine, the incorporeal sphere. This divine fire can be said to be primarily the fire of the Divine Word, of the Divine Reason immanent in rational beings, which never ceases to endeavour to restore them to their original fiery purity."
Cf. also Rius-Camps, "Origenes y Marcion", p.10, where he says, with reference to bodily and natural evils (so-called), that according to Origen, "before participating in the Word made flesh, it is necessary to be purified in the appropriate manner from any obstacles interposed by one's previous sinful life."

[38] *Frag. in I Sam.* IV. (GCS 3.296.1-3, 12-15, 25-28). Cf. Pitra A.S. III.215 (Ps.CV.45).

[39] *Hom. in Jud.* II.4 (GCS 7.477.25-478.2). Cf. *Frag. in Joh.* LI (GCS 4.526.4-8); *Comm. in Rom.* I.16 (PG XIV.862C-863A); Pitra A.S.III.130 (Ps.LXXVII.65). Cf. also Primmer's discussion of this topic in op. cit., pp.24-26.

[40] *Contra Cels.* IV.99 (GCS 1.373.13-21); *Frag. in Eph.* XXII.9-14 (*JTS* 3.556). Cf. Primmer, op. cit., pp.48 and 49, and Pannenberg, op. cit., Vol.II, pp.161 and 162.

[41] *Comm. in Rom.* IX.1 (PG XIV.1207C, 1208A). Cf. Ruth Carter Stapleton, *The Experience of Inner Healing*, (Hodder & Stoughton, 1978), p.37 where a distinction is made between "the per-

fect will of God" and "the circumstantial will of God"... "The perfect will of God is that sickness be replaced with health in everyone. But human factors such as faithlessness, carelessness and sloth can block this perfect will, so God's circumstantial will is that the condition remains unhealed. Under the circumstances, God cannot heal. But given man's faith and faithfulness, healing would be realised."

42 *Comm. in Matt.* XVII.17 (GCS 10.635.16-30).
43 Ibid.XVII.20 (GCS 10.641.10-22). Cf. Crouzel, *L'Image*, p.260.
44 *Comm. in Joh.* I.36 (GCS 4.46.13-15).
45 Ibid. (46.17-23); *Comm. in Ezek.* VII.10 (PG XIII.791AB). Cf. *Sel. in Ps.* XC.10 (PG XII.1552C).
46 *Hom. in Num.* IX.9 (GCS 7.67.12-18). Cf. also ibid.XVII.6 (GCS 7.166.11-14), where, with reference to Num.xxiv.9, Christ is said to be a "lion" in those who are mature, and a "young lion" in those who are as yet immature in the Faith.
47 Cf. Koch, op. cit., p.118, where E. Hatch is quoted as saying that "the cosmology of Origen was a theodicy." On the other hand, the present writer considers that Koch goes too far in saying (on p.139) that the educative value of punishment is the key to Origen's whole theological system, from the creation of the visible world to its disappearance and the continuation of instruction in future worlds. Surely punishment is not in Origen's view the highest mode of instruction, but only a preliminary mode. This is made clear by E. de Faye when he says (op. cit., Vol.III, pp. 216,217) that whereas the Christ of the Gnostics is Revealer rather than Instructor, the Christ of Origen is *par excellence* Instructor. De Faye also says (op. cit., p.50) that "Origen saw a purely punitive infliction of punishment as a form of vengeance unworthy of God. In his opinion, suffering only has meaning if it is intended to bring about the amendment of the sufferer."
48 *Comm. in Ezek.* VII.3 (PG XIII.789AB).
49 Cf. Crouzel, *La Conn.*, p.455.
50 *De Princ.* I.3.8 (GCS 5.61.5-11, 16-20). Cf. Balas, op. cit., pp.14, 15, and J. Rius-Camps, "Comunicabilidad", (*OCP* 36,1970), p. 219.
51 *De Princ.* III.3.1 (GCS 5.256.19-257.8). Cf. Mme. Harl, op. cit., pp.163,164, where this passage is quoted, and Koch, op. cit., p. 65.
52 *Hom. in Gen.* XIII.3 (GCS 6.118.11-26). Cf. ibid.XIII.4 (6.119.

5-8).
[53] *Hom. in Lev.* XVI.5 (GCS 6.500.13-18). Cf. also *Hom. in Ps.* XXXVI.IV.3 (PG XII.1357B).
[54] *Comm. in Matt.* XII.14 (GCS 10.97.17-30).
[55] Op. cit., p.377: "For Origen, Platonism and Christianity differ not so much in religious theory . . . but rather in manner of exposition, which is dependent upon their respective audiences. Platonism speaks to a little, select company, Christianity to all men." Again, p.379: "According to Origen, Christianity and Platonism both represent ideally the same lofty standpoint; but Christianity, to its great advantage, is able to express this in such a way as immediately to capture even the masses . . . Christianity simply says what is both true and seems to be clear for the many, though naturally it is not as clear for them as for the few who devote themselves to a philosophical study of these things."
[56] Op. cit., pp.318,319.
[57] See also on this subject Ch.VI, pp.205-210.
[58] Op. cit., p.177.
[59] In his article "Glaube, Gnosis und Mysterium" (*JLW* 15 (1941)).
[60] See on this subject Ch.II, pp.39-41.

CONTENTS

CHAPTER V

SECTION 1

THE SELF-HUMILIATION OF THE DIVINE WORD

The Word took upon Himself the form of a slave for the redemption of mankind — 105

He did so to display the example of perfect obedience — 105

The example, however, is that displayed by the soul which was united to the Word — 106

The Son was as closely united to the father during the Incarnate life as He had been before — 107

The Son became inferior to the Holy Spirit as the result of the Incarnation — 108

The Incarnate Son derives all His power from the Father — 109

The Resurrection is due to the Father's act — 109

The Son's identity with the Father derives from the union of their wills — 110

Therefore the Son did not need to utter explicit prayer (though Origen takes a different view in certain passages) — 112

SECTION 2

THE KENOSIS DOCTRINE IN ORIGEN'S THOUGHT

Origen appears in certain passages to think of the Word as having divested Himself of certain attributes in order to become incarnate — 115

But His essential goodness and honour are not affected by the Incarnation	115
And even His diminished wisdom and power were superior to any possessed by human beings	116
The First Coming of Christ only gives us an inkling of what the Second Coming will be like	117
It was at the time of the Crucifixion that Our Lord underwent the extremity of His humiliation	118
But sometimes Origen regards the Divine Nature of the Word as in no way affected by the Incarnation	119
It was only the soul which He assumed which underwent development	122
The Word of God was not confined within the person of the human Jesus	123
The Word assumed a human form so as to enable human beings to apprehend His higher form	127
Origen sometimes implies that it was not the Word Who became incarnate, but the soul which had become united to Him	128
Strictly, one should speak of the νοῦς of Christ rather than of His ψυχή	131
It was the human soul of Christ which suffered human hardships	137
That soul descended to human conditions of its own free will	141
But sometimes Origen regards the Divine Nature of Christ as susceptible to feelings	142

Has each individual two souls? (with reference to
Origen's analysis of the personality of the Incarnate
Jesus)   144

Summary   154

Appendix   157

NOTES on Chapter V   159

CHAPTER V

SECTION 1

THE SELF-HUMILIATION OF THE DIVINE WORD

For the purpose of redeeming mankind the Divine Word took upon Himself the form of a slave, with the result that the words "You are my slave" recorded in the Book of Isaiah could be addressed to Him by the Father. The goodness of the Son is thus seen to resemble that of the Father more fully in so far as He humbled Himself even to death than if He had thought equality with God a thing to be clutched at. [1] In a very striking passage in *Hom. in Lev.*, Origen points out that when Christ assumed a servant's form, the Immortal died, the Incapable of suffering suffered, the Invisible One was seen, and since death and every other fleshly weakness resulted from our state of sin, He Who was made in the likeness of man offered His unstained flesh as a victim to God. [2] For although He suffered death, He did so willingly, and not, as we do, by the necessity which sin imposes. [3] In humbling Himself in this way as in others, He fulfilled the will of the Father Who gave Him up on behalf of sinners rather than His own will, and in this way showed Himself to be the image of the Father's goodness. [4] Thus Joshua foreshadowed Jesus the Christ as "the servant of Moses" in so far as Jesus the Son of God was born "under the law" (Gal.iv.4), and thus became "the servant of Moses." [5]

In fact it was only because Jesus Christ took human nature upon Himself and thus adopted a status different from that which was His in the beginning that He was able to bestow the help which the Father desired to impart through Him. [6] Origen also says that if sin had not entered the world, the Son of God would not have needed to take upon Himself human flesh and be crucified, but would have remained what He was in the beginning, the Word of God. [7] Thus it is said elsewhere that although there was originally only one nature in Christ, namely His Divine nature as the Only-begotten Son of the Father, none the less in recent times He took upon Himself human nature in order to fulfil the Divine purpose. [8] It is likewise said that the Son of God emptied Himself and took the form of a servant in order to teach obedience to those who could be saved only by the example of the Incarnate Son. [9]

So far, what Origen says is in accordance with traditional doctrine; but now comes a statement which betrays his distinctive outlook: "The man whom He assumed was the most honourable and purest of all, and was thus qualified to receive Him, just as we can, if we make sufficient room for Him in our own souls."[10] This strange language expresses Origen's notion, expounded more fully in *De Princ.* that the Son of God did not become incarnate directly, but united Himself to a soul which had never become rebellious, and finally became incarnate in order to act as an instrument of the Word of God. It was possible for this soul to act thus because it had so firmly chosen to love righteousness that it became no longer capable of a change of attitude, or in other words what had formerly depended upon the will was as the result of long custom changed into something natural.[11] This soul is in fact said to have "become the image of the Image of God" because of its virtue (διὰ τὴν ἀρετήν). [12]

Origen thus suggests that the followers of Christ do not in fact receive the pattern by which their lives are moulded from the Divine nature of the Word of God, because that is far superior to all the actions and attitudes which require imitation, but rather from the soul which He assumed *(anima quae assumpta est ab eo)* and which was characterised by the highest perfection.[13] This is the explanation which Origen gives of why St. Paul speaks of being "conformed", not to the Son of God, but to "the image of the Son" (Rom.viii.29). To quote Origen's own words, "he who desires the fullness of perfection and blessedness must aim at attaining a likeness to that *anima* which is chiefly and above all others the *imago Filii Dei*."[14]

The same doctrine also underlies the statement elsewhere that those who sought to kill Jesus, even though they might succeed, could only kill a man, and that any who thought that the being against whom they plotted was Divine would scarcely continue to plot against Him, because they could do nothing more than kill His body.[15] This statement is repeated in *De Princ.* where it is said that the invisible spirits who rule over the nations saw that the Saviour had come to abolish the doctrines which they had implanted in the minds of their subjects, and thus laid snares for Him, not knowing Who was concealed within Him *(quis obtegeretur intrinsecus ignorantes)*.[16] Elsewhere Origen suggests that the Lamb of God spoken of by John the Baptist as destined to take away the sins of the world was the man assumed by the Son of God, and He Who led the Lamb to the sacrifice was the God Who resided in the man and uttered the words "No one takes my ψυχή from me, but I lay it down of my own accord, just as I take it up of my own accord."[17] Origen even suggests that what appears to be the same person can speak at one time as a man and at another time as a Divine being, inasmuch as He can say at one time "Now you seek to kill me, a man who has told you the truth", and at another time "I and the Father are one", "I am the Truth and the Life", "I am the Resurrection."[18]

It is worth referring to the passage in *Comm. in Rom.* where Origen interprets St. Paul's words "whom God set forth (προέθετο) to be a propitiation" (iii.25) as meaning that God "arranged beforehand" that the soul of Jesus should be a propitiation, ie. before that soul existed, whereas this could not be said of the Word of God, Who has existed eternally.[19] It must be admitted, however, that this is a conspicuous instance of Origen's tendency to twist the natural meaning of words so as to use them in support of ideas formed independently.

It is passages such as the ones just referred to which led de Faye to say [20] that according to Origen "the victim who died on the cross was not the Word of God Who was in Jesus Christ, but exclusively the man Christ Jesus." I feel that D'Alès' criticism of de Faye's statement [21] shows that he has not really grasped Origen's Christology in the way de Faye has. D'Alès seems content to interpret that Christology in the light of the later Conciliar definitions, according to which the incarnate Word of God had two natures, Divine and human. But that does not seem to have been Origen's real view, whatever certain passages might suggest. When D'Alès says that there is no reason to make Origen into a Nestorian, he is taking the easy way out. A careful study of such texts as have been quoted would seem to give considerable ground for that suggestion, in so far as the Word of God and the man Jesus seem to be presented as two distinct beings.

It is indeed true that there are passages where Origen seems to say roundly that the Word of God Himself was subject to mortality. For instance, in *Comm. in Joh.* the blood-dipped robe with which the Word of God seen on a horse is clothed is regarded as a symbol of the death of the Word on the Cross and the subsequent piercing of His side by the soldier's spear.[22] In other words, Origen finds it difficult to emancipate himself from the traditional doctrine of the Incarnation, as he also does when he says that even during His incarnate life the Son was still as closely united to the Father as He was before He became incarnate.[23] It is true, says Origen, that from one point of view the Son of God in becoming incarnate came, as it were, out of Him Who sent Him; but from another point of view the Father remained with the Son and was in Him as the Son was in the Father.[24] (On the other hand, unless the Son could be thought of as being in the Father in a manner other than He was before He came forth from God, there would appear to be a contradiction in the statement that He both came forth from God and yet remained in God even after coming forth from Him.) It is in conformity with this outlook that Origen says in *Comm. in Rom.*[25] that St. Paul speaks of the Son of God as having the likeness of sinful flesh (Rom.viii.3), but not sinful flesh itself, because although he possessed a human body, He did not contract the defilement of sin which is caused by the sexual desire from which conception normally results.

One paradoxical result of the Incarnation is that during the time of our Lord's life on earth He became inferior to the Holy Spirit, even though by nature He is not so. Origen applies to Christ the words of the prophet Isaiah (xlviii.16) which state that "the Lord and His Spirit have sent me."[26] Origen is no doubt thinking of passages in the Gospels where our Lord is said to have been full of the Holy Spirit or led by the Spirit. Thus it is said in one place[27] that after His Baptism our Lord was led by the Spirit into the wilderness because He was the unique Son of God, just as (according to St. Paul) all those who are led by the Spirit of God are the sons of God. Elsewhere it is said that the Holy Spirit would not descend on us if He had not first descended (at our Lord's baptism) on One Who shared in His own nature.[28] Likewise in *Comm. in Matt.*,[29] in the passage where the little child set by our Lord before His disciples is compared to the Holy Spirit, it is said that the Holy Spirit humbled Himself for the salvation of mankind, and the passage from Isaiah is quoted as evidence that the Spirit was sent as well as the Son, although Origen admits that the passage is ambiguous. In *Contra Cels.*[30] it is also said that the episode of the Spirit descending upon Jesus in the form of a dove is enough to show that Isaiah's words mean that the Father sent both Christ and the Holy Spirit. On the other hand, the tension existing in Origen's mind between the idea of the Son as becoming incarnate in one place and the doctrine of the Son's omnipresence becomes evident when he suggests that the account of the descent of the Holy Spirit in the form of a dove is not to be interpreted literally, because the Holy Spirit is inseparable from the Son and therefore cannot pass from the Father to the

Son.[31]

It is made perfectly clear that in His incarnate life the Son derives all the powers that He possesses from the Father.[32] Origen says that if our Lord had replied to the question put by the Jewish priests "In what power do you do these things?" (Matt.xxi.23), He would have explained in what surpassing power (ἐξουσίᾳ) He did the marvellous things witnessed by the people, a power given to Him not by any being inferior to God, but by the Father Himself.[33] Again, Origen says that when the crowds praised the God of Israel for Christ's miracles, they showed that they were unaware that Christ Himself possessed all the power possessed by the Father, in so far as it is through Christ that the Father performs all things. An ordinary man who performs a miracle does so simply as God's instrument, whereas Christ performs miracles in the power inherent in His own nature as God's Vicegerent.[34] Origen recognises that the Son of God only claims to be able to give life (whether spiritual or physical) by virtue of the power which the Father has given to Him: after all, the Son Himself states that the life which He has in Himself is imparted to Him by the Father.[35] Origen thus deplores the mistake of those who condemned to death the Source and Origin of all life, and did not recognise through the testimony of so many who had risen to new life the Fountain from which life flows to all that live, a life which none the less is given by the Father (St. John v.26).[36] But even in other matters, the Son declares that He does nothing of His own accord, because He seeks not His own will, but the will of the Father Who has sent Him.[37] When the Pharisees asked Him, "Whom makest Thou Thyself?", they displayed a failure to recognise that the Father alone had accorded to Him the status He occupied; accordingly, He replied that He was in no position to give honour to Himself, but merely received it from the Father.[38]

Origen admits that it might be inferred from the text "Destroy this temple, and in three days I will raise it up" that the Son is able to act on His own initiative; indeed, says Origen, some might derive from this saying the Sabellian doctrine of a God Who appears in different aspects and so is spoken of as Father and Son at different times. But in fact, says Origen, Christ's words must be understood as implying that He was able to raise up His body from the dead only because the Father granted Him this privilege (τοῦ πατρὸς αὐτῷ τοῦτο χαριζομένου), so that the Father remained the principal Agent in the raising up of Christ from the dead.[39] In the same way, Origen compares the Son of God to a lion's whelp who lay down and slept but was afterwards aroused by the Father (with reference to Gen.xlix.9).[40]

In another passage, Origen explicitly states that the reason why the Son is able to claim identity with the Father is that the Son's will differs in no way from that of the Father. It is not that the Son obeys particular commands of the Father; it is rather that the Son is always in harmony with the Father, and so transforms the world into what the Father would have it be. Origen even goes to the length of saying that the will of the Father "takes up its seat" in the son (γενόμενον ἐν τῷ υἱῷ), and so brings it about that the Father's will is accomplished. It is thus because the entire will of the Father is carried out by the Son and by no one else that the Son can be called "the Image of God."[41] (There are in fact various passages in Origen's works where the Father is described as "dwelling in" Christ, or having Christ for His temple or His throne.)[42] Thus elsewhere Origen says that the Father's image is reproduced in the Son by the very fact that the Son does all things just as the Father does, quoting St. John v.19 "All things that the Father doeth, these also doeth the Son likewise."[43] The task of Christ Incarnate may in fact be said to be that of bringing human wills into conformity with the Divine Will.[44]

Maydieu, in his discussion[45] of the passage referred to in note 41, appears to make an unwarrantable distinction between the way in which the Son resembles the Father through carrying out the Father's will and the resemblance resulting from the bringing forth by the Father of the Son as His Word or Self-expression. It is not just a matter of the Son's voluntarily acting in conformity with the Father's purpose: such action is inevitable because of the unique derivation of the Son. At least, that is what Origen would say. Thus it is not really true that at one time Origen appears to maintain the identity of Image and Model while preserving the separate reality of each, and at another regards the First-born Son as only a defective image of the Father.[46] Rius-Camps appears likewise to credit Origen with an Arian view of the Son's relationship to the Father when he says[47] that "Origen makes use of certain terms such as ὄνομα, χάρις, δόξα, δύναμις, ἀπορροή, θεότης, to preserve on the one hand the transcendence of God, and on the other hand to express a certain degradation inherent in all intermediate beings", apparently including even the Only-begotten Son.

There is one passage in which Origen stresses that the Son alone has a perfect knowledge of the Father's will. In *Hom. in Ezek.*, he says that the Saviour eats food which no one else can eat, this food being the knowledge of the Father's will, but that He invites others to share a meal with Him, at which He bestows such food as His guest is capable of receiving *(excellens quippe ab universa conditione natura eius, et ab omnibus segregata, facit eum quotidianum panem de Patris natura comedere)*. Each of us desires daily bread, and in doing so does not receive the same bread or bread in the same quantity as the Son of God, but in sincere prayer and in a clear conscience and in righteous actions we all receive our daily bread. But if anyone is less pure, he eats his daily bread differently. It is also said, with reference to the closed door mentioned in Ezek.xliv.2, that there are certain facts known only to the Son of God, and not to any creature. For the Son does not reveal to this world all that He Himself knows *(non capit creatura quod capit Deus)*. Nor is every creature capable of receiving an equal amount of knowledge: Paul could receive more than Timothy, and Timothy more than I. There are certain things which Christ alone can receive. [48]

But Origen has to face the fact that there is one famous occasion when the will of the Son appears to have been out of harmony with that of the Father. Hence in *Exhort.ad Mart.* he insists that the Son has on occasion to defer to the will and judgement of the Father, as proceeding from superior knowledge and wisdom, as when He asked that the cup of suffering of which He was about to drink might be taken from Him, but was denied His request.[49] In *Matt. Comm. Series* Origen underlines this fact with reference to the same episode, when he says that the cup could pass from Jesus in two ways, inasmuch as if He were to drink it, it would afterwards pass from Him and from all mankind, but if He were not to drink it, it would perhaps pass from Him, but not from mankind, but would remain with them until it had made an end of them *(donec perfeceret eos)*. He therefore wished to drink it so that it might pass from Him and from the whole human race, rather than to act against His Father's will by evading the drinking of it.[50] Völker, in discussing this passage,[51] points out that Origen contradicts himself in the matter of Gethsemane. He admits that it is difficult to harmonise with the nature of the Divine Word, and so attributes it to the human side of the Incarnate Word. Even so, he tries to diminish the element of fear implicit in the request of Jesus by suggesting that He was really asking for a severer form of suffering.[52] In another passage, Origen seems to try to have it both ways when he suggests that our Lord asked that the cup might pass from Him because of the immediate consequences, ie. the disciples' abandonment of Him, Peter's denial of Him, and the rejection by God of the Jewish nation (the implication being that He did not know the ultimate consequences). But He preferred the Father's will, in so far as all were allowed to disobey so that as the result of the successive disobedience of all, mercy might be successively shown to all, and that through the fall of Israel salvation might come to the Gentiles.[53]

It was because the will of the Son was in entire harmony with the will of the Father that the Son did not need to utter explicit prayer, because the Father foresaw what that prayer would be. It can indeed be said to those who pray in a Christian manner, "While you are yet speaking, I will say, Here I am" (Is.lxv.24); but the Father would have said to His Son *"Before* you are speaking, I will say, Here I am." Hence at the raising of Lazarus from the dead, an act of thanksgiving took the place of the prayer which Christ might have been expected to make for the raising of Lazarus, because before He uttered His prayer, He saw in His spirit that Lazarus' soul was restored to his body.[54]

Sometimes, Origen almost seems to suggest that Christ prayed in order to present the appearance of being human.[55] Thus he says that the Lord gave thanks to the God Who is His Father (with ref. to Matt. xi.25) in so far as He was fashioned in like manner to His slaves and transmitted the thanks of the slaves to the Master. Elsewhere Origen says that the Saviour lifted His eyes to heaven before the feeding of the five thousand so that we may believe in Him as Divine ($\dot{\omega}\varsigma$ $\theta\epsilon\tilde{\omega}$) from the wonderful thing which He did, but admit Him to be human because He gave thanks and looked up to heaven.[56]

On the other hand Origen takes a different view in *De Oratione* of the place which prayer occupied in the life of the Incarnate Christ. It is there said that Jesus might not have obtained His requests without prayer ($\tau\acute{\alpha}\chi\alpha$ $o\mathring{v}\kappa$ $\mathring{\alpha}\nu$ $\alpha\mathring{v}\tau\grave{\alpha}$ $\epsilon\mathring{\iota}\lambda\eta\phi\grave{\omega}\varsigma$ $\chi\omega\rho\grave{\iota}\varsigma$ $\epsilon\mathring{v}\chi\tilde{\eta}\varsigma$), and then follows a list of the Gospel references to the occaisons when Jesus is said to have spent time in prayer. The final reference is to the act of thanksgiving uttered before the raising of Lazarus, in which the Lord said that "the Father always hears Him" (John xi.41), a statement which Origen here (as distinct from the former passage referred to!) interprets as meaning that he who always prays is always heard ($\pi\acute{\alpha}\nu\tau\sigma\tau\epsilon$ $\epsilon\mathring{v}\chi\acute{o}\mu\epsilon\nu\sigma\varsigma$ $\pi\acute{\alpha}\nu\tau\sigma\tau\epsilon$ $\epsilon\pi\alpha\kappa\sigma\acute{v}\epsilon\tau\alpha\iota$).[57] Elsewhere it is said that Christ in His human nature was heard at the very time he invoked God, not after He had invoked God; for to those who are holy and listen to the Divine commands, the promise is made "While you are yet speaking, I will say, Here I am." (Is.lviii.9).[58] Again, with reference to St. John i.51, Origen says that it was likely that the Saviour actually prayed that Nathanael might have such faith as to see the heavens opened, etc.[59] Again, Origen says that after the feeding recording in St. Matthew, our Lord went up a mountain by Himself to pray (Matt.xiv.23), probably both for the crowds, that they might continue to behave as His followers should, and also for the disciples, that they might have a safe journey to the other side of the lake.[60] In yet another passage Origen actually suggests that at certain times the Son may not have needed to pray for the granting of His requests, but may have needed to do so at other times.[61]

Perhaps the dilemma which is thus presented to us as to whether the Son of God needed to pray or not is resolved by thinking of Him as needing to pray in so far as He is human, and therefore partly ignorant of the Father's will, but as not needing to pray in so far as He is Divine and therefore fully cognisant of the Father's will. It was in His Divine capacity that He said to the palsied man "Son, thy sins are forgiven thee" (Matt.ix.2). Origen thus says that others could obtain remission of sins by their prayers, but Christ alone by His power *(ceteri . . . precibus peccata, hic solus potestate dimisit).*[62] On the other hand one cannot help observing that it is hard to see how these two states of mind could really co-exist in the same person. He cannot surely change from being Divine to human, and then from being human to Divine, because that is almost what Origen's theory of our Lord's prayer life amounts to.

CHAPTER V

SECTION 2

THE KENOSIS DOCTRINE IN ORIGEN'S THOUGHT

No discussion of the self-humiliation of the Divine Word in Origen's thought would be complete without an examination of the doctrine of the Kenosis. This is based on St. Paul's well-known statement in Philippians (ii.6.7) that Jesus Christ was originally in the form of God, but did not regard equality with God as something which He should hold on to, but "emptied Himself" by taking the form of a servant and becoming like other human beings. [63] This statement appears to be echoed by Origen in one or two passages, in the sense that our Lord is thought of as having literally divested Himself of some of His attributes as a man might take off a suit of clothes, with the result that He became inferior to what He originally was. Thus in *Comm. in Cant.* Origen compares our Lord to the stone said by the prophet Daniel (ii.34) to have been cut out from the mountain without hands, and to the "drop" which according to his version of Micah ii.12 would gather together the nations which could themselves be compared to a drop in a bucket. [64] In *Hom. in Jos.*, the knives made of rock used by Joshua to circumcise for the second time the Israelites who had come from Egypt are said to stand for the Word of God which cleanses the hearts of its hearers from spiritual impurity and is derived from that Rock which was cut from a mountain without hands and has filled the world and bestowed its spiritual gifts on believers.[65]

After all, says Origen, what was the Lord not made for our salvation? We were void of understanding *(inanes)*, and He emptied Himself *(exinanivit seipsum)*, taking the form of a servant. We were a foolish and senseless people (Deut.xxxii.6), and He was made "the foolishness of preaching" (I Cor.i.21), so that "the foolishness of God might be made wiser than men" (I Cor.i.25). [66]

But Origen stresses that whatever other qualities the Divine Word might have put off, His goodness and honour were unaffected, because goodness and honour are part of His essential nature. And even though He came to this vale of tears and woe, He was not in fact unhappy, because He was thus carrying out the Father's will.[67] Origen instances a doctor who has to familiarise Himself with the less pleasant aspects of human life in the form of diseases and wounds. From one point of view he would naturally prefer not to have anything to do with such things, but none the less he concerns himself with them so as to bring healing to his patients. Moreover, since he himself shares in human weakness, it is always possible that he may be infected with the diseases which he tries to treat. Not so the Word of God, Who is only able to heal the wounds of our souls because sin is utterly foreign to His nature.[68]

Elsewhere, Origen suggests that it was really a matter of our Lord's bringing with Him into the world as much of the Divine wisdom and power as was necessary for Him to fulfil His purposes, just as a person might pack as much of his property as possible into a trunk before going on a journey.[69] Origen thus feels able to say that the wisdom brought by Jesus Christ into the world, though vastly inferior to that which He possessed by nature, and therefore deserving the name of the "foolishness of God", was immeasurably superior to the wisdom possessed by any human being, with the result that St. Paul could say that "the foolishness of God is wiser than men",[70] yes, than the very wisest men, such as Peter and Paul and John.[71] Thus Origen asserts in two passages that Christ's Divinity was shown by His extraordinary awareness of what was going on in people's minds.[72] He likewise empties Himself of the fullness of His power, but none the less brought with Him enough power to enable Him to perform actions which no ordinary man could have performed — the actions we call miracles.[73] This power, being limited, was liable to fail as the result of the cruelty of His enemies, with the result that the prophet Isaiah could say, "With His stripes we are healed."[74] On the other hand, if He did succumb to the plots of His enemies, that was only because He was willing to do so, because He could have overcome them if He had wished.[75]

Origen thus feels able to say that the power and glory with which our Lord first came, even though they enabled Him to work miracles, were vastly inferior to the power and glory which will attend Him at His Second Coming; for the power which marked His First Coming was the power of one who had emptied Himself.[76] Origen likewise says elsewhere that in condescending to our poverty, the Lord obscured His unique glory,[77] but none the less the Lord is His Name; for even though He became man, God did not cease to be the Lord.[78] There is also a curious passage in which, in reply to the suggestion that our

Lord could easily have supplied food miraculously to His disciples instead of leaving them to go and buy it (John iv.8), Origen says that though our Lord had become a man, He would not have been recognised as such if His Divinity had overshadowed all that He did as man.[79]

It is with these considerations in mind that Origen interprets the words in the song of triumph over Pharaoh which run: — "Let us sing to the Lord, for He has been outstandingly glorified." (Exod.xv.1). He says that in taking flesh from His Virgin Mother for our salvation, and also in submitting to the Cross, Jesus Christ has been glorified, but not outstandingly; but when He shall come in the glory of His Father and the holy angels to judge the world, then He will be outstandingly glorified, and "all will honour the Son as they honour the Father" (John v.23).[80] It was because His glory was veiled in His incarnate state that the devil underestimated His power to resist temptation, supposing that He had attained to the status of Son of God through His own merits.[81] Again, Origen speaks of the First Coming of Christ as being likened to a "shadow" in Scripture (Lam.iv.20), and as providing us with hints and foreshadowings of those things which we shall only experience fully when He comes again.[82] In *De Princ.* Origen elucidates this statement by saying that though the Son of God was brought within the very narrow limits of a human body, He yet gave indications, through the likeness of His power and works to those of God the Father, of the unbounded and invisible greatness that was in Him.[83] The passage in Lamentations is also quoted in another place, where Origen suggests that just as the shadow of our body is inseparable from our body, so the earthly actions and movements of Christ can be regarded as His "shadow", and that the truth to which they are intended to lead us will only be fully apprehended in that state where the glory of God and the causes of His actions will be fully revealed, although even in this life we can obtain an inkling of that revelation in so far as St. Paul says that even if we have formerly known Christ after the flesh, yet henceforth we know Him no more in this fashion (II Cor.v.16).[84] Origen likewise explains the apparent contradiction between the passage in Romans (v.2) in which it is said that "we rejoice in the hope of the glory of God" and the passage in II Cor. (iii.18) where it is said that "we with unveiled face behold the glory of the Lord" by saying that the latter glory was revealed in the Incarnation of the Saviour, whereas the former is the glory which will be revealed at His Second Coming. It follows that those who have already seen the glory of the Only-begotten Son with the full understanding of faith must none the less direct their minds to the glory of the Second Coming of Christ, and so progress from the present glory to the future glory which is the object of their hope. [85] Origen also says that the Second Coming of Christ will be the prelude to the state in which His disciples will live in accordance with the laws of the "eternal gospel", which will supersede the laws and the modes of worship at present binding on Christians. [86]

When discussing the cry of dereliction uttered on the Cross, Origen interprets it as meaning that our Lord had in fact descended from the condition of being in the form of the invisible God and in the likeness of the Father when He took the form of a servant, and that the extremity of His humiliation occured when He was crucified.[87] Thus it is said elsewhere that Christ implores the Father to have mercy upon Him, because man tramples upon Him, although He is God.[88] Origen even goes to the length of saying that it is true that God alone possesses immortality, because Jesus Christ died for all apart from God (χωρὶς θεοῦ) (Heb.ii.10).[89] It was in fact supremely at the time of the Crucifixion that it became true that, in Origen's words, our Lord "assumed human nature in all respects" (πάντη ἄνθρωπον ἀνειληφέναι) by "descending as far as human flesh" (μέχρι σαρκὸς ἀνθρωπίνης καταβεβηκέναι). [90] Origen asks why, if Christ did not experience human infirmity in the very act of dying, was His soul *(anima)* troubled, and sad even unto death? Surely, he says, it was as a genuine man that Christ said: "The spirit is willing, but the flesh is weak." [91] In fact, those who try to explain away His Crucifixion as only apparent, on the ground that He was incapable of human feeling (τὸ ἀπαθές) and so superior to all human calamity, are in fact depriving us of our only means of salvation, because they deny His true humanity.[92] It was for the sake of souls still in a state of growth that He condescended to be crucified, so that these souls might love Him and draw Him to themselves after He had emptied Himself of His Divine glory. [93]

So far, Origen appears to take St. Paul's words about Christ's self-emptying literally. Jesus Christ did not come into this world in the fullness of His Divine Majesty, but laid aside some of it so that those to whom he came might be able to endure His presence. Thus Origen says that "if the Only-begotten Son had not emptied out the fullness of the Divine Spirit and humbled Himself to a servant's form, no one would have been able to receive Him in the fullness of His Deity." [94] Origen likewise says elsewhere that the brightness of the Divine Light, this brightness being the Son (Heb.i.3), at first falls softly and gently on the weak eyes of human beings, and then gradually trains and habituates them, so to speak, to endure the Light in its full glory by removing all that obscures and hinders their vision (cf. Matt.vii.5).[95] Origen elsewhere points out, with reference to the statement that "no one knows the Son except the Father" (Matt.xi.27), that no one can fully know the Son in His various aspects of wisdom, truth, and reason except Him from Whom the being of the Son is derived. For this reason it was necessary that the Son of God should "empty Himself" of His majestic condition so as to become a man, and give evidence of His Divinity through the words of grace which He spoke and the extraordinary acts which He performed.[96]

But there are other passages which seem to indicate that in Origen's view the self-emptying of the Divine Word was only apparent. To put it crudely, it was not so much a case of travelling light as of travelling incognito, in the sense that a king remains what he is even though he disguises himself for the purpose of keeping his subjects in ignorance of His identity.[97] In one passage [98] the Divine nature of our Lord is regarded as in no way affected by the Incarnation, that is, by His assumption of human nature and of the flesh which according to St. Paul lusts against the spirit.[99] It is here as much as anywhere that Origen reveals himself as not being a systematic theologian, because he does not really attempt to reconcile the disparate elements of His thinking. I can thus hardly agree with Mme. Harl [100] that "in Origen's coherent (if not organised) system, the lines of thought reveal themselves regarding all-important problems, whatever may be the fluctuations or contradictions which the writer allows to exist among secondary hypotheses."

There are numerous examples of the way in which the Divine Nature of our Lord could exercise itself at will. Thus in various passages it is implied that He knew all the time what was going on in men's minds,[101] and therefore did not ask questions (when He did) in order to gain information, but for some other reason.[102] Thus when at Lazarus' graveside He asked Martha whether she believed that He was what He claimed to be – the Resurrection and the Life [103] – He did not ask because He did not know, but so that we and those present could learn her state of mind from her reply.[104] Again, when He sat weary with His journey by the well of Sychar, although He thus showed that His body was liable to experience the feelings common to all human bodies, He was not ignorant of the impending arrival of the woman of Samaria who drew water from the well, nor of the benefits which He was going to confer on her.[105] Again, with reference to the statement in St. Matthew (xxiv.36) that the Son of God does not know the hour when the final judgement will take place, Origen says that it is only as man that He does not know it, seeing that He has the power not to know it just as He has the power to eat or drink![106]

So far as human feelings are concerned, Origen in at least two passages takes refuge in paradox by asserting that the Word of God, though not liable to such feelings, did in fact experience them, whether they were feelings of compassion or feelings of pain.[107] Indeed in another passage Origen roundly asserts that just as a shepherd will naturally feel compassion towards his own sheep, even so it is characteristic of the Saviour of the world to be compassionate towards the product of His fashioning.[108] As we shall see later,[109] the problem of how feelings, however commendable, can be reconciled with the unchangeability of the Divine Word is one with which Origen never adequately copes.

Again, it was only the flesh of Christ which was born of the Virgin Mary, just as it was only the flesh of Christ which suffered death.[110] Even when apparently in the womb of the Virgin Mary, He transmitted power through her to his cousin who was also in his mother's womb.[111] When tempted, He made it clear to the devil that to Him, the Only-begotten Son of God, the prophecy that Divine protection would be afforded in the hour of danger did not apply; if it applied at all, it was to His human nature only.[112] Likewise, even though it might appear that it would be easy for His enemies to arrest Him, they were incapable of doing so until the predestined time arrived (John vii. 30).[113] And even when it did arrive, it is made abundantly clear in the Gospel that if He had not wished to be taken captive, He would not have been taken captive; for when He announced to those who confronted Him that He was Jesus of Nazareth whom they were looking for, they went backward and fell to the ground.[114]

Again, it was by the hidden power of His Divinity that He was able to bend the elements of nature to His will.[115] In a passage commenting on the stilling of the storm of the Lake of Galilee, Origen asserts that in the body Christ was asleep, but so far as His Deity was concerned, He was awake, and in fact caused the sea to be troubled so as to have the opportunity of displaying His power to His Apostles by calming it again.[116] So far as His own body was concerned, although He was prepared for food to be brought to Him, He did not Himself need the nourishment which He bestowed on others.[117]

Finally, — and this is in some ways the most significant of Origen's attempts to assert the complete independence of the Divine Nature of Christ — Origen declares that Christ only gave up His life when He wished to give it up, unlike other men, who give up their life because it is required of them.[118] It was because He wished to make it clear to His disciples that the manner of His decease was exceptional that He said: "No one takes my ψυχή from me, but I lay it down of my own free will" (John x.18). None of the Old Testament worthies could have said this: Jesus alone could say it.[119] In fact His final words "Into Thy hands I commend my spirit" show that He gave up His life of His own free will.[120]

All these considerations go to show that, as Origen says explicitly in one passage,[121] he regards the Divine Nature of our Lord as in no way affected by the Incarnation, that is, by His assumption of human nature and of the flesh which according to St. Paul lusts against the spirit. We can thus scarcely fail to agree with Eichinger[122] when he says that "there is no real unity in Origen's thought between the Divine Word and the human nature which He assumed. Hence in his Christology there is no real inner tension between the Divine and the human elements in Christ. In the last analysis the Divine Word, even in His revelatory function, remains unaffected by the human nature which He assumed." Or in Wintersig's words:[123] "The Incarnation of the Word of God is for Origen not a genuine entry of the Word into the company of fallen humanity." What Grillmeier says[124] of Clement of Alexandria is in fact equally true of Origen. He says that "if the Divine Word has personally taken up his dwelling in (the human) Christ, He must according to the Stoic-philonic teaching of Clement about the soul be the all-powerful Controller of the human nature of Christ. But where the prototype (ie. the Word) appears, the image (ie. the human soul) must necessarily lose its place and function. The ψυχή, the lower soul of Christ, remains entirely an instrument in the service of the governing Word of God . . . . The power of the Word invades the corporeal nature of the Lord and transforms it . . . . The human soul of Christ can no longer have any genuine theological significance in such a presentation of Christ. A full understanding of the role of the humanity of Jesus in the work of human salvation is absent from the works of Clement."

In fact, during the incarnate life of Christ the Divine Nature was in control all the time, operating the human nature in the way in which a marionette is operated. He thus did not need to discipline Himself in the way in which John the Baptist needed to.[125] Indeed, in one place Origen interprets the white horse on which the Word of God is said to ride in Rev.xix.11 as being the body which He assumed and used for His own purposes, or else as being the life which He said Himself that He was able to lay down and take up again at will (John x.17).[126] The purpose of this activity was that human beings should gradually come to recognise the Power that had descended into human nature and human circumstances (περιστάσεις), and had assumed a human soul and body together with the Divine characteristics in order to bring salvation to believers.[127] Thus, with reference to the passage in Joshua where the Lord is said to have "exalted Joshua in the sight of all the people" (iv.14), Origen says that in the presence of the Father Christ was always exalted and set on high, but that it was needful that He should be exalted in our sight also. This comes about when the sublimity of His Divine Nature is revealed to us.[128]

Elsewhere, Origen asserts that though the immortal Word of God assumed both a human body and a human soul, and might thus appear to be subject to change, the Word none the less remains essentially the same, and undergoes none of the experiences of the body or the soul. In other words, the Divine Word cannot possibly experience the development of mind and spirit which marks the career of a normal human being. It is a matter of His coming down to the level of those who cannot look on the radiance of His Deity, and thus so to speak becoming flesh, until those who have accepted Him in this form are uplifted by Him so as to be able to contemplate Him in His chief form (τὴν προηγουμένην μορφήν).[129] Elsewhere, Origen says that whereas it is chiefly the Father Who remains unchangeable (ἄτρεπος) and unalterable (ἀναλλοίωτος), the Word of God also retains these characteristics, even if He becomes incarnate and lives amongst human beings. He is thus neither taken captive nor ever seen, but simply continues to urge everyone to drink of that inexhaustible fount of wisdom which He Himself is.[130] Prat in his book on Origen[131] remarks that "the distinction of the two natures Divine and human could not be more clearly expressed. The eternal Divine Word remaining what He was, and without any change on His part, takes a mortal body and a human soul capable of suffering." Prat then goes on to say that "the interchange of qualities *(communicatio idiomatum)* which is established between the two natures shows that the union is not accidental, but has for its result the bringing into being of a single Person." Mme. Harl on the contrary observes with some justice [132] that Origen seems to evade rather than answer the question how the Incarnation can be reconciled with the changelessness of the Divine Nature.

In fact, it is not really true that the Word became flesh: the Word of God, according to Origen, simply disguises Himself as a person made up of flesh and bones so as to enable those capable of it to penetrate beneath the imposture and discover the real Person. Thus in *Contra Celsum*,[133] while he at first rejects the suggestion of Celsus that the Divine Word gives a false impression to those who see Him, he goes on to suggest that just as in medicine the patient may lawfully be misled for his own sake, the same may be true in the process of salvation.[134] Thus Origen states that in his exposition of doctrine it is his custom to say that Jesus Christ is not simply a man *(Christum non purum hominem dicimus)*, but rather both God and Man. The suggestion is that Divinity and humanity are separate elements which are somehow brought together in Jesus Christ.[135] A striking illustration of this view is forthcoming in the passage[136] where Origen says that if the Saviour associates Himself with those who are ignorant of the day and hour of the end of the world, that may be because the Son on His human side *(homo, qui secundum Salvatorem (est))* is understood to have made progress beyond all others in knowledge and wisdom, but did not attain full maturity until He had fully accomplished His appointed task. Hence it is not remarkable if the day and hour of the end was the only thing He did not know before His final exaltation. Thus to the extent that the soul *(anima)* of Christ was capable of developing, it was of one kind with all human souls.[137]

From what has been said so far, we can infer that, as Origen says, even though the prophets foretold that a certain "effulgence and image"[138] of the Divine Nature would come into human life together with the incarnate soul of Jesus, these rays were not enclosed in the human Jesus alone, so that the light of the Divine Word, from which these rays proceed, existed nowhere else.[139] (Curiously enough, Origen slips into the more primitive way of thinking about the Heavenly Christ when, in discussing the soul's progress through the heavenly spheres, he says that in fact Jesus Christ is everywhere and pervades all things, and we must thus *no longer (nec ultra)* think of Him as being restricted to the limits within which He once lived on earth.[140] This statement, taken by itself, appears to ignore the original omnipresence of the Divine Word before the Incarnation, and also to leave it an open question whether the omnipresence continued throughout the Incarnate Life). Likewise in *De Princ.* Origen declares with reference to the Incarnation that we must not suppose that the Word of God, Who is also the Wisdom, Truth and Life of God, was separated from the Father and confined within the compass of a human body in such a way that He existed nowhere else. Origen quotes the statement of John the Baptist "There stands one among you whom you do not know" (John i.26) as showing that even though Jesus might not be present in the body, He would be present invisibly.[141] Likewise, if our Lord had asked the centurion why he had not brought his paralysed servant to be healed (Matt.viii.6), the centurion would have replied that there was no need to show his servant to One Who sees everything, nor to bring him into the presence of One Whose power is not limited or enclosed or excluded from anything.[142] Again, once our Lord had declared that the Canaanite woman's request on behalf of her sick daughter was granted, the healing was not delayed, for since He was Divine, His word was effective everywhere ($\pi\alpha\nu\tau\alpha\chi o\tilde{v}$).[143]

Again, if Mary, the sister of Lazarus, said to our Lord "If you had been here . . .", that shows that she and her sister had not made sufficient spiritual progress to know that He was in fact present invisibly; for whether human beings are aware of it or not, He is among them.[144] Likewise, when discussing the parable of a man going into a far country,[145] Origen says that although our Lord is compared to such a man, that does not contradict His omnipresence, because it was only as embodied that He became absent; as the Only-begotten Son of God Who is not confined within a body, He is present with all who are gathered in His Name *(secundum hanc divinitatis suae naturam non peregrinatur, sed peregrinatur secundum dispensationem corporis quod suscepit).*[146] When St. Paul says that while we are at home in the body, we are absent from the Lord (II Cor.v.6), it is only His humanity which is absent, for His Divinity is always with us, although we may not be aware of it.[147] Even when Jesus went away to suffer on the Cross, He remained invisibly with His disciples in order to keep alive their faith even after they had seen Him die.[148]

Mme. Harl sums up very effectively what has been said in this section when she observes [149] that Origen tends to think of the Incarnation as intended to be a sign of the spiritual activity of the Divine Word rather than a full realisation of that activity; indeed she goes so far as to say that Origen finds it hard to think of the Word of God as being genuinely present in the humanity of Christ. In fact, Origen's doctrine of the Incarnation appears to be of a definitely Docetic character, in so far as the Divine Word appears in different forms in the way in which an actor may change from one suit of clothes to another.[150] The strange conclusion is thus reached that the Transfiguration as narrated in the Gospels is the exact opposite of the truth, which was that so far from being changed into a more glorious form, the Divine Word allowed His true form to appear to those of His disciples who were qualified to apprehend it; whereas the people down below, who were unable to receive Him as He was, were content to say: "We saw Him, and He had no form or beauty."[151] Thus Eichinger observes that Origen does not allow for the possibility of an actual process of Transfiguration in the case of our Lord, but only of a spiritual progress of human beings from the apprehension of "the form of a servant" to that of "the form of God."[152] He likewise says elsewhere that "the distinction affirmed by Origen between the forms of the Divine Word is not to be understood as a statement about the constitution of the Word Himself, but as a closer definition of the Word with reference to His revelatory function."[153] Miura-Stange puts the matter even more vividly when she says that "the true self-emptying of the Divine Word consists in the fact that He continually abandons His own Divine Being for individual men, and takes on veil after veil of lowliness in order to minister to His creatures with a being which is not His own being. He is thus a complex formation of appearances which have only a relative value; His true and absolute appearance we understand as little as we understand God Himself . . .. (Thus) the final form is always the Divine Word, which acts through all things and so shines through all forms. A 'Gnostic' could always have seen God in the Jesus of the gospels. The Man would have dissolved as a cloud before his deeper glance."[154]

Origen himself says roundly that "the Word appears to each individual in the way most beneficial to the person himself, and does not reveal Himself more fully than the viewer can see Him.[155] Hence Peter was not allowed to stay on the mountain side in contemplation of the Divine Word, but was required to descend together with his Master so that His Master might be seen in the form in which those below were able to see him[156] — those who called Him "Son of David" and regarded Him indeed as the Christ, but knew Him only after the flesh because they were still "babes" ($\nu\acute{\eta}\pi\iota o\iota$).[157] In fact the natural way in which Christ could begin to be known is as the Power and Wisdom of God; but because of our frailty we cannot begin to know Him in that way, but only as the incarnate and crucified Christ[158] (It is to be observed, however, that in at least one passage Origen declares that it was only after the Crucifixion and Resurrection that Jesus appeared in a way adapted to the capability of each person who saw Him; before those events He appeared in the same way to all.[159] On the other hand, this statement may simply be a concession to the traditional view of Jesus Christ.)

Origen elsewhere declares that the Word became flesh for the sake of those who through cleaving to the flesh had become as flesh, and were thus incapable of seeing Him as He actually is — namely as the Word Who is with God and is God.[160] Grillmeier thus seems right in observing [161] that because in Origen's thought the Divine Word was regarded as the governing principle in the incarnate Jesus, "the genuine manhood of Jesus could never be fully appreciated. Body and soul appear in the last resort as transitory realities which are swallowed up in the Divinity. They were to so great an extent taken up into the Divinity of the Word of God that the Word ceased to be human. In particular, the distinctive act of the human Jesus, the saving death, was depreciated."

Again, Origen says that the Christian preacher needs to adapt his message to the state of mind of his hearers. If they are fleshly-minded (σαρκίνοι), we must preach the bodily gospel (σωματικὸν εὐαγγέλιον), in so far as we preach the Christ Who became incarnate and was crucified; but when they have progressed spiritually and desire heavenly wisdom, we must reveal to them the Divine Word Who has been restored to His pre-incarnate state.[162] In another passage, it is stated that those who are spiritually mature apprehend the glory of the Divine Word and the fullness of the grace and truth with which He is endowed; but these things cannot be grasped by those who require "the foolishness of preaching" (I Cor.i.21) in order to believe.[163]

Crouzel [164] seems to minimise the extent to which the Incarnate Christ should according to Origen be transcended in the spiritual progress of the believer. He says, in contradiction to Hanson, that religious experience does not dissolve the Incarnation, and that "the Incarnation is not simply a means, a mere stage in the process of the Divine plan, but rather the unique fact whose consequences unfold until the second Coming of Christ . . .. If the facts of Christ's life should be interpreted with reference to His presence in the heart of the Christian, if, that is, Jesus must be born and grow in each person as He was born and grew in His body and His human soul . . . what is more appropriate than this to make plain the unique character of the

Incarnation?" On the contrary, it appears to the present writer that the genuine development of the incarnate Jesus is something which it would be so awkward for Origen to admit that on the whole he prefers to allegorise it.[165]

It is curious that Origen is prepared to admit that Judas himself recognised his Master's greatness, that is, the greatness of the wisdom and grace that was in Him, but none the less says that Judas did not see the full extent of it; otherwise he would not have betrayed Him to His enemies.[166] It is difficult to see how Origen can be acquitted of the charge of trying to have it both ways in this passage. Crouzel,[167] when he refers to Origen as saying that neither Pilate nor Judas nor the Jews who clamoured for our Lord's crucifixion saw God in Jesus, does not seem to have fully weighed the purport of this passage.

But it is not just a matter of apprehending the Word as He originally was and as He again became after His earthly life: it is also a matter of being transformed into His likeness. The "metamorphosis" which occurred in the case of the Son of God must also occur in the life of the believer. Thus Origen says that the Son assumed a physical form so that He might transform those whom He calls to Himself, first into the likeness of the Word Who became flesh, and then introduce them to Himself as He was in the beginning.[168] Thus it was that even during His sojourn on earth, He did not limit Himself to His primary form,[169] but led those who were qualified to the spiritual high mountain and showed them His glorious form and the radiance thereof.[170] There is a striking passage in *Comm. in Rom.*[171] in which, with reference to the phrase "conformed to the likeness of the Son of God" (Rom.viii.29), Origen says that those who love God and for whom all things therefore work together for good are conformed to the likeness of the Son in so far as He is in the form of God; in them are implanted the Divine qualities of Christ, His truth and wisdom and righteousness and all the others. Whereas those in the early stages of discipleship are conformed to the Word of God in so far as He is in the form of a servant, because they "receive the primary elements of Divine knowledge in a spirit of fear." Origen actually suggests that though Jesus Christ was still in His mother's womb when she visited the mother of John the Baptist, He conferred His own Divine form on His cousin, with the result that later on one was confused with the other.[172] In another passage Origen says that it was necessary for the Son of God to come in a lowly form so that He might introduce human beings to His glorious form and indeed assimilate them to that form.[173] For those who experience this second coming of the Word, the present age comes to an end, because in St. Paul's words "the world is crucified to them and they to the world." [174]

The Transfiguration in fact seems to be treated allegorically rather than literally by Origen, in so far as he takes it as symbolising the spiritual ascent of the believer to a more enlightened apprehension of the Divine Word. [175] In fact any suggestion that God descended to this world should be interpreted as meaning that He concerned Himself with human problems. Thus the Divine Word did not really abandon His invisible condition when He took the form of a servant; even then He could be seen as what He really was by His chosen Apostles, but was seen as a mere man by the crowds and Pharisees whose sins He reproved. [176] Again, with reference to Matt.xvi.28, Origen says that not all who stand by Jesus are said not to be destined to taste death till they see the Son of Man coming in His kingdom. For when people are first introduced to Him, He does not appear glorious or great; only if they are prepared to follow Him up the high mountain do they see His kingly glory. [177]

The full extent of Origen's Docetism is clearly seen when he states that the very body of Jesus appeared in such a form as was appropriate to the individuals who saw it.[178] The extraordinary result of this outlook is that Origen considers that the crowd led by Judas failed to recognise our Lord in the Garden of Gethsemane because He appeared in a form different from that to which they were accustomed.[179] Eichinger justly asks, when discussing this passage,[180] why our Lord should not have appeared to His captors in a form appropriate to them. It seems to be going beyond the evidence, however, to say with Hanson [181] that Origen thought it possible that "the Jesus of history could during His life on earth occasionally dissolve into the Jesus of religious experience." That would be Docetism in a more extreme form even than that which Origen seems to adopt.

It is also the case that in many passages Origen declares that it was not the Word of God Who became incarnate at all, but rather the preexistent soul who had become spiritually united to Him, and to whom alone it really appertained to be united to a human body.[182] Only through the hypothesis of a pre-existent soul could Origen attempt to take account of the human development of Jesus. In one fragment [183] Origen says that "there is such a Person as the Son of God, Who is the Image of the invisible God, and there is also an image of the Son of God, which we consider to be the human soul which the Son of God assumed, and which became through its virtue (διὰ τὴν ἀρετήν) the image of the image of God.[184] In another fragment he applied the first Psalm to the man united to the Saviour (τοῦ κατὰ τὸν Σωτῆρα ἀνθρώπου), inasmuch as he abstained from evil and practised goodness, and hence became like (ἐξομοιώσει) the Only-begotten Son.[185] Crouzel is really whitewashing Origen[186] when he says that "he has no clear idea of the concept of 'personality', and therefore could not foresee the criticism which would be made of his conception of the soul of Jesus, in so far as he attributed to the Incarnate Word a double personality, that of the Word on the one hand, and on the other that of the man whose chief part is the soul as possessor of free will." There is really no reason why we should regard Origen as incapable of understanding the meaning of "personality." Crouzel also says[187] that although Origen's speculations about the soul of Jesus have a Nestorian appearance, that soul is no more than a metaphysical principle which does not imperil the unity of Christ's Person, as many passages bear witness (though the present writer would say that many passages would suggest the opposite). Lieske[188] seems to have grasped Origen's thought more fully when he says that "since the soul (of Christ) is one with the Divine Word, its entry into the material world implied the incarnation of the Son of God. Through the soul the Divine Word took human nature from the Virgin Mary and was thereby united to a body." As Grillmeier says:[189] (According to Origen) the unity of Christ comes about in so far as the soul of Christ acts as intermediary between flesh and the Word, because these two cannot otherwise be united by the Platonic dualism of Origen."

In one passage[190] Origen says that whereas the Word of God as spiritual Bridegroom may have a number of brides, in so far as all rational beings have the power to apprehend Him, with the result that He takes them to Himself, none the less there is one soul which is called the perfect dove (τελεία περιστερά) because it receives special honour. In another passage[191] we learn that Origen considers that the man who was united to the Divine Son of God existed prior to his birth from the Virgin Mary. Elsewhere,[192] Origen says that "the man thought of as Jesus" (τῷ κατὰ τὸν Ἰησοῦν νοουμένῳ) was not merely united with the Firstborn of all creation but in every respect became one with Him, inasmuch as he who is joined to the Lord is one spirit (ἓν πνεῦμα) with Him." Origen also says[193] that since it is reasonable to suppose that each soul (ψυχή) enters a body appropriate to it, it is probable that the soul of Jesus, seeing how beneficial its incarnate life was going to be, needed a body superior to all others.

In *Hom. in Num.*[194] Origen compares Jesus Christ to Aaron who as priest "stood between the living and the dead" when a plague had broken out among the Israelites (Num.xvi.46-48), and likens the censer which Aaron held to the human flesh which Christ assumed, and the fire from off the altar which was put into the censer to "that stupendous human soul" *(anima illa magnifica)* with which He was born, and the incense to His "immaculate spirit."[195] Origen says elsewhere[196] that this soul was in its nature like our souls, but in intention and virtue like the Word of God Himself, and therefore such as could unfailingly carry out the plans and wishes of the Word Himself. It was this soul which Origen in one passage declares to have emptied itself and to have taken the form of a servant, "so that it might be restored to the form of God by superior examples and teachings, and recalled to the fullness of which it had emptied itself."[197] This statement is somewhat puzzling, because it could be taken to imply that this soul became incarnate as a punishment for its disobedience, whereas in fact it descended to the human state for the sake of those who had fallen to that state. Presumably Origen means that though this soul became incarnate without being obliged, none the less it could not resume its original state until it had done all that was required for the salvation of human beings.

It is to be observed, however, that Origen does not always express himself in such a way as to emphasise that it was not the Word of God Himself, but only the soul united to Him, which assumed a human body. Thus in one passage the Virgin Mary is spoken of as the mansion of the Only-begotten Son and the house of God *(domum Dei)*.[198] Elsewhere there is a reference to "Jesus the God" Who has arisen as a Light for those who sit in darkness.[199] Again, Origen speaks of the just men of the Old Dispensation as desiring to see what the Apostles saw, that is "God Who took human flesh" ($\theta\epsilon\grave{o}\nu$ $\dot{\epsilon}\nu\alpha\nu\theta\rho\omega\pi\dot{\eta}\sigma\alpha\nu\tau\alpha$), and to hear "the voice of God substantially united to flesh" ($\theta\epsilon o\hat{v}$ $\dot{\epsilon}\nu\omega\theta\dot{\epsilon}\nu\tau\sigma\varsigma$ $\sigma\alpha\rho\kappa\grave{\iota}$ $\kappa\alpha\theta$'$\dot{v}\pi\dot{o}\sigma\tau\alpha\sigma\iota\nu$).[200] Again, Origen declares that it must not be thought that He Who took human nature upon Himself is someone other than Him Who is invisible and extends to every man and even to the whole world ($\delta\iota\dot{\eta}\kappa o\nu\tau\alpha$ $\dot{\epsilon}\pi\grave{\iota}$ $\pi\dot{\alpha}\nu\tau\alpha$ $\ddot{\alpha}\nu\theta\rho\omega\pi o\nu$ etc. . .)[201] There is one passage [202] where the two ideas — that of God becoming man and that of a man being united to God — are combined inexplicably, as though Origen did not really know his own mind on this matter. First, he refers to the Word of God as having taken human flesh and having become to each created being what each required in order that the Word might gain them all, and then as having been restored to His original state of glory; but then he refers to "the man thought of as Jesus" (τὸν κατὰ τὸν Ἰησοῦν ἄνθρωπον νοούμενον) who became united to the Word of God to a greater extent than anyone else did.

One wonders whether the distinction made between the Son of God as Doctor and Shepherd and Redeemer on the one hand and Wisdom, Reason and Justice on the other [203] corresponds to the distinction between the human soul of Christ and the Divine Word Himself. I do not feel that Laeuchli is right in dismissing this conjecture as readily as he does [204] when he says that "the Son of God as Wisdom and Reason and Justice is only a part of Him Who made Himself incarnate in Jesus", and asserts that there is no question of "the incarnate Christ being subordinated to the timeless Word of God." In fact Laeuchli hints at the end of the very same sentence that the reason why the Son of God bestows His help in different ways to different people is that the soul of Jesus is united to the Divine Word, the soul of Jesus assisting those at a lower stage of spiritual development, and the Divine Word assisting those at a higher stage.

Strictly speaking, however, it is inaccurate to speak of the "soul of Christ", although Origen freely uses the word "soul" (ψυχή or *anima*), because according to him the "soul" is "mind" (νοῦς) in its degenerate form, that is, mind which has gone astray from its Creator, or to put it another way, has "grown cold" in its love towards Him (hence the word ψυχή, derived, according to Origen, from ψύχεσθαι, to grow cool).[205] Whereas the soul of Christ had never lost its original fervour, and hence remained united to Him.[206] So it is only by an extension of the meaning of the word ψυχή to indicate "mind" or "spirit" that the word can be used of the earthly agent of the Word of God at all.[207]

The highest element in human nature is in fact called by Origen indifferently πνεῦμα or νοῦς. Thus he says[208] that those who excelled in virtue are said in Scripture to have become χοϊκούς and to act no longer according to reason, and to have made earthly (ἀπογεώσαντας) the πνεῦμα which is the chief part of them. Again, he asserts[209] that the ψυχή, which becomes σάρξ because of sin, can be changed and become πνεῦμα. He likewise asks [210] what is more seemly than a ψυχή which is joined to the πνεῦμα and united to it in such a way that it no longer remains ψυχή but becomes what the πνεῦμα is. Again, it is said [211] that the just man, though distinct from Christ, can be said to be one with Christ, the reference being to I Cor.vi.17. For even though the just man is of an essence inferior to that of Christ, none the less they form ἓν πνεῦμα. Again, Origen says with reference to John xi.38 that our Lord was distressed in spirit (τῷ πνεύματι) when he was at a distance from the tomb of Lazarus, but on drawing near to the tomb, He kept His distress within himself, so that we may learn that He became a man who was unchangeably like us.[212] Again, when in I Sam.xxviii.13 the witch of Endor stated that "she saw gods ascending out of the earth", Origen refers to these beings as πνεύματα.[213]

There are also passages where the highest element in man's nature is termed νοῦς. Thus Origen says that "the tabernacle of the name of God" is the νοῦς of the individual, and that this is polluted when it becomes earthly (γήϊνος) instead of heavenly (ἐπουράνιος).[214] Again, with reference to Luke xii.35 "Let your lights (λύχνοι) be burning", Origen says that since our earthly life is as night, we need a candle or lamp, and this is provided by the νοῦς, which is the eye of the ψυχή.[215] This statement is repeated and amplified in another fragment, where, with reference to Matt.vi.22.23, Origen says that the νοῦς is the eye not only of the rest of the ψυχή but of the body itself.[216] Elsewhere Origen says that the νοῦς only acquires full perception when it is a partaker of Him Who said "I am come into the world as light."[217] In fact, it is incumbent upon us to take care of our faculty of understanding (τῆς ἐν ἡμῖν νοητικῆς δυνάμεως), so that the νοῦς may perform its intended function of enlightening soul and body alike.[218] How, asks Origen, did the two blind men recognise Christ, if they did not have the mind (νοῦν) which led them to follow the Good Shepherd?[219] The Saviour Himself, says Origen, did not experience the mindless state of infants (τῇ τῶν νηπίων ἀνοίᾳ); for even when He was being suckled, He knew how to place His hope in Him Who had taken Him from His mother's womb.[220]

It would seem that Crouzel does not fully establish his contention that Origen distinguishes πνεῦμα from νοῦς in the sense that he regards πνεῦμα as "the Divine element present to the soul."[221] The passages just referred to hardly seem to give him much support. He says elsewhere: "We scarcely any text which attributes intellectual functions to the πνεῦμα; it is represented as exterior to the soul which should be conformed to it. The νοῦς and the λόγος in each person stand for the superior and spiritual ("pneumatique" in the French) part of the soul, that which conforms itself to the πνεῦμα."[222] The passage which Crouzel quotes from *De Oratione*[223] which appears to distinguish νοῦς from πνεῦμα surely means by νοῦς something different from what Origen normally means, ie. it means "intelligence" in the ordinary sense.[224] Nor do I think that Dupuis[225] really proves that there is a firm distinction between πνεῦμα and νοῦς in Origen's thought. He asserts, with Crouzel, that the πνεῦμα is "the Divine element present to the soul", and also describes it as "a gift of grace."[226] But surely whether the Divine gift is present to the soul depends on whether the soul is prepared to receive it. It can thus be bestowed or withdrawn; it is certainly not an inalienable part of the human personality.[227] Dupuis similarly tries to have it both ways when he says[228] that "on the one hand, the πνεῦμα is the Divine element present in man, and on the other, as the highest element in his threefold constitution, it belongs to him as his own." F. Rusche, in his *Das Seelenpneuma*,[229] rightly, in my view, identifies πνεῦμα with νοῦς. He also does this in *Blut, Leben und Seele*.[230] Rius-Camps says[231] that Origen, even when he uses Platonic terms, confers a new content on them, and thus, by identifying τὰ νοητά with τὰ πνευματικά he makes the Biblical sense prevail over the philosophical.[232]

It is also worth referring to Origen's two interpretations of the parable of the unjust stewards, who are said to be "cut asunder" and "their portion" to be "placed with the unbelievers" (Luke xii.46). In the first interpretation, he again uses the word "soul" of the spirit of man in its unfallen state, when he says that if a spiritual gift has not been used as it should be, the gift of the Holy Spirit will be withdrawn from a man's "soul", and the portion which remains, ie. the essence of the soul, will be placed with the unbelievers, now that it has been cut asunder from that Divine Spirit with which it ought to have been united.[233] But it is surely a straining of language to suggest that the spirit of man and the Divine spirit are united in such a manner that the resultant entity can be split into portions; in fact this is a thoroughly materialistic attitude.

In the second interpretation, he makes a distinction between the two portions of the soul itself, the better portion being that which was made in the image of God, and the other portion being that which "was received" (adsumpta est) through the misuse of freewill in a condition contrary to the nature of its original purity.[234] But here again, it is utterly incongruous to conceive of the spirit of man as itself divided into portions, Origen's avowed doctrine in fact is that the spirit itself degenerates through the misuse of freewill, and is thus changed into something which can be called "soul", because the ardour of its love for God has cooled. Once again, Origen slips into the habit of naming "soul" what was originally unfallen.[235]

Verbeke refers to this passage in his book,[236] but in my opinion does not draw the right conclusions from it. It is not the case that a *portion* of the πνεῦμα becomes cold and is thus imprisoned in the body:[237] the *entire* πνεῦμα becomes cold in the love of God, and the lower soul is thus *added*, ie. that element which is susceptible to higher and lower suggestions, ie. from the πνεῦμα and from the σάρξ respectively.[238] The lower ψυχή is *not* "the source of evil tendencies";[239] Origen makes it clear that the source of these tendencies is the flesh, and the lower soul simply responds or not as it is inclined. It might indeed appear that according to Origen the lower soul is a "material breath"[240] if attention be paid only to De Princ. III.4.2;[241] but if we read further on in the chapter,[242] we realise that it is only called "material" because it comes into being together with the body, and we also realise that in fact it is not the seat of the bodily desires; it simply responds to them favourably or unfavourably.

There are two other passages in which Origen overlooks the strict doctrine that the spirit of man in its unfallen state should be termed πνεῦμα and only becomes ψυχή when its love of God has grown cold. In one of them, with reference to Lamentations i.1a, he compares the city of Jerusalem to the ψυχή, the multitude of its people to the richness of its contemplations, and the multitude of the nations to the abundance of its good deeds. The ψυχή now sits solitary, because she, the bride, is separated from the Word, her Bridegroom, and has thus become a widow.[243] Again, the disciples of Christ are said to have been, so to speak, His ψυχή, and thus at the time of His Passion they are said to have grown sick and thus to have sinned by forsaking Him, and Peter in particular by denying Him.[244]

On the other hand, in *De Orat.* Origen states that the soul which ascends to a higher level and follows after the Spirit of God and is emancipated from the body ceased to be a soul and becomes spiritual (πνευματικὴ γίνεται).[245] Völker[246] quotes this passage as showing that the same thing happens to the fully-developed Christian as to the Lord Himself, in so far as the Lord's ψυχή became πνεῦμα. And yet it had never really degenerated into the condition of being a ψυχή, because its original ardour continued unabated. And the conclusion certainly does not follow that the Lord's ψυχή lost its identity and was absorbed into His Divinity, any more than the human ψυχή is.[247] Again, in *Exhort. ad Mart.* Origen recommends those to whom he writes to lose their souls by enduring martyrdom so as to save them and even receive them back as something better than a soul.[248] Elsewhere in the same treatise, he asks; "How can the soul be slain when it has been given life by the very fact of martyrdom?"[249]

However, in one Greek passage which refers to what is commonly called "the soul of Christ" the word νοῦς (mind) is actually used, as appropriate to a being who "remained steadfast in the love and contemplation of God."[250] It is also worth noticing that Origen modifies his strict doctrine of the placing of individual spirits in positions of service appropriate to their degree of nearness to God or departure from God when he says that "some beings who are of higher merit are required to suffer with the rest and to perform a duty to those below them for the sake of improving the state of the world *(ad exornandum mundi statum)*."[251] In certain places this seems to be asserted of the heavenly bodies; but with vastly more reason could it be asserted of the "soul of Christ", which of all creatures did not deserve *of itself* to enter the material world and endure the hardships resulting therefrom.[252]

On the other hand, some of the statements which Origen makes about the incarnate soul of Christ are not very easy to reconcile, at any rate if taken in their *prima facie* sense, with the statements he makes about that soul in its pre-incarnate state. Thus he says that after the Incarnation the soul and body of Jesus became very closely united with the Divine Word. Origen cites the instance of the believer who according to St. Paul is "one spirit" with the Lord (I Cor. vi.7), and then suggests that in a superior and more Divine way, that which was at one time a composite being in relation to the Word of God became one with Him.[253] This statement only becomes compatible with Origen's doctrine of the indissoluble union existing between the pre-incarnate soul of Jesus and the Divine Word if we understand it as meaning that before the Incarnation the Divine Word did not use the soul and body of Jesus as His instrument in the way He did afterwards.

Aeby in his article "Les missions divines",[254] while he refers to the chapter in *Contra Cels.* in which this statement is contained, does not attempt to deal with the difficulty which the statement raises: he contents himself with saying that "by the entire adherence of the soul of Christ to the Divine Word, it becomes the indispensable link which unites the Divine and human natures of Jesus." P. Nemeshegyi interprets this passage as meaning that the union of the soul of Christ with the Divine Word was increased by the accomplishing of Christ's redemptive work.[255] But Origen has said in *De Princ.*[256] that the human soul of Jesus was fully united to the Word of God even in its preexistent state.[257]

Refoulé[258] refers to the excerpt from Justinian's letter to Mennas[259] where the human Jesus is said to have "become Christ" by reason of his goodness (Ps.xlv.7 is quoted here) as proving that he was anointed with the oil of gladness because he loved righteousness and hated iniquity. But whereas this passage by itself might naturally be interpreted of the incarnate Jesus, the context shows that it refers to the preexistent soul which continued steadfast in its adherence to the Divine Word. Such a notion appears to leave no room for the idea of development of character in the incarnate Jesus.[260]

It is curious that Origen regards the human Jesus as at certain times speaking in his own person, and at other times as a mouthpiece of the Divine Word. Thus Origen regards our Lord's words "I am the Way, the Truth, and the Life" as only referring to the Divine element of His nature; whereas when He said "But now you seek to kill me, a man who has told you the truth", He was referring to Himself as a man enclosed in a fleshly body. In fact, our Lord is described in this passage also [261] as a "composite being", [262] but here in the sense that He was not a single personality, but rather consisted of the Word of God and a human soul used as His agent.[263] The same idea seems to be suggested in the passage in *Contra Cels.*,[264] where the Being to Whom the wise men offered gifts is said to have been "a combination of God and mortal man" (συνθέτῳ τινί ἐκ θεοῦ καὶ ἀνθρώπου θνητοῦ).[265] Nemeshegyi seems to be in error when he suggests [266] that whereas the Father is a Being distinct from the Son and vice versa, the "man" in Jesus is not a being other than the Word, ie. they are not distinct in essence, but only as different aspects of the same being. Some passages in Origen's works might suggest this view;[267] but it certainly does not appear to be the main outlook of either *De Princ.* or *Contra Cels.* Indeed, Nemeshegyi himself suggests that Origen thought otherwise at times.[268] The same criticism can be made of Lieske,[269] when he asks the question whether the union of the soul of Christ and the Divine Word is a matter of the union of the Divine and human natures in a single person, or whether it is a matter of a moral union of two persons, the Word of God and the man Jesus? The phrase σύνθετον κτῆμα as used in *Contra Cels.* I.66 (referred to in n.263) suggests the second answer.

Again, Origen points out that although the Synoptists represent Jesus as being tempted by the devil, St. John, who described His "spiritual nature", does not speak of Him as being tempted, because the Truth, the Life, and the Resurrection cannot be tempted. He was tempted in the human nature which He had assumed *(secundum hominem quem susceperat)*.[270] Likewise, in reply to the suggestion of Celsus that a man who was Divine could not be led away under arrest or be betrayed and deserted by His companions, Origen asserts that neither the body nor the soul ($τὴν\ ψυχήν$) of Jesus was Divine, the soul of which He said "My soul is exceeding sorrowful even unto death"; it was rather the Word Who spoke in Jesus, saying "I am the Way, the Truth, and the Life", Who was Divine.[271] The suggestion seems to be that the human Jesus was a uniquely inspired man through whom the Word of God spoke, just as He spoke through the Jewish prophets. This is presumably the notion which prompted Origen to interpret as referring to Christ the passage in Psalm xlv where the tongue of the person addressed is said to be "the pen of a ready writer", and "grace" is said to have been "poured on his lips."[272] (On the other hand, in one passage Origen appears to accept the view that it was the Divine Word Himself Who towards the time of His death was so distressed as to utter the words quoted above;[273] but perhaps Origen is simply stating the apparent meaning of the Gospel in order to introduce his own interpretation later in the same chapter.)

Again, it seems obvious, says Origen, that when the prophets spoke of the Suffering Servant as "having no form of comeliness" and as "a man of sorrows, and acquainted with grief", they were not foretelling the crucifixion of God Himself.[274] Likewise, Origen says elsewhere that although the Saviour suffers all that His Body the Church suffers — hunger, thirst, sickness — He cannot suffer anything so far as His Divinity is concerned.[275] In another passage, Origen quotes the text "He Himself took our weaknesses and bore our diseases" (Matt. viii.17), and interprets these weaknesses as being those of the hidden man of our heart (I Peter iii.4), but at the same time says that it was His $ψυχή$ which was distressed and troubled (Mark xiv.34) as the result of the weaknesses and diseases of which He has relieved us.[276]With reference to the parallel passage in St. Matthew (xxvi.37), where it is said that "He began to be sad and distressed", Origen agrees that our Lord shared in human nature to the extent of beginning to be distressed and afraid, so that He might show His disciples that He Himself needed the help of God because of the weakness of the flesh; but

Origen none the less stresses that His Divine Nature was far removed from feelings of distress or fear.[277] In the same way, although Origen thinks that the words of Jeremiah "Woe is me, mother, that you have borne me as a man who is condemned and judged by all the earth!" (xv.10) can fittingly be applied to the Saviour, none the less it is as man, not as God, that He says this, because His soul ($\psi v \chi \dot{\eta}$) was human, and could therefore be troubled and distressed, whereas the Word Who was with God in the beginning could not undergo these feelings.[278] Again, Origen states [279] that when at the time of His Passion Satan and his minions made war against the Saviour, His soul ($\psi v \chi \dot{\eta}$) was distressed in a human fashion ($\dot{a}v\theta\rho\omega\pi\dot{\iota}v\omega\varsigma$), not because He feared death, though this would have been human, but because He feared defeat. For Christ allowed this $\psi v \chi \dot{\eta}$ to undergo the feelings natural to it, and therefore His $\psi v \chi \dot{\eta}$ was grieved and distressed, though not overwhelmed by the distress because it was only momentary.

Again, in *Matt. Comm. Series* Origen goes to great pains to point out that it was our Lord's human nature which quailed at the prospect of the Passion. It was because of His human nature that he began to be sorrowful and afraid, and it was because of His human nature that He asked for the cup of suffering to be taken from Him. Origen interprets the crucial passage ". . . not as I will, but as Thou wilt" (Matt. xxvi.39) by attributing it not to His Divine and impassible nature, but to his human and frail nature.[280] Origen has already said that Christ led His three disciples near to where He prayed in Gethsemane so that they might recognise that human power to endure suffering comes from God alone, and is only bestowed in answer to prayer.[281]

Origen also makes it clear that after the death of our Lord on the Cross, it was His $\psi v \chi \dot{\eta}$ which entered the realm of departed spirits. Even if the Saviour appeared to sleep in death, that sleep was not a state in which His $\psi v \chi \dot{\eta}$ was inactive; it was only His body which ceased to be used.[282] It was thus as a disembodied $\psi v \chi \dot{\eta}$ that He associated with departed spirits and converted some of them.[283] This ministry of reconciliation, says Origen, was actually suggested to the Saviour by the Divine Word.[284] And even now it is the $\psi v \chi \dot{\eta}$ of Jesus which complains of the ingratitude of those for whom He died.[285]

It is worth remarking that in *De Princ.* Origen points out that the intervening agent through whom the Son of God entered into human life is differently referred to in different contexts. When it is a question of suffering or distress befalling Him, the name used is "soul", as in John xii.27, Matt.xxvi.38, and John x.18; but when the reference is to something unconnected with suffering or distress, the word used is "spirit", as in Luke xxiii.46 and Matt.xxvi.41. On the other hand, the words which follow, ie. "From which it appears as though the soul were something intermediate between the weak flesh and the willing spirit", suggest that the word "soul" may here be used as meaning one part of a tripartite personality; but that is not the way in which the phrase "the soul of Christ" is normally used in Origen's writings.[286] Curiously enough, in one passage Origen makes use of the idea of the soul as something liable to suffer as a means of suggesting that "the soul of God", which is occasionally mentioned in the Bible, is His Only-begotten Son, in so far as it was He Who descended to this vale of tears and woe. But that immediately brings back the idea of the Word of God has having *directly* become incarnate as the Father's Representative.[287]

So far as his general outlook is concerned, however, Origen does not altogether escape the reproach levelled by Nemeshegyi[288] against the God of the Platonists in so far as that God was thought of as "lacking a genuine love of the world, and a genuine personal interest in human affairs . . .. He resembles a splendid object of which one takes possession, rather than a living God Who makes an appeal to us . . .. The idea that this God should reveal Himself to man by a personal intervention in history was inconceivable for Greek philosophy." Nemeshegyi later in his book displays the contradiction in Origen's thought on this point when he says that according to Origen, "even to this perfect God one thing is lacking, ie. the salvation of man and of all other rational creatures."[289] Miura-Stange points out[290] that the manhood of Jesus was an embarrassment to Origen when it was a matter of proving His Divinity, as is shown by his complaint against Celsus that Celsus keeps silence about what reveals His Divinity,[291] and yet continually reveals what appertains to the manhood (in particular, the Agony in Gethsemane), even though the Gospel writers could have kept silent about it if they had not been such lovers of truth.[292]

It is thus not surprising that Origen should make the very revealing statement that "there is a quite different account to be given of the Divine Person and His essence from the one to be given of His human nature." [293]This suggests the Nestorian doctrine of a human being united spiritually to the Divine Word, with the exception that in Origen's view the human soul of Jesus was already united to the Divine Word before the Incarnation, whereas in the Nestorian view this union only gradually came about during the earthly life of Jesus. Origen thus declares that although originally there was a distinction between the soul of Jesus and the Divine Word, they became joined together so closely that the relation of the one to the other is no longer that of two separate beings.[294] Völker uses this passage [295] as a means of establishing his contention that the union between the Word of God and the soul of Jesus was more than purely ethical; but the metaphor used by Origen and quoted by Völker on the very same page, that of marriage, to describe that union, would seem to show that in Origen's view the two entities retained their separate natures, the soul not being absorbed into the Word, even though it is in perfect harmony with the Word. Refoulé observes[296] on the contrary that "it was not possible for Origen to explain satisfactorily the union of the human and Divine natures of Christ. In *Convs. with Her.* he criticises Adoptionism as an impious doctrine. He also affirms in various places that 'the man in Jesus' is not a being other than the Divine Word, that they are not distinct from each other except as different 'aspects' of the same unique being .... It remains true, however, that Origen could not conceive the union of the pre-existent soul of Christ with the Divine Word otherwise than on the lines of mystical union . . . . This union attains in Christ so high a degree of intensity that the soul loses its individuality and is blended with the being of God; but it does not appear that Origen regarded this union as strictly speaking ontological. He remains dynamic in his outlook. To put it another way, the union between Christ and the Word is, when strictly defined, a moral union.'[297]

This is certainly the impression we gain from the statement by Origen that in so far as Jesus was a man who above all others was "adorned by sublime participation in the very Word and Wisdom Himself,[298] He endured as a wise and perfect man all that was needed for the sake of human beings."[299] In the same way, when it is stated that the Word of God came to the prophet Ezekiel, Origen declares that this formula can be used of the Saviour Himself, if one thinks of the Word of God, Who always remained in the Father, as coming to him who was born of a Virgin, ie. the man Jesus, so that both might be one, and so that the man whom He had put on *(induerat)* for the sake of the salvation of mankind should be united to the nature of the Only-begotten Word of God.[300]

Curiously enough, when Origen discusses the Incarnation in *De Princ.* he claims that his purpose is not to divide the personality of Christ, but rather to show how each nature — Divine and human — can exist in one and the same person *(in uno eodemque)*, without anything incongruous being ascribed to the Divine nature, and without regarding the events of His earthly life as being illusory.[301] In fact, however, Origen cannot manage to bring the two elements together without interposing a "soul" which can somehow reconcile them within itself. Thus Origen says that this soul is entitled to be called both "Son of God" and "Son of Man", both "Christ" and "Jesus", according to the aspect from which it is viewed. In particular, it can thus be said that the Son of God died, and that the Son of Man will come again in the glory of the Father.[302] On the other hand, in *Exh. ad Mart.*[303] Origen quotes our Lord as saying in St. Matthew's Gospel with reference to the man who acknowledges Christ by dying for His sake, "I will also acknowledge him before my heavenly Father" (x.32), whereas the words as given in St. Luke are "Him shall the Son of Man also acknowledge before the angels of God" (xii.8); and he thus concludes that it is the Word Who is the Image of God Who will acknowledge His disciple before the Father, whereas it is the man who was born of human stock and became the agent of the Word who will acknowledge his disciple before the angels.

As has already been stated,[304] Origen also believed that the Divine Word did not cease to be omnipresent because of the Incarnation, which is another sign that Origen did not regard any genuine "self-emptying" as having taken place. Thus he states that He Who said "I am the Way, the Truth, and the Life" was not circumscribed in such a manner that the Word did not exist anywhere outside the soul and body of Jesus.[305] Elsewhere, it is suggested that Jesus has not been assigned any particular place like the gods mentioned by Celsus who possess human form, but rather "pervades the entire world",[306] and gathers together by the power of His Divine Nature any whom He finds to be inclined towards living the good life.[307]

There are numerous passages which emphasise a cardinal element in Origen's thought, namely that it is degrading for an immaterial spirit to become encased in a body and experience the feelings associated with the body, but that none the less the soul of Jesus consented to do so, seeing that it was inconceivable that the Divine Word Himself should descend to such a state.

Thus Origen speaks of the Divine Word as "bringing down" a Saviour to the human race, that Saviour being the soul of Jesus, which did not undergo any change of essence, but was none the less affected by the body and the surroundings which it entered. That soul was not, however, brought down without its own consent; rather, of its own free will it descended into our midst and accepted the miseries of humanity for our sakes.[308] We may observe that this can be regarded as the supreme example of what Origen describes as the appointed destiny of certain superior souls, namely that they should descend to a lower level than that to which their merits entitle them in order to minister to the needs of souls inferior to them, so that (in Origen's words) "they may thus become sharers in the endurance *(patientiae)* of the Creator."[309] Elsewhere, Origen says that the words recorded in St. John's Gospel "I did not come of my own accord, but the Father sent me,"[310] were spoken by the soul of Jesus, who, though it left nothing to be desired, none the less came forth from God as God's messenger, and took human flesh; whereas other souls do not come in this way from God, that is, they are not sent in accordance with God's will.[311] For instance, those unseen powers who lead astray those little ones who believe in Jesus are liable to be saddled with a mortal body which weighs down the soul, so that in this way their pride may be humbled and they may thus derive spiritual profit.[312]

It was thus from the Divine Word that the human soul of Jesus derived the power of converting and healing and improving the human race.[313] In discussing the utterance "O my Father, if it be possible, let this cup pass from me" and the words which follow, an utterance which above all others bears witness to our Lord's participation in feelings natural to human beings, Origen stresses that the Lord was speaking in His humanity, and thus revealing both the weakness of the flesh and the willingness of the spirit.[314] Elsewhere, Origen makes the significant statement that Pilate had power over Christ's human nature alone,[315] because it was not consistent with the dignity of the Divine Word to become subject to a human governor.[316] Likewise, Origen condemns the suggestion of Celsus that Christians consider Jesus as God when He is being tortured and punished. The truth rather is, says Origen, that the Divine Nature of Jesus is not susceptible to these experiences.[317]

On the other hand, Origen seems on occasion to think that it is to make too great a dichotomy between our Lord's Divine Nature and His human nature to say that as Divine He is devoid of feelings. For the Saviour, he says, descended to the earth out of pity for mankind, and thus underwent our feelings before He condescended to take upon Himself our flesh. His precise words are: *"Primum passus est, deinde descendit et visus est."* Origen goes on to say that the Father Himself is not without feelings, because if prayer is made to Him, He feels our pain, and experiences those feelings which are strictly out of keeping with the grandeur of His Nature — feelings which are properly human.[318]

Adolf Primmer discusses at length[319] the whole subject of the impassibility of the Father and the Son. Primmer seems to think[320] that this quality is safeguarded if Divine compassion is not thought of so much as a feeling, but is rather thought of as an attitude which shows itself in action, but is it possible to make an absolute distinction of this kind? It is interesting that he points out [321] that the Stoics insist on the universal activity of the Logos as Reason, and thus deprecate emotion as irrational and therefore as hindering the undisputed sway of the Logos; but surely emotion is one aspect of the activity of the Logos itself?

Later in the thesis [322] Primmer shows how Origen is as it were caught on the horns of a dilemma. In so far as he starts from the conception of an impassible God, he must inevitably think of the Son as also impassible. Whereas if he thinks of the Son as affected by the sin and suffering of the world, he is bound to transfer these feelings to the Father Himself, because Father and Son co-operate for the salvation of the world in the closest possible manner. This really shows the fatal defect in Origen's soteriological system, in so far as he starts from assumptions which do not harmonise with all the facts.[323] Perhaps the solution of the dilemma (which Primmer does not seem to indicate) is that although there is feeling in God, it is always obedient to right reason, and is therefore not allowed to manifest itself in an uncontrolled manner, as it so often does in human beings.[324]

Pannenberg likewise indicates the dilemma in which Origen involved himself when he says[325] that "the concept of a God Who is by nature immutable . . . constitutes the background for the idea of the impassibility of God which so fatefully determined the Christology of the early Church right down to the theopaschitic controversy." Later on, Pannenberg observes [326] that "immutability, timelessness, simplicity, propertylessness, and namelessness have repeatedly forced the concept of God into an unbridgeable distance from the contingent changes of historical reality in which the salvation of man is decided, and the assertions of faith regarding God's historical acts of salvation were purchased only at the expense of violating the strict sense of those attributes."

It seems at this point worth analysing further Origen's conception of the personality of the Incarnate Jesus with reference to the chapter in *De Princ.*[327] discussing the question whether each individual has two souls. It is true that Origen does not profess at the end of the chapter to come to any definite conclusion; [328] but his outlook as expressed elsewhere seems to necessitate the doctrine of two souls, the higher of which can be called "spirit" (πνεῦμα), and existed before the body, and the lower of which is produced by the generative processes by which the body itself was produced.[329] Origen's discussion of the way in which this doctrine can be reconciled with St. Paul's statement that flesh and spirit war against each other (Gal.v.17) is extremely involved and difficult; but it does seem to emerge that in Origen's view the lower soul has no will of its own other than the desire to remain inactive, and thus either conforms to the will of the spirit or else yields itself up to that of the flesh, the will of the flesh consisting not only of the desires closely associated with the body but also the other feelings listed by St. Paul under the heading of "works of the flesh" (Gal. v.19-21).[330]

It remains to indicate in more detail by reference to other passages in the works of Origen how πνεῦμα and ψυχή are related to each other. In *Comm. in Joh.*[331] he enquires why in one place it is said that our Lord was troubled in His ψυχή [332] and in another that He was troubled τῷ πνεύματι.[333] He first says that Scripture makes a distinction between πνεῦμα and ψυχή (one wonders whether the distinction is everywhere observed!) and that whereas the πνεῦμα does not admit of anything evil, the ψυχή is regarded as morally ambiguous, ie. as admitting of both virtue and vice, for the noblest things are said in Scripture to the the "fruits of the spirit" (which Origen interprets here as meaning the human spirit), whereas the "works of the flesh" carried out as the result of the subservience of the ψυχή to the flesh are said to be altogether blameworthy. Now in the Incarnate Jesus the πνεῦμα was in perfect control of all the other elements of His nature; and so when it is said that "He was troubled τῷ πνεύματι", the meaning is that the feeling of distress was perfectly under the control of His πνεῦμα. Granted, the feeling itself could be said to have originated in His ψυχή; but it was not allowed to develop beyond due limits.[334]

There are also certain passages in *Comm. in Rom.* where Origen expounds the view of the ψυχή as being intermediate between πνεῦμα and σάρξ. In one place he says roundly that the *spiritus* is a higher part of human nature than the *anima*, and it is thus the *spiritus* to which the Spirit of God is said to bear witness in Rom.viii.16;[335] elsewhere he declares that the *anima*, which is intermediate between flesh and spirit, can ally itself to either of these two elements.[336] Again, with reference to Rom.i.9, Origen points out that St. Paul says that he serves God not in the body, nor in the *anima*, but in the highest part of his being, ie. the *spiritus*.[337] Again, Origen identifies "conscience" to which St. Paul refers as that which rebukes deeds that are bad with the *spiritus* which co-exists with the *anima* and is meant to instruct it and to rebuke it when necessary. In those who are righteous, the *anima* is joined to the *spiritus* and is obedient to it in all things; but where the *anima* is disobedient and insolent towards the *spiritus*, it is divided from it at death. This is how Origen interprets the passage in Luke xii.46, where it is said of the evil servant that the Lord on His return will divide him and appoint his portion with the unbelievers.[338] In a curious interpretation of Rom.xiii.1, Origen suggests that only the *anima*, not the *spiritus*, could possibly be recommended to be subject to earthly powers; it is only to the Lord Himself that the *spiritus* can be said to be subject. The *anima* is only bidden to be subject to the powers of this world if our *anima* is still linked in some way to this world and so not completely under the dominion of the *spiritus*.[339]

Origen also has much to say about the problem of freeing the *anima* from its entanglement with the flesh and subordinating it to the *spiritus*. It almost appears from some passages [340] as though the *anima* is like a rope in a tug-of-war, in so far as both *spiritus* and *caro* seek to gain possession of it. The ψυχή is also compared to a woman who is the object of seduction, in so far as Origen thinks of the "law of the flesh" mentioned in Rom.vii.23 as something which commits adultery with the ψυχή.[341] But Origen elsewhere represents the *anima* as capable of making its own decisions, in so far as it is regarded as capable of guarding against the attacks of the flesh, and thus making such progress as to be held fast to God by the sweetness of His love.[342] On the other hand it is the Word of God Who takes the initiative in severing the connexion between ψυχή and σῶμα so that the ψυχή may surrender itself to the πνεῦμα and so be reconciled to God.[343] In fact Origen suggests that the measures taken for this purpose may be painful, even though they are taken with the best intentions.[344] After all, says Origen, "it can never be that the *anima* is without a king; and it must be ensured that it has Christ as King, Whose yoke is easy, and Whose burden is light."[345] Elsewhere Origen varies the metaphor, saying that "the souls of the impious are widows, since they are deprived of the bridegroom who is Christ."[346] On the other hand, Origen also ascribes to the Holy Spirit a share in the work of freeing the ψυχή from evil influences; for in a note on Eph.iv.30 (a reference to being "sealed with the Holy Spirit") he says that we were sealed with the Spirit so that we might become holy as the Spirit is holy, and this applies to both πνεῦμα and ψυχή.[347] Likewise, with reference to the passage in I Cor.v.5 where St. Paul says he has judged it right to deliver the immoral Corinthian to Satan for the destruction of the flesh, so that his πνεῦμα may be saved in the day of the Lord Jesus, Origen suggests that St. Paul is referring to the salvation of the whole man, πνεῦμα, ψυχή and σῶμα alike, by referring to his highest part, because it is not the flesh itself which is destined to be destroyed, but only the "mind of the flesh" (τὸ φρόνημα τῆς σάρκος).[348]

There is however a passage in *Comm. in Joh.*[349] where Origen appears to make no distinction between the πνεῦμα and the ψυχή, but simply contrasts our main substance (ἡ προηγουμένη ὑπόστασις) which is made in the Divine image with the substance deriving from our (pre-incarnate) guilt, which consists in the material element of our nature. It is "our superior nature" (κρείττων οὐσία) which will take on the image of the earthly if we forget it and become subject to our material nature; but if we incline ourselves towards Him in Whose image we were made, we shall attain to the Divine likeness, inasmuch as we shall have abandoned all affinity with any created thing. In this passage Origen inclines towards the more usual view of the soul as a single entity composed of various elements. But elsewhere [350] he reverts to his distinctive view of regarding a human being as composed of different entities which are in a state either of tension or of harmony with each other. He says that when the flesh is said to lust against the spirit and the spirit against the flesh (Gal.v.17), the *anima* is intermediate between the two and inclines itself to one or to the other. The spirit is said to recall to itself the *anima* which is intermediate between spirit and flesh, and to be aided by all the good angels and by the Lord Himself, Who laid down His own *anima* for His sheep. Such is the result of Origen's theory of a pre-mundane fall; it involves him in the fanciful supposition of two entities, πνεῦμα and ψυχή, which exist in each individual person and act independently of each other.[351]

There is also a passage [352] where the trichotomist and dichotomist views of human personality appear to exist side by side. Origen begins by saying that in inferior human beings the ψυχή is dominated by sin and simply carries out the desires of the body. It is only when sin has been ousted from its supremacy that "the σάρξ lusts against the πνεῦμα and the πνεῦμα against the σάρξ." But when the πνεῦμα has won the victory it imparts its own life to the body, and a harmony begins to exist between them, with the result that a prayer is sent up alike from the heart which believes unto righteousness and from the mouth which makes confession unto salvation.[353] Elsewhere, however,[354] it would appear that Origen regards the ψυχή as ultimately responsible for its own destiny. With reference to the text in Galations (vi.6) where St. Paul says that "he who sows in the flesh shall reap corruption from the flesh, and he who sows in the spirit (interpreted by Origen as the human spirit) shall from the spirit reap eternal life," Origen says that it is the *anima* which sows either in the spirit or in the flesh and can thus either fall into sin or be converted from sin. "For the body is the agent of the *anima* in doing whatever it appoints, and the spirit leads the *anima* to virtue, if the *anima* desires to follow it."

Origen feels able on the strength of the foregoing exposition of the relationship between πνεῦμα and ψυχή to explain in his own way the passages of Scripture in which sin is said to have death for its result. He explains the fragment of the early Christian hymn preserved in Eph.v.13 "Awake, thou that sleepest, and arise from the dead" as not addressed to one being, as might at first appear, but rather as addressed to the πνεῦμα and the ψυχή, since the πνεῦμα cannot die, though it can fall asleep, whereas the ψυχή is liable to die, in accordance with the Scriptural dictum "The soul that sinneth, it shall die."[355] This death is the opposite to that which in I Cor.iii.22 is said to belong to Christians, because the latter death is the death to sin which results in living with Christ.[356] In *Comm. in Joh.*[357] Origen suggests that the life which the πνεῦμα (here interpreted as the human πνεῦμα) is said to give is not the ordinary kind of life but the Divine life; just as the death which the latter causes is not the ordinary kind of death which consists in the separation of the ψυχή from the σῶμα, but that which consists in the separation of the ψυχή from God.

There are however other passages where the function of the πνεῦμα in imparting the Divine life is not mentioned, and where the suggestion seems to be that the ψυχή can enter into direct fellowship with Christ. Thus in commenting on the word "death" as used in Rom.vii. 38, he says that the death to which reference is there made is that which separates the *anima* from the love of God.[358] In the same way he elsewhere says that those who put a stumbling-block in the way of others and so cause their *anima* to be separated from God can be called homicides, in so far as they cut off the *anima* of others from its true source of life.³⁵⁹ Indeed, in another passage Origen explicitly says that the life of the *anima* is derived from Christ, Who is Himself Life;³⁶⁰ not that the substance of the *anima* can be destroyed, but it can none the less turn away from the source of the true life and so make itself mortal.³⁶¹

From the above survey it will be clearly seen how great are the difficulties in which Origen lands himself as the result of his peculiar doctrine of "two souls", the higher and the lower. He cannot come to a distinct conclusion as to how harmony between the two is brought about, ie. whether it is as the result of the initiative of the πνεῦμα or that of the ψυχή. Of course the dilemma stems from his equally strange doctrine of the pre-existence of souls, according to which the πνεῦμα becomes incarcerated in a body as the result of its premundane fall from grace, and in the process acquires a lower soul to which alone the name of ψυχή is strictly applicable and which is liable to link itself either to the σάρξ or to the πνεῦμα. The question now arises: If the πνεῦμα is itself in a defective state, how can it reconcile the ψυχή to itself? On the other hand, if it is the ψυχή which is liable to sin, must it not be the πνεῦμα which recalls it from sin?

There are certain passages where Origen appears in the light of these considerations to abandon his doctrine of an individual πνεῦμα appertaining to each person and to understand the word πνεῦμα in the sense of mere "inspiration" or "influence." Thus, with reference to the statement that John the Baptist would go forth "in the spirit (πνεύματι) and power of Elijah" (Luke i.17), Origen says that the πνεύματα of the prophets are spoken of as the possessions of the prophets because they are given to them by God, as is clear from the texts "the spirits of the prophets are subject to the prophets" (I Cor. xiv.32) and "the spirit of Elijah has rested on Elisha" (II Kings ii.15), and that therefore there was nothing absurd in speaking of John as Elijah who was to come, because it was in the spirit and power of Elijah that he reconciled fathers to children and children to fathers.³⁶² In the same way he says elsewhere that the πνεῦμα of Elijah can be regarded as so to speak the clothing (ἔνδυμα) of the ψυχή of John the Baptist.³⁶³ In another passage ³⁶⁴ he interprets the words in Genesis which state that "God breathed into the first man's face the breath of life, and he became a living soul" as referring to the Divine πνεῦμα which confers life on the ψυχή, and states that he who is deprived of the Divine πνεῦμα becomes earthy (χοϊκός), but he who is qualified to receive it is renewed and thus saved. We may compare the *Frag. in I Cor.* [365] where Origen states that only with the aid of Divine πνεῦμα (without the article) can the human ψυχή explore the depths of God's own nature (the reference is to I Cor.ii.10).

Indeed, there are various passages in which Origen uses the word ψυχή to refer to the chief element in the soul, the element normally called πνεῦμα. Thus he says in *Convs. with Her.* that the image of God in which we are made resides in the ψυχή.[366] Again, Christ is said to have given His disciples power over unclean spirits in order that as a result of their expulsion ψυχή and σῶμα might be in harmony and praise the God Who united them.[367] Again, with reference to Eph.v. 28,29, Origen says that just as Christ nourishes and cherishes the Church, so *animae* cherish the bodies over which they are set so that they may follow their husbands without being bowed down by any weakness.[368] Origen in two passages explicitly identifies the ψυχή with what he normally calls the πνεῦμα. In one,[369] he describes the ψυχή as containing "the faculties which perceive Divine and intelligible things", and in the other [370] Origen says that the ψυχή was made by God alone, and was made "free from wickedness" (κακίας ἐκτός). Finally, in a most curious passage in *Frag. in Matt.,*[371] the last words of Christ on the Cross "Father, into Thy hands I commend my spirit" are taken to mean that the ψυχαί of the saints are no longer in Hades but are with God, because this happened in the case of Christ as first fruits.

From what has been said so far, it would appear that Crouzel is correct in suggesting,[372] in his diagram showing the relationship between the part of a human being created in the Divine likeness and the earthly part, that in the works of Origen the word ψυχή is used in two senses, namely that of the πνεῦμα which is the highest part of human personality, and that of the animal soul which is the seat of impulse and perception, and which is associated with the body. Crouzel has pointed out on the previous page that the earthly part of man was acquired as the result of the (premundane) fall, and thus although it is not evil in itself, it is a means of testing the individual, in so far as the highest part of man — that made in the Divine image — is meant to control it, and not be controlled by it.[373] But neither Crouzel nor Rahner[374] really brings out the fundamental discrepancy between the two accounts which Origen gives of the way in which sin originates. On the one hand, he depicts it as resulting from the rebellion of pure spirits against their Creator, and on the other, he suggests that it is due to the animal soul making common cause with the body against the spirit. The second would appear to the commonsense account of evil, the first is purely theoretical, and involves Origen in difficulties regarding the way in which man comes to be as he now is. The πνεῦμα waxes cold in its love of God, and so becomes ψυχή; but another ψυχή, the animal soul, needs to be added to the higher soul so as to complete the constitution of man as it is on earth.

Bürke says [375] that (according to Origen) "in the transition from νοῦς to ψυχή there is in no way involved a substantial alteration of the being of the subject in question", and goes on to say that "ψυχή is nothing other than a defective mode of being of νοῦς." That is true of the ψυχή in one sense, but not of the ψυχή in another sense, and it cannot really be said that Bürke effectively distinguishes the two senses.[376] On the previous page Bürke[377] seems to have contradicted himself by first pointing out that according to Origen the ψυχή is the πνεῦμα whose love of God has become cold, and then going on to say that the soul is intermediate between πνεῦμα and σάρξ, and follows either one or the other. To quote Bürke himself: "(According to Origen) the ψυχή is the meeting place of πνεῦμα and σῶμα, and is thus the place of freedom and decision."

Origen's outlook is in fact defective in so far as whereas in the pre-existent state the πνεῦμα is thought of as exercising choice either by adhering to God or by departing from Him, in the incarnate state it is the lower part of the ψυχή which chooses (or at least this seems to be his normal viewpoint). While it may be true to say of the incarnate state, as does Dupuis,[378] that in the threefold structure of man it is only "the (lower) soul . . . which represents the person . . . for this soul chooses, and on its choice depends its eternal destiny", that is not true of the pre-incarnate state, because the lower soul had not then come into being. In fact Dupuis himself says elsewhere [379] that the νοῦς in its pre-existent state represented the person by itself, and only after the fall was it amalgamated with new elements.[380]

It is now time to show how the two elements known as πνεῦμα and ψυχή found their place in the personality of the incarnate Jesus. The most noteworthy passage is in *Convs. with Her.*,[381] where it is said that our Lord and Saviour, because He wished to save man in his entirety, took on all the elements of human nature – πνεῦμα, ψυχή and σῶμα. These three elements were separated at the time of the Passion, and brought together again at the time of the Resurrection. At the time of the Passion, each element went its separate way – the σῶμα to the tomb, the ψυχή to Hades, the world of departed spirits, and the πνεῦμα to the Father, with Whom the Lord had deposited it just before He expired on the Cross. On the other hand, it had been said in the Psalms, "Thou shalt not leave my ψυχή in Hades"; and if the πνεῦμα had been deposited with the Father, the intention was that it should be received back. But this took place shortly after the Resurrection, for when Mary Magdalene met Him, He bade her not touch Him, because He desired that He should be touched in His entirety, so that the person touching Him might be benefited in all three elements of human nature by coming into contact with all three elements of the Saviour's nature. In fact it was only after ascending to the Father that He reclaimed His πνεῦμα.[382]

After all, says Origen,[383] can the Divine Nature of the Word of God have been given as ransom to the devil: would the devil have been capable of receiving it? It was only His ψυχή which was given as a ransom by the Saviour; but that does not alter the fact that Jesus Christ and His ψυχή and His σῶμα were united to the First-born of all creation in a closer manner than that in which the believer is united to His Lord so as to form one spirit with Him.

On the other hand, we encounter the same confusion in the use of the words πνεῦμα and ψυχή with reference to Jesus Christ as we did in the general discussion of human nature. In one passage[384] the words are actually used interchangeably. Origen says in that passage that when Christ commended His πνεῦμα into the Father's hands, He intended to indicate on what terms the departure of His ψυχή occurred; for "I commend (παρατίθεμαι)" implied that He would receive it back again. Again, Origen refers to the visit of Christ to the spirits imprisoned in Hades "with His spirit" (μετὰ πνεύματος), quoting I Peter iii. 18-20.[385] Dupuis[386] does not really overcome the contradiction between this passage and the one from *Convs. with Her.* by saying that according to Origen, it was after the price of redemption had been paid by the ψυχή of the Saviour that His πνεῦμα announced deliverance to the spirits in the prison of Hades: for in the latter passage it is clearly stated that it was after the Resurrection that He claimed back His πνεῦμα.

There is one passage in *Comm. in Rom.*[387] where Origen interprets Rom.i.3,4 on his own lines. He first makes a distinction between what is born of the seed of David, and is therefore "according to the flesh", and what is appointed in power according to the spirit of holiness, ie. the Son of God Who is of one substance with God. He then asks why the *anima* of Jesus is not mentioned in this passage together with the flesh and the spirit of holiness — the *anima* which was at one time troubled and at another time sorrowful unto death, the *anima* which He separated from Himself after His death and which descended to the lower regions. Origen says that since the *anima* cannot be thought of as included in what is according to the flesh nor in what is appointed to be the Son of God with power, the Apostle is simply bearing in mind that the *anima* is placed between the flesh and the spirit and joins itself either to the one or to the other, and he thus refrains from mentioning the *anima* in the case of Jesus Christ, because that *anima* is joined to the Lord and is thus made one spirit of holiness with Him.

It would indeed appear to be the case that in Origen's view the lower part of the soul, called *anima* or ψυχή, would of necessity have been assumed by Christ at the time of His Incarnation, but would at all times have been submissive to the will of Christ's spirit (πνεῦμα), that spirit which was perfectly united to the Word of God. We may compare Origen's insistence in *Hom. in Num.*[388] that the Holy Spirit not only descended upon the human Jesus, as He did upon others, but "remained upon Him", with reference to the statement of John the Baptist in John i.33. It is to be noted that in the passage in *Comm. in Rom.* referred to above Origen applies to the spirit (πνεῦμα) of Jesus language which strictly only refers to the Divine Word, eg. "the Son of God in the substance of God", and there he speaks of the *anima* of Jesus as "joined to the Lord" *(sociata Domino).* But this is only in accordance with the principle of "interchange of attributes" *(communicatio idiomatum)* which Origen declares to be legitimate so far as the (higher) soul of Jesus and the Divine Word are concerned.[389]

From what has been said it would appear that Origen's Christology is profoundly affected by his attitude to the body and the material world. Although there is a section in *Contra Cels.*[390] in which he is less inclined to think of matter and its manifestations as merely the result of the fall of immaterial spirits, he cannot be said to have entirely emancipated himself from the outlook which caused him to deprive himself in his early manhood of his virile powers, namely the feeling that man's true destiny is to escape to a higher sphere. He is thus torn between acceptance of the passages in St. Paul which envisage a Divine self-emptying, and reluctance to admit that the Word of God could ever have undergone the changes and limitations involved in becoming incarnate.

Mrs Williamina Macaulay[391] states that "the idea of Incarnation in

Origen's thought is not inconceivable in view of the peculiar quality of the Logos-Son to transmit divinity to lesser beings." But surely such transmission does not involve self-emptying, whereas a true Incarnation does. Mrs. Macaulay goes on to say that "even on grounds of pure logic as opposed to faith, one could well postulate as the ultimate hypothesis of such a system (what system?) a perfect human being able to participate fully in the Godhead offered to him." But the idea of a human being participating in Divinity is surely the exact opposite of the idea of the Divine Word becoming human. Mrs. Macaulay does not really explain how according to Origen a Divine being can become genuinely human.[392]

It would perhaps be true to say that there is a tension in Origen's mind between the idea of the Word of God as becoming personally incarnate and the idea of His using His human soul as a mediator between Himself and human beings. This tension corresponds to the tension between two divergent ideas of the ultimate destiny of bodily matter. Has it a permanent place in the scheme of things, or is it a temporary feature of the universe, brought into existence as the result of the fall of immaterial beings? J. Armantage[393] is inclined to think that Origen held the first view. But though passages suggesting this can be found in *De Princ.* and elsewhere, his main view appears to be the second one. Armantage says that "for the opponents of the resurrection of the body, to define religion as the involvement of God in the this-worldly life of the individual violated the fundamental canons of divinity."[394] But this in fact appears to be the view of Origen himself: man's destiny is the contemplation of the immaterial Divine Word, and thus ultimately of the Father Himself, and a body is not needed for this purpose.

Origen seems at heart to agree with the Hellenistic outlook that salvation consists in being emancipated from bodily entanglements.[395] Armantage appears right in saying that according to Origen, "the correct view does not extend the present into the future, but rather brings the future into the present."[396] But this future is a future in which the body has no place; it is only anticipated here and now in so far as the individual sits loose to the demands of the body as far as possible. Armantage, in order to defend his view of Origen's outlook, credits Origen with a totally unnatural conception of the body, in so far as he sees Origen as not regarding it as necessary to limit the notion of the body by the character of corporeality as understood in this life.[397] He adduces as an argument for this view Origen's reference to the *eye* of the person who endeavours to apprehend spiritual truth as being something other than the eye of the flesh. But the fact that Origen regards the bodily senses as having spiritual faculties corresponding to them has nothing in itself to do with his notion of the body, and certainly does not justify Armantage's assertion that according to Origen, body is defined by function, not by substance.[398] It may be true, as Armantage says, that it is the body which according to Origen offers to each soul its own path back to the source of nature;[399] but that does not alter the fact that Origen's main view seems to be that the body will be annihilated when it has served its purpose.

And so the lines of the Christmas hymn which run:-
The Word in the bliss of the Godhead remains,[400]
Yet in flesh comes to suffer the keenest of pains.
are lines with which Origen's distinctive philosphy of matter and spirit would never have allowed him to concur.

I would conclude by suggesting that although Origen departs from traditional Christology in one direction by separating the Divine Word from human experiences, he also indicates a defect in traditional Christology itself, in so far as if the Divine Word is what He is, the possessor of Divine attributes, any real Divine self-emptying is logically inconceivable. It seems to me fantastic to suppose that during the incarnate life of Christ the Divine Word remained on the one hand at the helm of the universe, ordering it and guiding it, and on the other hand reduced Himself to the compass of a human being and underwent the development natural to such a being.[401] As a matter of fact, many distinguished Christian theologians who in theory have adhered to the Christological statements contained in the Nicene Creed have in fact considered that the Incarnation of the Word of God was only apparent, because he retained all the qualities bound up with His Divinity. It was not that He really developed as a human being, but rather that He gave the impression of doing so. And that, I submit, is all that we can say, if we adhere to the traditional view of our Lord's Person.

This is a difficulty not really faced by J. C. D'hotel,[402] who is at pains to point out that in Origen's view only the human nature of the Incarnate Lord can be said to have been sanctified, whereas the Divine nature possessed sanctification by nature. In his own words, "the Saviour needed to be sanctified in His humanity, that is, to receive from the Father the Holy Spirit, so as to be able in His turn to sanctify His brothers by giving them the same Spirit in the manner in which

He Himself received it."[403] But we are still left wondering how the Incarnate Lord can really be said to have "grown in grace" as every normal human being has to do, if He were already perfectly holy by nature? How can growth and perfection be ascribed to one and the same Person?[404] D'hotel says that Nestorius rightly saw that "sanctification is the transformation of a person and not of a nature",[405] and so regarded the Word of God and the human Jesus as two separate persons: but none the less D'hotel appears to adopt the Nicene point of view regarding the Incarnate Christ.

T. E. Pollard[406] rightly points out that Origen never really explained the Person of Christ in such a way as to bring out the soteriological aspect of His Nature as distinct from the cosmological. And although Arius, in his modification of Origen's outlook, failed to give a satisfactory account of the Son as Saviour in so far as he distinguished Him from the Divine Word and so made Him a creature (albeit one created before the universe came into being), neither did Athanasius, in spite of his identification of the Incarnate Son with the Divine Word, really explain how the Word could become truly human. Pollard asserts that according to Athanasius, "only one who is eternally God and yet at the same time really incarnate can save mankind";[407] but how can the same Person be thought of in both ways?

R. L. Wilken, when he describes[408] the course of the dispute between Cyril and Nestorius about the Person of Christ, rightly points out that it will not do to say with Athanasius that the passages of Scripture which attribute human feelings and experiences to Christ are to be ascribed to His human nature only. If Christ is one Person, they must be ascribed to the Divine Word, and that makes Him inferior to the Father. The view of Nestorius is more consistent with logic, but at the same time one wonders whether the hypothesis of a pre-existent Divine Word is really necessary on his view (ie. would it not suffice to say that the human Jesus entered into ever closer fellowship with the Father?). Wilken regards Nestorius as in effect asserting that "the uniqueness of Christ does not lie in some innate quality or capacity, for he is like other men in every respect. Rather, his uniqueness lies in what he did; he lived a perfect life and offered to God a perfect sacrifice."[409] This statement would appear to need qualifying in so far as all human beings are not alike; each one is unique, though all have certain qualities in common. And so it is true to say that Christ, although a man, was unlike any other man in so far as he performed what no other man could perform — the saving work of reconciling man to God.

It cannot be denied that if we treat Him as a genuine man, we can more easily conceive of Him as gradually entering into fuller union with God, so that in the end His personality was completely expressive of the Divine Nature, so far as it can be expressed in human terms. We could thus apply to Him the analogy employed by Origen in describing someone who desires to obtain Divine truth. Origen instances a man wishing to paint a picture, who first sketches the outline of what he proposes to depict, and then inserts the detailed features, so that the resultant portrait may be balanced in character. Even so, says Origen, the faint form and outline of Divine truth in inscribed on "the tablets of our heart" (II Cor.iii.3) by the pencil of our Lord Jesus Christ.[410] But if this is the spiritual history of the believer, how can it fail to have been that of his Lord, if the Lord Himself was truly human?

I would even make bold to say that two of the main schools of thought in the Church of England — the Tractarian and the Evangelical — are based, even though unconsciously, on two opposed conceptions of our Lord's Nature. To speak of our having been made partakers of the Divine Nature through Baptism is to hold the Monophysite view of Christ's own Person, according to which His Divinity was unaffected by His assumption of humanity. Whereas to hold that baptism is a sign of the grace of God which is thereafter given in so far as it is desired is to take the Adoptionist view of Christ Himself as having become progressively united to God as the result of His aspirations towards such unity.

APPENDIX TO CHAPTER V

ORIGEN'S CONCEPTION OF THE RELATION BETWEEN THE VARIOUS DISCLOSURES OF THE LAW OF GOD

It is noteworthy that in at least one passage the Law of Moses is said by Origen to hold a "shadow" of the "good things made known at the Coming of Christ."[411] The Mosaic Law is said to have contained the truth, but hidden as it were under a veil, in so far as the spiritual nature of that law was not yet understood.[412] Hence, according to Origen, there are three stages in the apprehension of Divine truth: first, the understanding of the Mosaic Law in its obvious sense; secondly, the understanding gained by acquaintance with Christ's earthly life; and thirdly, the full understanding to be gained in a future state of being.[413] But he would doubtless agree that the three stages cannot be strictly distinguished, but rather shade off into one another.

There is a striking sentence in *Hom. in Num.* where Origen says that the Old Covenant is not to be regarded as a legal code if it is spiritually understood *(nec Vetus Testamentum tunc nomino legem, si eam spiritualiter intelligam).*[414] But oddly enough he states elsewhere that it is the spiritual interpretation of Scripture which has "the shadow of good things to come."[415] In a comment on St. John's words "Of His fullness have we all received" (i.15), he says that those in this life share Christ's fullness in the sense that they know in part and prophesy in part, but will not possess that fullness (if they ever do) until after this life is over.[416] Likewise in *Hom. in Lev.* he says with reference to Ps.cxix.105 that the "lamp" of the Divine Law is lit for those in this present world, whereas the "eternal light" is reserved for those who are entitled to it in the future age;[417] and in a note on the Psalms he says that only when we live with the angels of God shall we meditate on the commandments of God, not in a shadowy fashion, but in accordance with the truth.[418] In another passage he says that the person who is free from sin and no longer requires the sacrifices prescribed by the Law may, when he is perfect, transcend even the spiritual law (τὸν πνευματικὸν νόμον) and dwell with the Divine Word Who is above that law.[419] And yet Origen asserts elsewhere that by the percepts of the Gospels, as contrasted with the Law of Moses, all things are brought to perfection, thus appearing to imply that there is no need for any further disclosure of Divine truth,[420] and that the "good things to come" consist in the spiritual interpretation of the Mosaic

Law.[421] He likewise asserts in another passage that whereas Christ spoke in the Law and the Prophets as well as in the Gospels, He teaches beginners through the Law, and those who are mature through the Gospels.[422]

Perhaps the contradiction in Origen's thought can be explained in so far as he had to take account of the traditional doctrine that Christ will be revealed in glory at some future date, but on the other hand thought of that glory as revealed in this life as a result of the progress of the Christian believer in spiritual insight.

NOTES ON CHAPTER V

[1] *Comm. in Joh.* I.32 (GCS 4.41.7-16). Cf. Nemeshegyi, op. cit., p.51, where this passage is quoted. Cf. also *Frag. in Luc.* 210.7.8 (GCS 9.318); *Comm. in Matt.* XVI.8 (GCS 10.497.23-32); *Frag. in Matt.* 52.1-3 (GCS XII.36); *Hom. in Gen.* I.13 (GCS 6.17.1-3).
[2] III.1 (GCS 6.300.15-32).
[3] *Comm. in Cant.* III (GCS 8.222.25,26).
[4] *Comm. in Joh.* VI.57 (GCS 4.166.3-7). Cf. *Hom. in Num.* XXVII. 3 (GCS 7.260.6.7), where it is said that Christ descended to our level not as a matter of necessity, but because He deigned to do so *(non necessitate, sed dignatione)*. Cf. also *Comm. in Rom.* V. 2 (PG XIV.1022C) and *Sel. in Gen.* XXII.6 (PG XII.117B). Cf. also Primmer, op. cit., p.90, where, after quoting the passage in the text, he says that the Father is thus credited with the quality of ἔλεος, and the idea of Divine impassibility is thus modified. On the other hand, Primmer has said on p.4 that "God's highest display of love for mankind, the offering of His Son, is quite irreconcilable with the categories of πάθος or εὐπάθεια; it is rather on the level of cosmic compassion."
On the other hand, there is a sense in which Christ died of necessity (χρειωδῶς), in the sense that if He had not tasted death on our behalf, we should not have been saved. This is what we are taught by the words "if it be possible" (Matt.xxvi.29) (*Frag. in Matt.* 531.1-3 (GCS 12.218).
[5] *Hom. in Jos.* II.2 (GCS 7.297.23-298.1).
[6] Cf. *Hom. in Luc.* XI, where it is said that Christ was willing to submit to being enrolled at the time of the universal census of the Emperor Augustus so that He might sanctify all men and offer them fellowship with Himself (GCS 9.71.1-22). Cf. also Mme.Harl, op.cit., p.297, where the passage in the text is quoted.
[7] *Hom. in Num.* XXIV.1 (GCS 7.226.7-10). See on this passage Rivière, "Théologie du sacrifice rédempteur" (*BLE* (1944), pp. 8-11).
[8] *De Princ.* I.2.1 (GCS 5.27.21-28.1). Cf. *Frag. in Matt.* 11.21-27 (GCS 12.19,20); *Frag. in Joh.* I (GCS 4.483.11-16); *Hom. in Matt.* I (GCS 12.243.8-11); *Contra Cels.* I.68 (GCS 1.123.4-7) and III.29 (GCS 1.226.26,27).
[9] *De Princ.* III.5.6 (GCS 5.277.3-7). Cf. Rahner, op. cit., p.200 where he says that according to Origen "not a self-initiated turn-

ing to God, but the gracious descent of God to us, is the central point of a true doctrine of man." Cf. also p.218. Cf. also *Comm. in Joh.* XXXII.3 (GCS 4.431.12-27); *Comm. in Rom.* VII.9 (PG XIV.1129A); *Frag. in Luc.* 151.14-24 (GCS 9.287); *Matt. Comm. Series* 75 (GCS 11.176.20-25); *Comm. in Matt.* XIII.8 (GCS 10.202.11-34); ibid. XIII.8 (GCS 10.200.17-29); *Comm. in Joh.* XXVIII.9 (GCS 4.414.5,6). Cf. also *Hom. in Ps.* XXXVII.I.2, where an unusual interpretation is given of the statement "The spirit is ready, but the flesh is weak", inasmuch as the weakening of the flesh is understood to mean self-denial and self-mortification (PG XII.1375D-1376B).

10 *Comm. in Joh.* X.6 (GCS 4.176.21-26).
11 *De Princ.* II.6.5 (GCS 5.144.24-145.2). Cf. also *Comm. in Joh.* XX.26,27 (GCS 4.377.10-25), and *Comm. in Rom.* III.8 (PG XIV.947B-948B), where the measurements of the mercy-seat described in Exodus are said to apply to the soul of Jesus, which is said to be midway between the Divine nature of the Trinity and the weakness of humanity. Crouzel in *L'Image* ... (p.134) refers to the passage in *Comm. in Rom.*, but says that the Word and the Holy Spirit, represented by the Cherubim whose wings stretch over the mercy-seat, seem to take the place of the spirit of Jesus. On the contrary, one would have thought that the word *anima*, as here used, is equivalent to the spirit (as distinct from the lower soul). Such also appears to be the opinion of Dupuis, op. cit., p. 79, n.115.

Lieske, op. cit., p.130 says that "Origen thinks of a kind of hypostatic union of the created spirit with the Divine Word in the final stage of full perfection. But there are essential differences between the God-Man and the created spirit which has the vision of God, in that while the soul of Christ is absolutely sinless, there is a possibility of sin even in a state of pure spirituality." This seems an illogical element in Origen's thought, because the soul of Christ is itself a created spirit, and to say that it is so closely united to the Word as to be incapable of falling away from God is simply to beg the question.

Cf. also p.169 of op. cit., where Lieske says (n.9) that "our union with the Son is the likeness or extension of the hypostatic union between the soul of Christ and the Divine Word." But the phrase "hypostatic union" does not correctly describe the thought of Origen, because according to him the soul of Christ and the Div-

ine Word were still two separate beings even after their union, which was a union of wills (Boon makes the same mistake in op. cit., p.26). Völker, op. cit., pp.111-113, also seems mistaken in thinking of the union between the Word and his human soul as anything more than a moral and ethical union. Knittel, as referred to in n.4 on p.112 of op. cit., seems to want to have it both ways, in so far as he says that the ultimate union was not moral, but physical, and yet seeks to preserve the distinctive features of the two natures, Divine and human.
Kelber, op. cit., pp.258,259, rightly points out that while Origen insisted that the soul of Christ was human, in fact he ascribed to it qualities which made it more than human, in so far as it only became incarnate out of pity for mankind, not because that was its own destiny, and could only become known by other human beings by emptying itself of its own being in order to become incarnate.
When Mrs. Macaulay, op. cit., p.184, says that Origen does not say that "there is any *essential* difference between the Incarnate Word or Christ Crucified and the Logos-Son", she shows that she has not studied all Origen's works, and not even the *Comm. on John* itself, as fully as she might have done. But in fact she says at the foot of that very page that the soul of Christ was pre-existent (ie. not simply assumed in order to become incarnate!).

[12] *Comm. I in Ep.ad Rom.* (Philocal. JAR 228.1-5). Cf. Crouzel *L'Image* ... p.226, and Mme. Harl., op. cit., p.281. Cf.pp.128,129.
[13] *Comm. in Cant.* II (GCS 8.153.14-19).
[14] *Comm. in Rom.* VII.7 (PG XIV.1123C-1124A).
[15] *Comm. in Joh.* XX.11 (GCS 4.340.8-17). Cf. *Contra Cels.* VII.16 (GCS 2.167.12-22). Cf. also Nemeshegyi, op. cit., p.79, where it is said that if Christ is said to suffer death, that is because the attributes of the human Jesus are assigned to the Divine Word on account of their personal union (cf. *Contra Cels.* III.41 (GCS 1. 237.7-10)).
[16] *De Princ.* III.3.2. (GCS 5.258.1-8).
[17] *Comm. in Joh.* VI.53 (GCS 4.161.30-162.1 and 162.9-12).
[18] Ibid. XIX.2 (GCS 4.299.14-21). Cf. ibid. XXVIII.18 (GCS 4.412. 27-413.7), and XX.11 (GCS 4.340.29-341.10), and XXXII.25 (GCS 4.469.29-470.12). Cf. also Crouzel, *L'Image* ..., p.79; Dupuis, op. cit., p.77; Boon, op. cit., p.26.
[19] III.8 (PG XIV.949C-950A).

[20] Op. cit., p.224.
[21] On p.264 of op. cit.
[22] *Comm. in Joh.* II.8 (GCS 4.62.19-26). Cf. also *Contra Cels.* I.61 (GCS 1.113.1,2); *Hom.in Ps.* XXXVI.V.4 (PG XII.1362A); *Hom. in Gen.* VIII.8 (GCS 6.84.5-9); *Comm. in Cant.* I (GCS 8.102.14, 15). The passage in *Comm. in Joh.* II.8 is in contradiction to *Comm. in Joh.* XX.11 (GCS 4.341.1-5), where Origen does not allow the expression "God the Word died" (quoted by Dupuis, op. cit., p.77, n.107). See the discussion of this passage in Völker, op. cit., p.103.
[23] It was this fact which Origen doubtless had in mind when he suggested that Jesus remained in the Temple because He held His true Father in higher honour than His earthly kinsmen (*Frag. in Luc.* 77 (GCS 9.259)).
[24] *Comm. in Joh.* XX.18 (GCS 4.350.23-351.4). Cf. *Contra Cels.* IV.5 (GCS 1.277.27-30), where it is said that when the Word of God comes to us, He does not leave His former abode, as though vacating one place and occupying another which He had not occupied before. Cf. also *Hom. in Matt.* I (GCS 12.239.12-16 and 240.12-17); *Sel. in Ps.* I.3 (PG XII.1088D); Pitra A.S.III.226 (Ps. CVIII.29-31). Cf. also the picturesque passage in *Frag. in Luc.* (59.7,8 (GCS 9.252)), which runs "When He was still an infant, the heavenly powers sang His praises as being in the bosom of the Father", on which Crouzel (S.C.87,pp.290,491) comments: "The Word of God in one way descends to the earth with His soul, but in another way He remains always in God Who is His abode." Cf. also *Hom. in I Sam.xxviii.3-25,8* (GCS 3.292.5-7), where Origen says that "Christ was still Christ, even when in Hades, and if I may so put it, even when He was below so far as place was concerned, He was above so far as His purpose was concerned" (τῇ προαιρέσει ἄνω ἦν).
Cf. also Primmer, op. cit., pp.35,36, and Schendel, *Herrschaft und Unterwerfung Christi* (Tubingen, 1971), pp.85,86, and Eichinger, *Die Verklärung Christi bei Origenes* (Vienna, 1969), pp. 148-150.
[25] VI.12 (PG XIV.1094D-1095A).
[26] *Comm. in Joh.* II.11 (GCS 4.66.17-21). On the other hand, in ibid. 66.28-67.8 it is said that although the Spirit as well as the Father sent the Son, the Spirit promised that He would descend at the appropriate time to co-operate with the Son for the salva-

tion of mankind.
27 *Hom. in Luc.* XXIX (GCS 9.167.14-20).
28 *Hom. in Ezek.* I.6 (GCS 8.331.4-7).
29 XIII.18 (GCS 10.227.27-228.24). Cf. the discussion of this passage, and that referred to in n.26, in Dupuis, op.cit., n.131, p.119.
30 I.46 (GCS 1.96.19-25).
31 *Frag. in Joh.* XX (GCS 4.501.15-23). See Aeby, op. cit., pp.153, 154, for a discussion of the points raised in this paragraph.
32 Cf. *Frag. in Luc.* 96 (GCS 9.265.18-21), where it is said that the devil, when he tempted Christ, recognised that Christ's power of changing stones into bread came from God.
33 *Comm. in Matt.* XVII.2 (GCS 10.584.16-25).
34 *Frag. in Matt.* 339.1-9 (GCS 12.146,147); cf. ibid.154.6-14 (GCS 12.77).
35 *Comm. in Joh.* XX.44 (GCS 4.388.20-29).
36 *Matt. Comm. Series* 112 (end) (GCS 11.233.31-234.2); cf.*Comm. in Matt.* XII.2 (GCS 10.72.9-12), and *Matt. Comm. Series* 132 (GCS 11.269.19-21).
37 Cf. *Matt. Comm. Series* 113 (GCS 11.235.6-10), referring to His teaching, and ibid. 99 (GCS 11.217.7-22), referring to His escape through the Father's help from His enemies when they threatened to cast Him down from the top of a hill.
38 *Matt. Comm. Series* 33 (already referred to in Ch.III, n.65). Cf. Ch.III, pp. 75 and 76, where this matter is dealt with more fully.
39 *Comm. in Joh.* X.37 (GCS 4.212.8-24). Cf. also *Contra Cels.* II. 58 (GCS 1.181.28-182.2), where it is said that the Resurrection of Jesus from the dead was more remarkable than the instances of boys raised from the dead by Elijah and Elisha, because the Agent Who raised Him was His heavenly Father. Cf. also *Comm. in Joh.* XXVIII.12 (GCS 4.403.33), and *Sel. in Ps.* III.8 (PG XII. 1129C). In *Sel. in Ps.* XXI.10 (PG XII.1253D) it is said that it was Christ alone Who was taken by the Father out of His mother's womb, because Christ alone was conceived through the Holy Spirit, whereas other men are not taken out, but come out.
40 *Comm. in Cant.* II (GCS 8.162.12-14). In *Hom. in Num.* Origen also recognises that in certain places (eg. Romans vi.4), Christ is said to be raised by the Father, but that He elsewhere says that He is able to raise "the temple of His own body" after three days (XVII.6 (GCS 7.166.14-17)).
41 *Comm. in Joh.* XIII.36 (GCS 4.260.29-261.20). Cf. also *Contra*

Cels. VIII.12 (GCS 2.229.10-230.4) discussed by Lowry, op. cit., *JTS* 37 (1936), pp.234,235; Mme. Harl, op. cit., p.270; Crouzel, *L'Image* . . ., pp.91,92; Rius-Camps, "Communicabilidad," *OCP* 36,1970, pp.209,212,213; Nemeshegyi, op. cit., pp.88,89; Lieske, op. cit., pp.198-200.
Cf. also the letter of Archbp. Wm. Temple to Ronald Knox set out in full in the former's biography (p.165), where Temple replies to Knox's criticisms of his explanation of our Lord's Divinity in terms of will. Knox has suggested that the distinction between the form and the content of a will (ie. between that which wills and that which is willed) is a distinction which can only be made in thought, so that in however close agreement two individuals might be, their wills would not be identical. Temple replied that since the form and the content of a will are inseparable, the form must be affected by the identity of content with that of another will.

42 *Comm. in Ezek.* III.12 (PG XIII.775A); *Sel. in Ps.* XVIII.6 (PG XII.1241CD); XXVI.5 (PG XII.1280D,1281A); LXIV.5 (PG XII.1493D); XXVII.2 (PG 1285A); XLVI.9 (PG XII.1437B); IX.5 (PG XII.1188C).

43 *De Princ.* I.2.6 (GCS 5.35.1-4). Cf. Lieske, op. cit., pp.192-194, and also 195, where he says "Because the Son is only begotten by the Father in so far as the Father conveys to Him His perfect likeness, because moreover this likeness consists in perfect knowledge and fulfilment of the Father's will, it follows that the Son is only begotten by the Father as His Likeness and Wisdom in so far as the Father imparts to Him the perfect vision and fulfilment of His will with the likeness."

44 Cf. *Hom. in Is.* IV.4 (GCS 8.261.26-262.5), where our Lord is compared to the seraph with a live coal in his hands sent for the purpose of purging away the sins of the prophet's lips. Cf. also *Sel. in Ps.* XV.3 (PG XII.1212A) and LXXXVIII.32 (PG XII.1549B).

45 Op. cit., pp.57-59.

46 Op. cit., p.61. Cf. Ch.II, p.47, where Maydieu's article is quoted as suggesting that Origen adopted an Arian view of Christ in so far as He is said to have become Divine by continually gazing into the depths of the Father's being.

47 "Communicabilidad", *OCP* 34,1968, pp. 7 and 8.

48 XIV.2,3 (PG XIII.767A-768C). Cf. Crouzel, *La Conn.* pp.86, 87,

and pp.168,169. Cf. also Ch.II, p.45, and Ch.III, pp.74 and 75, where the extent of the Son's knowledge is discussed.
49 Section 29 (GCS 1.26.10-13).
50 95 (GCS 11.213.5-15,17-27).
51 Op. cit., p.26, n.5.
52 *Exh. ad Mart.* 29 (GCS 1.25.2-23), to which (oddly enough) Völker does not explicitly allude.
53 *Frag. in Matt.* 530 II. 1st col. 1-6 (GCS 12.217).
54 *Comm. in Joh.* XXVIII.6 (GCS 4.395.9-32).
55 Cf.pp.116 & 117, where the veiling of Christ's Divinity is discussed.
56 *Frag. in Matt.* 239.3-5 (GCS 12.112), and ibid. 321.2-4 (GCS 12.141). Cf. C. J. Cadoux, *The Case for Evangelical Modernism* (Hodder and Stoughton, 1938), p.85, where he says: "Thomas Aquinas taught that the prayers of Jesus were intended merely for didactic and examplary purposes. What are we to say of a doctrine (ie. of our Lord's Person) which necessitates such a conclusion as that?"
57 XIII.1 (GCS 2.325.20-326.11).
58 *Sel. in Ps.* IV.2 (PG XII.1133D-1136A); cf. *Frag. in Jer.* 68 (GCS 3.231.20-25).
59 *Frag. in Joh.* CXX (GCS 4.567.19-21).
60 *Comm. in Matt.* XI.6 (GCS 10.43.15-24).
61 Ibid.XVI.5 (GCS 10.480.23-481.1).
62 *Hom. in Num.* XXIV.1 (GCS 7.227.7-9; cf. 226.15-19).
63 Cf. II Cor.viii.9.
64 II (GCS 8.169.17-170.3). Cf. also ibid.III (206.11-14); *Hom. in Cant.* II.3 (GCS 8.45.3-9); *Hom. in Lev.* VII.2 (GCS 6.375.8-11). Cf.also Lomiento, article "Cristo didaskalos di pochi e la comunicazione ai molti secondo Origene" (*VC* 9 (1972)), pp.25,26.
On the other hand, Origen is not everywhere consistent in his interpretation of the text in Daniel about the stone cut out of the mountain without the work of human hands. In *Hom. in Cant.* II.3 it is made clear that the mountain is understood as our Lord's Divine Nature, whereas in the sixth Homily on Exodus it is interpreted as human flesh and human nature as such, from which the Lord took a small portion at His Incarnation *(istud est sanctimonium carnis assumptae, et sine manibus, id est, absque opere hominum, de monte humanae naturae et substantiae excisum). Hom. in Ex.* VI.12 (GCS 6.203.1-6).
The subject of the Kenosis of the Divine Word is discussed by

Mme. Harl, op. cit., pp.229-233. I cannot help feeling that she misrepresents Origen by asserting that "Origen does not consider that the Divine Word is stripped of His Divinity, but interprets the Kenosis either in the sense of the accommodation of the Divine to the human, or else by referring it to the man Jesus, who did not claim immediate equality with the Father, but chose to die in order to be exalted afterwards." How can "the Divine be accommodated to the human" without a measure of self-emptying?

[65] XXVI.2 (GCS 7.459.22-460.3).

[66] *Hom. in Cant.* II.3 (GCS 8.44.20-45.18). Cf. *Sel. in Jos.* V.2 (PG XII.821C). Cf. also Crouzel, *L'Image,* p.141. Cf. also p.126.

[67] Cf. p.110.

[68] *Contra Cels.* IV.15 (GCS 1.284.29-285.14). Cf. *Hom. in Matt.* II (GCS 12.248.16-21), and *Hom. in Lev.* VIII.1 (GCS 6.393.18-21 and 394.4-6,14-19). Cf. also *Frag. in Matt.* 11.14-21 (GCS 12. 19), where, with reference to the distinction between the two words γένεσις and γέννησις, Origen declares that although Christ possessed the sinlessness of Adam as he originally was, He also shared in the suffering which Adam subsequently underwent because of his sin. Two other passages declare that Christ was born of a Virgin because He was sinless *Hom. in Matt.* I (GCS 12.240. 9-11) and *Frag. in Matt.* 14 (GCS 12.21).

[69] Cf. p.118.

[70] I Cor.i.25.

[71] *Hom. in Jer.* VIII.8,9 (GCS 3.61.32-63.11). Cf. *Hom. in Is.* VI.1 (GCS 8.280.5-13). Crouzel in *La Conn.*, p.344, says that Origen is developing St. Paul's thought in speaking of "God's foolishness" in this way, and not misrepresenting it; but in fact St. Paul is not contrasting the entire wisdom possessed by Jesus Christ with that wisdom which He brought into the world; he is simply contrasting human so-called "wisdom" with the Divine wisdom which appears to be foolishness to those content with human wisdom (cf. also op. cit., pp.482,483). See also Molland, op. cit., p.148, where he says, referring to the passage in Origen quoted above, that "Origen does not hear the irony in these words, nor does he hear the paradox in the Apostle's mouth."

[72] *Comm. in Joh.* X.46 (GCS 4.224.34-225.3), and *Comm. in Matt.* XII.6 (GCS 10.77.18-25).

[73] *Matt. Comm. Series* 50 (GCS 11.110.7-11). Cf. *Hom. in Matt.*

III. (GCS 12.261.33-262.1); *Comm. in Matt.* XI.17 (GCS 10.64. 1-4,7-9); *Sel. in Ps.* XXIX.8 (PG XII.1296A); *Comm. in Joh.* X. 27 (GCS 4.200.28-31). Cf. also Mme. Harl, op. cit., p.247,where she says that according to Origen, "the miracles reveal the Word by way of Jesus. They serve to underline the astonishing character of the man who is Jesus, but they should also lead to the discovery in Him of the Son of God."

[74] *Hom. in Jer.* XIV.9 (GCS 3.113.25-114.15).

[75] Cf. *Comm. in Joh.* XIX.10 (GCS 4.309.24-310.1), and XXVIII. 12 (GCS 4.402.30-403.15).

[76] *Matt. Comm. Series* 50 (GCS 11.110.11-17). Cf. *Hom. in Cant.* II.3 (GCS 8.44.20-45.11). It is noteworthy, however, that Origen asserts in the *Hom. in Num.* that the Saviour will have the same form at His Second Coming as at His First, in so far as He will possess a human body and a human soul (IX.5 (GCS 7.61.1-3)). Cf. also *Matt. Comm. Series* 70 (GCS 11.164.6-9). On the other hand, in another passage, it is said that the First Coming of Christ was accompanied by human feelings (ἀνθρωποπαθέστεραν), whereas at His Second Coming He will have no humanfeelings bound up with His Divinity (οὐδὲν ἐπιπεπλεγμένον τῇ θειότητι ἔχουσαν ἀνθρωποπαθές) *Contra Cels.* I.56 (GCS 1.107. 1-8).

[77] τὴν οἰκείαν συνεσκίασε δόξαν.

[78] *Sel. in Ps.* LXVII.5 (PG XII.1505C). Cf. also ibid. IV.9,10 (PG XII.1168C), and *Frag. in Luc.* 140.5-8 (GCS 9.283).

[79] *Frag. in Joh.* LIII (GCS 4.527.3-23). Cf. p.112.

[80] *Hom. in Exod.* VI.1 (GCS 6.192.10-193.3). Cf. Pitra, A.S.III. 195 (Ps.CI.16,17), where it is said that when Christ became flesh and dwelt among us, He built the Church, the spiritual Sion; but He will be seen in His glory, when after He has dwelt among us we shall behold His glory, full of grace and truth. Cf. also Molland, op. cit., p.156.

[81] *Frag. in Luc.* 96.1-11 (GCS 9.265).

[82] *Hom. in Jos.* VIII.4 (GCS 7.339.12-20). Cf. *De Princ.* IV.3.13 (GCS 5.343.23-344.7). Cf. Daniélou, "L'Unité des Deux Testaments" (*RvSR* (1948)), pp.53,54. Origen also quotes Lam.iv.20 in *Hom. in Num.* XXVII.12, but there understands the "shadow" which Christ affords as protecting us against the heat of temptation (GCS 7.277.13-16).

[83] I.2.8 (GCS 5.39.6-8).

[84] *De Princ.* II.6.7 (GCS 5.146.10-19,147.7-14). Fitzgerald, op.cit., p.188, understands this statement of the soul of Christ in its preincarnate state. Admittedly, it is the present writer who has inserted the adjective "earthly" before "actions and movements" on p.117; but surely it is impossible for this phrase to have any real meaning when applied to a disembodied spirit. Cf. Crouzel, *L'Image*, pp.139 and 251, and Dupuis, op. cit., p.194. Cf. also *Hom. in Ps.* XXXVIII.II.2 (PG XII.1402D-1403A); *Sel. in Ps.* LXXVI.11 (PG XII.1540B); *Comm. in Rom.* VII.4 (PG XIV. 1109AB); ibid.VI.3 (PG XIV.1061C-1062B). On the last passage referred to see Crouzel, *L'Image*, p.231; Mme. Harl, op. cit., pp. 197,198,212-214; Dupuis, op. cit., p.195, n.147; Crouzel, *La Conn.*, pp.340,341; Molland, op. cit., p.150; Gruber, op. cit., pp. 58,59. Cf. Ch.VI, pp.210-213, where the distinction between the knowledge of the earthly Christ and that of the heavenly Christ is more fully expounded.

[85] *Comm. in Rom.* IV.8 (PG XIV.991B-992D).

[86] *De Princ.* IV.3.13 (GCS 5.343.20-24), and also Jerome, *Ep. ad Avitum* 12, which purports to quote Origen's own words (lines 1-8 of note immediately under text on p.344). Cf. also *Comm. in Rom.* I.4 (PG XIV.847B); *Comm. in Joh.* I.7 (GCS 4.12.8-16), and Molland, op. cit., p.147, where this passage is referred to. It will be pointed out in Ch.VI, pp.205-215 and Ch.VII, pp.235-240, that Origen seems to suggest that some of Christ's disciples can even now have experience of His Second Coming, in so far as they progress from knowledge of the Incarnate Jesus to knowledge of the Eternal Word of God. Cf. also pp.127,128, and the Appendix to this Chapter.

[87] *Matt. Comm. Series* 135 (GCS 11.279.5-16,21-24).

[88] *Sel. in Ps.* LV.2 (PG XII.1469B).

[89] *Convs. with Heracl.* 27.4-8 (Scherer p.106). Cf. *Comm. in Joh.* I. 35 (GCS 4.45.19,20) and XXVIII.18 (GCS 4.412.18-20). Cf. Ch. IV.p.89, where the passage in *Comm. in Joh.* I.35 is also referred to.

[90] *De Princ.* IV.2.7 (GCS 5.319.8,9).

[91] *Frag. in Gal.* (PG XIV.1296D). Cf. the further discussion of this subject on pp.137 and 138.

[92] *Comm. in Joh.* X.6 (GCS 4.176.16-21). Cf. pp.115,116.

[93] *Comm. in Cant.* I (GCS 8.102.2-8). Cf. on this subject Rius-Camps, "Comunicabilidad", *OCP* 36, 1970, pp.226,227.

94 *Comm. in Cant.* I (GCS 8.107.25-108.2). Cf. Völker, op. cit., pp. 898,899, and Mme. Harl, op. cit., p.201, section headed "La chair comme 'voile'." On the other hand, His "fullness" can be understood in more than one sense, as Origen makes plain. It can on the one hand mean all the Divine attributes which He laid aside at the Incarnation; it can on the other hand mean the fullness of grace which He came to impart to all men, with the result that St. John could say that "of His fullness we all have received" (i. 16) (cf. *Comm. in Cant.* I (GCS 8.107.19-25)). It is the second type of fullness to which Origen alludes when he interprets the words "Thy Name is as ointment poured forth" as alluding to the activity whereby the Gospel of Jesus Christ is proclaimed to the world (*Hom. in Cant.* I.4 (GCS 8.33.11-13,21-30 and 34.7-9)). Origen thus says elsewhere that the anointing of Christ with the oil of gladness is not the same as the anointing of His "companions" (Ps.xlv.8), that is the prophets and apostles. The soul of Christ contained the ointment of whose odour the prophets and apostles partook, in proportion to their spiritual closeness to the soul of Christ (*De Princ.* II.6.6 (GCS 5.145.24-146.9)).

95 *De Princ.* I.2.7 (GCS 5.37.14-20). Cf. also ibid.I.2.8 (GCS 5.38. 26-39.4), where it is said that the Son becomes the brightness of God *to us* by emptying Himself of His equality with the Father, so that through looking on the brightness we may have a means of viewing the Divine Light. Cf. also Mme. Harl, op. cit., pp.114 and 309.

96 *De Princ.* II.6.1 (GCS 5.140.2-18).

97 Cf. pp.116 and 124,125.

98 *Contra Cels.* IV.15 (GCS 1.285.14-22).

99 Cf. Laeuchli's thesis, *Probleme des Geschichtlichen bei Origenes,* in which (p.225) he says that "for Origen, the abstract Word of God is a metaphysical entity which, as in Philo's thought, reveals itself now more and now less in a personal manner on earth. In this case we are imprisoned in the Greek cycles once again. We encounter the continually repeated manifestations of the Word of God in different ways, and behind this naturally stands the Platonic presence of the Ideas in the world of the senses." Laeuchli quotes in support of this statement *Hom. in Jer.* XIV.7 (GCS 3.112.11-13), where it is stated that the Word of God does not admit of death, and that it is only the human element ($\tau\grave{o}$ $\mathring{\alpha}\nu\theta\rho\omega$-$\pi\iota\nu o\nu$) which does.

100 Op. cit., p.333.
101 *Frag. in Joh.* XXXIII (GCS 4.508.22-509.3); *Frag. in Matt.* 70.1-6 (GCS 12.44).
102 *Frag. in Matt.* 344.4 (GCS 12.149); *Hom. in Matt.* II (GCS 12.251.25-28); *Comm. in Matt.* X.14 (GCS 10.16.13-15); *Frag. in Joh.* LXXXIII (GCS 4.549.8-12).
103 John xi.25,26.
104 *Frag. in Joh.* LXXXI (GCS 4.548.14-17).
105 *Frag. in Joh.* LII (GCS 4.526.11-21).
106 *Frag. in Matt.* 487 (GCS 12.200).
107 *Comm. in Matt.* X.23 (GCS 10.33.3,4), and *Sel. in Ps.* XXI.2 (PG XII.1253A).
108 *Frag. in Matt.* 188 (GCS 12.91).
109 See pp.142,143.
110 *Frag. ex Tom.I. Matt. Comm.* 2.8-11 (GCS 12.4) and *Frag. in Matt.* 8 (ibid.12.18); *Hom. in Gen.* VIII.9 (GCS 6.84.18-85.2).
111 *Comm. in Joh.* VI.49 (GCS 4.158.24-29); cf. *Sel. in Ps.* LXX.1 (PG XII.1517D,1520A).
112 *Frag. in Matt.* 65 (GCS 12.41,42); *Matt. Comm. Series* 102 (GCS 11.223.11-15).
113 *Frag. in Joh.* LXXV (GCS 4.542.7-9); *Comm. in Joh.* XXVIII.23 (GCS 4.418.16-24).
114 *Comm. in Joh.* XXVIII.23 (GCS 4.419.15-28).
115 *Hom. in Matt.* III (GCS 12.259.13,14).
116 *Hom. in Matt.* II (GCS 12.257.24-30).
117 *Frag. in Joh.* LIX (GCS 4.531.18,19). In Grillmeier, *Das Konzil von Chalkedon* Vol.I (Wurzburg, 1951), p.63, Clement of Alexandria is quoted as taking a similar view, viz. the view that in the Lord the food assimilated did not undergo the normal process of digestion and consequent breaking-down into its component parts.
118 *Comm. in Joh.* XIX.16 (GCS 4.316.8-13).
119 Ibid. (GCS 4.316.13-27); cf. *Contra Cels.* II.16 (GCS 1.145.22-146.1) and III.32 (GCS 1.229.2-13). Cf. also pp.106,107.
 D'Alès (on p.234 of op. cit.,) misunderstands de Faye when he criticises him for saying (op. cit., pp.118,119) that according to Origen "the Divine Word leaves and returns to the body of Jesus at will, on the ground that the Lord says, according to St. John, that He has power to give up His ψυχή and power to reclaim it." How, asks d'Alès, can the giving up of His ψυχή be equivalent to

a departure from the body of Jesus? Has de Faye confused the Divine Word with the soul which He gives up and receives back? The answer is that de Faye's words must not be taken too literally. The Word of God is surely not thought of by Origen as actually entering and leaving a human body; it is rather a matter of using the body of Jesus as His instrument for as long as He sees fit. Admittedly, de Faye has expressed himself rather carelessly. See also the passages from de Faye quoted on pp.239 and 240. At the foot of p.240, the statement of de Faye is quoted that there is an organic union between the Word of God and the man Jesus, as the result of which the nature of the man undergoes a transformation. Yes, but that must not be interpreted, as d'Alès does, as a hypostatic union; the Divine Word and the man Jesus still retain, according to Origen, their separate identities.

120 *Frag. in Luc.* 253,9,10 (GCS 9.334).
121 *Contra Cels.* IV.15 (GCS 1.285.14-22) (already referred to in n. 98).
122 Op. cit., pp.201,202.
123 Op. cit., p.76. Cf. also Grillmeier, *Christ in Christian Tradition*, 2nd ed., (London, 1975), p.148, where he says that "Origen exposed himself to the charge that his system left no room for a full appreciation of the humanity of the Lord."
124 In *Das Konzil von Chalkedon*, Vol.I, pp.62,63.
125 *Frag. in Matt.* 235.1-3 (GCS 12.111).
126 *Comm. in Cant.* II (GCS 8.152.11-16). It is interesting that this metaphor of a rider on a horse is applied also to the relation between Christ and His disciples, and also to the relation between the devil and those who serve him (*Hom. in Exod.* VI.2 (GCS 6.193.5-19), and *Comm. in Cant.* II (GCS 8.153.10-14). From this point of view, Judas changed riders. The metaphor is inadequate because it suggests that those regarded as "horses" are bereft of the power of judgement, just as the comparison between the human nature of Christ and the "white horse" of the Apocalypse is inadequate because it does not make allowance for the normal development of human personality. It is worth mentioning that in *Hom. in Num.* the Church is compared to the ass on which at first Balaam sat and which Christ instructed His disciples to set free so that He might mount it and upon it enter the heavenly Jerusalem (XIII.8 (GCS 7.119.10-29)).
127 *Contra Cels.* III.28 (GCS 1.226.9-13). Cf. Eichinger, op. cit., p.

189, where he says that "the revelation of the Divinity of Christ in all its glory is not the result of a movement ascending from the humanity of Jesus to His Divinity, so that the humanity could express the Divinity, but it is the result from the movement from the Divinity which encroaches on the humanity and lifts it up and transfigures it, so that the Divinity gives itself expression in the humanity."

[128] *Hom. in Josh.* V.3 (GCS 7.317.2-11).

[129] *Contra Cels.* IV.15 (GCS 1.285.14-22); cf. ibid.VI.67 (GCS 2.137.18-21), and VI.68 (138.6-17).

[130] *Comm. in Joh.* VI.38 (GCS 4.147.7-11). But contrast ibid.II.17, where it is said that none but God possesses ἄτρεπτον and ἀναλλοίωτον ζωήν, for not even Christ possessed the Father's immortality (GCS 4.74.34-75.3). See also Ch.IV,p.89, where this passage is also referred to.

[131] P.49, n.3.

[132] Op. cit., p.310. The same point is made by Hal Koch, op. cit., p. 71. Cf. also the discussion of this matter in Eichinger, op. cit., pp.170,171, and Loofs, "Das altchristliche Zeugnis gegen die herrschende Auffassung der Kenosisstelle Phil.ii.5-11" (*TSK* 100 (1927-28)), pp.10 sqq., where Origen is seen as appearing to suggest in a few passages that "the form of God" was abandoned when "the form of a slave" was assumed, but on the other hand his main view is seen to be that "the form of a slave" is a means whereby human beings could first become acquainted with the Divine Word and then finally be introduced to His Divinity. Loofs sees Origen as viewing "the form of a slave" in two ways. He sometimes regards it as simply veiling the Divinity. But elsewhere he thinks of it in a more positive manner as a means whereby the Divine Word performs His saving activity among human beings. Loofs actually seems to suggest that Origen interpreted the statement of St. Paul that the Divine Word "emptied Himself" and became obedient unto death as meaning the exact opposite of what it appears to mean, because despite all appearances the Divine Word does not suffer what His human nature suffers!

[133] IV.19 (GCS 1.288.18-25).

[134] Cf. Hanson, *Allegory and Event,* (London, 1959), p.285, where he quotes with approval Crouzel's statement that Origen envisaged the mediatorship of Jesus Christ as lying in His Divine

Nature, quite apart from the Incarnation, with the result that the Incarnation was simply "a device adopted to transfer souls from involvement in matter to a post-material existence."
135 *Hom. in Jos.* VII.7 (GCS 7.335,19-21).
136 *Matt. Comm. Series* 55 (GCS 11.124.20-125.16).
137 *Hom. in Lev.* XII.5 (GCS 6.464.11,12).
138 Wisdom vii.26.
139 *Contra Cels.* VII.17 (GCS 2.168.14-23). Cf. also ibid.V.12 (GCS 2.13.1,2), where it is said that "when God in His goodness descends to mankind, this occurs not spatially, but in accordance with His plan." Cf. also *Hom. in Lev.* IX.5 (GCS 6.427.20-428. 8); *Comm. in Rom.* VIII.2 (PG XIV.1162A); *Hom. in Matt.* I (GCS 12.240.19-24); *Frag. in Joh.* XL (GCS 4.515.22-24).
See Marcus, op. cit., p.163, where, after quoting the passage first referred to, he goes on to say: — "That this is a matter of the subordination of the Son to the Father in pursuance of the Divine plan, is clear
(a) from the natural subjection of all things created out of nothing to the God Who exists by virtue of His own nature;
(b) from the fact that to the Divine Word is assigned the saving function of being a cause of judgement to all created rational beings as a result of His Kenosis, in so far as they must decide either for truth and knowledge or else for falsehood and darkness;
(c) from the fact that to the Divine Word is assigned the saving function of displaying the Divine immanence in all created things, whereas the Father performs the saving function of displaying the Divine transcendence over all created things."
140 *De Princ.* II.11.6 (GCS 5.190.15-191.4). Mersch, op. cit., p.358 n.2, interprets this passage as referring to the human nature of Christ, which was not fully united to the Divine Word till the time of the Resurrection, but was then in so perfected a state that the Divine attributes were communicated to it, and through it spread abroad in human beings. Mersch seems to read far more into this passage than is warranted by the text; no distinction is there made between the Divinity and the humanity of Christ.
141 *De Princ.* IV.4.3 (GCS 5.352.14-29). Cf. *Contra Cels.* II.9 (GCS 1.136.14-24). Cf. Kelber, op. cit., p.263; "For Origen, the Divinity of the Word of God remains, even in respect of the quality of omnipresence, during His incarnate existence." Cf. also Ch.IV,

[142] p.87.
[143] *Hom. in Matt.* II (GCS 12.251.21-25); cf. ibid. 252.23-25.
[144] *Frag. in Matt.* 338 (GCS 12.146).
[145] *Frag. in Joh.* LXXXII (GCS 4.548.25-549.5).
[146] Matt.xxv.14 sqq.
[147] *Matt. Comm. Series* 65 (GCS 11.152.17-24). See Mme. Harl, op. cit., p.239, where this passage is quoted (in n.84), and Aeby, op. cit., pp.152,153.
[148] *Frag. in Matt.* 504 (GCS 12.206,207).
[149] *Matt. Comm. Series* 83 (GCS 11.195.9-18).
[150] Op. cit., p.154. Cf. also Aeby, op. cit., pp.162,163.
Cf. Miura-Stange, *Celsus und Origenes; das Gemeinsame ihrer Weltanschauung* (Giessen, 1926), p.148: "At any rate Origen has certainly found a possibility of dissolving the corporeality (of Jesus) which he could so realistically understand, as we see in his teaching about the various ways in which Jesus appeared, teaching which comes near to Docetism." Contrast the view expressed in the S.C. edition of *Hom. in Luc.*, p.125, n.1, where it is said that "Origen's conception (of the Incarnate Christ) bears no trace of Docetism: before the Resurrection, the body of Jesus is a human body like all others." Surely a careful study of the relevant texts hardly supports this assertion!
[151] *Contra Cels.* IV.16 (GCS 1.285.26-286.6). Cf. ibid.II.64,65 (GCS 1.185.26-187.19), and *Comm. in Cant.* III. (GCS 8.175.8-14). Cf. also Kelber, op. cit., pp.265-7.
[152] Op. cit., p.167. But see Mme. Harl, op. cit., p.251, first para.
[153] Op. cit., p.164. See also p.137. Cf. also op. cit., pp.250-254, and Crouzel, *La Conn.*, p.471.
[154] Op. cit., pp.153,154.
[155] *Comm. in Matt.* XII.36 (GCS 10.152.9-13). Cf. Koch, op. cit., p. 69, especially n.1, where this passage is quoted in Greek. Cf. also Hirschberg, op. cit., p.209, and Mumm, op. cit., pp.78,79, where Origen's treatment of the Transfiguration is discussed.
[156] *Comm. in Matt.* XII.41 (GCS 10.163.30-164.5).
[157] *Frag. in Matt.* 187.I.1-3 (GCS 12.89). Cf. Miura-Stange, op. cit., pp.159,160, where she says: "The open lack of embarrassment with which Origen occasionally pronounces his judgment (sc. that Jesus won over the multitudes by the fascination of His personality) shows that he in no way thinks that he is degrading Christ Himself thereby. In so far as the Word of God reveals

Himself in different presentations to different levels of mankind, these presentations are themselves limited and relative, and the true and genuine appearance of Christ is not affected thereby. Thus the radiation emitted by Christ in His various forms enabled Origen to include the form of the historical Jesus in a remarkably unrestricted way."

[158] *Comm. in Joh.* I.18 (GCS 4.22.21-23.5). Cf. Mme. Harl, op. cit., p.228, where Origen is quoted (*Comm. in Joh.* II.8 (GCS 4.62. 24-26)), as saying that even if we arrive at an exalted contemplation of the Divine Word, we must not neglect the introduction which is given by His assumption of a human body. Cf. also Hirschberg, op. cit., pp.218 sqq; Gögler, "Die christologische und heilstheologische Grundlage der Bibelexegese des Origenes" (*TQ* (1956)), pp.4 and 5; Refoulé, "La christologie d'Evagre et l'origénisme," *OCP* 27, 1961, pp.236,237, where Origen's influence on Evagrius, in this respect as in others, is emphasised. Cf. also *Frag. in Matt.* 54.7-9 (GCS 12.37).

[159] *Contra Cels.* II.66 (GCS 1.188.16-20); cf. *Frag. in Luc.* 255.2-6 (GCS 9.335).

[160] *Contra Cels.* VI.68 (GCS 2.138.6-11). Cf. *Sel. in Ps.* CXVII.27 (PG XII.1584C-1585A), and *Frag. in Joh.* XVIII (GCS 4.498.12-17). Cf. also Mme. Harl, op. cit., p.114, where she points out that Origen seems to declare that the Incarnate Christ only conveys the truth by way of image, since the world of sense into which He entered itself belongs to the order of image, and not that of intelligible reality. Cf. also Rius-Camps, "Comunicabilidad," *OCP* 38, 1972, p.448, where he says that according to Origen, it is not because the Only-begotten Son is in Himself any easier to comprehend than God the Father that He became incarnate. (But the question then arises, how do we pass from the comprehension of the Incarnate Word to that of the Divine Word? Origen nowhere satisfactorily answers this question. Surely the only intelligible way of thinking is to regard God as manifested *by way of* the Incarnate Jesus, rather than as being revealed after the veil of the humanity of Jesus has been removed.)

[161] Op. cit., p.66.

[162] *Comm. in Joh.* I.7 (GCS 4.13.3-10). Cf. Lebreton, op. cit., pp. 273,274, where this passage is quoted. Lebreton appears justified in suggesting that Origen's attitude savours of Gnosticism,

because it is impossible to separate people into rigid categories in this way. Such a passage as this casts doubt on the accuracy of Crouzel's description of Origen's outlook (in "Origène devant l'Incarnation et devant l'histoire" (*BLE* 61,1960), p.104) as not being concerned with the Word from whom His flesh has been removed, but with the Word Who appears by way of (à travers) His flesh. The passage in *Comm. in Joh.* II.8 (quoted in note 22, and also quoted by Crouzel) does not really lend itself to Crouzel's interpretation. See Fitzgerald, op. cit., pp.74 and 75, for a discussion of the passage.

163 *Comm. in Matt.* XII.30 (GCS 10.133.15-134.5). Cf. *Comm. in Joh.* I.37 (GCS 4.48.30-49.2), and *Frag. in Matt.* 464.2-4 (GCS 12.191,192). Cf. Mme. Harl, op. cit., p.194, where she says that the two realities which are "above" and "below" do not constitute, for Origen, "two Christs." If he distinguishes the Word Who was with God and His shadow here below, that is through an analysis of the internal structure of Christ. Lebreton, op. cit., p.286, after quoting *Comm. in Matt.* XII.30, comments (justly, in my opinion) that "it displays the rash idealism which thinks it can approach God while losing sight of the humanity of Christ." Cf. also Ch.VI, p.206.

164 In his article "O. dev. l'Inc. et dev. l'hist.", p.95.

165 Eg. *Hom. in Lev.* XII.2 (GCS 6.456.18-24); *Prol. in Cant.* (GCS 8.85.10-16); *Comm. in Cant.* I (GCS 8.111.17-19); ibid. II (GCS 8.164.2-10); ibid. III (GCS 8.206.6,7); *Comm. in Matt.* XIII.26 (GCS 10.250.24-251.9). In *Hom. in Jer.* I.7 (GCS 3.6.20-31), and *Hom. in Luc.* XX (GCS 9.123.3-14), Origen seems to suggest that our Lord's development was only apparent. Origen however takes it literally in *Hom. in Jer.* XIV.10 (GCS 3.114.27-115.1), and *Matt. Comm. Series* 55 (GCS 11.124.27-125.3).
De Faye, op. cit., p.160, likewise says that "the thought of Origen owes nothing to the Jesus Who lived, spoke and acted."

166 *Comm. in Joh.* XXXII.18 (GCS 4.457.17-27).

167 In *La Conn.*, p.111.

168 Cf. Crouzel, *La Conn.*, p.108, and Koch, op. cit., p.70. Cf. also Mme Harl, op. cit., p.255, where she says that it is on the distinction of the humanity and the Divinity of Jesus Christ that Origen bases his certainty that there is a progress in the knowledge of Christ. If Christ reveals God in the manner of an instructor, that is because of the interplay of the human and Divine ele-

ments united in Him. Cf. also pp.282-285. On the other hand Wintersig, op. cit., p.77, points out (justly, in the present writer's opinion) with reference to *Contra Cels.* VI.68 (mentioned in n. 170 below) that "the humanity of Jesus has in Origen's system only a transitory significance; it serves above all else to make the Invisible One visible, so as to give emphasis to His esoteric instruction." Cf. Kelber, op. cit., pp.263,264. Cf. also Hanson, op. cit., p.284, where, after quoting the passage from *Contra Cels.*, he says that one must conclude that "the Incarnation was to Origen no more than a necessary device employed by God as an important stage in the process of fully revealing Himself."

[169] οὐκ ἔμεινεν ἐπὶ τῆς πρώτης μορφῆς.

[170] *Contra Cels.* VI.68 (GCS 2.138.18-21). Cf. the discussion of this passage in Eichinger, op. cit., pp.177-179. The passage is also discussed on pp.39 sqq., with particular reference to the meaning of "being transformed into the likeness of the Word Who became flesh." It is to be doubted whether Origen means, as Eichinger asserts him to mean, that the Divine Word deters men from sin in the first place by threatening them with the consequences of sin. That conception indeed appears in Origen's writings, but it does not seem to be what he has in mind here. It is in fact not part of the work of the *Incarnate* Word. Origen appears to mean rather that men first recognise the Incarnate Word as expressing in His life the principles of action to which they acknowledge that they should themselves conform. Cf. also op. cit., pp.59-61, and Crouzel, *La Conn.* p.472.

Cf. Pitra, A.S. III.245 (Ps.CXVII.25-27), and *Hom. in Luc.* III (GCS 9.21.12-22.4), where Origen says that not all who saw Christ in His earthly life saw the Word of God – not Pilate or Judas or the multitude which thronged Him, but only those whom He thought worthy of contemplating Him.

[171] *Comm. in Rom.* VII.7 (PG XIV.1122A-C).

[172] *Comm. in Joh.* VI.49 (GCS 4.157.27-158.1).

[173] *Comm. in Matt.* XII.29 (GCS 10.132.21-133.14).

[174] *Matt. Comm. Series* 32 (GCS 11.58.16-59.3). Cf. pp.117,118.

[175] *Frag. in Luc.* 140.8-11 (GCS 9.283), and *Comm. in Matt.* XII.39 (GCS 10.156.3-11). Cf. Ch.VII, pp.239,240.

[176] *Hom. in Gen.* IV.5 (GCS 6.55.15-28). Cf. Origen's attitude to the prophets (Ch.II, pp.39-42).

[177] *Comm. in Matt.* XII.32 (GCS 10.139.19-140.6,20-27); cf. *Ex-*

178 cerpt. in Cant. VI.4 (PG XIII.207C), and *Frag. in Matt.* 357.11-15 (GCS 12.153). Cf. also Crouzel, *La Conn.*, p.486.

178 *Contra Cels.* VI.77 (GCS 2.146.14-29). Cf. *Matt. Comm. Series* 35, where it is said that "perhaps the Word appears with diverse kinds of glory, depending on the capacity of the soul which sees Him" (GCS 11.65.28-30).

179 *Matt. Comm. Series* 100 (GCS 11.219.7-17).
180 Op. cit., pp.106 and 107, n.193.
181 Op. cit., pp.274-276, where this matter is discussed.
182 *De Princ.* II.6.3 (GCS 5.141.25-143.2).
183 *Frag. in Rom.* I.38-41 (*JTS* 13.211).
184 Cf. p.106.
185 *Sel. in Ps.* I.1 (PG XII.1085A). Cf. ibid.XLII.3 (PG XII.1421A).
186 In *L'Image*, p.135, first para. of n.44.
187 On p.243 of op. cit.
188 Op. cit., p.125.
189 In *Das Konzil von Chalkedon*, Vol.I, p.64.
190 *Excerpt. in Cant.* VI.7 (PG XIII.209B). Cf. Pitra, A.S.III.173 (Ps.XCII.1,2).
191 *Comm. in Joh.* I.32 (GCS 4.42.10-14).
192 *Comm. in Matt.* XIV.7 (GCS 10.290.16,17,24-31), and ibid.XVI.19 (GCS 10.540.23-29). Cf. Pitra A.S.III.46 (Ps.XLVII.3), where it is said: ῥίζα δὲ αὐτοῦ (ie. Χριστοῦ) ὁ Θεὸς Λόγος, ὁ ἐν αὐτῷ. Cf. also ibid.330 (Ps.CXXXI.7), where it is said that "by Christ I here refer to the λογικὴ ψυχή which together with the Word of God entered the life of men."
193 *Contra Cels.* I.32 (GCS 1.84.19-26).
194 IX.5 (GCS 7.60.18-24).
195 It does not seem clear, however, that there is any firm distinction to be drawn between the "soul" and the "spirit" of Christ, as will shortly appear.
196 *De Princ.* IV.4.4 (GCS 5.353.10-13).
197 Ibid.IV.4.5 (GCS 5.355.14-356.5). See Fitzgerald's discussion of this passage in op. cit., pp.190-192. It is however to be observed that Fitzgerald seems to contradict himself when he denies on p. 191 that the Word Himself became incarnate, and yet on p.192 asserts that the Word was involved with Christ's human soul in the "self-emptying" entailed in the Incarnation.
198 *Hom. in Matt.* I (GCS 12.242.27).
199 *Contra Cels.* VI.66 (GCS 2.136.28).

200 *Frag. in Matt.* 288.2,3 (GCS 12.128).
201 *Comm. in Joh.* VI.30 (GCS 4.140.17-22).
202 *Comm. in Matt.* XV.24 (GCS 10.419.30-420.13).
203 *Comm. in Joh.* I.20 (GCS 4.25.16-20).
204 Op. cit., pp.227,228.
205 *De Princ.* II.8.3 (GCS 5.156.22-26, and 157,12-158.2). Cf. also 158.22-159.2). Cf. Cadiou, op. cit., p.8.
206 Ibid.II.6.3 (GCS 5.142.2-10).
207 Indeed, Origen has to admit that certain passages of Scripture speak of the "soul of God" (Lev.xvii.10, Is.i.13,14 and xlii.1), so that his derivation of the word "soul" does not harmonise with all the uses of it (*De Princ.* II.8.1 (GCS 5.153,25-29)). In fact, the idea of the soul as something which has lost its original perfection is introduced quite abruptly in *De Princ.* II.8,2, where reference is made to the "soul-like man" whom St. Paul contrasts with the "spiritual man" in I Cor.ii.14 (GCS 5.154.18-24). Cf. Eichinger, op. cit., pp.87 sqq., and Gruber, op. cit., p.150.
208 In *Frag. in Lam.* LIII (GCS 3.258.10,11).
209 *Sel. in Ps.* LXIV.3 (PG XII.1493B).
210 *Frag. in I Cor.* XXXIX.57-59 (*JTS* 9.510).
211 *Convs. with Heracl.* 3.12-20 (Scherer's ed., pp.58,60).
212 *Frag. in Joh.* LXXXIV (GCS 4.549.17-21).
213 *Hom. in I Sam.xxviii.3-25* 7 (GCS 3.290.1-10).
214 *Sel. in Ps.* LXXIII.7 (PG XII.1529D).
215 *Frag. in Luc.* 195.1,2 (GCS 9.310).
216 *Frag. in Matt.* 125 (GCS 12.65).
217 *Frag. in Luc.* 121.20-25 (GCS 9.276). Cf. Lieske, op. cit., p.104.
218 Ibid.186.1-5,17-24 (GCS 9.305,306). Cf. *Frag. in Matt.* 265.1-3 (GCS 12.121).
219 *Frag. in Matt.* 187.II.3,4 (GCS 12.89).
220 *Sel. in Ps.* XXI.10 (PG XII.1253D-1256A).
221 See Crouzel, *L'Image*, pp.131 and 157.
222 Ibid., n.86 on p.159.
223 II.4 (GCS 2.301.25-302.6).
224 The same applies to the distinction made between πνεῦμα and νοῦς in the passage from *De Orat.* (XIV.5 (GCS 2.332.18-25)) referred to by Dupuis on p.74, n.80, and in *Frag. in Eph.* XIX.42-48 (*JTS* 3.419).
225 Op. cit., pp.10-13.
226 Op. cit., p.12.

[227] Cf. also Crouzel, *La Conn.*, pp.463,464, where he makes the same distinction between πνεῦμα and νοῦς, and declares that the πνεῦμα is "grace." Lieske in n.56 on pp.143 and 144 similarly identifies πνεῦμα with "the grace bestowed by the Holy Spirit", even though he admits that Origen treats the πνεῦμα as νοῦς.
[228] On p.256 of op. cit.
[229] pp.40,41 and 45.
[230] pp.414,415 and 417.
[231] In "Comunicabilidad," *OCP* 38,1972, p.433.
[232] The same view is taken by Teichtweier, op. cit., p.270: the whole chapter entitled "Der Geist des Menschen" is relevant to this theme. Cf. also p.253 of op. cit., where the author says that "in general it must be said that Origen understands by the term πνεῦμα that element in man which is directed to God and enlightened by Him and strives to free itself from evil." H.Rahner also appears to identify πνεῦμα with νοῦς; see op. cit., p.209.
[233] *De Princ.* II.10.7 (GCS 5.181.1-13). Crouzel in *L'Image*, p.145, does not interpret this passage in the way I do; he appears to suggest that the "spirit" of those who have not used the gifts of the Holy Spirit aright will return to the God Who gave it, whereas the rest of the soul will go to hell. But surely Origen means that the entire soul (including the "spirit") of these persons will be separated from God. The same criticism can be made of Dupuis, op. cit., pp.213,214.
[234] *De Princ.* II.10.7 (GCS 5.181.13-19).
[235] Cf. the quotation from Irenaeus given on p.65 of Crouzel, op. cit.
[236] p.457 of *L'Évolution de la doctrine du Pneuma du Stoicisme a Saint Augustin* (Paris-Louvain,1945).
[237] p.459.
[238] *De Princ.* III.4.3 (GCS 5.267.23-268.17).
[239] pp.457,467,468.
[240] p.458.
[241] GCS 5.265.6-13, referred to in n.130 on p.458 of op. cit.
[242] III.4.2 (GCS 5.266.27-267.5).
[243] *Frag. in Lam.* VII (GCS 3.237.10-18).
[244] *Sel. in Ps.* XL.6 (PG XII.1413B).
[245] IX.2 (GCS 2.319.4-8). Cf. Rahner, op. cit., pp.219 and 220, where this passage is quoted. Crouzel in *La Conn.*, pp.145 and 146 understands the word "spirit" (πνεῦμα) in this passage to refer to the human spirit. The quotation from Ps.xxiv.1 in the

passage would seem to indicate that it is the Divine Spirit Who is referred to. Cf. *Comm. in Joh.* I.28 (GCS IX.36.12-14), where Origen refers to the soul becoming united with the Holy Spirit, with the result that each of the saved becomes spiritual (πνευματικός). Cf. Cadiou, *Frag. in Ps.* CXVIII.81 (p.112), where it is said, with reference to the verse "My ψυχή fades away (ἐκλείπει) for Thy salvation", that the writer would not have said "My πνεῦμα fades away"; for the ψυχή which is joined (κολλωμένη) to the πνεῦμα ceases to be a ψυχή and becomes one with the πνεῦμα.

246 Op. cit., pp.115,116.
247 Cf. also op. cit., p.125, where it is said that "the stage of mystical union with Christ corresponds to the future close contact with the Ascended Lord which in the condition of the soul of Christ and its full blending (Verschmelzen) with the Divine Word is clearly expressed." Cf. also the last sentence of the para. ending on p.130 of op. cit.
Cf. also Grillmeier, op. cit., p.65, where it is suggested first that the union of the soul of Christ with the Divine Word is "eine wirklich ontische Einheit", which presumably means that the soul loses its separate identity, and secondly, that "Christ is in the last resort only a special instance of the general relation of the mature Christian to the Divine Word." I would agree with the second statement, but not with the first.
248 Section 12 (GCS 1.12.23-25).
249 Section 34 (GCS 1.31.17,18).
250 Anathema 6a of the Second Council of Constantinople, quoted in *De Princ.* II.8.3 (GCS 5.160,15-18).
251 *De Princ.* II.9.7 (GCS 5.171.15-17).
252 Cf. Eichinger, op. cit., pp.89.90.
253 ἕν ἐστι τὸ ποτε σύνθετον πρὸς τὸν Λόγον τοῦ θεοῦ. *Contra Cels.* II.9 (GCS 1.136.30-137.3). Cf. Fitzgerald, op. cit., 77-79, and also n.46 on p.113, where, however, he makes what seems an entirely unacceptable deduction from this passage that there was no separation between the Word and the soul of Christ before the Incarnation, in the sense that the soul shared in all the operations of the Word. The union which Origen insists on is surely a union of wills only.
254 p.152. Boon interprets the passage in a *prima facie* manner when he says (op. cit., p.26) that "notwithstanding the co-existence of

both natures in Christ, there is in the Incarnation an element of deification of the human nature since this is taken up into the Divine Nature. Thus both the soul and the body of Jesus Christ become a unity with the Word of God."

[255] Op. cit., p.165; the same point is made on p.178, n.3.

[256] *De Princ.* II.6.3 (GCS 5.142.2-10). See also *Comm. in Joh.* XX. 19 (GCS 4.351.25-28), where Origen says that "perhaps the soul of Jesus in its perfection was in God and in His fullness; it came forth from thence, sent by the Father, and took flesh in the womb of Mary."

[257] The same criticism can be made of Crouzel's interpretation in *La Conn.*, p.461, n.1.

[258] Op. cit., p.340.

[259] Inserted in *De Princ.* II.6.4 (GCS 5.143.18-23).

[260] Cf. p.201 and Ch.VI, n.9. It is interesting to observe that according to Refoulé, op. cit., p.239, Gregory of Nyssa is caught in the same dilemma as Origen when he says that the human Jesus was only exalted as Lord and Christ after His Passion, and yet also regards the union of the Divine and human natures as essential and not merely moral. If the union were "essential", there could be no question of the human Jesus becoming after His Passion what He had not been before it.

[261] As well as in the one referred to in n.253.

[262] σύνθετον κτῆμα.

[263] *Contra Cels.* I.66 (GCS 1.119.16-21); cf. ibid. (120.20-121.2), II. 25 (GCS 1.154,16-155.6), and VII.16 (GCS 2.167.12-168.10). Cf. p.137.

[264] I.60 (GCS 1.111.20-22).

[265] Cf. Wintersig, op. cit., pp.77,78.

[266] On p.165 of op. cit.

[267] Eg. *Comm. in Joh.* I.28 (GCS 4.36.24-26) quoted in Nemeshegyi, op. cit., p.73.

[268] On p.156 of his book.

[269] Op. cit., pp.119-121.

[270] *Matt. Comm. Series* 126 (GCS 11.263.2,3).

[271] *Contra Cels.* II.9 (GCS 1.135.3-28). Cf. Miura-Stange, op. cit., p. 148, third para.

[272] *De Princ.* IV.1.5 (GCS 5.299.4-7).

[273] *De Princ.* II.6.2 (GCS 5.141.1-3).

[274] *Contra Cels.* VII.16 (GCS 2.167.13-19).

275 *Matt. Comm. Series* 73 (GCS 11.172.21-27). Cf. Lieske, op. cit., pp.140 and 154, and Kelber, op. cit., p.262, where he says: "The idea of a suffering God, which first presented itself through the description of the genuine being of Christ, has no place in the thought of Origen. The Word of God cannot suffer. Suffering was the lot of the soul of Jesus. The Word can take this suffering into His consciousness, indeed, but not as a soul which is itself capable of undergoing feelings." Cf. also *Sel. in Ps.* LXVIII.3 (PG XII.1512B), where it is said that although the Word of God may send up prayers to the Father to be rescued from His distress, He is simply making His own the feelings of the man whom he took to Himself (ἰδιοποιούμενος τὰ καθ' ὃν εἴληφεν ἄνθρωπον πάθη).

276 *Comm. in Joh.* II.26 (GCS 4.83.13-17).

277 *Matt. Comm. Series* 90 (GCS 11.205.24-206.16). Cf. Mme. Harl, op. cit., p.241, where she quotes this passage, and admits that the reality of the Incarnation is somewhat diminished thereby. Cf. also p.358, where she says that "leaving the sufferings to the man, ie. to the agent of salvation, Origen reflects above all on the glorious scenes in which the Divinity of the Son of God was proclaimed."

278 *Hom. in Jer.* XIV.5,6 (GCS 3.112.5-10); cf. XV.4 (128.8-13), and *Hom. in Ezek.* I.5 (GCS 8.330.4-6). But strangely enough, in *Exhort. ad Mart.* 29 (GCS 1.25.2-23), Origen suggests that at the time when the Saviour asked that "this cup" should pass from Him (Matt.xxvi.39), He cannot be supposed to have been afraid, because He was assured of the powerful protection of the Father and was therefore afraid of no one. Origen seems here to revert to the idea that it was the Word of God Himself Who became incarnate. In order to reconcile this assertion with the prayer quoted, Origen claims that "*this* cup" must be distinguished from martyrdom as such, because that is called "*a* cup" of suffering, and says that our Lord was asking that He be martyred in a manner more severe than crucifixion, so as to benefit mankind to a greater extent. But such was not the Father's will. Cf. also pp.111,112.

Teichtweier, on p.307 of op. cit., quotes *Hom. in Jer.* XIV.5,6, but does not recognise that the part of the soul of Jesus which experienced feelings was not the pre-existent soul, but the part which was assumed at the Incarnation (midway between "spirit"

and "flesh"). How can Teichtweier say that "the soul of Jesus in no way became pure spirit"? Surely it always was pure spirit, and never became anything inferior. See pp. 143 - 148 for a detailed discussion of the two types of soul.
279 *Frag. in Joh.* LXXXVIII (GCS 4.552.14-22). Cf. *Sel. in Ps.* LXI. 2 (PG XII.1484D,1485A); XVII.5,6 (1225B); LIV.4 (1464C).
280 92 (GCS 11.208.13-15,26-29). But see Pitra A.S.III.86 (Ps. LXVIII.14,15) for a different view, in fact a view which is more in accordance with traditional teaching about the Incarnate Jesus. It is there said that when Christ said "Let this cup pass from me", He was not intending to deceive Satan nor to make the will of worldly people His own, but in His own Person Christ spontaneously implored the Father with a loud cry and with tears and sweat, even though He was the Son of God.
281 *Matt. Comm. Series* 91 (GCS 11.207.22-26).
282 *Sel. in Ps.* III.6 (PG XII.1128BC).
283 *Contra Cels.* II.43 (GCS 1.166.8-11).
284 *Hom. in I Sam.xxviii.3-25.*8 (GCS 3.292.18,19).
285 *Comm. in Matt.* XVI.21 (GCS 10.546.30-547.17); cf. *Frag. in Matt.* 558.1-14 (GCS 12.229).
286 *De Princ.* II.8.4 (GCS 5.162.11-21); cf. ibid.IV.4.4 (GCS 5.353. 19-354.3). Cf. also *Hom. in Num.* IX.5, referred to on p. 130, and comment made in n.195. But see *Convs. with Heracl.*, 6.20-7.7 (Scherer, pp.68,70), referred to again on pp.150,151. For a discussion of the soul of Jesus as conceived of by Origen, see Teichtweier, pp.306-308.
287 *De Princ.* II.8.5 (GCS 5.163.7-11).
288 Op. cit., pp.24,25.
289 Ibid., p.49.
290 Op. cit., p.148.
291 *Contra Cels.* II.34 (GCS 1.161.3-7).
292 Ibid.II.24 (GCS 1.153.10-16).
293 ἄλλος δήπου ὁ περὶ τούτου καὶ τῆς οὐσίας αὐτοῦ λόγος ἐστι παρὰ τὸν περὶ τοῦ νοουμένου κατὰ τὸν Ἰησοῦν ἀνθρώπου (*Contra Cels.* VII.16 (GCS 2.167.26-28)).
294 *Contra Cels.* VI.47 (GCS 2.119.4-15); cf. ibid.VI.48 (GCS 2.120. 2-9).
295 Op. cit., p.114.
296 Op. cit., pp.262,263.
297 See also notes 3 and 4 on p.262 of op. cit.

298 κεκοσμημένος τῇ ἄκρᾳ μετοχῇ τοῦ αὐτολόγου καὶ τῆς αὐτοσοφίας.
299 *Contra Cels.* VII.17 (GCS 2.168.26-29); cf. V.39 (GCS 2.43.26-44.2).
300 *Hom. in Ezek.* I.10 (GCS 8.333.20-24). Cf. Eichinger, op. cit., p. 195, where he says that "Jesus in the body which He assumed, even when this is transfigured, is never the Self-revelation of the Divine Word, but as the Bearer of a mystical content He merely has an inner relationship to the revelation of the Word." Cf. also Mme. Harl, op. cit., pp.203,204.
301 II.6.2 (GCS 5.141.12-15).
302 Ibid.II.6.3 (GCS 5.143.2-9). Cf. Primmer, op. cit., pp.84,85.
303 Section 35 (GCS 1.32.15-24).
304 See pp.123,124.
305 *Contra Cels.* II.9 (GCS 1.136.13-18).
306 διῆκον ἐπὶ πᾶσαν τὴν οἰκουμένην.
307 *Contra Cels.* VII.35 (GCS 2.186.8-11).
308 εἰς τὰς ἀνθρωπίνας κῆρας καταβᾶσα (*Contra Cels.* IV.18 (GCS 1.288.1-10)). Cf. *Sel. in Ps.* XXIX.7 (PG XII.1293D,1296A). Cf. also Kelber, op. cit., p.257, and Eichinger, op. cit., p.145, who quotes the passage and also refers to the question introducing it – "Does the Word of God undergo anything inappropriate by bringing down the Saviour to the human race out of His great love for mankind?" – as involving "a surprising change of subject", presumably meaning that the Word and the Saviour appear to be treated as two separate beings. Cf. also pp.86 and 87 of op. cit. Cf. also Cornelis, op. cit., p.49, where he says that according to Origen, "souls as such are incorporeal, and thus integral parts of the invisible world, but they have left their fatherland. The soul of Jesus was an exception to this: though it was a real ψυχή, it did not deserve to be brought down to an inferior level in the hierarchy of values, for nothing belonging to the higher world is of small account."
309 *De Princ.* II.9.7 (GCS 5.171.15-18). See also *Comm. in Joh.* II. 31 (GCS 4.88.12-18), and XIX.22 (324.13-16). Cf. also *De Princ.* III.5.4 and 5 (GCS 5.275.5-9 and 20-23, and 276.1-6). It is worth remarking that Origen is inconsistent with himself in the first and last passages referred to in *De Princ.* III.5. In the first, he suggests that the souls who were brought down from higher conditions to serve those who on account of their own defects were placed on a lower level were brought down

against their own will (*licet non volentes* (5.275.9)). In the third passage, he allows that some may have been willing and some unwilling (*vel volentes vel inviti* (5.276.4)). In any case, if they were unwilling, that would be a sign that they were not in a state of perfect harmony with God and therefore *deserved* to be deprived of unmixed fellowship with Him. Cf. Aeby, op. cit., pp. 148,149 (esp. n.4 on latter page), and Cadiou, op. cit., pp.61,62. I suppose the solution would be to say, not that they were unwilling, but that they did not desire to be brought down from their state of bliss, but none the less consented to sacrifice their own desires to the Divine Will, just as our Lord sacrificed His human will in the Garden of Gethsemane.

Perhaps this provides a clue to the solution of the problem of whether the Incarnate Jesus had two wills. The "orthodox" view is that He had two wills — Divine and human; but in order to avoid the corollary of a split personality, it could be said that the human will was not independent, but simply consisted of inclinations and feelings, which might on occasion be out of harmony with the Divine Will, but could never prevent it from being put into effect. See also Fitzgerald, op. cit., p.179.

[310] St. John viii.42.

[311] *Comm. in Joh.* XX.19 (GCS 4.351.24-30). A distinction seems necessary here between what might be called God's "primary" will, that is, what He requires of those in fellowship with Him, and His "consequent" will, that is, what He inflicts on those who have to a greater or less extent departed from that fellowship.

[312] *Comm. in Matt.* XIII.17 (GCS 10.226.2-17). Teichtweier on p. 308 of op. cit. discusses the difference between the soul of Jesus and other human souls, and quotes with approval Redepenning's statement that "such a soul (as that of Jesus) is not a real soul in the sense which Origen's system demands", because it had never grown cold in its love for God, and thus did not deserve to be implanted in a human body.

[313] *Contra Cels.* VI.45 (GCS 2.116.14,15).

[314] Ibid.II.25 (GCS 1.154.21-25).

[315] κατὰ τοῦ ἀνθρωπίνου αὐτοῦ.

[316] *Contra Cels.* VII.43 (GCS 2.194.15,16).

[317] Ibid.VIII.42 (GCS 2.256.27-31).

[318] *Hom. in Ezek.* VI.6 (GCS 8.384.16-385.3). Cf. also *Frag. in Ezek.* XVI.8, where it is stated that God is not without feelings

(οὐ γὰρ ἄσπλαγχος ὁ θεός) (PG XIII.812B). Cf. also *Sel. in Ps.* XLI.10, where it is said that Christ declares Himself to be of a sad countenance because He is forsaken by God (PG XII.1420A), and *Sel. in Ezek.* VII.27 (PG XIII 796A) where it is said that the sentence "the King shall mourn" is not translated in the Septuagint, perhaps because the translators did not think the Saviour would mourn, though Origen himself would say that this is not an unreasonable idea if the Saviour mourned over Jerusalem. Cf. also Crouzel, "O. dev. l'Inc. et dev. l'hist.", p.83.

[319] Op. cit. The passage from *Hom. in Ezek.* VI.6 is quoted on pp. 75 and 76 of that work.
[320] pp.68-70.
[321] On p.21, op. cit.
[322] On pp.85 and 86, op. cit.
[323] Cf. also what Primmer says, op. cit., p.89: "The love of the Word of God for His Bride the Church is the fundamental idea on which the view of God as feeling the emotion of pity (ἔλεος) rests."
[324] Cf. Temple, op. cit., p.269 n.1: "It is truer to say that there is suffering in God than that God suffered. The Greek conception of the impassibility of the Divine wrought fearful havoc in the theology of the patristic period. If Christ is the revelation of God, then God is not impassible. But to say boldly that He is passible is not true either. There is suffering in God, but it is always an element in the joy of the triumphant sacrifice."
[325] Op. cit., Vol.II, p.162.
[326] Ibid., p.180.
[327] III.4.
[328] Section 5 (GCS 5.270.27-29).
[329] Section 2 (GCS 5.264.13-265.4). Rüsche in *Das Seelenpueuma: Seine Entwicklung von der Hauchseele zur Geistseele* (Paderborn, 1933) seems to give a misleading account of Origen's description of the animal soul. It is surely not in his view "material", even though it is closely associated with the body. Rüsche correctly observes that Origen parts company with the Stoics in so far as he declares the primal νοῦς in each person to be non-material (p. 45). But it seems fanciful to suggest that what Rüsche calls the "Blutpneuma" originates, according to Origen, from the cooling of the ethereal body which he supposes Origen to have associated with the νοῦς in its pre-existent state (ibid.). See also Rüsche,

Blut, Leben, and Seele (Paderborn, 1930) pp.418 sqq., for a discussion of *De Princ.* III.4.
See also Lot-Borodine, op. cit., *RHR,* 1932, CVI, p.533, and also 1933, CVII, n.1 on pp.32 and 33, where he points out that the Eastern mystics from the time of Origen considered the deiform νοῦς as perfectly independent of the ψυχή which is set under it, including the rational part of the ψυχή.
Hirschberg seems to be wrong when on p.173 of op. cit., he asserts that Origen does not suppose that the soul's fall from its original state through sin has added to it another and inferior substance.
Teichtweier on p.321 of op. cit., seems mistaken in holding that Origen rejected the idea that the animal soul originated with the body.
Javierre in his article "Hacia una definicion plena del 'soma' origenista" (*RET* 9 (1949)), when he discusses Origen's conception of the ψυχή on pp.379-382, makes no reference whatever to *De Princ.* III.4, which one would have thought vital for a full understanding of Origen's doctrine. In particular, if he had studied this chapter, he would not have asserted that "Origen declares that the ψυχή did not depend essentially on matter at the time of its creation."

330 Sections 2 and 3 of *De Princ.* III.4 (GCS 5.265.2-268.23). Cf. *Frag. in Rom.* XXXI.5-11 (*JTS* 13.365). Cf. Teichtweier, pp. 318,319.
331 XXXII.18 (GCS 4.455.12-456.13).
332 St. John xii.27.
333 St. John xiii.21.
334 Cf. Mumm's comment on this passage in n.341 of op. cit., where he says that "one has the feeling that Origen has created a difficulty and distinction which does not really exist in John, and then has resolved it by a bit of ingenious and subtle argument which overreaches itself." Cf. also Dupuis' discussion of this passage in op. cit., pp.84 and 85, and that of Verbeke in op. cit., pp.456,457.
Cf. also Teichtweier, pp.271,272 and 300. The statement of Origen that "the human spirit does not admit of anything evil" is shown by Teichtweier to be in contradiction to the view of Origen expressed elsewhere, when Teichtweier says (p.274) that according to Origen, "what disappears in the encounter of the

human spirit with the Spirit of God is only the state of imperfection and sin which the human spirit has against its own nature appropriated to itself." Origen in fact fails to realise that sin can hardly be said to originate in the human spirit (in his sense), but rather in the lower part of the soul which asserts itself against the (unawakened) spirit. The contradiction is made still more apparent in another statement (p.254) to the effect that "the human spirit according to Origen remains good even after the Fall; it retains the power to remember its former state and finally to win it back. There lives in it the unbroken power of its initial state, and its danger is that it may leave that power unused, and allow itself to be overcome by earthly things." Teichtweier himself admits (on p.301) that there is a contradiction in this aspect of Origen's thought.

Cf. also Gruber, op. cit., p.154, n.56, where this contradiction is also admitted, and also pp.178,179, where the passage from *Comm. in Joh.* XXXII is quoted and commented on, and n.12 on pp.179 and 180, where the contradiction in Origen's thought is also alluded to.

335 *Comm. in Rom.* VII.3 (PG XIV.1106A).
336 Ibid.VI.1 (PG XIV.1057A). Cf. *Frag. in Rom.* XXXI 16-18 (*JTS* 13,366).
337 Ibid.I.10 (PG XIV.856A).
338 Ibid.II.10 (PG XIV.893B-D). This is the second of the interpretations of St. Luke xii.46 suggested in *De Princ.* II.10.7 (see pp. 133,134). Cf. Crouzel, *L'Image*, p.133.
339 Ibid.IX.25 (PG XIV.1226A-C). Such a passage as this seems to refute Teichtweier's suggestion (op. cit., p.330) that an individual has two souls in addition to the "spirit", namely the "soul of the flesh" and a higher soul, which enters the individual from outside, and which can fulfil either the will of the spirit or the will of the flesh. Origen does not suggest that the "flesh" has a soul of its own, though he does suggest that the soul which is distinct from the spirit can yield to the solicitations of the flesh.
340 Eg. *Comm. in Rom.* VI.9 (PG XIV.1089A).
341 *Frag. in Matt.* 274.6-9 (1st col.) (GCS 12.123). Cf. *Comm. in Matt.* XII.4 (GCS 10.75.3-5), and *Hom. in Jud.* IV.4 (GCS 7.491. 18-21).
342 *Comm. in Rom.* VII.12 (PG XIV.1137A).
343 *Frag. in Matt.* 214.2-5 (GCS 12.102). Cf. *Comm. in Joh.* I.32

344 (GCS 4.40.31-41.2), and Pitra, A.S.II.458 (Ps.VII.13).
Comm. in Rom. VI.6 (PG XIV.1069A).
345 Ibid.V.6 (PG XIV.1034D,1035A).
346 *Frag. in Jer.* 10 (GCS 3.202.2,3).
347 *Frag. in Eph.* XXI.15-18 (*JTS* 3.556).
348 *Frag. in I Cor.* XXIV.2,3,9,11-13,16-18 (*JTS* 9.364).
349 XX.22 (GCS 4.355.9-17).
350 *Comm. in Rom.* I.17 (PG XIV.866A-C).
351 Cf. Rahner, op. cit., pp.213-215, where this passage is quoted, and Dupuis, op. cit., pp.47-49,65,67,184 n.114,p.185.
Cf. *Frag. in Rom.* XXXI.16-18 (*JTS* 13.366), where it is said that "the ψυχή itself does not seem to remain in one state, but either becomes σάρξ through wickedness or πνεῦμα through virtue."
Cf. Cadiou, *Frag. in Ps.* CXLI.8 (p.131), where it is said that the ψυχή which is freed from material things and from the body is led out of prison by God.
Cf. also Pitra A.S.III.32 (Ps.XXXVIII.11,12), and 62 (Ps.LVII.5), where it is said that when wrath (θυμός) prevails, the ψυχή becomes bestial; when desire (τὸ ἐπιθυμητικόν) prevails, it becomes a horse or a mule; but when ὁ νοῦς prevails, it becomes angelic and Divine.
Cf. ibid.119 (Ps.LXXVII.19-25), where it is said that those who are occupied with mundane matters are sick in soul (νοσοῦσι τὴν ψυχήν) because of the divided state of their soul (διὰ τὴν διψυχίαν αὐτῶν). Cf. ibid.126,127 (Ps.LXXVII.48-51).
352 In *Comm. in Matt.* XIV.3 (GCS 10.278,29-279.27). Cf. Pitra A. S.III.136 (Ps.LXXX.3).
353 In *Frag. in Rom.* XXXI.6-11 (*JTS* 13.365), Origen says that St. Paul in listing "heresies" among the works of the flesh (in Gal.v. 20) prevents us from thinking that some sins are not works of the flesh, but of the ψυχή or νοῦς. If heresies are included among the works of the flesh that is because they arise ἀπὸ τοῦ νοῦ τῆς σάρκος.
354 *Hom. in Lev.* II.2 (GCS 6.292.25-293.4). Rahner, op. cit., p.222, quotes *Sel. in Ezek.* XIV.4 (PG XIII.805D) as stating that in so far as the ψυχή inclines to one or the other field of influence (ie. the body or the spirit), the individual becomes either a bestial man (κτηνώδης ἄνθρωπος) or a more rational man (λογικώτερος ανθρωπος).
355 *Frag. in Eph.* XXVI.13-18 (*JTS* 3.563).

356 *Frag. in I Cor.* XVII.4-6 (*JTS* 9.353).
357 XIII.24 (GCS 4.247.16-20).
358 *Comm. in Rom.* VII.12 (PG XIV.1134AB). Cf. *Frag. in Rom.* LII.7-17 (*JTS* 14.20,21). See E. Schendel, op. cit., pp.83-85 (section entitled "Die Vernichtung des Todes"). Cf. also Pitra, A.S.II.479 (Ps.XXII.4).
359 *Comm. in Rom.* III.4 (PG XIV.936A).
360 *Hom. in Lev.* XII.3 (GCS 6.460.1,2).
361 Ibid.IX.11 (GCS 6.439.23-440.4).
362 *Comm. in Joh.* VI.11 (GCS 4.120.5-22). Cf. Pitra A.S.III.52 (Ps. L.13) where it is said that the Spirit of God is the source of τὸ προφητικὸν πνεῦμα. On the other hand, Origen appears to revert to his usual view of the πνεῦμα as part of man's natural endowment when he says in Cadiou, *Frag. in Ps.* CV.32,33 (p.92) that the πνεῦμα of Moses which the Israelites provoked is the spirit of man which is in him, and that perhaps the spirit of Elijah in John the Baptist is this kind of thing (the implication being that John the Baptist was a re-incarnation of Elijah).
363 *Comm. in Joh.* VI.20 (GCS 4.130.16-18).
364 Ibid.XIII.24 (GCS 4.247.26-31).
365 X.6-10 (*JTS* 9.239).
366 Scherer's ed., 23.2-7.
367 *Frag. in Matt.* 193.11-16 (GCS 12.93).
368 *Frag. in Eph.* (PG XIV.1297,1298). Cf. *De Orat.* XXXI.2 (GCS 2.396.10-14).
369 *Frag. in Eph.* XXXIII.24,25 (*JTS* 3.571).
370 Pitra A.S.III.344 (Ps.CXXXVIII.14-16).
371 560.8-13 (GCS 12.230).
372 In *L'Image*, p.264.
373 Cf. *Frag. in I Cor.* XXXV.12,13 (*JTS* 9.503), where with reference to St. Paul's statement in I Cor.vii.9 that "it is better to marry than to burn", Origen takes the "burning" (πύρωσιν) to be "the desire of the flesh" (τὴν ἐπιθυμίαν τῆς σαρκός) which in the sinner is not quenched by reason, but overcomes his ψυχή. Mme. Harl in op. cit., p.116, does refer to the alternatives possible to the lower soul – that of obeying the πνεῦμα or yielding to the σάρξ – but oddly enough she makes no reference to the chapter (*De Princ.* III.4), where the matter is fully discussed. She also seems to fail to distinguish between the two meanings of "soul" in Origen.

374 Op. cit. (see n.351 of this chapter).
375 Op. cit., p.20.
376 Cf. also Mumm, who in op. cit., (pp.250,251) indicates a contradiction in Origen's view of the soul, but apparently does not recognise it as such (ie. he recognises that in some places Origen considers "soul" to be "fallen spirit", but in other places considers it as an entity on its own).
377 Op. cit., p.19.
378 Op. cit., pp.258,259; cf.p.135.
379 Op. cit., p.36; cf. also p.34.
380 It is worth observing that the problem of how the soul could choose evil in an incorporeal state was raised by Methodius of Olympus, who denied the pre-existence of the soul for this reason (see Cornelis, op. cit., p.207; cf. also p.61). Teichtweier (op. cit., p.327) also quotes Plotinus as saying that in so far as the soul is liable to lapse, that is due to its composite character; if the spiritual part of it were its whole being, it could not lapse.
381 6.20-8.17 (Scherer pp.68,70,72). See Fitzgerald's discussion of this passage, op. cit., pp.140-142. Fitzgerald makes the interesting suggestion that the reason why Origen failed to complete his argument against those who set at nought the salvation of man's soul and spirit by the Incarnate Christ is that he held views about Christ's assumption of a human soul and spirit which were by no means universally acceptable, because in Origen's view the spirit of Christ was not identifiable with the Divine Word.
382 Ch.VI, pp.216-218, where this matter is discussed further.
383 *Comm. in Matt.* XVI.8 (GCS 10.499.21-501.4). Cf. Crouzel's discussion of this passage in *L'Image* . . ., p.135,n.4, 2nd para. Cf. also Wintersig, op. cit., p.79, where he says that when Origen says that the Lord handed over His soul (Seele) to the evil spirits, the reference was only to the animal soul connected with the body (die animalische Leibseele), and not to the spirit (Geist).
384 *Frag. in Matt.* 562 (GCS 12.231).
385 *Comm. in Joh.* VI.35 (GCS 4.144.11-16).
386 Op. cit., pp.86-88.
387 I.4 (PG XIV.849C-850C).
388 VI.3 (GCS 7.33.25-34.2). Cf. also XVIII.4 (GCS 7.173.26-174.5.). See also Molland, op. cit., pp.110,111.
389 *De Princ.* II.6.3 (GCS 5.143.2-9).
390 IV.54-end (GCS 1.326.21-373.21).

391 In op. cit., p.185.
392 Cf. Refoulé, op. cit., p.253, where, after quoting various statements of Evagrius regarding Christ in the "Gnostic Centuries", he says that the first group of statements could be regarded as Nestorian and the second group as Monophysite, and goes on to say that the relevant texts in Origen display the same apparent contradiction.
393 In his article "Origen's defence of the resurrection of the body" (*M*,1973).
394 Op. cit., p.8.
395 It is rather significant that the title of Rius-Camps' article referred to in n.19 on p.9 of Armantage's article is "The final destiny of corporeal substance according to the P.A. of Origen, a formulation fluctuating between revealed truth and the philosophical assumptions of a system."
396 p.11.
397 p.15.
398 Ibid.
399 p.22.
400 H.R. Bramley's hymn beginning "The great God of heaven is come down to earth", (E.H., N.29).
401 Though this is suggested by eg. Archbp. Wm. Temple op. cit., pp. 140-143. Cf. C.J. Cadoux, op. cit., pp.87-89.
402 Op. cit.
403 Op. cit., p.524.
404 Thus Archbp. Temple seems to contradict himself when he says in op. cit. that "Christ's obedience, always perfect at each stage, yet deepened as He advanced from the Boy's subjection in His home at Nazareth to the point where He 'became obedient unto death' "(p.148). Temple seems to express the truth more clearly when a little later (p.150) he says that "there are two wills in the Incarnate in the sense that His human nature comes through struggle and effort to an ever deeper union with the Divine in completeness of self-sacrifice."
405 p.525.
406 In his article "Logos and Son in Origen, Arius and Athanasius" (*TU* 64 (1957), pp.282-287).
407 p.287 of op. cit.
408 In his article "Tradition, Exegesis and the Christological Controversies" (*CH* 34 (1965), pp.123-142).

[409] Op. cit., p.133.
[410] *De Princ.* II.11.4 (GCS 5.187.22-30).
[411] Cf. Heb.x.1.
[412] *De Princ.* IV.1.6 (GCS 5.302.7-10; 301.13-15). Cf. ibid.IV.2.2 (GCS 5.308.8-11); *Comm. in Matt.* XIV.18 (GCS 10.329.4-8); *Frag. in Rom.* XXXV.13 (*JTS* 14.10); ibid.XXXVI.32,33 (*JTS* 14.11); ibid.XXXVI.63-67 (*JTS* 14.12); Pitra A.S.III.210 (Ps. CIV.45). Cf. Rius-Camps, "Origenes y Marcion", p.5, where he says that "with the coming of Jesus, the Divine content of the O. T. prophecies and the spiritual meaning of the Law shone out." Cf. also Daniélou, op. cit., p.41; Crouzel, *La Conn.*, p.288; de Lubac, op. cit., p.553.
[413] Cf. Crouzel, *L'Image* . . ., p.139, n.72. See also Mme. Harl, op. cit., pp.140-145, and Crouzel, *La Conn.*, p.325, where he says that "the N.T. has brought us the truth, and put an end to the images of the ancient Scriptures. But the temporal Gospel is still an image of the truth . . .. It is the truth in the sense that it is substantially identical with the eternal Gospel, but it is still an image for us, in so far as we remain in the knowledge by way of a mirror which is linked to our earthly condition . . .. But in accordance with our spiritual progress, the N.T. ceases progressively to be an image of the truth and becomes increasingly the truth itself, even though it does not here below perfectly attain the state of direct apprehension." Cf. also op. cit., p.335; "Although Christ has taken from the O.T. the veil of the letter, our temporal Gospel is itself also enclosed in the letter." Cf. also p.354; "The knowledge conveyed by the temporal Gospel is of the same nature as that conveyed by the O.T., ie. progressive, partial, always capable of being exceeded."
Cf. also Daniélou, op. cit., pp.54-56, and Rius-Camps, "Comunicabilidad", *OCP* 38,1972,p.446, where he says: "Origen seems to help Christians overcome any kind of literalism in the interpretation of Scripture, and every kind of anthropomorphism in their conception of God, of blessedness, and of the way which leads to it."
[414] *IX*.4 (GCS 7.59.9,10). Cf. *Contra Cels.* II.2 (GCS 1.129.2-7), II. 6 (GCS 1.132.24-31), and V.60 (GCS 2.63.20-29); *Comm. in Joh.* I.6 (GCS 4.11.8-14), X.28 (GCS 4.201.22-28), and XIII.47 (GCS 4.273.12-17); *Hom. in Gen.* VI.1 (GCS 6.66.9-18); *Hom. in Lev.* I.1 (GCS 6.280.5-18); *Comm. in Matt.* XII.5 (GCS 10.76.14-

18); *Frag. in Matt.* 99.2-6 (GCS 12.56); *Convs. with Heracl.* 17.2-6 (Scherer's ed.,p.90); Pitra A.S.II.448 (Ps.II.3) and 474 (Ps. XVIII.8); A.S.III.117 (Ps.LXXVII.19-25) and 290,291 (Ps. CXVIII.102); *Comm. in Ps.* L (Philocal. JAR 35.15,16).
Cf. Crouzel, *La Conn.*, p.291; Verbeke, op. cit., pp.460-463; Gögler, op. cit., pp.7 sqq. (section entitled "Christus, das Mysterium der Schrift").
See also de Lubac, op. cit., where it is made clear that not only must the N.T. be interpreted in the light of the O.T., but the O.T. itself is only fully intelligible in the light of the New. Thus on p.558 he says: "By the soul which opens itself to the Gospel and which clings to Christ, all Scripture is perceived in a new light. All Scripture, through Christ, is transfigured." On p.548 he says: "If Christianity is a body of doctrine, the interpretation of the O.T. is not a garment thrown over it later on; it is part of the body itself, of which the unifying spirit is the present reality of the Saviour." In note 1 on the same page he says: "Every thought, in order to come into existence, needs a mode of expression which links it, by analogy or contrast, to a thought previously expressed. . ... This is supremely true when it is the concern of the human spirit to express in a human fashion, so as to obtain a reflective knowledge of it and somehow to 'grasp' it, the Object of Divine revelation . . .. There will as a consequence be so much more room for symbolism." On p.570 he says: "All the O.T. Scriptures make plain the mystery of the Cross, but they are themselves in turn made plain by it alone." On p.563 he says that "the religious understanding of Scripture (ie. the understanding possessed by the Scriptural writers and the persons whom they describe) and the spiritual understanding come together in many respects . . .. They have need of one another, the one so as not to lose its foundation, the other so as not to remain too limited . . .. The spiritual interpretation must not interfere in a rash or premature manner with the work of the historian."

[415] *De Princ.* IV.2.4 (GCS 5.312.15-313.1). Cf. *Comm. in Joh.* II.17 (GCS 4.74.7-11) and XIII.48 (274.12-275.12); *Comm. in Matt.* XV.12 (GCS 10.380.23-381.2); *Frag. in Luc.* 171.4-8 (GCS 9. 298) and Crouzel's note on this passage in Sources Chrétiennes 87, pp.522,523; *Convs. with Heracl.* 27.14-28.16 (Scherer pp. 108,110); Cadiou, *Frag. in Ps.* CXVIII.44a,p.108.

[416] *Frag. in Joh.* X (GCS 4.492.27-493.1).

[417] XIII.2 (GCS 6.469.21-470.2).
[418] *Sel. in Ps.* CXVIII.117 (PG XII.1613B).
[419] *Comm. in Matt.* XII.4 (GCS 10.74.8-19).
[420] *De Princ.* IV.3.2 (GCS 5.343.12-16).
[421] *Comm. in Matt.* XI.12 (GCS 10.54.14-24).
[422] *Hom. in Gen.* XIV.1 (GCS 6.122.20-22). Cf. *Frag. in Luc.* 204.9-22 (GCS 9.315,316). See Koch's comments on this subject in op. cit., p.60.

CONTENTS

CHAPTER VI.

THE HUMAN AND DIVINE ASPECTS OF CHRIST'S PERSONALITY

The Divine Word has always enjoyed God's favour; the human Jesus earns it   199

The Son of God took human nature so that the sovereignty of God might be fully accepted   203

The two types of disciple correspond to the two aspects of the nature of Christ: —
1. Those apprehending invisible realities
2. Those who do not progress further than sensible realities   205

It was the human nature of Christ which needed cleansing after the victory won by the Crucifixion   216

NOTES on Chapter VI   221

CHAPTER VI

THE HUMAN AND DIVINE ASPECTS OF
CHRIST'S PERSONALITY

It is by distinguishing between the human and the Divine aspects of the personality of Jesus Christ that Origen can assert on the one hand that Jesus earns God's favour, and on the other that He has always enjoyed it. It is to Jesus Christ as Man that Origen applies the psalmist's words "Thou hast loved righteousness and hated iniquity; wherefore God, even thy God, hath anointed Thee with the oil of gladness", because as Man He is elevated to a position of kingship on account of His obedience to the Father's will. On the other hand, in so far as He is Divine He has always been in the position of King. Elsewhere, Origen also says that the human Jesus became entitled to the name of "Christ" (the Anointed One) because of His goodness, with the result that the psalmist's words could be applied to Him.[1] Origen in fact speaks of two images: the Son Who is the Image of God, and the being who is said (according to Origen's interpretation!) to be the Image of the Son in Romans viii.29, ie. the human soul which the Son assumed and which became the Image of the Son through its virtue ($\delta\iota\grave{\alpha}$ $\tau\grave{\eta}\nu$ $\dot{\alpha}\rho\epsilon\tau\acute{\eta}\nu$).[2] Origen likewise suggests in *Contra Cels.* that although those who take as their model the life of Christ and teach His doctrine have been anointed with the oil of gladness by God the Father, it was Christ Himself Who was anointed first of all, because He loved righteousness and hated iniquity more than His companions, who simply share in His anointing as far as they are able.[3] In another passage Origen raises the question whether the word $\alpha\dot{\upsilon}\tau o\sigma o\phi\acute{\iota}\alpha$ (wisdom in itself) should be attributed to the so-called "Son of Man" as well as to the Son of God, in so far as the former has been made one with wisdom ($\dot{\epsilon}\kappa$ $\tau o\hat{\upsilon}$ $\dot{\eta}\nu\hat{\omega}\sigma\theta\alpha\iota$ $\tau\hat{\eta}$ $\sigma o\phi\acute{\iota}\alpha$).[4]

It is passages such as these which lead one to wonder whether the observation made by Refoulé[5] about Origen's disciple Evagrius does not also apply to Origen himself, when he says: "Does it (ie. Origen's Christology) not amount to affirming two Christs, and does it not relapse into a form of Adoptionism?" Pennenberg also pertinently observes that "above all, . . . the concept of the immutability of God necessarily leads to the consequence that the transition to every innovation in the relationship between God and man has to be sought as much as possible on the side of man. Thus the idea of God becoming man has to recede into the background behind that of God assuming human nature. In addition to this, the concept of God's immutability pressed in the direction of conceiving this 'assumption' of a man by God in terms of the scheme of assimilation to God, and thus finding this realised in the ethical striving of Jesus, a tendency which is traceable from Origen and Paul of Samosata right on into the later Antiochene Christology."

On the other hand, Origen elsewhere represents the Son as anointed by the Father on His entry into the world, in so far as the Holy Spirit compounded all the elements of His human nature into a single person – the Holy Spirit being regarded as the oil of gladness.[7] In another passage, Origen represents Christ as the Bridegroom sent by God the Father and coming already anointed to His Bride the Church. To Him it is said "Thou hast loved righteousness and hated iniquity " etc.[8] Elsewhere, it is the pre-existent soul of Christ which is said to have been "anointed with the oil of gladness above its fellows", because it was united in an unspotted fellowship with the Word of God and therefore alone among all souls became incapable of sin.[9] We thus gain an insight into the tension in Origen's thought between his preconceived notion that the pre-existent soul of Christ was already perfect and the necessity of admitting spiritual growth and development in the incarnate Christ.

In one passage, Origen shows that he is himself aware of the difficulty. In discussing Psalm xlv, in which he considers the person addressed to be Christ, he asks how the Firstborn of all creation can be anointed as King through loving righteousness, seeing that He is righteousness in itself. Surely, says Origen, His kingship is bound up with His nature, and not something conferred upon Him later. The solution to the problem, says Origen, is to be found in calling to mind "the man who is Christ", ie. the soul which was on occasion distressed and agitated because it was human. This soul is the "king's son" referred to in Ps.lxxii, to whom the psalmist asks God to give His righteousness, whereas the "king" to whom the psalmist asks God to give the power of judgement is the Firstborn of all creation, Who is entitled to it on account of His unique status.[10] The soul is also spoken of in this passage as "the man whom He assumed, who was moulded and fashioned according to righteousness by the Divine Nature" of the Son of God. But Origen none the less shelves the problem of reconciling the ideas of changelessness and change by saying that since the psalmist afterwards refers to one person instead of two, this shows that both beings are brought together in one Divine Word. [11]

There is a passage in *Comm. in Rom.* [12] where the man Christ Jesus is explicitly stated not to have been made equal to the Son of God till after the Resurrection. The passage in Hebrews [13] where the human Jesus is said to have been made "perfect through sufferings" is quoted in support of this view. Origen says that as the result of the Resurrection, to which the sufferings were a necessary preliminary, "all that is in Christ is now the Son of God" *(omne quod in Christo, iam nunc Filius Dei est)*, seeing that the Word and the flesh are indissolubly united, so that all that belongs to the flesh is ascribed to the Word, and what belongs to the Word is referred to the flesh.[14] We can only comment that in suggesting that the human nature of Christ was not perfectly united with His Divinity until the Passion and Resurrection, Origen is not consistent with his general outlook, which is that the human soul of Christ, which became incarnate, was indissolubly united to the Word of God, in its pre-existent state. In the same vein, Origen states in *De Orat.*[15] that it was after the Resurrection that the "man" whom Christ assumed said: "All power is given to me in heaven and on earth", thus indicating that His human nature shared the power which appertained to His Divine nature.[16]

What has been quoted so far would appear to lend support to Lieske's assertion that the union created between the Man Jesus and the Divine Word foreshadows the union which is brought about between the individual disciple and his Lord. To quote his own words: "Just as the human nature of Christ attained to personal unity with the Divine Word inasmuch as it ascended to Him in the vision and love of God and formed with Him the unique God-Man, even so each being who has attained to the vision of God is likewise made Divine and is united to the Word of God."[17] And again: "Origen understands the union of the soul of Christ with the Word of God, in spite of the uniqueness of its position, simply as the highest achievement of the real union with the Divine Word in the vision of God which is accomplished in those who are perfect." [18]

On the other hand, there is a most baffling passage in *Comm. in Joh.* [19] in which Origen appears so anxious to safeguard the unity of the two elements – Divine and human – in Jesus Christ that he appears to want to have it both ways so far as the changelessness of the

Divine Word is concerned. He first stresses that it is the Son of Man Who was exalted, because He became obedient unto death, whereas the Divine Word did not admit of being exalted. The exaltation (ὑπερύψωσις) consisted in His being no longer other than the Word of God, but rather identical with Him.[20] Origen then goes on to say: "He Who did not consider equality with God as something worth holding on to (ref. to Philipp.ii.6) was highly exalted, but the Word remained in His unique position of glory or else was restored to it, when the Divine Word, Who was also human, returned once more to God."[21] With reference to this passage, Eichinger points out [22]the uncertainty shown by Origen as to whether the Divine Word Himself was exalted at the Resurrection. He also points out that the question is involved as to whether, and how, the Divine Word participated in the descent to the human level which is clearly affirmed of the soul of Jesus. Gögler observes,[23] after quoting this passage, that "through the exaltation (of the human element in Jesus) the Divine and the human became one πνεῦμα. The δόξα (of the Divine nature) has grasped and magnified the τὸ κατὰ σάρκα . . .. The *communicatio idiomatum* is now complete." But surely it was complete before the Incarnation, according to Origen's theory, because what became incarnate was the pre-existent soul of Christ.

The same criticism can be made of Kelber's statement [24] apropos of the passage which has been quoted, that according to Origen "the original Transubstantiation which was brought about by the indwelling of Christ (should it not be rather "the Word of God"?) in the body and blood of Jesus of Nazareth and which was complete on Golgotha, was transformed into full union with the Divine Word by the exaltation of the manhood of Jesus." It is true that Origen appears to say in the passage quoted that the human Jesus became progressively more closely united to the Divine Word during His earthly life: but though this statement seems reasonable, and in fact necessary to safeguard the genuine humanity of Jesus, it does not accord with Origen's general outlook.

The dilemma is very well presented in another passage from Origen,[25] where it is said that Christ is firstborn (ie. presumably from the dead) according to the flesh (πρωτότοκος κατὰ τὴν σάρκα), and Only-begotten according to His Divinity (μονογενής κατὰ τὴν θεότητα), but is none the less one Son of God with both attributes. He is told to sit at God's right hand, not as the Only-begotten, because in this respect He is co-eternal with the Father, but rather as the firstborn from the dead and heir (κληρονόμος) to the privilege in store for Him. In other words the seat at God's right hand is assigned to Him διὰ τὴν σάρκα, ie. because He was human and thus did not have this privilege beforehand, and not διὰ τὴν θεότητα, because as Divine He possessed it by nature. Once more, if the pre-existent soul which became incarnate was already linked with the Word of God in the closest possible fellowship, how could that soul fail to enjoy already the privileges resulting from that fellowship?

Elsewhere,[26] Origen states that the Son of God took human nature upon Himself precisely in order that the sovereignty of God might be accepted as fully on earth as it is in heaven. In so far as He is Divine, the Word of God had supreme power over all things in heaven and on earth before His Incarnation: but that power was not acknowledged by all mankind, and therefore the Word took human nature upon Himself, and, to quote Origen's exact words, "received, as man, power which He had not had before."[27] Apparently Origen understands the words in Psalm 2 where the Lord invites His Son to ask Him to give Him the nations for His inheritance, etc., as referring to the power of judgement granted to the Son of God in His human aspect.[28]

The same idea is expressed even more vividly in a passage[29] which states that Christ as Man was appointed Heir of all things (ref. to Hebrews i.2) so that He might rescue, as His own inheritance, those scattered impiously on earth by evil powers. "See then", says Origen, "how He ascends even in the flesh to the riches appertaining to Him by nature" (κατὰ φύσιν). But how, says Origen, if human beings belonged to the Divine Word as well as to the Father, could He be bidden in the second Psalm to ask for them as His inheritance? The answer is that mankind has revolted from the allegiance it owed to God, and so the Father sent the Son into the world so that He might be welcomed as a man, even though His real nature remained all the while unchanged. Hence it was only as Man, says Origen, that He is said to have received all things as heir. But Origen might have gone on to say that only through taking human nature could the Son of God obtain the allegiance of human beings. In the same way, Origen says that although in the angel's message to the Virgin Mary it is said that only in the future will He be great and be called the Son of the Most High and receive the kingdom of David, none the less in so far as He is Divine, His Kingship is eternal.[30]

It is to be observed that in one passage [31] Origen interprets the words of the psalm "Worship before the footstool of His feet, because it is holy" as meaning that the flesh (ie. the human nature) of Christ is entitled to the honour due to His Divine Nature.[32] In *De Orat.* [33] it is the Church which is taken to be indicated by "the footstool of His feet" as contrasted with Christ Himself, Who is indicated by the word "heaven", regarded as God's throne (Isaiah lxvi.1; cf. Matt.v.34,35); but the Church can be regarded as those human beings who share the sonship possessed by the human Jesus. In *Frag. in Eph.*[34] it is suggested that the Church is called by St. Paul "Christ's body" because it is animated ($\psi υχούμενον$) by His Divinity. If this is so, His human element (τὸ ἀνθρωπικώτερον αὐτοῦ) will, says Origen, itself be part of the whole body, because it is animated by the same Divine power which animates the Church. Once more, the suggestion seems to be that the Word of God could only obtain the allegiance of other human beings after He had taken possession of the human Jesus and employed him for carrying out the work of God.[35]

This indeed seems to be the way in which the apparent contradiction between the passages already cited and those about to be cited can be reconciled, in so far as the second group appears to suggest that the Divine Word did not have authority over all things, even so far as His Divine Nature was concerned, until His earthly work was done. Thus in one passage [36] it is stated that Christ originally had authority (ἐξουσίαν) in heaven, and also an authority on earth confined to the people of Israel. It was only after He had completed His "rational contests" (ἄθλους) on behalf of human beings that He obtained authority throughout the earth, so that He might reconcile all things to God through His blood shed on the Cross. The same idea is presented even more vividly in the statement [37] that by His Crucifixion, Christ triumphed over the hostile unseen powers and won control of all things.[38]

Another passage [39] makes it clear that what Origen really means by saying that the Word of God did not have authority over all things before the Incarnation and Resurrection is that He did not have it *de facto*, but only *de jure*. Origen states that the Lord Who by His own power hung the world on nothing (cf. Job xxvi.7) hung fastened with nails to the Cross and stretched His hands on the Tree so that he might thus bring to nothing the hostile powers and draw the ends of the world to Himself (cf. John xii.32). It will be seen, however, in the next section that Origen is only repeating here the traditional doctrine of the Church about the Crucifixion; in his own distinctive thinking he does not accord it nearly so important a place.

In fact, this is made clear in the passage where Origen says that corresponding to the two aspects of the nature of the Son of God are the two types of disciple. Those who apprehend invisible realities are governed by the Divine element in the Son of God, whereas those who do not progress further than sensible realities are governed by that element of His nature which the Psalmist speaks of as "anointed."[40]

Referring to the parable of the treasure hidden in a field,[41] Origen likens the field to Christ, and the treasure concealed in it to the invisible things which Christ contains, the "treasures of wisdom and knowledge" referred to by St. Paul. A little further on, Origen says quite plainly that the Person of Christ is composed "both of what is open and of what is hidden."[42] In another passage,[43] Origen makes a subtle distinction between the gospel which St. Paul preached to all and sundry and "the revelation of the mystery which has been kept hidden throughout all ages."[44] The revelation is only intended for those few chosen ones who are capable of receiving the wisdom and knowledge of God. Elsewhere,[45] Origen states that this wisdom can only be unfolded to those who are versed in discriminating between good and evil. Origen goes so far as to say that even after Christ's Incarnation He has not really come to those who are immature and are thus not really prepared for His Coming. Only the forerunners of Christ come to them, ie. discourses adapted to childish minds; whereas further preparation is necessary for those who are going to receive His Divinity into themselves.[46] Origen makes the same observation in a different form[47] when he distinguishes between the things we need and "those things which form part of riches and luxury." So far as religious matters are concerned, the things which we need are those which admit us to the life which Christ supplies; the things superior to what we need are the spiritual riches which are the rewards of acquiring wisdom. If it is said that there is a contradiction between this passage and the previous one, inasmuch as it is suggested in this passage that even elementary instruction can introduce us to Christ, the answer seems to be that there is a distinction between knowing Christ "after the flesh"[48] and knowing Him as the invisible Word of God. Even if we know Him in the former manner only, we can still derive benefit from that knowledge in so far as our conduct is improved:[49] but only if we know Him in His Divinity can we obtain the full benefit which He desires to bestow.

The question now arises: what place does the Crucifixion have in the thought of Origen? Is it simply one of the outward events in the life of Christ which needs to be transcended in order to arrive at the deeper truths which Christ came to reveal, or does it in itself contain this deeper truth? Does it veil the truth, or is it a vehicle of the truth? The thought of Origen is ambiguous on this point, although it could be plausibly said that in the main he comes down on the side of the former position. Let us substantiate this suggestion by reference to various passages.

In *Contra Cels.*[50] Origen suggests that it is better to accept doctrines after rational thought than with bare faith, and that it was only as a makeshift device that the Divine Word was prepared for belief to rest on bare faith. He adduces I Cor.i.21 in support of this view, since he interprets it as meaning that God intended that He should have become known through the wisdom which He supplies, but since this was not possible for many people, He decided to bring salvation to believers through what St. Paul calls "the foolishness of preaching", this being the preaching of Christ as crucified, as is made clear (according to Origen) in the following verses. It seems obvious that St. Paul is being misinterpreted by Origen so as to be made to conform to his point of view, because St. Paul expressly asserts that the preaching of the Cross is not foolishness in itself, but is only regarded as such by those who do not accept the Gospel (I Cor.i.18,23).

Origen makes the same point by the employment of other metaphors. With reference to the saying quoted in St. John's Gospel, "When you have exalted the Son of Man, then you will know that I am He",[51] Origen observes that no one exalts Him while he is as yet being fed spiritually with milk rather than solid food; and so St. Paul says to such a person, "I thought it right not to know anything among you except Jesus Christ, and Him crucified" (I Cor.ii.2). To such a person the minister of the Gospel comes "in weakness and fear and much trembling", as St. Paul goes on to say. Here again, Origen is misinterpreting St. Paul, because St. Paul is not contrasting elementary Christian instruction with more advanced instruction, but rather contrasting Divine wisdom with human wisdom, as is made clear in verse 5.[52]

Again, Origen takes as an analogy the Jewish practice whereby the priest wore different garments for the offering of sacrifice and for going forth to the people. Likewise, says Origen, when St. Paul was in the company of the mature, he wore the garment of perfection and said: "We speak wisdom among the mature . . . the wisdom of God hidden in a mystery" (I Cor.ii.6,7). But when he came out to the people he changed his robe and said the words already quoted: "I thought it right to know nothing among you, except Jesus Christ, and Him crucified." Just as Jesus Christ spoke in parables to the multitudes and afterwards explained those parables to His disciples, so the Christian minister gives inferior teaching to those incapable of receiving higher teaching.[53] We can thus scarcely disagree with Eichinger when he says: "Even is a transfigured mode of bodily appearance is ascribed to the transfigured Word of God, the Word Who became flesh and was crucified remains for Origen always foolishness, and is not, as such, the Wisdom of God."[54] Crouzel also justly observes,[55] with reference to Origen's exegesis of I Cor.ii.6-8, that it "distorts the Apostle's intention: in preaching Jesus as crucified, Paul does not intend to adapt himself to the weakness of his readers, but rather to cause offence to human wisdom."

Muira-Stange takes the same view when she says [56] that "both to Celsus and to Origen redemption (Erlösung) is a bare concept ... Sin, the human need of grace, one's own helplessness, the power of God's grace, are ideas which do not affect the central beliefs of either of them ..... The operations of the Redeemer are limited by Origen to the second level, ie. those called 'sinners'; to the sin-free Gnostics is sent instead the Word as Teacher of Divine mysteries."[57]

On the other hand, as has already been observed, Origen has to reckon with the fact that the Crucifixion was regarded by the Church of his own time, as by the Church all down the ages, as of greater importance than any other event in the earthly life of Christ; and this would scarcely be the case if truths did not reside in this event which could not be discovered in any other way. Hence in one passage in *Comm. in Matt.*[58] Origen remarks that is is necessary in preaching Jesus Christ to preach Him as crucified. Any other form of preaching would be inadequate. Even if none of the other marvellous events of His life were mentioned, the omission would not be so important as that of the Crucifixion. In another passage,[59] Origen points out that our Lord commanded His disciples not to announce that He was the Christ and the Son of the living God even after Peter had acknowledged Him as such, but desired rather that this announcement be deferred till after the Crucifixion. The implication was that the meaning of the title "Christ" could only be understood as the result of the more advanced teaching which could only be based on the Crucifixion. The proclamation of the teaching and actions of Jesus was a more elementary form of teaching.

In two other passages the Greek verb δεικνύειν is used as a means of showing that the event of the Crucifixion contains more than meets the eye, in fact that its significance is only apprehensible as the result of the use of reason. It is one thing to see with one's bodily eyes the sufferings which Christ endured at the hands of the Jewish leaders; it is quite another to see the full significance of those sufferings. And so when it is said that Jesus began to show (δεικνύειν) to His disciples that He must go to Jerusalem and suffer and die (Matt.xvi.21), what is meant is that He explained why this was necessary.[60] In another passage, Origen says that a person can obtain perfect knowledge of the mysteries of Christ's sufferings and death in the sense of seeing with his mind's eye what is shown (τὰ δεικνύμενα) as the result of rational demonstration (ἀπὸ λογικῆς δείξεως).[61]

Two other passages underline the fact that for Origen, in some moods at any rate, the Passion has a hidden meaning, and is not just one event among others which merely belong to the outward appearance of Jesus Christ. In the first it is stated[62] that He offered Himself as Victim not only on behalf of earthly beings, but also on behalf of celestial beings. For men He poured out the bodily substance of His blood; but for the priests who minister in heaven, if there be any such, He sacrificed the living energy of His body *(vitalem corporis sui virtutem)* as a kind of spiritual sacrifice. Perhaps this means that some human beings (those more advanced in spiritual insight) can appropriate the benefits of His Passion more fully than others can. Elsewhere, the giving of the shewbread to David is said to be a prophecy of the fact that the priestly and royal dignities were going to be united in the Person of Him Who on the human side was descended from David.[63]

Molland observes,[64] with reference to the former passage, that "knowing Origen's strongly spiritualising tendency, and his distinction between the two Gospels (ie. the temporal and the eternal), we should expect him to consider Christ's Passion on earth in the form of a servant as belonging only to the bodily and temporal Gospel .... But we are surprised to see that Origen finds a place for the Passion of Christ in the eternal Gospel. This fact proves how central is the idea of Christ's sacrifice in Origen's conception of the Gospel. He has not been led by his philosophical scheme — bodily-spiritual, temporal-eternal, imperfection-perfection — to despise or neglect the Passion of Christ."

It has to be admitted, however, that Cadiou[65] does indicate an oscillation in Origen's thought between regarding the preaching of the

Cross as merely *introducing* the hearer to a higher form of preaching, and regarding the preaching of the Cross itself as taking different forms, a more elementary and a more advanced. To quote Cadiou's own words expressing the second point of view, "if there is a dissimilarity in the way in which (according to Origen) human souls meditate on the Passion, it springs from different degrees of faith." Perhaps this oscillation corresponds to the uncertainty shown by Origen in different passages as to whether the Divine Word Himself really underwent the sufferings of the Cross.

Mme. Harl, [66] after quoting the passage referred to in note 58, points out that in suggesting that the preaching of the crucified Christ is a higher form of preaching than that of His words and actions, Origen is contradicting what he says elsewhere about the preaching of the crucified Christ. She resolves the contradiction by suggesting that for Origen, to be acquainted with the crucified Christ is (at any rate in this passage) to be acquainted, not with Jesus the Man, but with the Son of God in the triumph of His Resurrection. Völker[67] points out that we must take Origen's insistence on the importance of the Cross more seriously than this; but at the same time[68] he tends to place the two outlooks — the one stressing and the other minimising the importance of the Cross — side by side, whereas surely Origen tends mainly to think of the perception of the crucified Christ as at most but one stage in the ascent to the perception of the glorified Christ, the Christ Who is the form of God.[69] Völker also points out that according to de Faye, the Cross plays no distinctive role in the thought of Origen.[70] Cadiou [71] seems to read too much into the passage referred to, inasmuch as he suggests that it proves that according to Origen the preaching of the Cross is the highest form of the preaching of Christ.

We can in fact scarcely fail to agree with Lebreton [72] that "the preaching of Christ crucified will never be for Origen other than an elementary form of Christianity, and the foolishness of the Cross is simply a means of help offered by God to those who are incapable of arriving at real wisdom." Schendel likewise says [73] that "Origen assigns less significance to the historical Jesus than to the eternal Word of God", and quotes Kettler as saying that "for Origen, the humanity of Jesus is something which needs to be overcome; it is not the foundation of the Christian hope." He also quotes Kettler[74] as saying that "the Christology of Origen is (in appearance) two-natured, but in its main concern Monophysite." Never a truer word spoken![75]

De Faye likewise observes [76] that "in Origen's doctrine of redemption there is no well-defined place for Christ's death on the Cross . . . . Would Origen have thought of inserting the Cross into his system if he had not had to take account of certain Biblical texts? . . .. One can consider it as a sort of appendix to his general doctrine of salvation." (It is true, however, that de Faye is thinking mainly of the expiatory theory of the Cross, according to which Christ bore the penalty which should strictly have been inflicted on those who had sinned.) The same verdict is passed by Wintersig, [77] who says [78] that "the saving death is in Origen's way of thinking so exclusively connected with Christ's humanity, that this death only stands in the loosest connection with the remaining saving work of the Word, and thus cannot be the distinguishing feature of an endless redemption." Nygren likewise says [79] that "according to Origen, neither the Incarnation nor the death on the Cross has any real meaning for the perfect Christian, the Christian Gnostic."

Kelber points out [80] that Origen expounds a mystique of the Cross, in so far as the earthly events connected therewith such as Crucifixion, death, burial and Resurrection are events in which Christ's followers are intended mystically to share.[81] But de Faye's criticism still holds good, in so far as even the mystical interpretation of the Crucifixion cannot really be harmonised with Origen's general outlook, which sees the believer as perfected by increasing enlightenment, not by increasing self-renunciation.[82]

Primmer refers [83] to the statement of de Faye quoted above, and says of him and Koch that they misunderstand the function of bodily realities as symbols of spiritual realities. The earthly entity still retains its own value in spite of pointing towards a higher entity. The various aspects ($\dot{\epsilon}\pi\dot{\iota}\nu o\iota a\iota$) of Christ which are apprehended by the more advanced Christian could not be understood apart from Christ's Incarnation and Crucifixion. But it may be replied that Origen does not explain *how* the events of the earthly life of Christ can guide us to this higher knowledge.[84] This remains true, even though, as Primmer points out, Origen does at times appear to recognise the significance which the Christian religion attaches to the Incarnation and the Passion as the gateway to the higher knowledge of God.[85]

There are several passages in which Origen underlines his contention that there are differing degrees of knowledge among Christians. In one passage [86] he states that even those who know Jesus to be the Christ do not know Him to an equal extent, because (for instance) Timothy was less enlightened in his knowledge of Jesus as the Christ then was St. Paul. In another remarkable passage,[87] Origen states that those who do not possess knowledge can wane in faith itself; this is the implication of St. Paul's statement "unless you have believed without cause" (I Cor.xv.2). There are in fact those who do not really seek an understanding of the truth in which they believe. It was because the Apostles recognised the difference between faith which is simply accepted on trust and faith illuminated by knowledge that they said to their Master, "Increase our faith" (Luke xvii.5); they wished to pass on from the former to the latter kind of faith. Origen also points out [88] that to believe ($\pi\iota\sigma\tau\epsilon\acute{\upsilon}\epsilon\sigma\theta\alpha\iota$) that Jesus is the Christ is inferior to knowing what is believed, as is clear from St. John's report of Jesus as saying to those Jews who believed in Him that "If you abide in my word, . . . you shall know the truth, and the truth shall make you free" (John viii.31,32).

These statements obviously tie up with the difference which Origen asserts to exist between those who only apprehend the outward semblance of the Passion and those who apprehend its inward meaning; but it may be questioned how far the distinction is as absolute as he asserts. It is very difficult to remain on the same spiritual level all the time.

It is now time to refer to certain passages which imply that there are some who have advanced no further than to an understanding of the outward events of Christ's earthly life. With reference to Cant.v. 4-6, Origen says[89] that when the bride lifts the bar of the door so as to open her soul to the Divine Word, He then simply shows His hand and some of His activities and then passes on, partly because the bride is not yet capable of a fuller vision, and partly so as to increase the extent of her love for Him. Again,[90] with reference to the Feeding of the Five Thousand, Origen says that the five loaves stand for the things perceived by the five senses, and the five thousand who ate of the loaves before the filling of the twelve baskets only attend to the things perceived by the senses. Somewhat curiously, however, he adds that the five thousand were men, and not women and children (these were additional), and concludes from this that the things perceived by the senses provide different forms of nourishment, some kinds being suitable for those who are babes in Christ,[91] and other kinds being suitable for those who have made an end of childish things. The implication seems to be that one can ascend from sensible things to spiritual things; whereas in another passage[92] reference is made to the fragments that remained, gathered up in twelve baskets, which are said to symbolise the nourishment which the ordinary disciples of Christ cannot receive, but only the more advanced disciples of Jesus. Are we thus introduced to an uncertainty in the mind of Origen as to whether material things are the gateway to spiritual realities, or whether the latter can be apprehended apart from the former? In other words, is the preaching of the Cross a necessary introduction to the deepest truths of Christianity, or is it simply a stage of discipleship which must be left behind? Is it by way of the Cross, or by superseding the Cross, that the essence of the Christian religion is apprehended?

It is on the whole true to say that Origen tends to regard the contemplation of the outward events of the life of Christ as merely an introduction to the apprehension of the deeper truths of the Faith, in other words as something which can be left behind. Thus he says that the crowds could not go to the other side of the lake (Matt.xiv.22) because only the disciples of Jesus can "go to the other side" in the sense of surpassing seen and temporal things and attaining to unseen and eternal things.[93] Elsewhere, he refers to those people who admire Jesus Christ when they become acquainted with His life story, but no longer believe when more profound doctrine than they are capable of receiving is unfolded to them. He is speaking with reference to the statement of our Lord to some of the Jews "Because I say the truth, you do not believe me" (John viii.45). They were people who believed in Him because of His miracles, but did not believe in His more profound teachings, as is clear from the words "Because I say the truth" when those words are taken in conjunction with the words "You shall know the truth" (John viii.32).[94] We can scarcely deny, when considering this passage and similar ones, that Mme. Harl is right when she suggests[95] that for Origen "there is a veil on the Gospel for those who are not converted, inasmuch as they find in the Gospel the body of the Divine Word but not His spirit, Jesus Christ crucified but not the Wisdom of God, the fleshly meaning but not the spiritual meaning." We must also agree with Lomiento when he points out the contrast[96] drawn by Origen between the *many* who rest content with the teaching of Christ in the sphere of conduct, and the *few* who attain to the contemplation of the Word of God.[97]   On the other hand Hanson seems to go too far in suggesting[98] that because Origen regards the movements and gestures of the historic Jesus as symbols of theological truths or of the spiritual state of the believer, therefore Origen is not interested in history as event, in history as the field of God's self-revalation *par excellence*. I think it is true to say that Origen regards the

Incarnation and the earthly life of Jesus as necessary for enabling the ordinary human being to apprehend the truths and attain to the spiritual states of which the events of that life were symbols. It is as though a man were to come into a room dressed in an ordinary suit of clothes and then disappear into another room and don a special uniform and then admit the viewers into the other room. Even so, according to Origen, God reveals Himself, however inadequately, through the senses before admitting human beings to a fuller knowledge of Himself. But the question then arises, if the two revelations are not bound up with each other, why should the earlier one need to be given before the later?

Fitzgerald in his thesis [99] highlights the problem when he contrasts the "spiritual coming" of Christ in His pre-incarnate state to the patriarchs and prophets with the visible coming in the days of His flesh, in so far as the latter coming was not a privilege confined to the perfect, but a grace offered to all men without distinction. He explains the meaning of this statement by describing [100] Christ's appearance in the flesh as "the condition and foundation of that universal economy whereby all men, even the 'simple' and 'common' souls who cannot rise above sensible realities to the invisible things of God, can be raised up to union with the Divinity of the Word, and through Him to the Father." Once more, how is it that the visible appearance of the Word can of itself provide the introduction to the apprehension of the invisible nature of God, if the visible appearance does not contain *within itself* the spiritual realities which are the object of Christian aspiration?

It is also true that there are various passages where Origen appears to suggest that Christians can be divided into two categories, according as they are or are not capable of receiving the deeper knowledge which Christ came to impart. He is very fond of employing the simile of "animals" to denote those less gifted intellectually, and "men" to indicate those better equipped to apprehend Divine mysteries. This is how he interprets the words of the Psalm "Thou, Lord, shalt save both men and beasts." Those who desire the Word of God and rational teaching are called "men"; those who live without these aspirations and are yet among the faithful are called animals, and yet clean animals. Moses and Elijah were men of God; but just as Ezekiel refers to the Lord's sheep, so does the Saviour Himself when he says in the Gospel "My sheep hear my voice" (John x.27), by which He meant that whereas men hear His word, sheep hear His voice only.[101] Origen likewise says elsewhere [102] with reference to John iv.12 that Jacob's well can be interpreted as the Law of Moses, and his flocks and herds can be understood to be those who possess a stable and gentle disposition without reason (ἄνευ λόγου).

Origen sometimes suggests that it was those gifted with greater spiritual perception whom Christ mainly came to save, because they are more akin to Him, and that He only chose those whom St. Paul terms "the foolish things of the world" (whom Origen regards as meaning the less perceptive) so as to put to shame "the wise" (whom Origen regards as meaning the more perceptive), in so far as He handed on to the less perceptive what St. Paul calls "the foolishness of the preaching", which was all they were capable of receiving, seeing that the more perceptive were opposed to the truth.[103] (It is scarcely necessary to point out that Origen is here misinterpreting St. Paul, who is not contrasting one type of disciple with another, but rather those who have accepted the wisdom which the world counts folly with those who are content with this world's wisdom).[104] The same suggestion is made elsewhere, when Origen interprets those who were originally invited to the wedding-feast recorded in Matt.xxii.1-14 as those well-endowed with understanding and perception; if these people refuse the invitation, the less well-endowed are invited in their place.[105]

Origen indeed likens the powers possessed by the Divine Word to food of which the quality is changed in accordance with the condition of those to whom it is administered, so that an infant requires food in the form of its mother's milk, and an invalid receives it in a specially prepared form, whereas a strong man receives it in its ordinary form. Origen ends by saying: "Surely the Word is not false to His own nature when He becomes food for each man in accordance with his capacity to receive Him." [106] There are various passages where Origen compares the elementary instruction which is given by the Word of God to milk, in so far as those who are children in spirit (παιδία τὴν ψυχήν) cannot assimilate anything stronger.[107] Elsewhere, those in whom the power of reason is as yet only partially developed and who therefore cannot receive more advanced instruction are compared to "dogs" who receive crumbs, and those in whom that power is more fully developed are compared to "children" who receive bread (ref. to Matt.xv.26,26).[108]

There is a rather curious passage in *Comm. in Joh.*[109] where Origen says that those who see what is incorporeal, the things called by St. Paul "invisible" and "not seen", inasmuch as in so doing they transcend sense-perceived things by the power of reason, are governed by the principal nature of the Only-begotten Son (ὑπό τῆς προηγουμένης φύσεως τοῦ μονογενοῦς), whereas those who advance no further than the knowledge of sense-perceived things and thereby glorify their Creator are also ruled by reason and so ruled by Christ. He does not specify the precise nature of that rule in the case of the second class of people; but he presumably means that they are guided by the example set by Christ in His earthly words and deeds without being aware of the spiritual realities of which those words and deeds are outward signs. (Origen nowhere makes it clear what these realities are; if they are moral qualities, they can surely also be apprehended by those on a lower intellectual level.) In the same way, in *Hom. in Exod.*[110] he says that there are certain people who can only receive the preaching of Jesus Christ as crucified (cf. I Cor.ii.2), whereas to others is revealed the wisdom of God hidden in a mystery (I Cor.ii.7) — the wisdom identifiable with Christ. The latter people are those who are invited to pass on from a fleshly understanding to a spiritual understanding of Christ, and to them it is said by St. Paul that "the Lord is Spirit" (II Cor.iii.17). (It seems worth quoting the comment of Hirschberg[111] that this attitude suggests theological relativism, ie. that Christian truth is not single, but manifold, in so far as it can only be grasped to the extent that the capacity of the hearer permits. To quote Hirschberg himself, "when this method (ie. the method of advancing from sensible objects to spiritual realities) is transferred from the philosophic to the theological sphere, and is thus made to suggest that instead of there being one Truth, there are many truths, it is out of harmony with the thinking of the Church. The method which is in itself right, springing as it does from the motive of adaptation (ie. to the needs of the undeveloped), must not be made into a form of teaching. But it is so made when Origen draws from it such deductions as that of lower forms of knowledge imparted by the Word of God in the form of the historical Jesus, or that of the inferiority of 'bare faith' (ψιλή πίστις"[112].)

Again, there is a passage in *Comm. in Joh.*[113] in which Origen refers to St. Paul's statement in Galatians that a man will reap what he sows, and also to Ps.cxxvi.5, where it is said that he who bears forth precious seed in tears will return brings his harvested sheaves in joy. Origen says that St. Paul's statement (Gal.vi.8), although it refers to different sorts of seed, does not tell us whence the seeds originated, whereas the Psalm appears to refer to the descent into this world of nobler souls (τῶν εὐγενεστέρων ψυχῶν), who enter this life with seeds which tend to salvation, but enter unwillingly and with weeping, but return in joy because the seeds with which they came have been well cultivated and so have come to maturity. A more arbitrary exposition of Scripture can scarcely be imagined — as though not all human beings have within them the seeds which can win salvation if tended, but only some! But at least this passage is in harmony with the thought contained in the passage from *Hom. in Exod.* already referred to on p.215, when it separates human beings into two categories. In the same vein, he refers to the heavenly Jerusalem as the city into which no one on earth ascends, in the sense that only those whose ψυχαί are naturally elevated and have a keen perception of intelligible things are citizens thereof. It is possible, however, for even the most well-endowed (τοὺς εὐφυεστάτους) to sin (presumably in the sense of losing sight of things unseen by the outward eye), and so lose their native nobility (τὴν εὐφυΐαν), and so become members not of Jerusalem but of cities alien to it, ie. remain unaware of the things which it is vital for their welfare that they should recollect, and become fast bound to the things of sense![114]

It has already been stated that those who apprehend invisible realities are governed according to Origen by the Divine element in the Son of God, whereas those who do not progress further than sensible realities are governed by the human element of His nature.[115] It is clearly to the latter element that Origen refers when he states that the Lord Who made an end of all His enemies by His Passion needed the cleansing which the Father alone could bestow on account of His exploits, and thus prevented Mary Magdalene from touching Him when He appeared to her after His Resurrection.[116] We may observe that this is the supreme instance of the fact recorded in *Hom. in Num.*,[117] where it is said that those who fight against the powers of evil and overcome them are defiled, and therefore need to be cleansed by the very fact of having had dealings with them. In fact the greater the achievements, the greater the purification needed (as in the case of St. Peter and St. Paul).[118]

On the other hand, in *Convs. with Her.*[119] a quite different reason is adduced for His refusal to allow Mary Magdalene to touch Him. There it is stated that He had not yet returned to the Father to claim His spirit (πνεῦμα), which had been yielded to the Father to be kept in trust for Him at the time of His crucifixion. It could however be said that only through claiming back His πνεῦμα could the other elements of His nature be cleansed.[120]

In order to understand the meaning of the "cleansing" which Christ is alleged to have needed after the Crucifixion, it seems desirable to refer to another passage, where Origen states that it was because our Lord submitted to death on behalf of mankind that He became worthy of the second place of honour after the God of the universe as an acknowledgement of His outstanding achievements alike in heaven and on earth.[121] It is clearly to the human element of our Lord's nature that this statement refers: so far as His Divine nature is concerned, the second place is accorded to Him by the very fact of His sharing in the Father's Divinity.[122] This perhaps gives us a clue to the meaning of the cleansing referred to by Origen as being needed after the Crucifixion. In so far as Christ was human, He could not be said to possess the full knowledge characteristic of the Word of God, and so while He was undergoing the suffering of the Cross, although He might have some inkling of the purpose of it, that purpose would not be fully apparent to Him, as the Cry of Dereliction makes clear. It was only after the pain and agony were over that He would be in a full position to appreciate why He had been obliged to suffer, and how the sufferings contributed to the end they were intended to serve. That could only come about when His $\pi\nu\epsilon\hat{\upsilon}\mu\alpha$ became fully self-conscious, ie., when it received the full influx of Divine enlightenment. It was as true of the human Jesus as it is of every human being that he needed to advance in self-knowledge, and that at no time in His life could it necessarily be said that the self-knowledge was complete. If His chief work was accomplished without His full awareness, that is simply equivalent to saying that God was in control of His life, but that being human, He did not fully understand how that control was exercised.

In *Matt. Comm. Series* it is stated that when Jesus hung on the Cross, there was inscribed over His head the text "This is the King of the Jews"; but when he ascended to the Father and received the Father into Himself, He gained possession of Him Who was really designated by the title inscribed above the Cross, and seeing that He had become worthy of Him, He became the Father's dwelling-place, He being the one Who was alone able to appropriate the Father completely.[123] "To gain possession of the Father" really means to accomplish to the full the Father's purpose, to have linked one's own will indissolubly to the will of the Father; but it is still possible to hold that even in the act of doing so, Christ in His human nature was not fully aware that this was what He was in fact doing, and only became so aware later on. In this sense, the human Jesus Himself progressed from "faith" to "knowledge",[124] inasmuch as He endured what He did endure in a state of uncertainty as to whether it was valuable, but in the end came to understand its value after emerging on to the "other side."

These considerations may help us to understand the meaning of the curious passage in *Hom. in Lev.*[125] where Origen refers to the purifications which Christ underwent. The first is suggested by the man who led the scapegoat into the wilderness in accordance with Jewish custom, and was obliged to wash his clothes at eventide because he had touched what was unclean; in the same way, Christ took human nature upon Himself, ie. flesh and blood, and washed it at the close of His earthly life in His own blood, and thus became clean. In other words He fulfilled in His own body the requirements of God when He suffered on the Cross, because previously He had not been able to fulfil them. On the other hand it is made clear that further purification was needed when He said to Mary Magdalene after His Resurrection when she wanted to hold His feet "Do not touch Me." After He had taken the powers of evil to a desert place in the power of His Crucifixion, it was necessary for Him to ascend to the Father and be more fully purified at the heavenly altar, so that He might bestow on our flesh, which He had not ceased to wear, the gift of perpetual purity. In other words, though He suffered to the full for our sakes on the Cross, He did not become aware of the extent of His achievements until it was all over and He could enter into uninterrupted communion with God and so be enlightened as to what He had in fact accomplished. Then, and only then, could He convey these benefits to others.

As a matter of fact, Origen is open to the charge of letting his intellectuals, who pride themselves on their ability to contemplate things not seen by the senses, get away with a lack of cleansing. The distinction between those who can see visible things only and those who can see with the mind's eye is surely invalid; it is really a matter of dealing with earthly affairs in accordance with the vision of spiritual realities made possible by Christ's act of sacrifice on the Cross. The person who has progressed from "faith" to "knowledge"[126] has no more right than Plato's guardians in the *Republic* had to rest content with his exalted state; he should apply that knowledge to the practical affairs of life and so improve the state of the world. That surely is the meaning of "redemption"; being made able to see the world with the eyes of God and so taking steps for its improvement and renovation.

It is also the case that even the same individual can waver from time to time between belief in the sense of accepting dogmatic statements about events alleged to have occurred (equivalent to resting content with visible realities in Origen's sense), and belief in the sense of recognising spiritual truths of which those outward events are the verification and confirmation (equivalent to the perception of unseen realities in Origen's sense). In the biography of Archbishop William Temple, [127] there is a letter written by him in 1930 to the then Bishop of Birmingham (Dr. Barnes) which shows a somewhat naive assumption that most Christians do not "build their faith on miracles", but rather accept the miracles "on the basis of a faith accepted in independence of miracles." He presumably means that Christians accept Christ as Divine because He displays the character which is alone worthy of God, and go on to accept the miracles because it seems appropriate that they should occur as features of His earthly life. It seems very doubtful if people who are not theologians give a sufficient amount of thought to their faith to arrive at that position. One would have thought that most of them base their faith — in so far as they enquire what basis it has — both on the miracles of our Lord and on His character, without stopping to enquire how the former are related to the latter. They thus cannot be said to come down definitely either on the side of a faith in visible realities or on that of a faith in unseen realities; their faith is thus immature.

It seems appropriate to refer to John vi.26,27, where our Lord reproves the crowd which had been miraculously fed by Him for not recognising that this miracle was a sign of something far greater than itself, that is, of the bestowing of spiritual nourishment. In that sense, a distinction can be drawn between those who are content with sensible realities and those who go on to the apprehension of something higher; but that does not seem to be the sense in which Origen makes this distinction.[128] His distinction is rather between those who use the life of Christ as a model for their own conduct and those who ascend in mind to the apprehension of unseen realities which are not identifiable with principles of action.

NOTES ON CHAPTER VI

1. *De Princ.* II.6.4 (GCS 5.143.18-21,144.1-3).
2. *Comm. I in Rom.* (Philocal., JAR p.228.1-5).
3. VI.79 (GCS 2.150.27-151.1). Cf. Pitra A.S.III.40.41 (Ps.XLIV. 3); Kelber, op.cit., pp.255,256; Rius-Camps, "Comunicabilidad", *OCP* 38, 1972, pp.451,452; Cadiou, op. cit., p.58.
4. *Comm. in Joh.* XXXII.28 (GCS 4.473.17-20).
5. Op. cit., p.249.
6. Op. cit., Vol.II, pp.162,163.
7. *Comm. in Cant.* I (GCS 8.98.7-13,99.23-100.11).
8. *Hom. in Cant.* I.2 (GCS 8.30.9-12). Cf. also I.3(32.1-3).
9. *De Princ.* IV.4.4 (GCS 5.354.11-18); cf.ibid.II.6.4 (5.143.18-23).
10. Cf. Ch.III, p.76. Cf. also *Hom. in Num.* XII.4 (GCS 7.106,12,13) and XIII.1 (108.26,27).
11. *Comm. in Joh.* I.28 (GCS 4.35.14-36.10). Cf. on this passage Eichinger, op. cit., pp.151 and 152; Schendel, op. cit., pp.86,87; and Fitzgerald, op. cit., pp.107,108. When Fitzgerald says that "the posteriority asserted in the present passage (ie. that of the assumption of kingly status by the human Jesus) may be regarded as one of logical sequence rather than one of time", he is really shelving the problem inherent in Christ's humanity instead of trying to solve it. See also ibid., pp.163-165. Cf. also the discussion of this passage on pp.82-84 of Franco's thesis.
12. I.6 (PG XIV.851D-852B). Cf. p.217.
13. ii.10.
14. It is to this passage that the remarks made by Mersch in op. cit.p. 358, note 2 really refer.
15. XXVI.4 (GCS 2.361.22-362.2).
16. Cf. Schendel, op. cit., p.88.
17. p.126.
18. p.127.
19. XXXII.25 (GCS 4.470.15-27).
20. τὸ μηκέτι ἕτερον αὐτὸν εἶναι τοῦ Λόγου ἀλλὰ τὸν αὐτὸν αὐτῷ.
21. ὑπερυψωμένου μὲν τοῦ μὴ ἁρπαγμὸν ἡγησαμένου τὸ εἶναι ἴσα θεῷ, μένοντος δὲ ἐν τῷ ἰδίῳ ὕψει ἢ καὶ ἀποκαθισταμένου ἐπ' αὐτὸ τοῦ Λόγου, ὅτε πάλιν ἦν πρὸς τὸν θεόν, θεὸς Λόγος ὢν ἄνθρωπος.
22. p.146; cf. also pp.104,105.
23. Op. cit., p.6.

24 Op. cit., pp.261,262.
25 Pitra, A.S.III, 227,228 (Ps.CIX.1-6).
26 *Hom. in Is.* I.2 (GCS 8.245.21-29).
27 Accepti potestatem homo Christus quam ante non habuit.
28 *Comm. in Joh.* XIII.1 (GCS 4.227.2-5). Cf. *Hom. in Num.* XVII. 5 (GCS 7.164.6-10). The words of Psalm 2 are likewise applied in *Hom. in Jos.* XI.3 (GCS 7.363,23-364.3), where it is said that the Father says these words to Him because He sees that the salvation of the Gentiles can only come about through Him, and thus lengthens the time available for their repentance. On the other hand, in the 8th. Homily on Exodus these words apparently refer to the Divine Nature of the Son of God (VIII.2 (GCS 6. 220.23-221.4)). In Cadiou, *Frag. in Ps.* II.6ᵃ(p.72), it is uncertain which nature is referred to. Cf. also II.8ᵃ(p.73). Cf. also pp. 200 and 201.
29 *Sel. in Ps.* II.8 (PG XII.1108A-C). Cf. Pitra A.S.II.447 (Ps.II).
30 *Frag. in Luc.* 25 (GCS 9.237); cf. also *Sel. in Ps.* CXLV.10 (PG XII.1676A), and Pitra, A.S.II.471 (Ps.XVII.40).
31 *Hom. in Is.* V.1 (GCS 8.263.21-23). Cf. *Sel. in Ps.* XCVIII.6 (PG XII.1557B).
32 Caro siquidem Domini honorem deitatis adsumit.
33 XXIII.4 (GCS 2.353.1-4).
34 IX.90.95 (*JTS* 3.401).
35 Cf. Mersch, op. cit., p.357, where he says that the Alexandrian teachers, of whom Origen was one, regarded Christ as the head of the Mystical Body in so far as He is God. Mersch considers this an error, because it is in His humanity that Christ is Head of the redeemed. The present writer agrees with Mersch, because he thinks that Origen considered that the humanity of Christ needed to be left behind in order to apprehend His Divinity, whereas in reality the humanity is the vehicle of the Divinity.
36 *Frag. in Matt.* 571.1-10 (GCS 12.235). Cf. *Sel. in Ps.* XV.5 (PG XII.1213A).
37 *Frag. in Matt.* 551.14.15 (GCS 12.226). Cf. *Hom. in Gen.* II.3 (GCS 6.30.14-27).
38 συνεκταθῇ τῷ παντί.
39 *Frag. in Matt.* 552.1-6 (GCS 12.226).
40 *Comm. in Joh.* I.28 (GCS 4.36.17-24). Cf. p.216 and also Ch.V, p.126.
41 Matthew xiii.44.

42 τὸν ἐκ φανερῶν καὶ κρυπτῶν συνεστηκότα. *Comm. in Matt.* X.5, 6 (GCS 10.5.21-24, and 6.8,9).
43 *Comm. in Rom.* X.43 (PG XIV.1290C-1291A). Cf. Mme. Harl, op. cit., p.92, where she says that according to the 2nd century philosophers, the chief condition of knowing God is that the intelligence be purified. If it is true that the senses are so designed as to become acquainted with sensible things, and the intelligence so as to become acquainted with intelligible things, it is needful that a person should detach himself from the senses to obtain a purely intellectual knowledge of God. See also Lieske, pp.45-47, op. cit.
44 Romans xvi.25.
45 *Frag. in I Cor.* IX.6-12 (*JTS* 9.238,239). Cf. ibid.XVIII.6-10 (354).
46 *Comm. in Joh.* I.7 (GCS 4.12.1-8). Cf. Hirschberg, op. cit., p. 194, where it is said that "the catechumen, after he has understood the initial principles and therewith the literal sense of Scripture, must strive ceaselessly to grasp the more recondite meaning of Scripture." See also Fitzgerald's discussion of this passage in op. cit., pp.74 and 75.
47 *Comm. in Joh.* XXXII.9 (GCS 4.440.20-441.1).
48 II Cor.v.16.
49 Cf. pp.214 and 215.
50 I.13 (GCS 1.66.8-23).
51 St. John viii.28.
52 *Comm. in Joh.* XIX.11 (GCS 4.310-28-311.5); See also *Comm. in Rom.* I.13 (PG XIV.859AB). Cf. Crouzel, *La Conn.*, pp.175, 449,459; Koch, op. cit., pp.68 and 69, where a passage from *Comm. in Matt.* XII.37 (GCS 10.153.8-23) is referred to; Bertrand, *Mystique de Jesus chez Origène* (Paris, 1951), p.31; Mme. Harl, op. cit., pp.155 (esply n.87), 192,196,258-261.
53 *Hom. in Lev.* IV.6 (GCS 6.324.15-325.14).
54 Op. cit., p.203; cf. also pp.57-59. Cf. also de Faye,op.cit., p.139.
55 *La Conn.*, p.175.
56 Op. cit., pp.155,156.
57 *Contra Cels.* III.62 (GCS 1.256.3-10) is quoted in support of this view. Cf. Teichtweier, op. cit., pp.254 and 255, where this passage is also referred to. Cf. also Vagaggini, op. cit., p.186, where he says that "Origen considers Christ as Teacher rather than as Redeemer by the blood of the Cross."

Cf. also the interesting discussion in Nygren, op. cit.,pp.377 sqq., of the reasons why Jesus Christ took human flesh. It was not for the sake of intellectuals, because they can ascend from visible to invisible realities; it was for the sake of those incapable of doing this, so that at least they may not be altogether bereft of the help which Christ can give. But Nygren does not sufficiently take account of the fact that Origen normally regards *all* human beings as in the end capable of ascending from "faith" to "knowledge".

[58] XII.19 (GCS 10.111.27-112.12).
[59] XII.18 (GCS 10.109.23-110.8).
[60] *Comm. in Matt.* XII.19 (GCS 10.112.27-113.4). Lebreton, who quotes this passage on pp.282,283 of op. cit., points out the danger inherent in Origen's distinction between those who see the events with their bodily eyes and those who understand the truths at which these events hint. No one in this life can pretend to have a completely direct knowledge of God which "miracles" (in the broad sense) do not help to convey.
See also Bardy,"La Spiritualité d'Origène" *VS* 31 suppl.(1932), pp.98,99, where this passage (and what follows it) is quoted.
[61] *Comm. in Matt.* XII.20 (GCS 10.113.13-24).
[62] *Hom. in Lev.* I.3 (GCS 6.285,1-9). See von Balthasar, op. cit., p. 48. On the following page, however, von Balthasar seems to interpret this passage quite unwarrantably as meaning that the self-offering of Christ is continued by the hands of earthly priests.
[63] *Frag. in I Sam.* X.6 (GCS 3.298.24-29).
[64] Op. cit., p.153. Molland also refers to *De Princ.* IV.3.13 (GCS 5. 344.8-345.4).
[65] "Le developpement d'une théologie: pression et aspiration (*RchSR* 23 (1933)), pp.420-422. Cf. Lebreton, op. cit., p.278, note 1.
[66] Op. cit., p.260.
[67] Op. cit., p.102.
[68] N.3 on p.102.
[69] Cf. what Hirschberg says on this point on pp.219,220 of op.cit.
[70] N.3 on p.136. Cf. also the remarks made by Puech on p.524 of his article "Un livre récent sur la mystique d'Origène" (*RHPR* 13 (1933)) on this topic.
[71] Op. cit., p.421.
[72] Op. cit., p.276, n.3. Cf. also Lot-Borodine, op. cit., *RHR* 106,

1932, p.561, and note thereon.
[73] Op. cit., p.104.
[74] Ibid.n.58.
[75] Cf. Molland, op. cit., p.143, which expresses the same opinion. Cf. also Casel, op. cit., p.191, where it is stated that "as Origen's whole theology shows, the Death of Christ on the Cross is simply a stage of transition to the revelation of Jesus as Christ the Word of God in the era of Resurrection; thus it is that the self-offering and the exaltation of Christ belong together."
[76] Op. cit., p.230; see also pp.224 and 242.
[77] Op. cit., pp.78 sqq.
[78] p.81.
[79] p.285.
[80] Op. cit., pp.267,268.
[81] The ref. is to *Contra Cels.* II.69 (GCS 1.190.9-20).
[82] See Ch.VII, pp.239 & 240. See also Hanson, op. cit., pp.284,285. On p.287 Hanson declares that "Origen says that Christ died at a point in history in order that we might be timelessly united to Him in Christian meditation and experience." Crouzel suggests on p.89 of "O. devant l'Inc. et dev. l'hist." that the adverb "timelessly" appears to exclude from history the coming of Christ to the Church and to the individual soul. In other words, the word "timelessly" obscures the fact that Origen believed that the destiny of the Christian was to grow in grace and to be progressively changed into the Divine Nature.
[83] Op. cit., pp.65 sqq.
[84] Cf. Ch.VII, p.260.
[85] Primmer quotes *Hom. in Jer.* X.2 (GCS 3.72.13-73.7); *Hom. in Exod.* XI.2 (GCS 6.254.7-9); *Comm. in Joh.* II.8 (GCS 4.62.24-26). In *Hom. in Ex.* XI.2 (GCS 6.254.2-9), Moses shows the people the Rock which is Christ; he leads them to this Rock so that they can drink from it and so quench their thirst. For, smitten with blows and nailed to the Cross, Christ has caused the sources of the New Covenant to flow out. If He had not been struck, and if water and blood had not come out of His side, we should all undergo thirst for the Word of God.
[86] *Comm. in Matt.* XII.15 (GCS 10.104.1-6,21-26).
[87] *Comm. in Rom.* VIII.1 (PG XIV.1159C-1160A).
[88] *Comm. in Matt.* XII.15 (GCS 10.103.22-34). Cf. Pitra, A.S.280, 281 (CXVIII.75), where the above text from St. John is quoted.

[89] *Excerpt in Cant.* V.6 (PG XIII.205B).
[90] *Comm. in Matt.* XI.2 (GCS 10.37.4-12).
[91] Cf. *Comm. in Matt.* XVI.17 (GCS 10.533.5-9), where it is said those who are beginners and initiates in the Church are His τεκνία and υἱοί. Cf. also Cadiou, *Frag. in Ps.* CXIII.21 (p.102).
[92] *Comm. in Matt.* XI.2 (GCS 10.37.1-4).
[93] *Comm. in Matt.* XI.5 (GCS 10.41.2-6).
[94] *Comm. in Joh.* XX.30 (GCS 4.367.28-368.7). Cf. Eichinger, op. cit., p.196, where the type of person he calls the "Man below" (Mensch-unten) is said to stand in a twofold relationship to the human element in Jesus. The *believing* Man below understands the human element in Jesus to be the first step towards the comprehension of His Divinity; whereas the *sinful* Man-below regards the human element in Jesus as the sole and final reality. On the other hand, it could be said that in so far as the "Man-below" recognises that there is a deeper reality underlying the human acts and words of Jesus, he is no longer the "Man-below", because he has an inkling, however vague, of something more advanced. It could also be said that such an attitude contradicts the suggestion that the "things which are seen" have to be transcended by the mature Christian, if the "things which are unseen" can already be apprehended, however vaguely, by the Christian who is as yet immature.
[95] Op. cit., p.155.
[96] Op. cit., pp.27,28. Cf. also p.34, and Lebreton, op. cit., p.284.
[97] Cf. also Kelber, op. cit., p.226, where he observes that "the Christianity of Origen had taken over the functions of both sections of the religious life of the ancient world, ie. popular religion and mysticism. Popular religion corresponded to the proclamation of the ideal humanity of Jesus Christ, and mysticism to enlightenment through the Divine Word."
[98] Op. cit., pp.276,277.
[99] p.100.
[100] Op. cit., p.219.
[101] *Hom. in Lev.* III.3 (GCS 6.305.4-18). Cf. ibid.XIII.3 (GCS 6.472.1-7), and *Sel. in Ps.* I.3 (PG XII.1089C), and *Frag. in Jer.* 20 (GCS 3.207.19-23). Cf. Crouzel, *L'Image*, p.201, where the passage from *Hom. in Lev.* III.3 is quoted, and also *La Conn.*, pp.173 and 476. Presumably when Crouzel says (in *La Conn.*, p.369) that "Jesus in His humanity and the N.T. Scriptures in their

literal sense bring salvation, even though the eye of the soul needs to accustom itself to see the Divine element which they carry within them", he is relying on such a passage as the one from *Hom. in Lev.* But surely full salvation can according to Origen only be obtained by apprehending the Divine element in the Person of Jesus, and the spiritual meaning of the Scriptures.

102 *Frag. in Joh.* LV (GCS 4.529.1-3).
103 *Comm. in Matt.* XI.17 (GCS 10.63.11-23). Cf. Bertrand, op. cit., p.29, and Crouzel, *La Conn.*, p.475, where he criticises those who suggest that Origen separates human beings into two classes, according as they are or are not capable to becoming acquainted with the mysteries of the Faith. (Cf. p.494 of op. cit., where it is said that "those who are spiritual or mature do not form a closed group; every Christian is called to that state".) But such a passage as the one from *Comm. in Matt.* appears to justify the opinion of Origen expressed by Lomiento, op. cit., p.35, when he says that according to Origen, "only some persons are capable of mingling their 'breath' increasingly with Christ in His work of redemption." On the other hand, Lomiento contradicts himself later on (p.39), when he says that "according to Origen, we can all be acquainted with this essential experience (ie.of the heavenly kingdom), in so far as we unite ourselves to the disciples at the highest point of their spirit."
Cf. also Hirschberg, op. cit., p.174, where he says that according to Origen, "simple-minded believers cannot develop further; for them it is decreed that they remain simple with a 'bare faith'."
Nemeshegyi agrees with Crouzel in so far as he says that "according to the Gnostics, natural endowments determine the moral possibilities of created beings, whereas according to Origen the moral dispositions of spirits determine their ontological condition" (pp.134,135 of op. cit.).
104 Cf. pp.206 & 207.
105 *Frag. in Matt.* 430.5-7 (GCS 12.179), and 433 (2nd Col.). 6-11 (ibid.180). Cf. *Comm. in Joh.* X.24 (GCS 4.196.20-23).
106 *Contra Cels.* IV.18 (GCS 1.287.22-24). Cf. *Comm. in Cant.* III (GCS 8.193.22-194.3); ibid.I (GCS 8.103.33-104.14); *De Orat.* XXVII.5 (GCS 2.366.8-15); *Hom. in Jos.* IX.9 (GCS 7.355.1-7); *Hom. in Exod.* VII.8 (GCS 6.215.6-8, 23-216.3); *Hom. in Num.* XVI.9 (GCS 7.151.30-152.6); ibid.XXVII.1 (GCS 7.256.1-8 and 257.12-19); *Frag. in I Cor.* XII.2-18 (*JTS* 9.341).

[107] Cf. also Mme. Harl, op. cit., pp.237,238; Crouzel, *La Conn.*, pp. 172,173; Marcus, op. cit., p.162.
Comm. in Matt. XV.6 (GCS 11.362.10-363.12). Cf. also *Comm. in Rom.* IX.36 (PG XIV.1235BC); *Hom. in Lev.* XVI.2 (GCS 6. 496.7-28); *Hom. in Jud.* V.6 (GCS 7.496.20-25); *Comm. in Matt.* XII.31 (GCS 10.137.29-138.32); *Contra Cels.* III.52 and 53 (GCS 1.248.12-249.6); ibid.59 (254.6-15); ibid.60 (255.1-8).
Cf. also Mme. Harl, op. cit., p.266, and A. Nygren, op. cit., pp. 378 and 379, in which he stresses that moral purity is necessary according to Origen for those to whom the higher knowledge of the Christian religion is going to be communicated.
[108] *Comm. in Matt.* XI.17 (GCS 10.64.11-15).
[109] I.28 (GCS 4.36.19-24), already referred to on p.205. Cf. *Comm. in Matt.* XVII.5 (GCS 10.590.27-33), and also *Comm. in Joh.* XX. 2 (GCS 4.329.4-6), where, with reference to John viii.37, Origen says that not all mankind are "the seed of Abraham", because not all men have the principles (λόγους) sown within their ψυχαί which could, if cultivated, make them the children of Abraham — surely a Gnostic view, and one akin to that of Heracleon with whom he disputes in *Comm. in Joh.*
[110] *Hom. in Exod.* XII.4 (GCS 6.267.13-25).
[111] Op. cit., p.214.
[112] Cf. ibid.p.217, where Hirschberg says that the contrast between Origen's esoteric outlook and that put forward by Jesus Himself (in Mark iv.10 sqq.) is obvious. The mystery of the Kingdom of God is the lowliness of the Kingdom which cannot be comprehended by the wise, and which reveals itself even in its hidden form, namely in the Cross; whereas according to Origen, the mystery is only discernible by the wise, and not by the unwise. Hirschberg is apparently thinking of such Scriptural passages as Matt.xi.25 and I Cor.i.27.
[113] XIII.43 (GCS 4.270.16-25).
[114] Ibid.X.23 (GCS 4.195.1-8). Such a passage as this provides a foundation for the Oriental conception of the ascetic life described by Lot-Borodine in op. cit., *RHR* 106,1932, pp.553,554, where the basis of such a life is said to be "the complete submission of the element of being which perceives with the senses to the intelligent, intuitive and purified soul."
[115] See p. 205.
[116] *Comm. in Joh.* VI.55 (GCS 4.164.22-28).

[117] XXV.6 (GCS 7.241.19-242.9).
[118] Cf. also *Hom. in Luc.* XIV (GCS 9.87.13-18), where it is said that the purification referred to by St. Luke (ii.22) shortly after the birth of Jesus was that rendered necessary by the defilement which a soul undergoes when it is clothed with a body.
[119] 8.5-17 (ed. Scherer).
[120] See Ch.V pp. 143,144.
[121] *Contra Cels.* VII.57 (GCS 2.206.24-26). Cf.p.201.
[122] Cf. pp.201-203.
[123] 130 (GCS 11.267.14-19).
[124] Cf. pp.210,211.
[125] IX.5 (GCS 6.424.15-24 , and 425,26-426.2).
[126] See pp.210,211.
[127] By F. A. Iremonger, p.491.
[128] Cf. pp.214,215.

CHAPTER VII

CONTENTS

THE EVENTUAL RECONCILING OF HUMAN BEINGS TO THE FATHER BY CHRIST, AND HIS CONSEQUENT SUBJUGATION TO THE FATHER

The ultimate goal of human beings is union with the Father, the work of Christ is a means to this end	233
In the meantime there has to be an ascent from the contemplation of the Incarnate Word to that of the pre-existent Word	235
The work of Christ is to complete the Father's work begun in creation by bringing rational creatures to perfection	240
It is only a matter of time before all rational creatures, including evil spirits, will be persuaded by the Son of God to accept the Father's rule	250
The Son desires to impart to others His own Sonship, and thus bring about their direct fellowship with the Father	257
NOTES on Chapter VII	267

CHAPTER VII

THE EVENTUAL RECONCILING OF HUMAN BEINGS TO THE FATHER BY CHRIST, AND HIS CONSEQUENT SUBJUGATION TO THE FATHER

The subordination of the Son to the Father, as conceived of by Origen, comes out most clearly in the passages which discuss the goal of Christ's earthly work, which is the reconciling of human beings to the Father. In one striking passage [1] it is stated that the spring of water arising in the believer as the result of Christ's gift (cf. John iv.14) may well ascend to the Father after it has ascended to everlasting life; for if Christ is the Life, He Who is greater than Christ is greater than life. In the same way, Origen states [2] that it is possible to interpret the words of Christ "Lo, I am with you always, even to the end of the world" as meaning that He Who is with His followers till the consummation of the ages is He Who emptied Himself (ie. Christ Incarnate); [3] whereas it will be, as it were, someone else, that is, He Who is in the state in which He was before emptying Himself, Who will be with His followers afterwards, until the time when the Father will have put all the Son's enemies under His feet; but after that time, when the Son delivers the kingdom to the Father, the Father will Himself say, "Behold, I am with you always."

Franco says, [4] with reference to the immediately preceding passage in *Comm. in Joh.*, [5] that Origen there appears to say that whereas Christ is merely *with* His disciples until the consummation of the world, when the world has been crucified to them and they to the world, they will say with St. Paul, "It is not I who lives, but Christ Who lives in me." In this passage, Origen says nothing about the surrender of the Kingdom to the Father. In the subsequent passage [6] (already referred to), Origen does not distinguish between "being with" and "being in", but between the different meanings of "I". But, says Franco, the two passages do not contradict each other, because even if it is the Father Who will be with Christ's disciples after the surrender of the Kingdom, that does not amount to saying that Christ will not be in them, even though Origen does not say this explicitly. [7]

There are several passages where the metaphor of "seeing" is used to denote the process whereby Christ introduces human beings to the Father. Thus with reference to the text "In Thy light shall we see light", Origen declares that by knowing Christ we shall eventually see God.[8] In the same way he says [9] that although the Son said "He who sees me has seen Him Who sent me", He would not have said "He Who has seen the Father has seen me", because it is after the soul has contemplated the Word of God that it ascends to the contemplation of God Himself.[10]

Elsewhere the metaphor of "sharing" is used to denote the relationship between the individual soul on the one hand and Christ and the Father on the other. Thus Origen prays [11] that his disciple Gregory may continually share ever more fully in the Spirit of God and the Spirit of Christ, so that he may not only say "We have become partakers of Christ" (μέτοχοι τοῦ Χριστοῦ), but also "We have become partakers of God" (μέτοχοι τοῦ θεοῦ). Such a passage as this justifies Völker in saying [12] that "the mystical notion of the marriage between the Divine Word and the human soul is itself only a transition stage and a necessary preparation for the summit consisting in mystical union with God, just as the whole system of Origen can be summed up in the idea of God being all in all."

Yet another metaphor employed in describing the process of reconcilliation of mankind with the Father through Christ is that of "ascent". Thus Origen says with reference to John xiii.36, where Our Lord tells Peter that he cannot follow Him to His destination at present, that even though a disciple of Jesus may not be in a position to follow his Master to the Father now, he may through diligence be able to do so later on.[13] Elsewhere, in a curious allegorical interpretation of Luke vii.37, where the woman in the Pharisee's house anointed the head of Jesus after His feet, Origen says that the more mature soul, when it has rendered fitting service to the Word of God, is free to approach the Head of Christ, Who is God.[14] Elsewhere, Origen says that if anyone is ready to ascend the spiritual mountain with Christ, as Peter, James and John did, He will not only be illuminated by the light of Christ, but will also hear the Father's voice.[15] Likewise, in *Hom. in Num.*[16] it is said that after Christ had come into the world, the Father recalled Him, so that a way might be opened up for those who wish to ascend from this world to God. In *Contra Cels.*[17] Origen says that he who has ascended to the God set above all things is he who gives his individual worship to that God through the Son, Who alone leads to God those who desire to have fellowship with God.

Elsewhere,[18] he says that just as Christ is said to have passed from this world to the Father in order to resume the fullness of which He had emptied Himself, so we, if we follow Him as Guide, will when we arrive at our destination be transformed from being spiritually empty to being spiritually full.

There are several passages in which Christ is said to "offer" to the Father those whom He reconciles to the Father. For instance, in *Hom. in Num.*[19] it is stated that in the early stages of spiritual development it is the angels who are deputed to take charge of human souls, but that in due course they offer the firstfruits *(primitiae)* of their cultivation to Christ, Who in turn offers them to God the Father, just as He offered Himself. The same sentiment is expressed in *Comm. in Rom.,*[20] where it is also stated that before human souls are mature enough to be offered to the Father, they call upon the Name of our Lord Jesus Christ as Mediator between God and man; but after the Spirit of God has entered their hearts and there cries "Abba, Father", the Spirit teaches them to call on the Name of the Father also. Elsewhere Origen prays[21] that he and his readers may be sufficiently pure in heart and upright in action to have a share in the Divine Sacrifice offered through the eternal Priest and Saviour, the Lord Jesus Christ.

It is noteworthy that this offering is in several places only regarded as adequate when it is corporate, ie. when it includes all mankind (we shall revert to this theme later).[22] Thus in *Comm. in Joh.* Origen says[23] that it would not be incorrect to say that no one now knows the Father to the fullest possible extent, even though he may be an apostle or a prophet, and that human beings will only attain to the fullest knowledge of Him when they attain to the unity which exists between the Father and the Son. Likewise in *Hom. in Jos.*[24] he declares that it is through the Spirit of Christ that we are enabled to attain to that unity of spirit which will enable us to make ourselves into a worthy offering to God the Father. But the clearest indication of the fact that it is a corporate offering which Christ makes to the Father occurs in the passage[25] where Origen says that when Christ shall have delivered His Kingdom to God the Father (I Cor.xv.24), all those living creatures who have already been made part of that kingdom will be delivered with the rest of it to the Father's rule, so that when God is all things in all creatures (I Cor.xv.28), they also, as being included amongst those creatures, may themselves be indwelt by God.

But before believers can be introduced by the Divine Word to God the Father, it is first necessary that they should ascend from contemplating the Incarnate Word to contemplating the pre-existent Word. Origen declares, as has already been indicated,[26] that there is a twofold coming of the Divine Word into the human soul. As first apprehended, He has no beauty or attractiveness, because He is apprehended by way of the "foolish preaching" as the Christ Who was born and crucified. But the second coming takes place when the believer no longer knows Christ "after the flesh" only, but comprehends Him in a more rational manner, with the result that he experiences the end of the world in so far as "the world is crucified to him, and he to the world."[27]

In another passage, Origen says that the Word in the opened heaven (Rev.xix.11) is called "faithful and true" in contrast to the shadow and image which the Word on earth is. It is by the shadow of the Word, and not by the true Word of God, that the great mass of those who are considered to be believers are taught.[28] It is interesting that Origen considers that just as the Word condescends to human infirmities by appearing as a man, so He condescends to the limitations of the angels by appearing amongst them as one of themselves. He makes this observation with reference to Genesis xxii.11,12, where an angel is said to have spoken to Abraham and later on this angel is shown to be God Himself.[29]

There is one passage where Origen appears to suggest that the contemplation of the pre-existent Word is not possible for those who are still imprisoned in the body.[30] He says in fact that for all who are in the body and are thus away from the Lord, the Lord Himself is away, because they walk by faith and not by sight, and that it is only when we are freed from the body that we shall be with the Lord and He with us and we shall thus walk by sight instead of by faith, that is, by seeing the Word in all His various aspects of wisdom, truth, righteousness, peace and the rest. But if we compare this passage with others, we can only say that Origen would allow that some Christians can transcend bodily limitations even in this life; otherwise how could any one attain to the contemplation of the Divine Word before physical death?[31]

In fact in another passage, which is worth quoting *verbatim*,[32] Origen implies that is is possible to apprehend the Divinity of the Word even in this life; for he says that "it is necessary that the Divine Word Who cleanses the soul should pre-exist in this soul, so that as a result of the purification which He carries out, all deadness and weakness may be removed, and unmixed life may come to exist in that soul, in so far as it is capable of receiving the Divinity of the Word."

There is also a rather curious passage which allegorises the story of the feet washing at the Last Supper. It is there said that the Lord "rises from supper, lays aside His garments, and girds Himself with a towel." Origen says that if there were no hidden meaning underlying these words, it is hard to understand why the Lord should not have washed His disciples' feet in His clothes. And so he interprets the clothes as the discourses He normally gave, and the towel as the more recondite teaching which could only be given when His disciples had been purified. [33]

There is also a passage where Origen's outlook is illustrated in the following striking way. He says that the soul apprehends God in various ways. Through its actions it apprehends Him as householder (that is, as being in charge of itself); through the study of nature as King (that is, as having charge of the whole world); but through the study of theology as God (that is, in His innermost nature and character). Origen also says that from the third mode of apprehension there follow the two previous ones, in other words they are implicit in it; but from the first the other two do not necessarily follow, in other words, there may be people who get no further than apprehending God as having the right to lay down what they should do.[34] Origen would say no doubt that those who are taught by the "shadow" of the Word, that is, the Word in His earthly form,[35] simply gain a clearer understanding of the actions which they are expected by God to perform, whereas in order to obtain an intimate acquaintance with God in Himself it is first necessary to apprehend the Word in His Divinity.

There are several passages where Origen leaves us in no doubt that he regards many Christians as not having advanced beyond the stage of being taught and governed by the Word in His earthly form, the Word Who was crucified. Thus he says[36] that some Christians are governed (κεκόσμηνται) by the Word of God Himself, but others by a Word united to Him and "appearing to be the primal Word" (strange phrase!). The second group know nothing but Jesus Christ, and Him crucified; they see the Word as flesh only. It is noteworthy that even Old Testament worthies are regarded as having been capable of entering into fellowship with the Word Who was in the beginning with God, whereas the generality of Christian believers are described as imagining that the entire Word consists of the Word made flesh.[37] And so Origen recommends that each Christian should receive the Divine message to the full extent of his capacity. If he is able to assimilate solid food, let him receive the wisdom which St. Paul spoke among the mature (cf. I Cor.ii.6); but he who is not ready for this should receive the teaching which conveys to him knowledge of nothing except Jesus Christ, and Him crucified.[38] It is interesting that when Origen refers[39] to the men who have joined the Christian Church after being steeped in what Christians call "wisdom after the flesh" (cf. I Cor.i.26), he says that some have passed on to the Divine wisdom — as though it was necessary first to divest oneself of human wisdom completely, as though it were wholly misleading, and simply accept elementary Christian teaching before going on to the more advanced! Such an outlook seems at variance with the opinion of Origen's predecessor Clement of Alexandria, which is that heathen thinkers had grasped fragments of the truth but had given then a one-sided emphasis.

Perhaps the main clue to the way in which Origen's mind works regarding the Crucifixion is given by Bertrand,[40] when he says that "the reproach levelled by Origen against simple believers is that they are not willing to go beyond the outward fact of the Crucifixion so as to try to penetrate the mystical aspect of it." Indeed, so much is suggested in *Comm. in Matt.*[41] when it is stated that one can become acquainted with the triumph of Christ on the Cross either by faith or by a higher form of knowledge." But as we shall see,[42] the mystical interpretation which Origen gives of the Crucifixion is not in line with the main stream of Christian thought, but is rather governed by his emphasis on the need to leave this sense-perceived world behind.

The distinction which Origen makes between faith (or belief) and knowledge apropos of the Crucifixion is in fact merely one example of the same distinction apropos of Christ Himself. Thus Origen says [43] with reference to John viii.31,32 that many believed in Christ, but not many knew Him. Only those believers who remained in His word and thus became His true disciples would come to know the truth which resided in Him; and the majority of believers would not advance further than believing Him. Origen says elsewhere [44] that the beginner believes in the Son of Man, but the one who makes progress ascends to believing in the Son of God also. In fact, after one's initiation there is need of advancing so that one may be seen and known by God, in accordance with St. Paul's words "but now having come to know God, or rather to be known by Him" (Gal.iv.9).

Origen expresses the same contention more fully when he says [45] that "those who are introduced to the Christian Faith receive the truth without the wisdom which acts as a confirmation of it, and without the Word of God Who demonstrates it . . . . For instance, an initiate is introduced to belief in one God, and is taught that Christ was sent for the benefit of mankind in order to put away sin by His own blood, and that after this life is over, the blessed will inherit a happy life, and sinners will inherit a life of punishment. This is truth, but truth which is not unfolded or established with wisdom and reason."

In view of what has been said, we can hardly fail to agree with Mersch [46] when he says that according to Origen, "Christ is Teacher rather than Life; Christianity has more the appearance of an immense and magnificent school, rather than that of an assimilation to God of the very substance of our race." We must also subscribe to the statement of Molland [47] that "the tendency in Origen to leave behind the historic revelation in his speculations is due to the influence of Platonism, which sometimes superseded the theology of the Incarnation in His thinking. When the Platonic line of thought is continued to its logical conclusion, all revelation within the sphere of this world becomes problematic, and he cannot retain his hold on the position of the Church; ὁ Λόγος σὰρξ ἐγένετο."

It is now time to refer to several passages in which Origen gives us his own mystical interpretation of the Crucifixion, which it will be generally agreed is rather forced. In a very obscure *Frag. in Luc.*[48] he interprets St. Paul's statement "I am crucified to the world, and the world to me" as meaning that the rational principle explaining the world (ὁ λόγος ὁ περὶ κόσμου) is perceived by me, and the Word (ὁ λόγος) is hence raised up and no longer lies below; for to him who does not understand the reason why the world was made the Word is not crucified. Origen goes on to say "For I think it right to be mystically crucified with Christ, as Paul was, in so far as the world (κόσμος) was to the mind of Paul lifted up and so understood." The general meaning seems to be that the mature Christian does not simply allow himself to become immersed in this world's affairs, but obtains a more detached view of the world by referring it to its origin and ruling principle, which is the Word of God.

Another striking passage [49] where Origen interprets the words of St. Paul in his own way is that in which he declares that the effect of the invisible entry of the Word of God into a person's soul is that the world is destroyed and brought to an end, in fact crucified to the person concerned, in the sense that worldly things have no attraction for him. The Word of God is able to enter the souls of those who having known Christ in an earthly manner ascend in order to grasp *(capere)* the glory of the Only-begotten Son of God. Once again, the Crucifixion is interpreted in terms of detachment from the world.

In an *obiter dictum* regarding the words "Heaven and earth shall pass away, but my words shall not pass away",[50] Origen declares that the place of the sinner referred to by the Psalmist when he says "Soon the wicked will be no more; you will look well at his place, but he will not be there"[51] is the present heaven and earth[52] — a clear indication of the fact that he regards the present material universe as only temporary and in fact the result of the fall of immaterial spirits. The Crucifixion is thus regarded, not as a means of redeeming the world, but as a means of transcending the world; it thus has the same message for Origen as the Transfiguration, which is mystically interpreted as symbolising what supervenes on the disappearance of this world, the previous six days referred to in St. Matthew's account[53] being understood as symbolising the bringing into being of this world.[54] In the same way, Origen says elsewhere that when we are exalted from earth to heaven by the Cross of Christ in fulfilment of His words "I, if I be lifted up, will draw all men unto me", we then truly magnify the Lord, Who magnified the Father by submitting to His will and so bestowing on believers, as far as He could, the highest conception ($\dot{\upsilon}\pi\acute{o}\lambda\eta\psi\iota\nu$) of the Father.[55] Origen is only repeating himself when he says elsewhere that even those who possess no more than "belief" can endeavour to worship God, but to see ($\theta\epsilon\omega\rho\epsilon\hat{\iota}\nu$) the Word, and to apprehend the Father in Him, is the prerogative not of all believers but of those who are pure in heart, and thus needs time and practice.[56]

In fact when it is said that the Son of God came to seek and to save the lost, what is meant is that the Father seeks true worshippers[57] through the son ($\delta\iota\grave{\alpha}\ \tau o\hat{\upsilon}\ \upsilon\iota o\hat{\upsilon}$), inasmuch as the Son by a process of cleansing and instruction makes human beings into true worshippers.[58]

It is now time to discuss the way in which the Divine Word helps people to develop the faculty of reason inherent in them, so as to enable them to offer adequate worship to the Father. For Origen, reason is the pre-requisite of virtuous living. In order to obtain $\dot{\alpha}\rho\epsilon\tau\acute{\eta}$, we must first pray for knowledge of how it is manifested, then we must find out how that knowledge can be applied to ourselves, and then we must knock at the door which is Christ (cf. Matt.vii.7) so that He may release us from the narrow and restricted way of self-will and lead us into the wide field of intelligent action.[59] There is an interesting passage in *Comm. in Joh.* where it is said that the gift of reason ($\lambda\acute{o}\gamma o\varsigma$) in which the human race participates can be understood first as consisting in the innate ideas (ἔννοιαι) which come into consciousness in those emerging from childhood, and secondly as the mature rationality found only in those who are fully developed (τελείοις).[60] Origen presumably means that the "innate ideas", presumably moral and ethical principles, need to be continually kept in mind and applied to practical situations so as to bring human life into some kind of harmony. In fact Origen says that before reason is fully developed, human life is defective and therefore blameworthy, inasmuch as the irrational elements (metaphorically called "sheep" in John x.8) are not fully obedient to reason.[61] Origen then makes a very surprising pronouncement; he says that perhaps in the first sense of "reason" the Word became flesh, and in the second sense of "reason" the Word was Divine. He could mean, of course, that the seminal reason inherent in all human beings is due to the activity of the Word of God, but that this activity is only fully manifested with the full development of reason in human beings;[62] but he could also mean that the Word of God Himself underwent the process of rational development to which every human being is subject. This, however, would be in contradiction to Origen's doctrine of the changelessness of the Divine Word, a doctrine which he firmly maintains in spite of St. John's insistence that "the Word became flesh." Dr. C. J. Cadoux maintains that in spite of the uniqueness of Jesus Christ, He was not exempt from the imperfection involved in the process of moral development. He says: "While we can distinguish *in the abstract* between conspicuous and indubitable sins committed against the light and in wilful disobedience to God, and unintentional imperfections or lapses incidental to all human life as it develops out of its initial immaturity, yet, in the actual experience of living, it is virtually impossible clearly to separate the one from the other . . . . So long as our conception of sin is clear only when sin is considered as a pure abstraction, we cannot treat the sinlessness of Jesus as if it were one of the obvious factual data on which our Christology must be based."[63]

It is noteworthy, however, that although Origen at times adopts the ordinary view of moral progress as being raised from a lower to a higher state of consciousness, he at times tends to make the notion of moral development conform to his own world-view, which regarded spirits who had originally been in perfect union with God as having later departed from Him through disobedience and as having thus become encased in material coverings. Thus he says in one place[64] that the captivity which Christ carries out is the return of a rational nature from sin and ignorance to virtue and knowledge. Elsewhere he says[65] that the destruction of a sinner is the separation of the rational soul (λογική ψυχή) from every kind of evil life. Origen indeed implies that the rational faculty inherent in spiritual beings was originally fully developed when he says[66] that these beings, though endowed with reason by God's bounty, transgressed the limits and commandments prescribed by reason, and thus deviated from what is right and just.

There are, however, two passages where he accepts the more commonsense account of moral progress as not so much a return to an original state of perfection as a progress from a lower to a higher state. With reference to St. Paul's statement that "we are saved by hope" (Rom.viii.24), he says that our adoption as sons and our redemption are at present received indirectly and through a mirror; but when we attain perfection, we shall obtain our adoption "face to face."[67] Elsewhere, in a rather curious interpretation of Genesis xx, where Sarah is represented as both Abraham's wife and his sister, Origen represents the acquisition of virtue as occurring in two stages. So long as we are not in complete possession of virtue it is fitting that it should be confined to us and enclosed within us, ie. be regarded as our wife. But when we have entered into complete possession of virtue, then it is that so far from keeping her to ourselves, we should share her with others who desire her, as though she were our sister.[68]

It would appear that the oscillation in Origen's thinking about moral progress to some extent derives from the fact that for him the exemplar of perfection is at one time the Word of God and at another time the historic Jesus. In the former case Origen thinks of moral perfection as consisting in contemplation only, after the removal of everything which obstructed it, sin being regarded primarily as that which interferes with the contemplation of God; in the latter case he thinks of moral perfection as consisting, in the words of the Collect, as "following the blessed steps of the most holy life" of the Incarnate Son. It is only if moral perfection be regarded as consisting in contemplation that moral progress can easily be regarded as a return to a former state; if it be regarded as necessarily manifesting itself in action, it is bound to be thought of as evolutionary in character. Thus Mme. Harl says:[69] "Is there not in Origen's conception of the role of Christ a constant ambiguity, which comes from the fact that his thinking is directed, in a not very explicit fashion, now to the Word Who is the illuminator of spirits, and now to the historic Jesus? What precisely is the imitation of Christ? Is it not the practice of the virtues? . . .

But is it not also conformity to the life of Jesus, seeing that, as the Pauline formulas express it, we are 'grafted' into Christ and share in his life?"

But in any case Origen would say that although all human beings possess the gift of reason, albeit not yet fully active, only the person spiritually united to the Word of God can be described as "rational" in the full sense. Thus he says that if it is true that only the person who (consciously) participates in the Word of God as λόγος (ie. reason) is rational (ie. λογικός), then it follows that only the ἅγιος is λογικός.[70] Elsewhere he says [71] that the τέλεως λόγος takes over him who has been under the law and the prophets and gives him his paternal inheritance (πατρική κληρονομία). Yet again,[72] he pronounces happy those who no longer need the Son of God as Doctor or as Shepherd or as Redeemer, but are able to receive Him in His capacity of perfect wisdom, reason, and justice, and whatever else is appropriate to those who are sufficiently mature to receive His best gifts.

There are indications that Origen regards the goal of full communion with the Divine Word as only attainable in the future life.[73] Thus he says [74] that so long as a person is in this life, his vision is only indirect and by means of a mirror, and he is hence like a sheep led by a Shepherd. Only when he is transferred to the future life, and is there acquainted with the truth face to face, will he have access to the spiritual table. In another passage, however, Origen seems to suggest that the transition from the one state to the other can be accomplished in this life.[75] He says indeed that when he who makes progress has reached the goal of becoming λογικός rather than a sheep led by his shepherd, he is admitted to the table on which God has prepared rational food (λογικῶν τροφῶν).[76]

Origen even goes on so far as to say that in their original state, men are comparable to beasts, because the gift of reason within them is undeveloped, and that only the Word of God can rescue them from that state.[77] It is curious that he does not regard the function of Christ as Shepherd in the way in which it is regarded nowadays, namely as that of guiding all those who accept Him as Lord, but in the more restricted sense of protecting disciples who are immature against rash courses of action and encouraging them in right courses of action without their fully understanding the reason why such actions are enjoined on them. Thus Origen says [78] that if, as the Psalmist says, God saves both men and beasts (Ps.xxvi.7), He saves the beasts whom He saves by granting a shepherd to those who cannot receive a king.[79] Later on,

Origen explains the meaning of this statement when he says that the Son of God, in His benevolence towards mankind, welcomes any kind of inclination of human souls towards what is better, even if they do not direct themselves towards the Word of God, but rather acquire a gentle and mild spirit which is devoid of reason, and so becomes their shepherd, for "the Lord saves both men and beasts."[80] Elsewhere, [81] Origen says that when the disciple's relation to his Lord is no longer that of a sheep to a shepherd, because he has now advanced to a more mature understanding of the Faith, it can be said that he is "converted" (Ps.xxiii.3).[82] It would appear that Origen is making a distinction between those who simply follow the example of the human Jesus, in so far as they model their actions on His, and those who ascend to the contemplation of the invisible Word of God, and so perceive the ultimate principle from which those actions proceed.[83]

There is a passage[84] in which Origen allegorises the story of the two wives of Elkanah — Anna and Peninna — in so far as the name of the first means "grace" and the name of the second means "conversion." "Grace" is joined to us by faith, and is the nobler gift; "conversion" follows on from it. But it is the second which first brings forth fruit, as in the case of Elkanah's two wives, because conversion produces the first shoots of righteousness in our actions; but those children do not wait on God, as Samuel did. In other words, the actions proceeding from conversion are not derived from intimate fellowship with God. Only when "grace" comes fully into its own do the children appear who wait on God and receive His word. In other words, only when the converted person is in full communion with the Word of God can that person perform actions which are fully acceptable to God. Origen quotes the episode of Martha and Mary in the Gospels: Martha does the works proceeding from conversion, but Mary sits at the feet of the Word of God and thus produces the fruits of grace.

On the other hand Origen is humble enough to recognise human limitations even when a person's rational powers appear to be in full exercise. "Compared with the true Word ($\tau\grave{o}\nu$ $\alpha\dot{\upsilon}\tau o\lambda\acute{o}\gamma o\nu$)", he says, "we are animal-like, and not only we, but beings much more rational and wise than we are." In fact Origen goes so far as to say that the reasoning faculty in the most mature of men, when compared with the true Word, is more distant from Him than is the life-principle ($\psi\upsilon\chi\acute{\eta}$) of an ass or a colt from that of a man.[85] Here Origen almost seems to be adopting the view already mentioned that full access to the truth enshrined in the Divine Word is only obtainable in the next life.[86]

At any rate he makes it clear that we can never be certain that we have transcended the relation of sheep to shepherd in our relation to the Divine Word. It might also be said that the same applies to the function of Christ as Physician; Origen says in one place that the outward miracles of Christ, such as the bestowal of sight and hearing, are symbolic of His cure of human souls.[87] In fact we can never be certain whether our wills are as stable as they should be, and whether the teaching of the Word of God will not again be necessary for rescuing them from sloth and wickedness and thus enabling them to bring forth their intended good works.[88] It is noteworthy that Origen regards angelic beings as appointed by the Father to protect immature souls until the time when those souls have the inner resources needed for their conflict with evil.[89]

There are numerous passages when Origen insists that it is necessary for the Divine Word to enter the $\psi v\chi \acute{\eta}$ of the person whom He helps to progress spiritually.[90] On the other hand, he also recognises that other agents prepare the way for that entry and enlarge it when it has been made. Thus he says that Christ does not enter the $\psi v\chi \acute{\eta}$ which is Jerusalem on His own, or with few companions: for there need to be many who precede the Word of God Who makes us perfect, and many who follow Him.[91]

In *Comm. in Cant.*[92] Origen states that the Word of God dwells as King in that soul which has arrived at spiritual perfection. It was of such a soul that the Lord said, "The Father and I will come and sup with him and make our abode with him." Origen pronounces blessed the breadth of that soul and the resting-place of that mind where the three Persons of the Divine Trinity recline and dine and make their abode.[93] Likewise in *De Orat.*[94] it is stated that God lives in the saints, and that this is what is meant by saying that God lives in heaven, because every saint bears the image of the Heavenly One. Elsewhere it is said that since every saint is obedient to the spiritual laws of God and has thus attained perfection of character, both the Father and the Son reign in his soul.[95] St. Paul's language about all Christ's enemies being subdued to Him and all forms of authority being abolished (I Cor.xv.24,25) can thus be applied to the individual soul, in so far as the power of sinful tendencies has been broken, and the Father and the Son thus take possession of the soul.[96]

There are several passages where Christ's work in the human soul is referred to in the same manner as the work which God is reported to have imposed on the prophet Jeremiah, ie. that of plucking up and breaking down, destroying and overthrowing, building and planting (Jer.i.10). The intention is that God's glory may be apparent in human souls. Thus in one passage it is stated that Christ is both a builder and a destroyer; He destroys the buildings erected in us by unclean spirits, and builds in us a temple of virtue and true beliefs in which God's glory can appear.[97] In another passage, the "glory" of God is held to the equivalent to His Divinity ($\dot{\eta}$ $\theta\epsilon\iota\acute{o}\tau\eta\varsigma$ $\alpha\dot{v}\tau o\hat{v}$). That Divinity, being so abundant, is difficult for created nature to comprehend; but from the riches of His Divinity He imparts a share to those to whom it is appropriate to receive it. This is brought about through Christ, Who, although He does not need individual souls as His dwelling-place, none the less dwells ($\kappa\alpha\tau o\iota\kappa\epsilon\hat{\iota}$) in those who partake of Him through faith.[98]

The help which Christ offers is often compared by Origen to nourishment. In his own words, "we feed on whatever discourse we hear, whether from the dragon, if we hear what is vain and useless, or from Christ, if we receive words which are edifying and helpful."[99] Elsewhere,[100] Christ is described as the Food which, though always consumed, always remains and indeed is augmented. For the more abundantly and eagerly a person receives the food which is the Word of God, the more richly will it enter that person. In an unusual interpretation of the phrase $\tau\grave{o}v$ $\ddot{\alpha}\rho\tau ov$ $\dot{\eta}\mu\hat{\omega}v$ $\tau\grave{o}v$ $\dot{\epsilon}\pi\iota o\acute{v}\sigma\iota ov$ in the Lord's Prayer, Origen says [101] that genuine substance ($o\dot{v}\sigma\acute{\iota}\alpha$) is what remains fixed, whereas bodily substance is fluid and disappears, and hence it is genuine substance which is nourished by the Divine Word Who is the Living Bread, from which the bridegroom's companions have to fast when they are deprived of the bridegroom himself, that Bridegroom Who nourishes invisibly the invisible soul ($\psi v \chi \acute{\eta}$) (cf. Matt.ix.15). Likewise Origen says that those who are humble in heart and poor in spirit are invited to the banquet provided by Divine Wisdom, and they thus escape the hunger which prevails on the earth (cf. Amos viii.11). The true Israelite is fed alike by the Law, the Prophets, and the Apostles. He is invited to recline on Abraham's bosom in the Father's kingdom, and there to eat the Tree of Life and drink from the true Vine which is Christ.[102]

Origen also says that food can actually be offered to Christ Himself, though it is only clean food if we have dined with Him previously.[103] This rather puzzling statement is elucidated in two other passages. In the first it is said that we must use the food which is given to us so as to prepare such food within ourselves as may worthily be set before the three Persons of the Divine Trinity Who desire to make their home within us. This food is interpreted as being such feelings as anger and desire which can be directed to right and wrong objects.[104] In the second, it is stated that we are the trees in Christ's garden (cf. Is.lviii.11) if we ourselves provide Him with nourishment, namely the salvation of our souls, as is suggested by the saying "My food is to do the will of Him Who sent me" (John iv.34), because the fruit which we produce consists in our own acts of choice ($\pi\rho o\alpha i\rho\epsilon\sigma\iota\varsigma$).[105] We can thus understand the meaning of the passage[106] where Origen says that a person who makes progress in virtue grants a place in his soul to the Son of God, Who thereafter fills it with His own wisdom and holiness, and finally brings His Divine Father with Him, so that together they can dine on the food which He Himself has provided.

There are, however, two other passages which raise a problem which Origen never satisfactorily solved – the problem of the original state of human beings. In the first,[107] he says that when Christ is spoken of as "reclining at the table" of a soul (Cant.i.12), this means that this soul is perfected in virtue; but where Christ reclines, there the Father also is, as is made clear in the saying "My Father and I will come and sup with him, and will make our abode with him." In the second, it is stated that when the human mind is nourished by the food of Divine Wisdom to the integrated and perfected state in which it was made in the beginning, it will be restored to the image and likeness of God.[108] In the meantime, as has been said already,[109] the Father seeks true worshippers through the Son ($\delta\iota\grave{a}$ $\tau o\hat{v}$ $v\iota o\hat{v}$), Who came to seek and to save the lost, whom by a process of cleansing and instruction He makes into true worshippers.[110] Elsewhere the Son declares that His mission is to "finish the Father's work" (John iv.34). This is at first a puzzling statement, because it implies that the work of God is imperfect, and how can that be so? Moreover, how can the Father's work be completed by Him Who said, "The Father Who sent me is greater than I?"[111] The dilemma can be resolved, says Origen, by saying that Christ is continuing the Father's work by bringing rational creatures to perfection. That was the purpose of the Incarnation. It would appear that beings who were originally perfect became imperfect through disobedience, and thus stood in need of One Who would restore them to perfection.[112] Hence, says Origen, the Saviour was sent to perfect the rational creatures who are the work of God, and thereafter accustom them to the solid food of true wisdom.[113] We have seen already [114] that if the work of the Son of God is limited to what the Incarnation was meant to bring about, it becomes easier to think of the process of redemption as distinguishable from that of creation; for whatever Origen may say, a being who was capable of transgressing the Divine Will could scarcely be said to be perfect, and the result would be that the process of bringing rational beings to perfection would be co-eval with the history of human beings. In fact Origen suggests in *Contra Cels.*[115] that God could have made human beings perfect at the beginning, but did not do so, in order to leave scope for freewill.

It seems quite clear that there is a contradiction between Origen's outlook in *De Princ.* and his outlook in *Contra Cels.* in so far as he seems to lay it down in the former work that all things were originally created perfect. Thus he says that since Christ, Who is the Word and Wisdom of God, is also perfect Righteousness, the result is that all that He has made has been made in that righteousness which is identifiable with Himself; and this means that there is nothing accidental, nothing unrighteous, in the things which have been made, but everything can be shown to be such as the principle of righteousness and justice requires.[116] But in that case, how did evil creep into the world? The answer is, says Origen, by the misuse of freewill, which resulted in different creatures receiving different positions in the universe.[117] But that appears too facile a solution if we recall that according to Origen himself, the act of creation did not take place at one definite time, but is a continuous process in which the Word of God is engaged everywhere in the universe.[118] This means that God's creatures are not as independent as they would like to think, because the omnipotent Word of God uses them as channels of His activity.

The solution of the difficulty would seem to be that whereas human beings were originally fashioned in a state of imperfection, the Divine Word leads them on to greater perfection, and more especially if they are conscious of His guidance.[119] Indeed, this is suggested by Origen himself in *De Princ.* (surprisingly enough) where he says with reference to Gen.i.27 that it was stated that God made man in His own "image" (as distinct from "likeness") because the "image" was only an inchoate form of the "likeness", which could only be acquired by man's own earnest aspirations after it. The "image" is in fact no more than the inherent possibility of acquiring the "likeness" through performing works acceptable to God.[120] Origen goes on to say that this happy consummation will come about through the pleading of the

Divine Saviour on behalf of human beings, as expressed in the words of the High-priestly prayer "As Thou and I are one, so may they be one in us" (John xvii.21). Origen here introduces a subtle distinction between "likeness" and "identity", and though "likeness" implies a measure of difference, whereas in the consummation of all things God's nature will be perfectly expressed in all things and creatures.[121] Elsewhere, Origen says that the perfection of human beings is attained when God is "all things" in each individual (with ref. to I Cor.xv.28). This means that the mind is purified from its vices and its powers of perception are unhindered by the clouds interposed by wickedness, with the result that all it feels or understands or thinks will be God, and God will supply the regulation of its every movement.[122]

It is also worth remarking that Origen stresses that since God's creatures are not co-eternal with Himself, they do not possess His attribute of changelessness.[123] But surely, if they were created perfect in the beginning, as Origen suggests in certain places, that would imply that they received the gift of changelessness. But Origen is compelled by the facts to deny this, because of the obvious imperfection of the world. He seems to be obsessed with the idea of evil as the result of deliberate choice, often stimulated by evil suggestion from outside, rather than as something resulting from an immature stage of spiritual development. Origen indeed says in one passage that "one who is always in the good and to whom God is all things will no longer desire to eat of the tree of the knowledge of Good and evil."[124] He is referring to the perfected state of human beings: but according to him, their perfected state is a restoration of their original state. So we are still left with the problem: how did evil originate? [125]

But whatever the defects of his explanation of evil, no one would surely wish to take issue with Origen's contention – already referred to and discussed [126] – that Jesus Christ is to be thought of as the Agent by Whom human beings are enabled to gain the Vision of God Himself. Origen here shows himself more ready to adopt the evolutionary account of moral progress. In his own words, "he who sees the Wisdom which God brought into being for the fashioning of His works, ascends from the knowledge of Wisdom to the Father of Wisdom. It is impossible to conceive the God of Wisdom without the introduction which (incarnate) Wisdom affords. It is the same with Truth . . .." [127] Origen then compares the process of becoming acquainted with the Father through the Son to the steps of the Temple which lead to the holiest place. The first step is His human nature, and then we travel through the other aspects of His Nature, the angelic and the rest.[128] From another point of view, we first encounter Him as the Way, and then as the Door, and again first accept Him as Shepherd in the manner of irrational creatures so as eventually to enjoy the benefits of His Kingship. Again, we first obtain the benefit of the deliverance from sin which He bestows as the Lamb of God, and then we eat of the true nourishment which His Flesh provides.[129] But all this is simply designed to enable us to advance towards our final goal of coming to know the Father.[130] Apropos of this passage, Koch begins[131] by pointing out that though Origen is a mystic, his mysticism is of a purely intellectual character, and consists in the knowledge of God, not in an ecstatic union with Him. He then goes on to say that Origen's understanding of the Divine Word is more closely connected with the philosophic conception of the Logos than with the historic Jesus Christ. None the less, says Koch, there is something additional, which consists not in the consideration of the Gospel story of His life, or even His sufferings and death, but rather in the fact that for Origen, the Divine Word is a personal Being, with whom one can enter into personal relationships. But this fact is rendered rather less significant when one considers that the ultimate goal for Origen is not a union of the will with that of God, but rather a mere knowledge of Him. This is true even if, as Koch says, Origen felt more at home with simple-minded Christians than with philosophers like Albinus and Numenius.[132]

It is the view of Origen that eventually all rational creatures will be persuaded by the Son of God to accept the Father's rule.[133] This is his interpretation of St. John's statement (xiii.3) that Jesus knew that the Father had given all things into His hands. This statement was anticipated by the psalmist in the words "The Lord said unto my Lord, Sit thou on my right hand, until I make thine enemies the footstool of thy feet." The enemies of Jesus were simply numbered among the things which Jesus knew that the Father had given into His hands, even though they did not yet appear to be subject to Him.[134] Origen then quotes the words "As in Adam all die, even so in Christ shall all be made alive" (I Cor.xv.22) as showing that what St. John meant was that all creatures would receive a share in Christ's risen life, though not all at the same time. The end will come when Christ, having put down all rule and authority (ie. the things which are objects of contention) shall deliver His Kingdom to God the Father.

The Lord in fact realised before His Passion that the persuading of

Judas by the devil to betray Him was only a means whereby the purpose of the Father might be fulfilled. Even though the Father had given all things into the Son's hands, it rested with the Son to subdue all things by His outstanding deeds, in accordance with His own words "Just as my Father has been at work till now, even so I must work." We thus see once more that Jesus came forth from God for the sake of those who had rebelled against God, even though He did not really wish to leave the Father's presence,[135] so that the creatures who had rebelled might come into the hands of Jesus in due order, and finally be brought back to God through following Jesus.[136]

There is of course a sense in which everything is already under the control of the Son of God, in so far as He brought all things into being and still exercises His providential care of them. And so although as St. John says in two places, the Father entrusts everything to the Son,[137] this must be understood in the sense of entrusting to Him the work of salvation, seeing that what He has made has gone astray from His protecting care. There never has been a time when the Son of God has not been concerned about the things which He has made; but special action was needed to make them aware of this concern and to persuade them to accept the enlightenment and healing which He provides. The believer is thus entrusted to the Son for his own benefit, and not for that of the Son.[138] This statement is amplified elsewhere,[139] in a passage where it is said that Christ's rule over all creatures is exercised partly in so far as He is Creator of all things and has power over all things, and thus rules over evil beings as well as good ones, and partly in so far as He persuades them to accept His rule of their own free will. To quote Origen's own words, "He persuades them by instruction rather than by command, by invitation rather than by torture." The supreme example of such persuasion was His death on the Cross, because in that way above all He bequeathed the example of obedience to those who are prepared to die to sin.[140]

Two observations may be made here. First, Origen seems to imply that if the Word of God so desired, He could exact obedience instead of requesting it. So much is implied in another passage,[141] where he says that Christians are persecuted when God permits them to be, and enjoy freedom from disturbance when God does not allow it, because the world only has power ($\iota\sigma\chi\acute{\upsilon}\epsilon\iota$) in so far as this is allowed by Him Who has received from the Father power to conquer the world. (This of course is a reference to John xvi.33 "I have overcome the world"; but Origen seems to invest these words with his own meaning, because our Lord's meaning surely was "I have not allowed myself to be affected by the attitude of the world.")

The second observation is that Origen states elsewhere that the Son of God does in fact employ chastisement as well as admonition for the improvement of human beings. We have seen this outlook fully set forth in an earlier chapter,[142] and we shall also allude to it later in this chapter.[143] Presumably Origen would say that as Man, Christ only exercises persuasion, whereas in so far as He is the Word of God and is therefore in ultimate control of all things, He exercises compulsion in the way in which the owner of a dog lets the animal move freely within the area to which the lead extends, but makes the animal sharply aware of his control if the animal tugs at the lead.

There is a rather curious passage in *Contra Cels.*[144] in which it is first stated that the Word of God is in one sense not in control of creatures who are unwilling to obey Him, but in another sense He is, just as we say that human beings can obtain control of irrational creatures not by subduing the principal part of their nature (τὸ ἡγεμονικόν), but in the way that a tamer gains control of lions and other wild beasts. The Word of God, however, takes all possible steps to exercise control through persuasion over those at present disobedient. One would have thought that the simile of "taming" was more appropriate to the influence exerted by the Divine Word upon those who are spiritually immature, inasmuch as they do what is right without fully understanding the reason for it. The simile of a dog on a lead seems more appropriate in the other case, as would that of a cage in which wild animals are confined, because Origen is surely wanting to suggest, not that those who are rebellious are won over to doing what is required of them by methods other than rational argument, but rather that they are prevented from doing what God does not want them to do. The simile of "taming" would, as has been said, be appropriate to the influence which persuades the spiritually immature to do what is right without fully understanding the reason for doing it.[145] (Indeed, Origen states in one place[146] that it must have been by the aid of supernatural power that Christ has converted so many people, not only among the wise, but also among the more irrational, so that they are no longer so liable to let their feelings run away with them.)

The tension between the control which Christ exercises over human beings in the one sense and that which He exercises in another sense is well brought out in the passage[147] where it is said that the reign of Christ over creation is not complete. True, He reigns in the sense that the reign of sin is gradually being diminished, even though it had previously extended over all mankind; and so it is true that as St. Paul says, "He must reign until He has subjected all His enemies" (I Cor.xv.25). But when this statement is set alongside the reminder that "We do not as yet see all things in subjection to Him" (Heb.ii.8), the statement "He must reign" is seen to mean "He must extend His kingdom."

Origen is now faced with the curious text of St. Paul in which it is said that when all things have been subjected to the Son, the Son will be subjected to the Father (I Cor.xv.28) — as though He were not already subjected to the Father! The solution to the problem, says Origen, lies in thinking of Christ as operating amongst His followers so as to transform them into His own likeness. In so far as He is at work in this way and persuades them to submit themselves to the Father, to that extent He Himself is subjected to the Father, because He indwells His followers.[148] As Origen himself expresses it, "Since Christ is the Head of the Body of which all human beings are members, it is true that He is not yet subjected to God, if His members are not so subjected." [149] As so often, Origen presses into the service of His own outlook a phrase of Scripture which he interprets in his own way. He refers to I Cor.xii.27, which is usually translated "You are the body of Christ, and individually (ἐκ μέρους) members of it ": but he understands it to mean "You are only partially members of the body", in so far as your wills are not yet in full harmony with Christ. Hence he feels able to say that when Christ has led the entire creation to the height of perfection and so completed His work, He himself will be said to be subject to the Father in so far as He is in those whom He has subjected.[150]

It is on similar lines that Origen interprets the passage where it is stated that the Son does not know the day and hour of the final judgement (Matt.xxiv.36). This statement at first sight appears inconsistent with the omniscience of the Divine Word; but once again Origen applies to Christ what strictly speaking is only applicable to His followers, in so far as when the Church, His Body, experiences that day and hour, He Himself will experience it, and not before (Origen defends this interpretation of the word "know" by reference to the text in which Christ is said to have "known no sin" (II Cor.v.21).[151]

As has already been stated in an earlier chapter,[152] Christ's method of subjecting human beings to Himself differs according to the state of those beings. Sometimes harsh methods are needed, and sometimes mere instruction will suffice. He is very fond of adducing Ps.xxiii.4 "Thy rod and Thy staff comfort me" in support of this contention.[153] The rod and the staff, says Origen, alike refer to beatings and punishments. The sheep who sins is chastised with a rod; the man who sins is chastised with a staff. The distinction seems to be between immature and mature Christians.[154] On the other hand, the person who is punished is consoled, because he knows that God scourges every son whom He receives. The same idea is expressed elsewhere[155] by saying that when God punishes, He is not an enemy of those whom He punishes; rather, He desires to help those who undergo the punishment, or failing that, those who witness it, ie. by discouraging them from sinning in the same way. Indeed Origen says,[156] with reference to the passage "Rule in the midst of your enemies", that Christ shows Himself to be the Image of God's goodness by bringing help to His enemies and so ruling them. An even more striking expression of the same idea is the statement [157] that the Saviour, because He is friendly towards mankind, brings to Himself by compulsion those who are no longer free to make their own decisions (ie. those who are sunk in sin and so spiritually dead). As elsewhere, Origen says [158] that the destruction of Christ's enemies is equivalent to their being turned into friends, because the power of sin within them is destroyed. To be subjected to Christ is in fact to "have the mind" of Christ.[159] In another passage, when reference is made to the text "He must reign till He has put all His enemies under His feet", Origen says [160] that Christ's kingly rule ($\beta\alpha\sigma\iota\lambda\epsilon\iota\alpha$) is the contemplation ($\theta\epsilon\omega\rho\iota\alpha$) of all the ages ($\alpha\iota\omega\nu\omega\nu$) that have occurred and will occur, and that through this contemplation even His enemies become His friends. In other words, Christ's enemies are converted from the assumption that other people exist to supply their wants to the recognition that they themselves are intended to promote the agelong purpose of God; in short, they see things *sub specie aeternitatis*.

To the question whether ultimately all creatures will submit to Christ of their own free will, or whether some will continue to be so stubborn as to require forcible subjection, Origen does not give the same answer in all the passages which deal with the question. Thus in *Contra Cels.*[161] he says that when each person by the exercise of his own freedom has chosen what is in accordance with the will of the Divine Word, and has adhered to that choice, the Divine Word will then have obtained control over rational creatures, because he will have changed them into His own perfection ($\tau\epsilon\lambda\epsilon\iota\acute{o}\tau\eta\tau\alpha$). Likewise, in a curious interpretation [162] of the passage "All power is given to Me in heaven and on earth", Origen suggests that at the end of the world all those on earth (ie. all those in a state of sin)[163] will submit to the persuasive power of the Son of God in accordance with the example of those who have already attained perfection by submitting to that power, and will thus attain a happy end. The subjection of the enemies of the Son of God is thus something which so far from being harmful to them, is beneficial to them, because it results in the restoration and salvation of those who are subjected.[164] In *Hom. in Jos.* Origen says that the Crucifixion was the episode when the power of the devil began to be brought to an end as the result of the availability of the spiritual life bestowed through the Crucified Christ.[165] It remains, however, for human beings to accept that gift of life, and so contribute to bringing to an end the devil's reign. The devil himself, in spite of the harm he has wreaked, will eventually accept the rule of God.[166]

On the other hand, there is also a passage in *Hom. in Jos.*[167] which appears to suggest that the time available for voluntary submission is limited, and that eventually those who still remain obstinate will be subjected by force. Origen interprets with reference to Christ the two statements made about the occupation of the land of Canaan by Joshua, the first being that "the land ceased from warfare as the result of Joshua's taking possession of the whole land" (Josh.xi.23), and the second being that "much of the land remained to be possessed" (xiii. 1). Origen says that our Lord at His first coming sowed the Word of the Gospel throughout the earth and so put to flight the hostile powers which had held sway over human minds; but in so far as there is still much which remains unsubdued, and He has thus not yet entered into possession of His entire inheritance, He needs to come again to subject by force those who still defy Him. But these latter will lack the blessing bestowed on those who voluntarily joined the Son of God in attacking evil powers. The same idea is expressed in a passage [168] where reference is made to those who despise the Word of God when they hear it, and are hence forcibly converted through punishments and chastisements.

It seems clear that Origen did not really know his own mind on the subject of whether all rational creatures will eventually submit voluntarily to the control of the Word of God. There is a passage in *De Princ.*[169] where this uncertainty seems to appear, in so far as Origen there says that there are two ways in which God exercises sway over all things through the wisdom which is Christ, one in so far as they cannot escape His ultimate control, the other in so far as they serve Him of their own free will. A little later, with reference to Philipp.ii. 10, Origen says[170] that if every knee bows to Jesus, it follows that it is through Him that all things are subjected to the Father in so far as their subjection is brought about by wisdom and reason, and not by force and necessity. Perhaps the view at which Origen eventually arrived is the one stated in the passage[171] where it is said that the world will not become subject to God through the compulsion of necessity, but rather by an appeal to the creature's own sense of what is right, though this does not exclude such warnings as are necessary for those who neglect their own spiritual welfare. In fact Origen seems to regard compulsion as an intermediate stage in obtaining the genuine submission of human beings; it is exerted in the expectation that it will soon be unnecessary.

Origen lays stress on the fact that those who are subjected to Christ of their own freewill have themselves won the victory over sin. Thus he says[172] that Christ ascribes the victory to those who are conquered by Him, because in so far as a person is conquered by Christ, he has conquered the sin which formerly adhered to him, and has blotted it out. For Christ as the Word of God conquers no one unwillingly; he only conquers by persuasion. In the same way, Origen says in *Hom. in Num.*[173] that although Jesus Christ is rightly called "King of kings" in so far as He exercises supreme oversight of the various communities of Christians, none the less Christians themselves can also be called "kings" in so far as through belief in Christ they have overcome the dominion of sin in themselves and have established the kingdom of righteousness. In one passage, however,[174] the ultimate fruits of the victory of Christians are postponed till the future age, in so far as Origen says that it is after the present world has come to an end that those who have won the victory under Christ's leadership will receive the kingdom prepared for those who have kept God's commandments.[175]

Origen indeed recognises that the victory over sin obtained by those who accept the Lordship of Christ is not accomplished all at once, but gradually. He says in fact that the Church on earth, while it is yet in the early stages of the worship of God and the knowledge of Christ, may be regarded as the footstool of Christ's feet (cf. Matt.xxii. 44), just as the sinful woman who came into the Pharisee's house remained at Jesus' feet at the beginning of her repentance because she could not yet pour the oil of her good actions on His head (Luke vii.

38).[176] In the same way, each of us must first become the footstool of Christ's feet when we have ceased to be the enemy of Christ, that is, the enemy of righteousness, truth, wisdom, and peace. On the other hand, even if we are relegated to that position, that is not done for our destruction but for our salvation, as St. Paul makes clear in I Cor.xv. 20-28.[177]

On the other hand there is no suggestion that we should remain in that position. In fact the Son of God desires to impart to others His own Sonship, and thus to bring about their direct fellowship with the Father. This Origen considers to be the real implication of the text in I Cor.xv (verse 28) in which it is said that the Son will eventually hand over His Kingdom to the Father. Thus he declares in *Comm. in Cant.* that the different ways in which Solomon is described in the opening words of Proverbs, Ecclesiastes, and Canticles respectively remind us that, first, Jesus Christ acquaints us with the commandments of God without as yet enrolling us in the company of His mature disciples; then after making further progress we are admitted into fellowship with the members of the heavenly Jerusalem, ie. with those who have abjured the things of this world; and finally, after all rational creatures have been reconciled by Christ to God, Christ ceases to bear rule as King Himself, and hands over kingly authority to the Father, and is thenceforth simply called "the peace-making One" (which is after all the meaning of the name "Solomon").[178] Later on in the same treatise, however, Origen shows that he is thinking more of individual rational beings than of rational beings collectively, because he says that the reason why at the beginning of Canticles the writer calls himself Solomon only is that in that book of the Bible the servant has been made as his Lord, the disciple as His Master, and the subject as His King.[179] Likewise in *De Princ.* Origen suggests that there are three stages in the way in which those destined for blessedness are supervised. First they come under the care of inferior governors (ie. human or angelic overseers); then they are taken over by Christ Himself so as to be instructed by Him in His capacity of Wisdom; and finally, when they have been made capable of receiving God Himself, they are handed over to the direct rule of the Father.[180]

On the other hand this statement must not be taken as implying that Christ ceases to have any relationship to those who are so handed over. Franco points out [181] that the apparent contradiction between the passages referred to above and the passage in *Comm. in Cant.* [182] where Christ is described as occupying the perfected soul as King is resolved by saying that "when the soul has arrived at perfection, Christ is not called 'King' in so far as that word implies struggle and conquest, but in so far as it implies overlordship and possession .... We can say that He ceases to be King in so far as being King is opposed to being Bridegroom, which amounts to saying, in so far as conquest is opposed to possession." Later on he says [183] that "if in the sphere of personal religion the reign of Christ is a transitory and supersessible phase, that is not in the sense that Christ ceases to influence the soul, but rather in the sense that His influence, which up to now has been external, is now so intimate that the soul forms 'one spirit' with Him." Curiously enough, Franco seems to think that this is true of the human soul of the Son of God Himself. In discussing [184] the passage in *Comm. in Joh.* [185] in which the relation between the Divine and the human nature of Christ is discussed, he points out that Origen says that the anointing of the human soul of the Divine Word as Christ was carried out because that soul loved righteousness and hated iniquity; in other words it was not received from the beginning of that soul's existence, but was, if it may be so expressed, a reward for effort made. On the other hand, the Kingship of the Word of God is eternal; otherwise He would not be what He is, ie. changeless. But in that case, when the condition which prevailed before the fall of created spirits is restored,[186] the Word of God will be King in the same sense as He was in the beginning, and will only cease to be King in so far as Kingship implies war and conquest rather than peaceful possession. It is also worth quoting Franco's statement elsewhere [187] that "the Word does not cease to influence souls when they attain to the highest stage of union with God and to the vision of the Father ... but it is precisely then that we can enquire whether this union is not of the same intensity as that of the soul of Christ with the Word of God." Aeby puts the matter very well when he says [188] that "the Word is the plenipotentiary Agent of the Father, and as such has the task of conducting all rational beings to the vision of God. He does so by becoming incarnate, by coming to dwell in them, by leading them to the contemplation of Himself, by transforming them into Himself and imparting to them His own Sonship so fully that finally those beings can, like Him, contemplate the Father face to face."

So far, Origen has considered the introduction of souls to the Father which Christ carries out from the point of view of mystical contemplation; but there are at least two passages in which he thinks of it in terms of a transformed way of living. In one of these passages [189] Origen points out that in Rom.xiv.10 St. Paul speaks of all human beings as standing at God's judgement seat, whereas in II Cor.v. 10 the judgement seat is that of Christ. The reason for the difference of language is that Christ as the Word of God has the function of reconciling the world to God through His Incarnation; but this reconciliation takes time because human beings are reluctant to accept the help which He offers, and so until He has finally subdued all His enemies He reigns as one who reveals those who are good and rewards the blameworthy according to their deeds; in other words, He is gradually conquering those opposed to Him. But when all human beings have been converted and reformed, He will deliver His Kingdom to God the Father in so far as He will have reconciled all human beings to God. Once again, the surrender of the kingdom to the Father does not mark the end of the work of Christ, but rather the completion of it, in so far as He completely indwells those whom He has converted. Origen expresses the matter in another way when he says [190] with reference to the individual that when a person is set free from sin, that is, when he becomes aware of his need of deliverance, he is first bound to become a servant of all the virtues so that he may make progress towards becoming a servant of God, even though in a sense he is serving God all the time. It is only later that he can become a servant of God in the full sense, that is, when he is perfected in virtue; it is then that Christ is said to deliver the kingdom to the Father, because only then is God "all in all" in the individual. We may compare the contrast which Origen makes elsewhere between those who are merely converted and those who wait on God.[191]

In another passage [192] Origen says that even though in one sense the Word of God and His servant cannot both be in the same place, in another sense they can be, because in so far as the servant is honoured by the Father the servant comes to be where the Word Himself is. The meaning seems to be that in so far as a human being endeavours to enter into fuller union with Christ, to that extent he receives honour from the Father, and the greater the extent of that union, the more fully is that person elevated to the level of Christ Himself and the more closely does the honour which he receives approximate to that accorded to the Son of God. Elsewhere,[193] with reference to John xii. 26, Origen says that when Christ promises that His servant shall be where He is, this must be understood primarily in a spiritual fashion; but it can also be understood corporeally and spatially, in so far as those outstanding in virtue will eventually be installed at the resurrection in the purest and most illuminated places, seeing that these places are most fitted for the contemplation of the Word of God. Origen seems here to recognise that the destiny of human beings is not that of disembodied spirits, but that of beings who will be able to enact through their bodies the vision which they have been able to perceive through spiritual purification. In the same way he says that Jesus as the Wisdom of God provides those who are truly wise with their heavenly dwelling-places, just as it was Joshua, and not Moses, who provided the Levites with their dwellings,[194] and that the members of the true Israel will share the glory of Christ, in so far as He is universal Ruler, at the time when they rise again with glorious bodies.[195] (On the other hand, Origen suggests that the Christian whose merit is greater will receive from Christ a greater reward in the future heavenly kingdom.)[196]

We may sum up the whole discussion of the effect of Christ's redeeming work by referring to Origen's comment on the passage in the Book of Numbers[197] where it is foretold that the people shall rise up like a lion's cub, and rejoice like a lion. Origen says[198] that the mature Christian has dominion over all things, just as a lion has dominion over all other animals, and therefore Christ, the Lion of the tribe of Judah, also grants the name of lion to all who believe in Him. The mature believer is no longer a servant of Christ, but a partner and fellow-worker, and thus has no need of the outward mediation of the Son of God, because he experiences His inward presence.[199] There is a passage[200] in which Origen states that whereas it is not possible for human beings to change their relationship to each other in the sense that a child becomes a brother, the person who was originally a child (τέκνον) of Jesus can become His brother. He instances the command of Jesus to Mary Magdalene to tell His "brothers" about His forthcoming ascension.[201] Indeed, there is a lower stage than that of being a τέκνον, ie. that of being a δοῦλος; for the disciples were spoken of as δοῦλοι in the Upper Room before they were addressed as children.[202] And so there are four stages through which the Christian believer passes, that of being a "slave", that of being a "disciple", that of being a "child", and that of being a brother of Christ and a Son of God. Elsewhere,[203] Origen says that the person who has reached the stage of being a "disciple" is in good health, presumably because he has overcome obvious sins, and therefore needs Jesus not as Physician, but in connexion with His other powers, ie. presumably as Enlightener.

We must now discuss the question whether in Origen's view the

Christian in the final stage of His discipleship can obtain a direct and unmediated vision of God the Father. Is this what is meant, in Origen's view, by the surrender of the Kingdom by the Son to the Father (I Cor.xv.24)? In one passage [204] it is stated that the fact that the Son sees the things of the Father directly is shown by the words "I speak what I have seen in the Father (παρὰ τῷ πατρί)" (John viii.38). Origen wonders whether the angels themselves (who in his view are simply human beings raised to a higher level) will one day see what is in the Father without any mediation. There is in fact a distinction between seeing the Father in the Son, as is done by a person who sees the Son and thus sees the Father Who sent Him, and seeing the Father and the things in the Father in the same way as the Son does and thus seeing the Father directly (αὐτόπτης ἔσται τοῦ πατρός).[205] In the latter case the person no longer obtains from the Image (εἰκών) an understanding of the things in Him Whose εἰκών the Son is. It is thus that God becomes all in all as the result of the surrender to the Father by the Son of the kingdom He has gained. In another passage [206] the same opinion is summarised in the statement that after the final consummation the one task of those who have attained to God by way of His Word will be to obtain an ever-increasing comprehension of God, so that they may through their knowledge of the Father be transformed into a single Son, inasmuch as they will know the Father as fully as the Son now does.

There has been much discussion of the meaning of the two passages just referred to by those who have commented on Origen's writings. Crouzel considers,[207] in my opinion rightly, that the Son is never rendered superfluous. He says that "if the vision of the Father is not now obtained by means of the Son, it is a vision similar to that of the Son; the soul is assimilated to the Son, and sees the Father in the same manner as He does. The Son is not a stage which one surmounts; the Son is He Who imparts continually to His brothers His unique attribute of being the Son of God." Elsewhere [208] Crouzel says, with reference to the same two passages, that "the mediation of the Son will be changed; from a connexion which is in some sense external, it will become a very intimate union. Human beings will not become 'one Son', except in so far as they are included in the unique Son of God."

Crouzel is in fact saying that although the Son will never cease to be the Agent whereby human beings are enabled to obtain the vision of the Father, the Son's agency will in the end be continuous instead of intermittent, and so human beings will scarcely be conscious of it.

At earlier stages of their development, their glimpses of God will be fitful and transient and they will be keenly aware that they only obtain these glimpses as a result of their acquaintance with Jesus Christ; but later on the influence of Christ will be less intermittent, and the vision of God thus granted to human beings will be more continuous and less interrupted.

Mme. Harl concludes[209] from the first passage that there is a knowledge of God which is superior to the knowledge obtained through the Son, and describes this as a weakness in Origen's theology. Crouzel's observations are worth bearing in mind in this connexion.[210] Dupuis takes the same view as Crouzel when he says[211] that when a person is described as αὐτόπτης τοῦ πατρός, it means that it is *in* the Word rather than *by means of* the Word that that person sees the Father. Dupuis refers to Nemeshegyi's work on Origen,[212] where it is said that "the Christian, being united to the Son, must not stop short at the Divinity of the Son, which, in spite of its equality with that of the Father, is merely derived from it; he must, by means of (à travers) this open door which is the Saviour, project himself in love towards the Father Himself." It is noteworthy that Nemeshegyi uses the phrase "à travers" to indicate the manner in which the believer ultimately views the Father by the Son's agency, whereas Dupuis rejects that phrase in favour of "dans"; but Nemeshegyi shows that he agrees with Dupuis and Crouzel when he says[213] that "the superseding (dépassement) of the mediation of the Son does not in any way mean that the Only-begotten Son ever becomes superfluous in the life of grace." Lieske takes the same view when he says[214] that "because the Word is the Head of all mankind and the Fullness of those who in Him attain salvation, He is also the Agent by Whom all are brought together into union with the Father."[215]

Völker also takes the same view[216] when he says that "mystical union with Christ, though a stage of transition to mystical union with God, has a value which is not superseded, but endures . . . As the Crucified Christ in some way plays a part in mystical union with the Divine Word, even so on the highest level of mystical union with God, the Word does not quite disappear."[217]

Schendel concludes the section[218] in which he discusses this matter by saying that "the return (ie. of created spirits) to their original unity . . . to the direct, restored vision of God, provided Origen with a foundation for his doctrine of the end of the sovereignty of the Son of God." And yet he also quotes[219] M. Eckart as saying that "even in the surrender of the Kingdom by Christ and His subjection to the Father, He remains Head of the Mystical Body which includes all created spirits. The final goal of union with the Father does not involve a breach of the relation of the redeemed to their Redeemer, but only an increased inwardness, ennobling, and exaltation of that relationship. In this sense the cessation of Christ's kingship is the supersession of the relationship of Lord and slave by a relationship of friends and brothers." [220]

Refoulé quotes [221] the passage from Origen referred to in note 202, but does not indicate whether in his opinion the mediation of the Son is still necessary in the direct vision of God. He does however raise [222] the important question of whether union with God is substantial in the case of Christ and accidental in the case of human souls. He considers, as against Lieske, that the logic of Origen's system compelled him to assimilate the final condition of all souls to that of Christ. But it remains true that Origen conceives of the possibility of a perpetual falling and rising again in the case of other souls,[223] and one is compelled to ask why in logic he should not have regarded this as equally possible in the case of the soul of Christ. In this instance, as in others, he seems to have wanted to try to have it both ways.[224]

It is of course a cardinal feature of Origen's system that the direct vision of God can only be obtained when out of the body. He appears to suppose that bodily entanglement is somehow an obstruction in the way of that vision. In his own words, "a person placed in the body cannot completely acquire the adoption of sons." He seems to suggest that the practice of the virtues is only preliminary to a state in which the struggle between duty and desire will be a thing of the past, in so far as those in that state will be free from bodily trammels. In a curious interpretation of St. Paul's description of himself as "a servant of Christ" in Romans i.1, Origen says that St. Paul is thinking of himself as in a state of slavery as contrasted with the liberty which he and his fellow-saints will eventually enjoy.[225]

The question now arises how far Origen's conception of the Christian goal is in line with the authentic Christian traditon. C. Vagaggini[226] seems to answer far too readily in the affirmative. He says that the question which concerned the Alexandrian Fathers was that of "salvation by a kind of assimilation to the Divine Nature. It is Gnosis (knowledge) which imparts this saving assimilation. This Gnosis includes as an essential element a knowledge of the philosophic type of which the objects are God, man, and other things; but this philosophic knowledge is here essentially at the service of a much wider process, which aims at a contemplative and joyful intuition bringing into play not only the speculative intellect, but all the vital forces of man." [227] Granted, Origen considers self-discipline and the cultivation of the good life as an essential preparation for this state: but to say that the final vision of God engages "all the vital forces of man" is to ignore Origen's dualism, according to which man tends to be thought of as "a ghost in a machine." [228]

Later on Vagaggini, [229] after quoting a passage in *Comm. in Joh.* [230] which states that "to know God in the final and perfect sense of that phrase should be understood as a mingling and union", says that "faith for Origen is not a mere conceptual acceptance of a body of doctrine, but implies the beginning of union with God, of sharing in the union between God and man which came into being in the Incarnation of the Son of God, a union which develops into perfect knowledge. From the fact that in Christ the Divine Word assumed a true human soul and body, Christ's disciples 'saw that in Him the Divine nature and human nature began to be united, so that human nature might become divine as the result of union with the more divine element, not only in Jesus, but in all those who together embrace the life which Jesus taught and which leads all those who live in accordance with the precepts of Jesus to friendship with God and union with Him'." [231] Yes: but the nature of that union is left ambiguous. Does it involve the whole of human nature and so express itself in action, or is it purely intellectual?

Still later, [232] Vagaggini says that Porphyry and others "did not consider the entirety of Origen's synthesis nor his method, in which the philosophic activity in connexion with the Gospel message does not determine that message but is determined by it, and is directed to the contemplative and joyful vision of the Word and of God. Although in Origen the philosophic, speculative, conceptual element is vastly more emphasised than in any other Father of the Church and though in him this element is derived from his Neo-Platonic environment, none the less Origen cannot in any way be considered as a Greek philosopher who lives in a Christian fashion. The synthesis of Origen is theological . . . but not in the Aristotelian sense nor in that of Thomas Aquinas, nor in the post-Tridentine sense; it is rather a theology which begins with faith and culminates in joyful contemplation, and in which the aspect of conceptual enquiry on the basis of philosophic concepts is considered only as an element in a vaster process. The intention is to arrive not only at intellectual vision, but also, as far as is possible in this life, at the salvation and blessedness of the whole concrete man."

I do not really think that a careful study of Origen really supports this suggestion: he was too much of an intellectualist to think along these lines. Man for him is not a spirit which exists to direct the body associated with it, but a spirit encased in a body and eventually destined to escape from it.

Von Balthasar expresses the essential outlook of Origen much more accurately when he says[233] that "Origen's passionate intellectualism did not allow him to think of the unity (ie. the final unity between God and created things) otherwise than as a light, vast but empty . . .. He displays a tendency to try to go beyond the Word of God Himself in order to gaze on the depths of the Father, to desire knowledge rather than life, to exaggerate the importance of the symbol of the Word and to underestimate the importance of that of love."[234] If, for Origen, the Word of God never became fully human, that was because he never really thought of the totality of human nature as capable of being redeemed. And this, I submit, is partly due to his own rash act in his later 'teens when he deprived himself of his virile powers and so created a dichotomy between his intellectual and his physical nature.

NOTES ON CHAPTER VII

1. *Comm. in Joh.* XIII.3 (GCS 4.229.7-10); cf. *Comm. in Matt.* XII. 9 (GCS 10.83.11-16).
2. Ibid.X.10 (GCS 4.180.6-14).
3. On the other hand in *Hom. in Num.* the words quoted are understood of the unseen Christ, in so far as they are taken to indicate that the Son of God protects us against the influence of evil spirits, and indeed in one sense deals violently with us so as to draw us in the direction of salvation (XX.3 (GCS 7.195.9-14)). On the other hand, Origen says in one place that these words of Christ were fulfilled even before the Incarnation, in so far as He visited Jeremiah and Isaiah and other Old Testament worthies (*Hom. in Jer.* IX.1 (GCS 3.63.23-64.5)).
4. Op. cit., p.98-100.
5. X.10 (GCS 4.179.25-180.2).
6. Already referred to in note 2.
7. Franco also says on p.100 of op. cit. that if there is a change in the position of Jesus (or the Word) with reference to His disciples, it is a change from external to internal influence, from union (being *with* them) to unity (being *in* them), though the oscillation of Origen's thought warns us that we should not emphasise this distinction too much.
Cf. *Euseb. De eccl. theol.* III.14 (GCS Euseb.4.170.30-171.2) where he says that when the Saviour said "I am with you always, till the end of the world", He did not say that He would not be with them afterwards, but He meant that after the end He will be with them in a fuller sense in so far as He will make them partakers of His kingdom.
Later, in III.16 (174.33-175.15) Eusebius says that if the Son is going to surrender His subjects to the Father, the Son will not cease to rule over them, nor will He abandon them, because that is not stated by the Apostle, but He will surrender them as a deposit (παραθήκην) received by Him, in so far as He will have perfected them and equipped them for the worship of the Father. They will thus not only enjoy the benefits of Christ's Kingship, but will also be filled with the unspeakable good things supplied by the Father.
It is worth observing that Marcellus of Ancyra understands St. Paul, when he says that Christ will deliver up the Kingdom to the

Father (I Cor.xv.24), to imply that the Son of God will lay aside His fleshly covering at the time of the final judgement, and be united once more to the Father (III.13 and 14 (170.19-26,171.20-28)). This idea has distinct affinities with the thought of Origen, even though Marcellus would presumably understand the idea of the doffing of the flesh literally, whereas Origen would tend to approach the matter more from the point of view of the disciple who first sees his Master in His fleshly form, and then goes on to view Him in His essential nature as the Word of God. Marcellus supports his argument by quoting the words in St. John (vi.63) "It is the spirit that quickeneth; the flesh profiteth nothing" spoken after the mysterious words about the necessity of eating the flesh and drinking the blood of the Son of Man in order to obtain eternal life (vi.51-58) (III.11 (167.21-32)). Eusebius suggests that the words "flesh" and "blood" do not refer to the physical flesh and blood of the Saviour, but to the words which he speaks and which he declares to convey life (vi.63b) (ibid.168.27-169.5). On the other hand, Origen would argue that unless He was referring to His actual flesh and blood, there would have been no point in introducing the words "flesh" and "blood", and that what Christ meant was that it was necessary to see the spiritual significance of Christ's earthly life, and in particular His death, in order to obtain the gift of eternal life which He came to bring.

[8] *Sel. in Ps.* XXXV.10 (PG XII.1316B). Cf. *Frag. in Matt.* 71 (GCS 12.44).

[9] *Comm. in Joh.* XIX.6 (GCS 4.305.3-9).

[10] It is on the strength of passages such as these that Koch declares (op. cit., pp.316,317) that Origen's ideal of the Christian life was not essentially different from that of the schools of philosophy. In both, he says, there was an endeavour to be purified through ascetic practices and to be freed from anything of a bodily nature, a search for truth in the knowledge of an unseen world. The distinguishing feature of Origen's exposition of the Christian outlook was the taking over of the Greek idea of God and of Greek teaching about the pre-existence of souls and about freewill, as well as the Greek idea of the method of God's instruction. In other words, Koch recognises that contemplation is what Origen considers to be the goal of the Christian life, and that this is not the authentic Christian view.

Cf. Maydieu, op. cit., p.63, where he says that according to Origen, "the life of action will disappear with the body to which action is linked; at the time of the restoration of all things, contemplation will be the sole occupation of the elect, ie. of those who will have been trained and instructed by the Divine Word." Cf. also Fitzgerald, op. cit., p.174, where he says that (according to Origen) "it is only through the Word that men can be raised to the contemplation of the Father's glory."

11 *Ep. ad Greg.* (Philocal. JAR.67.15-19).
12 Op. cit., p.109.
13 *Comm. in Joh.* XIX.14 (GCS 4.313.25-32).
14 *Frag. in Luc.* 113.1,2 (GCS 9.273). Cf. pp.256 and 257.
15 *Hom. in Gen.* I.7 (GCS 6.10.3-5).
16 XVII.6 (GCS 7.165.4,5,9-12).
17 VIII.4 (GCS 2.223.18-224.5).
18 *De Orat.* XXIII.2 (GCS 2.350.19-25).
19 XI.2 (GCS 7.81.5-18), and XI.4 (7.85.26-31). Cf. also XI.5 (7.86.30-87.1).
20 VIII.5 (PG XIV.1166C-1167A).
21 *Hom. in Lev.* V.12 (GCS 6.358.14-16).
22 See pp.250-256.
23 I.16 (GCS 4.20.21-23).
24 IX.2 (GCS 7.347.26-348.4).
25 *De Princ.* I.7.5 (GCS 5.94.9-13).
26 See Ch.V, pp.127 and 128.
27 *Matt. Comm. Series* 32 (GCS 11.58.16-59.3), already referred to in Ch.V, n.174.
28 *Comm. in Joh.* II.6 (GCS 4.60.13-23). It is noteworthy that in one passage (*Comm. in Joh.* II.3 (GCS 4.55.25-29)) Origen suggests that he who cannot receive the Word Who was in the beginning with God will be in one of three conditions. He may be joined to the Incarnate Word; he may be associated with one of those who do in fact participate in the true Word; or else he may fall away even from this state, and may thus reside in a λόγος so called which is quite alien to the true Λόγος (by which presumably is meant that he will allow his life to be governed by a false principle of action).
29 *Hom. in Gen.* VIII.8 (GCS 6.83.10-14).
30 *Matt. Comm. Series* 65 (GCS 11.153.12-22). Cf. p.243.
31 Cf. Crouzel, *La Conn.*, p.353, where he says that "the first com-

ing of Christ is for each person a point of departure for an ascension which, without arriving here below at a direct union, approximates to it more and more, in proportion to his progress in contemplation and virtue."

32   *Comm. in Joh.* II.18 (GCS 4.76.4-8).
33   Ibid.XXXII.4 (GCS 4.431.18-30).
34   *Sel. in Ps.* CXXVI.1 (PG XII.1641D,1644A).
35   See passage referred to in n.28.
36   *Comm. in Joh.* II.3 (GCS 4.57.20-23).
37   Ibid. (GCS 4.56.29-57.2). Cf. Jules Gross, *La Divinisation du Chrétien d'après les Pères Grecs* (Paris, 1938), p.79: Crouzel, *La Conn.*, p.364; Bertrand, op. cit., p.31. This passage is also referred to in Cadiou, op. cit., p.420, and contrasted with *Comm. in Matt.* XII.17 (GCS 10.107.22-108.2), 18 (GCS 10.109,28-36 and 111.3-9), and 19 (GCS 10.111.27-112,12), which suggest to Cadiou that Origen eventually regarded the Crucifixion, not as an item of teaching preparatory to what was more advanced, but as part of that advanced teaching itself. I do not think that the respective passages necessarily bear out this conclusion; it could be said that the Crucifixion was simply the climax of the more elementary teaching.
It is to be noted that while Cadiou regards *Comm. in Matt.* as representing a later stage in Origen's thought than *Comm. in Joh.*, and one more inclined to orthodoxy, Origen makes just as rigorous a distinction between the human and Divine nature of Christ in the former work as in the latter. In *Comm. Series* 92 (referred to in Ch.V, note 280), he insists that the Divine nature, the one not liable to suffering, must not be regarded as responsible for the plea to be let off the suffering of the Cross; it was the human nature which was the source of that plea. It would therefore be natural to suppose that even at this stage in his development, Origen regarded the Crucifixion as a phase of teaching which must be transcended so as to pass from the contemplation of the Incarnate Jesus to that of the Divine Word.
38   *Comm. in Rom.* II.14 (PG XIV.917C).
39   *Contra Cels.* VI.14 (GCS 2.85.2-5).
40   Op. cit., p.32.
41   XII.18 (GCS 10.111.6-9).
42   pp. 239 and 240.
43   *Comm. in Joh.* XIX.11 (GCS 4.310.21-26). Cf. *Frag. in Joh.*

44 LXXIII (GCS 4.540.15-18).
   Frag. in Joh. LXXI (GCS 4.539.19-540.2).
45 Cadiou, *Frag. in Ps.* CXVIII.160 (pp.117,118).
46 Op. cit., pp.361,362.
47 Op. cit., p.134.
48 257 (GCS 9.336.10-17).
49 *Matt. Comm. Series* 35 (GCS 11.65.13-27).
50 Luke xxi.33.
51 Psalm xxxvii.10.
52 *Hom. in Ps.* XXXVI.II.5 (PG XII.1333C).
53 xvii.1.
54 *Frag. in Luc.* 139.8-13 (GCS 9.283).
55 *Sel. in Ps.* XXIX.2 (PG XII.1292BC).
56 *Frag. in Joh.* XCIII (GCS 4.556.13-21).
57 Cf. John iv.23.
58 *Comm. in Joh.* XIII.20 (GCS 4.244.3-6). Cf. Nemeshegyi, op. cit., p.163, where he says that "the true adoption of human beings as sons of God results from a continual and gradual influence exerted by Christ, the God-Man, Who raises them, purifies them, and unites them to Himself."
59 *Frag. in Matt.* 138 II (2nd Col.) 5-15 (GCS 12.70).
60 *Comm. in Joh.* I.37 (GCS 4.48.18-30). Cf. Lieske, op. cit., p. 210, where he says: "Just as the bare state of being rational (λογικὸν εἶναι) implies a real though rudimentary presence of the Divine Logos in our ἡγεμονικόν, so the completion of our real union with the Logos can only consist in the perfect vision of the Father."
61 Contrast the interpretation of "sheep" given in *Hom. in Lev.* III. 3 (referred to in Ch.VI, n.101).
62 Cf. *Hom. in Gen.* I.13 (GCS 6.17.16-20). Lieske, op. cit., pp.10-12, criticises Völker for not recognising that mystical union with Christ is a higher stage of development of an already deeply founded essential relationship with God, and not simply an experiential union consisting in knowledge and love. Völker does not take into account the union with the Divine Word which already exists in so far as all human beings partake of reason through the indwelling Word of God. Cf. also the last paragraph of p.31 and the second paragraph of p.113.
63 Op. cit., pp.136-138.
64 *Sel. in Ps.* LXVII.9 (PG XII.1508C).

[65] Ibid.CXLIV.20 (PG XII.1673BC). Cf. *Comm. in Ezek.* XXX.4 (PG XIII.823D).
[66] *De Princ.* I.5.2 (GCS 5.70.1-3).
[67] *Comm. in Rom.* VII.5 (PG XIV.1116C).
[68] *Hom. in Gen.* VI.1 (GCS 6.66.18-67.12).
[69] Op. cit., p.287.
[70] *Comm. in Joh.* II.16 (GCS 4.73.11-14). Cf. Crouzel's discussion of the meaning of the terms λόγος and λογικός in the early Christian Fathers in *L'Image*, p.172, note 176. Crouzel there points out that even Platonists thought of the human faculty of reason, termed λόγος in Greek, not as directed towards the universe, but as a participation in the Word and Wisdom of God (though of course they are supposed to have borrowed this idea from the Biblical Wisdom literature).
[71] *Frag. in Matt.* 227.8-10 (GCS 12.108).
[72] *Comm. in Joh.* I.20 (GCS 4.25.16-20). Cf. Pitra, A.S. III.181 (Ps.XCIV.6.7). Cf. also Nemeshegyi, op. cit., p.170, where he says: "Just as the will of the Father, received actively and perfectly by the Son, ensures of itself the conformity of all the outward actions of the Son to their source which is the Divine Will, so the perfections of Christ, received actively by the righteous man, produce in him the deeds and actions which conform to the Divine Word." Cf. also Fitzgerald's comments on *Comm. in Joh.* I.20 in op. cit., pp.151-154.
[73] This matter has already been discussed on p.236.
[74] *Sel. in Ps.* XXII.5 (PG XII.1264A).
[75] Ibid. (PG XII.1264C).
[76] Ibid. (PG XII.1261D). Cf. Pitra, A.S. II.480 (Ps.XXII.5). Cf. Crouzel's discussion of the transition which according to Origen needs to be made from being the σπέρμα of God, in the sense of being potentially rational, to being the τέκνον of God in the sense of having developed the germs of reason innate in oneself (*L'Image . . .*, pp.219-221 and 237).
Cf. *Sel. in Ps.* IV.3 (PG XII.1140C), where, with reference to I. Cor.xv.47, Origen says that he who is on a lower spiritual level can be a son of man on the level of the earthly man, but that he who is converted can become a son of man on the level of the heavenly man.
Cf. also *Matt. Comm. Series* 93 (GCS 11.211.20-24), where he points out that to come to Jesus is to escape temptation, and

that those who come to Jesus are drawn to Him by the Father, so that they may be raised to life by Him *(ut resuscitetur ab eo)*. Cf. Lomiento, op. cit., p.42, where he says that according to Origen, "the disciples of Christ strive to gather together the 'breath' of Divine sonship in everyone whom they meet, so that it may not become extinct as the result of being suffocated by the material element, but expand itself into all their being."

77 Cf. Pitra A.S.III.545 (*in Ezek*. XIV.4); *Frag. in Luc*. 155 (GCS 9. 288); *Frag. in Jer*. 25 (GCS 3.210.15-19); *De Princ*. IV.3.12 (GCS 5.342.6-10).

78 *Comm. in Joh*. I.20 (GCS 4.25.8-11).

79 There is no need to deduce, with Hirschberg, from such passages as this one that there is a class of believers who cannot advance in insight, and must remain on the level of simple faith (ψιλή πίστις). Most of the passages which Hirschberg quotes could be interpreted as referring to believers at an early stage of their discipleship (op. cit., pp.221-224).

80 *Comm. in Joh*. I.27 (GCS 4.35.7-13). Cf. *Comm. in Cant*. II. (GCS 8.135.10-17); *Hom. in Num*. XIV.4 (GCS 7.127.6-15); *Sel. in Num*. XXIII.1 (PG XII.580C). Cf. also the passage from *The Brothers Karamazov* quoted on p.17 of Carroll Simcox's *Living the Ten Commandments* (Dacre Press, 1957): "We have corrected thy work (the Grand Inquisitor is speaking to Christ) and have founded it upon miracles, mystery, and authority. And men rejoiced that they were again led like sheep, and that the terrible gift (ie. of Christian freedom) that had brought them such suffering was, at last, lifted from their hearts."

81 *Comm. in Cant*. II (GCS 8.138.10-130).

82 Cf. *Convs. with Heracl*. 14.8-16 (p.84, Scherer's ed.), and *Comm. in Joh*. I.28 (GCS 4.36.14-16). Cf. also Koch, op. cit., p.32, where he says that according to Origen, God's purpose is to evoke the original nature of each man, and awaken his better self to life; in fact what needs to be achieved is the unfolding of the divinity immanent in man. Cf. also Schendel, op. cit., p.87.

83 This subject has already been discussed in Ch.VI, pp. 213-215.

84 *Hom. in I Reg*. I.5 (GCS 8.8.14-9.19).

85 *Comm. in Matt*. XVI.16 (GCS 10.527.22-33). Cf. Crouzel, *L' Image* . . ., p.109, note 186, where this passage is quoted.

86 See p.243.

87 *Sel. in Ps*. IV.6 (PG XII.1161D). Cf. *Comm. in Matt*. XII.24

[88] (GCS 10.123.16-19).
Comm. in Cant. III (GCS 8.227.7-13). Cf. Carroll E. Simcox, op. cit., p.22: "In God's ordering of history it was expedient that the people of God should live for an age under a dominion of moral law in order to prepare them for the freedom which Christ would bring (ie. the freedom which springs from loving God). This statement holds true also of the individual Christian's experience. We need the preparatory discipline of the law . . . . Who can dispense with it? Who is, at all times and in all his being, fit for the full freedom?"

[89] *Hom. in Jud.* VI.2 (GCS 7.500.1-3), and *Hom. in Gen.* VIII.8 (GCS 6.83.16-18).

[90] eg. *Hom. in Lev.* XVI.7 (GCS 6.506.22-507.3); *Comm. in Matt.* X.14 (GCS 10.17.28-30); *Hom. in Jud.* VI.3 (GCS 7.501.10-14); *Sel. in Ps.* CXVIII.32 (PG XII.1593D).
Cf. Beskow, *Rex gloriae: the Kingship of Christ in the early Church* (Stockholm, 1962), p.227; Rahner, "Die Gottesgeburt: Die Lehre der Kirchenväter von der Geburt Christi in Herzen der Glaubigen" (*ZKT* 59 (1935)), p.351; Aeby, op. cit., pp.164-168, 171 and 176, where he expresses Origen's view as follows: "The coming of Christ into me, which displays itself by the conformity of my actions with His, is thus the prolongation in me of His Incarnation." Cf. also p.177, where he says that according to Origen, "the fact that all men are sinners demands that Christ should always come into them to cure them."
Cf. also Lieske, op. cit., pp.5-7, where he refers to Origen's comparison between the union of the human soul with the Divine Word and that of a wife with her husband. Cf. also pp.68,69. Cf. also Kelber, op. cit., pp.252 sqq., in which that union is said to result from the birth of the Word of God within the human soul.

[91] *Comm. in Joh.* X.28 (GCS 4.201.26-202.2).

[92] II (GCS 8.165.2-11).

[93] See Franco, op. cit., pp.77-79, where this passage is discussed, and where the contrast is drawn between kingship in the sense of conquest and kingship in the sense of possession.

[94] XXIII.4 (GCS 2.352.15-17).

[95] Op. cit., XXV.1 (GCS 2.356.30-357.9).

[96] Op. cit., XXV.3 (GCS 2.358.29-359.7). See Franco, op. cit., pp. 73-75, where this passage and the two previous ones are discussed, and where the author says that "according to Origen, both the

reign of Christ and the reign of God in the soul are described as things which grow and develop and attain perfection, but with a clear subordination of the reign of Christ to the reign of God, as of means to end, or of acquisition to possession. The reign of God is the logical consequence, the completion of the reign of Christ."

97 *Frag. in Jer.* 23 (GCS 3.209.21-28). Cf. Pitra, A.S.III.539 (in Jer. i.10); *Hom. in Jos.* XIII.1,4 (GCS 7.371.10-13 and 374.8-13); ibid.XV.1 (GCS 7.381,20-24); ibid.VI.1 (GCS 7.321.12-17).

98 *Frag. in Eph.* XV.15-22 (*JTS* 3.411). Cf. Nemeshegyi, op. cit., pp.180,181, where he says that "faith is for Origen the beginning of an ontological and spiritual contact with Christ, accomplished by the effect of the Saviour's grace . . .. But faith itself only receives its full perfection in the life beyond." Cf. also Rahner, op. cit., p.354: "The typical outlook of Origen is that the dormant grace consisting in the indwelling of the soul by the Divine Word is an immanent principle of an ever-advancing life. The indwelling Word will awaken: He must daily increase."

99 *Sel. in Job.* (PG XII.1048B). Cf. *Hom. in Ps.* XXXVI.I.4 (PG XII.1326A); ibid.I.2 (1324D); *Frag. in Jer.* 19 (GCS 3.207.15-17); *Hom. in Num.* XXIII.6 (GCS 7.218.15-28).

100 *Hom. in Num.* XI.6 (GCS 7.88.11-15). Cf. *Hom. in Gen.* XVI.3 (GCS 6.139.18-22).

101 *Frag. in Matt.* 122.4-10 (GCS 12.64).

102 *Hom. in Gen.* XVI.4 (GCS 6.141.4-8,13-18). Cf. the comments made on this passage by Crouzel, *La Conn.*, p.333.

103 *Comm. in Ezek.* IV.9 (PG XIII.779D).

104 *Hom. in Gen.* II.17 (GCS 6.22.7-10 and 20.22-21.3).

105 *Excerpt. in Cant.* VI.1 (PG XIII.206A). Cf. Rahner, op. cit., p. 353, note 23, where this passage is quoted.

106 *Hom. in Jos.* XXIV.3 (GCS 7.451.4-11).

107 *Comm. in Cant.* II (GCS 8.165.2-8). Cf. Beskow, op. cit., p.229, where reference is made to this passage.

108 *De Princ.* II.11.3 (GCS 5.186.11-13).

109 See p. 240.

110 *Comm. in Joh.* XIII.20 (GCS 4.244.3-6). Cf. Nemeshegyi, op. cit., p.163, where he says that "the true adoption of human beings as children of God results from a continual and gradual influence exerted by Christ, the God-Man, Who raises them, purifies them, and unites them to Himself."

[111] Cf. Crouzel's discussion of this passage in *L'Image*, pp.221,222. He points out justly that there is a contradiction implicit in Origen's thought, in so far as on the one hand he conceives of the history of the individual as the recovery of the original perfect state lost by disobedience, and on the other hand thinks of it as a process of evolution from a lower to a higher state.
Völker, op. cit., pp.109,110, sees the whole world view of Origen as based upon the backward progress of souls from Christ to the Father, and thus as a reversal of the process whereby the world arrived at its present state. He sees the inner development of the πνευματικός as an anticipation in this life of the future transformation of the world itself. But the question remains: how did God's creation lose its original perfection?
Cf. Rahner, "Das Menschenbild des O.", pp.232,233, where he says that the anti-gnostic reply to the question "Whence and to what purpose did evil appear?", namely, that evil comes from the created free wills of human spirits, does not satisfy Origen, even though in one sense it is the final answer; for God's overflowing grace could without compulsion have prevented this freely-chosen Fall. Cf. also Bürke, op. cit., pp.5 sqq.

[112] Cf. Lieske, op. cit., pp.59,60, especially the following passage: "If the original perfection of the soul's likeness to the Word of God is destroyed, that likeness is not lost; for the Word of God dwells in each human being, even in the unbelieving, but only becomes awake in one who is holy." Koch, op. cit., pp.31,32, stresses that the Incarnation was only one of the many measures taken by Divine Providence for the instruction of mankind; the appearance of the Incarnate Word is not the final stage in God's dealings with man. Cf. also Boon, op. cit., p.31.
Cf. also Teichtweier, op. cit., p.263, where he says: "Rational beings (λογικοί) are by their own nature equipped with reason through being endowed with νοῦς, but need to take possession of the eternal Logos in order to achieve their true nature as spiritual beings (Geistwesen)."

[113] *Comm. in Joh.* XIII.37 (GCS 4.261.32-262.25). Cf. the discussion of this passage in Koch, op. cit., p.105, and in Franco, op. cit., pp.102,103, and note 120 on latter page.

[114] See Ch.I, p.13.

[115] IV.3 (GCS 1.276.12-19).

[116] II.9.4 (GCS 5.167.26-31).

[117] Ibid.II.9.6 (GCS 5.169.25-170.5).
[118] *Comm. in Joh.* VI.38 (GCS 4.146.12-22). See also Ch.I.pp.11 and 12.
[119] Cf. Rahner, "Die Gottesgeburt", p.356, where he says: "Origen continually insists that the marvellous birth of the Divine Word in the heart of the believer is useless, unless it continually renews itself in moral growth."
[120] Cf. Ch.II, pp.48 and 49, where it is suggested that originally God made man in His "likeness" as well as in His "image".
[121] *De Princ.* III.6.1 (GCS 5.280.10-281.5). Cf. Völker, op. cit., pp. 126-128, where this passage is discussed. Völker appears to consider that this passage implies that in Origen's view the individuality of the soul is eventually obliterated, even though at the stage of mystical union with the Divine Word this has not yet taken place. Such a conclusion does not seem warranted by Origen's actual words, as Bürke points out in op. cit., p.9.

Franco on p.87 of his thesis seems to suggest that if the union of souls with the Divine Word grows progressively so as to be equivalent to the union of the soul of Christ with the selfsame Word, it would follow that there is a hypostatic union of all humanity with the Divine Word and the consequent loss of individual personality. Franco also suggests that this would not imply loss of personal consciousness (see p.89), and that loss of individual personality is not altogether foreign to Origen's thought, although he does not offer a definite solution to this problem (see p.90). On the contrary, if the union of other souls with the Word of God became as close as the union of the soul of Christ with the Word, that would not seem to imply loss of personality, for the simple reason that the soul of Christ itself does not lose its personality and individuality.

It seems worth quoting Franco's comment on *De Princ.* III.6.1 in n.132 on p.106 of his thesis, that "the Father will be in us in so far as we are transformed into the Son, because it is in the Son that the Father is."
[122] Ibid.III.6.2,3 (GCS 5.283.10-21).
[123] Ibid.II.9.2 (GCS 5.165.17-21). Cf. Gronau, op. cit., pp.78,79.
[124] Ibid.III.6.3 (GCS 5.284.1-3).
[125] Cadiou, op. cit., pp.49 sqq., suggests that Origen demands more than a mere forgetfulness of heavenly things as the cause of the fall of the soul, and insists that this cause consists in the act of

the will, the admission of evil into the soul itself. But if evil as such is "non-being" — deficiency in goodness — how can it be the cause of the fall of the soul?
The problem of evil is also discussed in Ch.I, pp.6 and 7, and Ch. II, pp. 48 and 49.

[126] See pp.233,235,236, and 257-259 and also Ch.II, p.51.

[127] *Comm. in Joh.* XIX.6 (GCS 4.305.10-14). Cf. Völker, op. cit., p. 98, and Hirschberg, op. cit., p.170, where he says that "the soul ascends the qualities of Christ, which lie upon each other in the form of steps, during its pilgrimage, as though it were ascending a staircase." Cf. also Schendel, op. cit., pp.102,103, where reference is also made to *Comm. in Joh.* XIX.6.

[128] Cf. *Hom. in Is.* IV.2 (GCS 8.260.1-4), where it is said, with reference to the vision recorded in Isaiah vi, that our aim should be to become partakers of the door and the lintel of the door which is Christ Jesus, the door being His flesh and the lintel the Divine Word.
Cf. also *Hom. in Jer.* XV.6 (GCS 3.130.18-21), in which it is said that the Son makes us partakers of His Divinity.

[129] Cf. Koch, op. cit., p.72, where this passage is quoted. Kelber, op. cit., p.267, makes the interesting point that Origen considers, with reference to our Lord's declaration that He is the Bread of Life, that "this statement must be understood symbolically, as is apparent from the statement that 'the Bread, of which the Divine Word says that it is His Body, is the Word as Nourisher of souls' (*Matt. Comm. Series* 85 (GCS 11.196.19,20))." Kelber goes on to say that "spiritual communion is thus treated as a stage in the inner development of the soul, a stage which has its rightful place between 'Way' and 'Door' inasmuch as the Word as Bread is nourishment along the way."

[130] *Comm. in Joh.* XIX.6 (GCS 4.305.17-34). Cf. *Comm. in Matt.* XVII.36 (GCS 10.702.27-31), and *Frag. in Luc.* 113.1,2 (GCS 9. 273), where it is said that the maturer soul, after rendering due service to the Word of God, is emboldened to approach the Head of Christ, Who is God. Cf. also *Matt. Comm. Series* 32 (GCS 11. 58.16-27).
Cf. Crouzel, *La Conn...*, pp.111,112.

[131] Op. cit., pp.320.321.

[132] See also on the same passage Fitzgerald, op. cit., pp.208-212. It would appear that Fitzgerald is reading into this passage his own

idea that Origen consistently held the view that Christ used a human soul as the means of becoming incarnate (p.208). On the other hand, on p.210 he says that "the humanity of the Word Incarnate is the proximate cause of our deification: God has become man that man may be a sharer in the Divine nature." On p. 211 he says that "His (ie. the Word's) visible humanity is the first point of contact between souls imprisoned in material bodies and the Divine nature adapted to their weakness by being veiled 'in the likeness of sinful flesh'." There is also an ambiguous statement on p.212 to the effect that "it is not Christ as the Word in His Divine Nature alone, but Christ, the God-Man, Who 'makes both one' in Himself, Who is 'all the steps' in the Christian's ascent to the vision of God."

133 Cf. *Contra Cels.* VIII.15 (GCS 2.233.21-24).
134 Cf. *Matt. Comm. Series* 8 (GCS 11.12.28-13.2).
135 Cf. Ch.V, pp.107 and 108.
136 *Comm. in Joh.* XXXII.3 (GCS 4.429.8-430.26). Cf. Rius-Camps, "Comunicabilidad", *OCP* 34,1968,p.37.
137 iii.35 and xiii.3.
138 *Frag. in Joh.* L (GCS 4.525.7-23). Cf. *Contra Cels.* VII.68 (GCS 2.217.15-218.2); *Sel. in Ps.* II.1.2 (PG XII.1104A); *Hom. in Num.* XVI.6 (GCS 7.144.23-30) and XVII.6 (165.12-15).
139 *Comm. in Rom.* IX.39 (PG XIV.1239BC).
140 This conception of the Cross is more in accordance with traditional teaching than is the one which Origen normally gives, ie. that it symbolises withdrawal from the world of sense.
141 *Contra Cels.* VIII.70 (GCS 2.287.7-14).
142 Ch.IV, pp.89-91.
143 See pp.253-255.
144 VIII.15 (GCS 2.233.11-22).
145 See passages referred to in notes 78,80 and 81. On the thought expressed in the passage referred to in note 144, cf. the comments in Marcus, op. cit., p.161, where the passage is quoted (in note 23): "In the order of being and creation, not only the world of rational creatures, but 'all that comes into being in consequence', ie. the whole created universe, is subordinate to the Word and is thus 'controlled' by Him. Of course, in the fulfilment of the general plan of creation through the freely-given loving service of the Son, the relation between the Word and rational beings and between the Spirit and holy beings has a decisive

meaning. The resulting apparent narrowing and abbreviation of the relationship of the Word and the Spirit to the created universe is thus a means of fulfilling the Divine purpose and is thus the highest possible intensification and the ultimate completion of that all-embracing plan."

[146] *Contra Cels.* II.79 (GCS 1.201.14-20).
[147] *Comm. in Rom.* V.3 (PG XIV.1028C). Cf. *Frag. in Eph.* IX. 103-108 (*JTS* 3.401).
[148] *Comm. in Rom.* VII.5 (PG XIV.1115A).
[149] *Hom. in Ps.* XXXVI.II.1 (PG XII.1329C-1330B). See Nemeshegyi, op. cit., pp.207,208, where this passage is quoted. Cf. also *Sel. in Ps.* LXI.2 (PG XII.1484C); *De Princ.* III.5.6 (GCS 5.277.15-17) and III.5.7 (278.1-18). See Franco, op. cit., pp.67-72, where this question is discussed. He says on p.78: "If the subjection of the Son to the Father is understood as the unity of all rational creatures in the Son, so that they may acquire, as far as possible, the same relation to the Father as the Son has, the surrender of the Kingdom is not to be understood as the transferring of it from the Son to the Father . . . .. In other words, it is not a matter of human beings being separated from the Word so as to be united to the Father, but of uniting them to the Father precisely in virtue of their union with the Son." Cf. also pp.71 and 72, where he says: "The subjection of Christ to the Father at the end of the ages is nothing more than the completion of the relation which the Son of God has had to the Father from all eternity, a relation which is not complete while any of the members of the Body of the Son has not submitted (ie. to the Father)."
[150] *Hom. in Lev.* VII.2 (GCS 6.376.12-19, 377.1-5, 379.5-8). See the discussion of this passage and of the longer one of which it forms part in Mersch, op. cit., pp.368-372. Mersch ends by saying that according to Origen "the unity between Christ and His followers, between the Head and the members, is so close that Scripture attributes to the one what in all strictness is only true of the other."
Cf. also Schendel, op. cit., pp.94 and 95, and also p.97, where he justly observes: "After the restoration of all things, the sovereignty of Christ must not be thought of in a temporal and soteriological manner, but as the expression of a relationship between the Divine Word and the spiritual beings who have been set free for the eternal contemplation of God."

[151] *Matt. Comm. Series* 55 (GCS 11.126.8-127.18, 128,1-10); *Frag. in Matt.* 485.1-3 (GCS 12.199).
[152] See Ch.IV, pp.89-91. See also p.252.
[153] *Sel. in Ps.* XXII.4 (PG XII.1260D-1261B). Cf. *Sel. in Ps.* II.9 (PG XII.1108D-1109A), and XLIV.7 (PG XII.1429D).
[154] Cf. Ch.VI, pp.213 and 214.
[155] *Frag. in Lam.* XLVI (GCS 3.255.26-28).
[156] Cadiou, *Frag. in Ps.* CIX.2b(p.97); cf. *Frag. in Lam.* CIV. (GCS 3.272.25-27).
[157] *Frag. in Luc.* 214.7,8 (GCS 9.320).
[158] *Sel. in Ps.* VII.7 (PG XII.1180C).
[159] *Sel. in Ps.* LXI.2 (PG XII.1484C).
[160] Pitra, A.S.II.464 (Ps.IX.37,38).
[161] VIII.72 (GCS 2.288.24-289.2).
[162] *De Orat.* 26.4 (GCS 2.361.10-15).
[163] Ibid.26.6 (GCS 2.362.28-373.1). Cf. *Sel. in Gen.* VI.7 (PG XII.104B).
[164] *De Princ.* I.6.1 (GCS 5.79.13-18), and III.5.7 (278.18-23). Cf. Schendel, op. cit., p.81.
[165] This conception of the Crucifixion – as something which makes available to believers a higher quality of life – is not in harmony with the main tenor of Origen's thought, as is clear from the exposition of it on pp.239 and 240 and in Ch.VI, pp.207-210.
[166] *Hom. in Jos.* VIII.6 (GCS 7.342.13-19) and VIII.4 (339.28-340.7); *De Princ.* III.6.5 (GCS 4.286.17-287.3). On the other hand Origen contradicts the doctrine of the devil's ultimate restoration in *Comm. in Rom.* VIII.9 (PG XIV.1185B), where he says that there will be no conversion even at the end of the world *(in fine saeculi)* of him who is said to have fallen from heaven (Is.xiv.12, and Luke x.18).
[167] XVI.3 (GCS 7.396.23-398.5).
[168] *De Princ.* III.5.8 (GCS 5.279.8-10).
[169] I.2.10 (GCS 5.43.8-10). *Per sapientiam enim, quae est Christus, tenet Deus omnium potestatem, non solum dominantis auctoritate, verum etiam subjectorum spontaneo famulatu.*
Cf. Cornelis, op. cit., where on the one hand (p.39) he suggests that according to Origen the law of the Divine Word is to be distinguished from all the other exercise of the powers within the creation, in that it acts by persuasion, in respecting the liberty of rational creatures; whereas in n.31 on p.43 it is said that the

170 Ibid. (GCS 5.44.5-8). In commenting on this passage Franco says (op. cit., p.105) that "the mission of Christ, the reign of Christ, ends when all that is irrational has been subdued, and everything has thus been subjected to Him, not by force, but by reason." He adds, however, in n.127 on that page, that "hardships are necessary while human beings are disobedient to reason. The fully mature perfect themselves μόνῳ τῷ λόγῳ."

171 Ibid.III.5.8 (GCS 5.278.24-29).
172 Sel. in Ps. IV.1 (PG XII.1133AB).
173 XII.2 (GCS 7.99.25-100.4, 100.24-101.9). Cf. also ibid.XXVIII. 4 (7.285.11-14). Cf. Beskow, op. cit., pp.226,227, where the passage in XII.2 is referred to.
174 Hom. in Jos. XIV.2 (GCS 7.380.24-381.9).
175 Cf. p.236, and also p.243.
176 Cf. p.234.
177 Matt. Comm. Series 8 (GCS 11.12.28-13.13). It is noteworthy, however, that in this very passage Origen does not regard the phrase "the footstool of God's feet" as necessarily implying the humiliation of those to whom it is applied. He quotes Lam.ii.1, where the daughter of Sion is described as having been "the footstool of God's feet" in heaven, and as having been cast down to the earth, and also Isaiah lxvi.1, where the description of the earth as God's footstool does not indicate its degradation but rather its glory, since God's feet are considered as His ultimate part. Cf. Ch.VI, pp.203 and 204, where passages are quoted where the phrase "the footstool of His feet" are applied to Christ's human nature and to His Church.
178 Prol (GCS 8.83.20-85.1).
179 Ibid.8.86.13-27.
180 III.6.9 (GCS 5.290.18-291.1). Cf. Völker, op. cit., p.109, where this passage is quoted. Cf. the passages quoted on p.236. Cf. also the discussion of this passage in Puech, op. cit., pp.524,525, where he says that according to Origen, the union of the Christian Gnostic with the Divine Word is analogous to the union of the soul of Christ with the Word.
Cf. also Cadiou, op. cit., pp.86,87, where he says that "it is from

the angle of the intelligence that we must look in the Alexandrian school for a point of connexion with a future theology of grace." A little later he says: "Salvation (according to Origen) consists in being enlightened by the Word of God. Origen's entire psychology demands a doctrine of illumination. It is to this light that he gives the name of grace, and it is from truth that this grace derives its strength."
In so far as the function of the Divine Word is thought of by Origen chiefly as illumination, Koch and de Faye seem justified in saying that "dogmatically considered, Origen's understanding of the Word of God has a closer link with the Logos-conception of philosophy than with the historical Jesus Christ", and that "in spite of all the Biblical terminology employed, the ideas formulated are really Platonic, and the Logos of Origen is thus that of philosophy" (quoted in Teichtweier, op. cit., p.264).

[181] Op. cit., pp.77-79.
[182] II. (GCS 8.165.2-11). Cf. p.245, where this passage is also referred to.
[183] Op. cit., p.80.
[184] Op. cit., pp.82-84.
[185] I.28 (GCS 4.35.14-36.26). Cf. the discussion of this passage in Ch.VI, pp.200 and 201.
[186] Franco refers to *De Princ.* II.1.3 (GCS 5.109.1-4) and I.6.2 (5. 81.19,20).
[187] Op. cit., p.96.
[188] Op. cit., p.181. Cf. Völker, op. cit., p.125, where he says that "just as for the pious person mystical union with Christ is but a transitory stage, so in the future life the task of the Divine Word consists precisely in making those who are united to Him worthy of and ready for the direct lordship of the Father, this being the summit of blessedness."
[189] *Comm. in Rom.* IX.41 (PG XIV.1243A-C).
[190] Ibid.VI.5 (PG XIV.1065CD). Cf. Rius-Camps, "Origenes y Marcion", p.25.
[191] See p.244.
[192] *Frag. in Joh.* LXXXVII (GCS 4.552.7-11).
[193] Ibid.CXXXIX (GCS 4.573.21-29). Cf. LXXXVII (4.552.2-7).
[194] *Hom. in Jos.* XVII.2 (GCS 7.403.24-27).
[195] *Hom. in Num.* XVI.6 (GCS 7.145.3-8).
[196] Ibid.XXVIII.2 (GCS 7.282.19-25), 3 (284.2-4), and 4 (284.25-

28).
197 xxiii.24.
198 *Hom in Num.* XVI.8 (GCS 7.150.26-151.7).
199 Cf. p.256, where it is said that mature disciples share the kingship of Christ.
200 *Comm. in Joh.* XXXII.30 (GCS 4.476.16-477.4).
201 John xx.17. On the other hand, Origen has overlooked the passage where Jesus is said to have addressed the disciples as "children" (παιδία) on the seashore before they hauled in the miraculous draught of fishes (John xxi.5).
202 John xiii.16.
203 *Comm. in Matt.* XI.4 (GCS 10.39.24-26). Cf. Eichinger, op. cit., pp.61 and 62, where this passage is referred to. Cf. also *Contra Cels.* III.61 (GCS 1.255.14-21).
204 *Comm. in Joh.* XX.7 (GCS 4.334.20-31).
205 Cf. Koch, op. cit., p.84, where he says that "the Christian life according to Origen is a continuous purification and resultant knowledge. This is what his intellectualism consists in. The intellectual element does not crowd out the moral element . . . but the crown of the work of the Christian is that souls return to the contemplation of heavenly things."
206 *Comm. in Joh.* I.16 (GCS 4.20.15-18). Cf. Lieske, op. cit., p.71, where this passage is quoted, and also Rahner, op. cit., pp.354, 355, and note 26 on former page. Cf. also Kelber, op.cit., p.254.
207 *L'Image,* p.82. Cf. also p.254, where both passages are referred to.
208 *La Conn.,* pp.497,498; cf. also p.108. Cf. also same author, "O. devant l'Inc. et l'hist.", pp.106,107.
209 In op. cit., p.185; see also p.339. De Faye interprets Origen in the same way; see op. cit., p.248, where he says that "it is Christ Who conducts the soul stage by stage to the Father, and does not leave it to itself until it is in a state to do without Him."
210 Gross, op. cit., p.183, appears to agree with Mme. Harl.
211 Op. cit., p.216, note 226.
212 Op. cit., p.201.
213 Ibid.
214 Op. cit., p.128.
215 Cf. *Comm. in Oseam* (Philocal. JAR 53.32-54.4), where Origen says: "That those who please God are one can be seen from the prayer which the Saviour made to the Father on behalf of His

disciples: 'Father', He said, 'grant that as Thou and I are one, so these may be one in us'."
216 Op. cit., p.110.
217 Cf. also Aeby, op. cit., p.181, note 3, where he says that "we must observe that the Son is not a stage which one traverses; He remains necessary for eternity."
218 Op. cit., pp.98-102.
219 In note 50 on p.102.
220 Cf. op. cit., p.205, where he says: "Christ remains even after His surrender of the Kingdom and His subjection to the Father in a purely spiritual sense 'Lord' in His relationship as the Word of God to redeemed spiritual beings, who are bound together in a common direct vision of God."
Cf. also Franco, op. cit., p.64, where he says that there is an aspect of the Son's mission which is contingent and essentially temporal, ie. that in which He is the Bestower of divinity, because He only bestows it in so far as the capacity of souls has not reached the level sufficient to receive the life of the Father directly. But in so far as the Son is the Source of reason, His mission is eternal, because it is precisely in so far as created beings participate in the Son as Reason that they are enabled to obtain the direct vision of the Father."
221 Op. cit., pp.264,265.
222 In note 6 on p.265.
223 Cf. Ch.IV, pp.88 and 89.
224 Cf. Franco, op. cit., pp.91-94, where this question is discussed, and where he concludes (p.94) that "the degree of union of other souls (than that of Christ) with the Word of God remains vague and uncertain, as is the question whether another material world will arise after the end which is described as definitive." He points out in note 101 on p.94 that in *Comm. in Joh.* XX.13 (GCS 4.344.29,30) Origen says that those who see the Son of God have a share through their vision in the power of not sinning any further, but this does not mean the impossibility of sinning, but merely the possibility of not sinning.
225 *Comm. in Rom.* I.1 (PG XIV.839C-840A). Cf. *De Princ.* I.7.5 (GCS 5.91.11-92.15); II.11.7 (191,20-192,3); III.6.1 (281.6-282. 20). See also pp. 243,249,256,257.
226 In op. cit.
227 p.173.

[228] Indeed Vagaggini himself puts forward this view of Origen's outlook on p.186.
[229] p.195.
[230] XIX.4 (GCS 4.303.2,3).
[231] *Contra Cels.* III.28 (GCS 1.226.13-18).
[232] On pp.196 and 197.
[233] Op. cit., p.64.
[234] Cf. also de Faye, op. cit., p.238, where he says that Origen "clearly tends to see in contemplation and transcendent knowledge the supreme degree of perfection." See also pp. 240 and 248.

CONCLUSION

One may begin by quoting the celebrated statement in *Hebrews* that "it was fitting that He, for Whom and by Whom all things exist, in bringing many sons to glory, should make the Pioneer of their salvation perfect through sufferings" (τὸν ἀρχηγὸν τῆς σωτηρίας αὐτῶν διὰ παθημάτων τελειῶσαι; Heb.ii.10). It is rather significant that in one of the modern translations of the New Testament the verb τελειῶσαι is not allowed to have its full force, but is translated "crown with suffering the life of . . .". In other words, the suggestion is that Jesus Christ was already perfect, as being the Divine Word of God, and therefore did not need any perfecting so far as His essential nature was concerned. It has been the purpose of this thesis to suggest that Origen, like other early Christian thinkers, is content to assume an original state of perfection from which creation has declined and to which it is intended to return, and that his contradictions and inconsistencies about the Person of Christ stem from that assumption.

In the first chapter it is shown that Jesus Christ in His Divine nature is conceived of not only as having created the universe but also as being the source of all that occurs within it (the σπερματικός λόγος of the Stoics). But this lands him in considerable difficulties when faced with the problem of evil because it thus becomes hard to set it in sharp opposition to good. It is rather to be thought of as a necessary ingredient in the bringing into being of the highest good.

We are anticipating here what will be more fully brought out when discussing the relation of the Divine nature to the human nature of Jesus Christ, but the present writer regards it as an unnecessary multiplication of hypotheses to credit the Divine Word with having brought the universe into being under the Father's direction, and as being immanent in it in a secondary capacity to the Father. Surely it is sufficient to think of the Father alone as the Creator and immanent principle, and as having in due course brought into being Jesus Christ as the most striking example of conformity to His will and purpose.

There appears to be no need to assert that the Father brought Jesus Christ into being directly, and left it to Jesus Christ to bring the rest of the world into being. It seems sufficient to describe God the Father as Creator and Sustainer of the universe, and Jesus Christ as having emerged during the course of human history to act as God's supreme Messenger to human beings. We can only succeed in thinking of Jesus Christ as genuinely sharing human nature if we think of Him as so opening Himself to the influence of the Divine Spirit as to partake of God's nature as fully as a human being can, and thereafter imparting that nature to others in accordance with their capacities. Indeed, Origen gives us a hint that he may be uneasy about the vast functions originally assigned to the Son of God by suggesting that His real function is that of bringing into full operation the rational faculty of beings endowed with it.

Only if we take fully into account the humanity of Jesus Christ can we really distinguish creation from redemption. Origen lands himself in hopeless tortuosities when he suggests that the Word of God was continually at work in the pre-Christian era revealing Himself to those who were qualified to glimpse Him; for he thus finds it very difficult to make it clear what the precise function of the incarnate Christ is. The Incarnation in fact becomes an awkward episode in the activity of the Divine Word — an episode which has to be taken account of because Christian tradition emphasises it.

In Chapter II there is a discussion of Origen's assertion that the Father used the Divine Word as an intermediary in communicating His plan to others, and in particular to the outstanding persons of the Old Testament. But once again, this seems an unnecessary multiplication of hypotheses. It is simply a matter of the Divine Spirit gradually imparting itself in fuller measure to the minds of human beings in so far as they are in a fit state to receive it. There is no need to ante-date the work of Christ; in fact if this is done the significance of the Incarnation is obscured. Nor is there any need to imagine that the prophets received knowledge which they did not impart to their contemporaries so as not to anticipate the Incarnation. Surely, if that knowledge would have been beneficial to their contemporaries, there is no reason why they should not have imparted it. Once more, Origen is influenced by his assumption that there was an original state of perfection from which creation has degenerated. The prophets are, as it were, regarded as receiving glimpses of that original state — glimpses denied to their contemporaries. But — all credit due — Origen has misgivings about this idea, misgivings which he occasionally voices. He recognises that it would seem absurd to suggest that the prophets were set so much higher spiritually than the other Jews, and he also recognises that it was only the Incarnation which revealed the truths adumbrated in the prophetic writings, and not fully understood even by the prophets themselves.

It cannot be denied that the view which Origen occasionally takes of the prophets, namely that they had an insight into the nature of the Divine Word, really implies that the Incarnation was unnecessary, because in the first place the unseen Christ can be apprehended apart from it, and in the second place even those who become acquainted with the visible Christ do not always pass on to the vision of the unseen Christ.

Origen says in one place that human co-operation is required in order that human beings may be transformed into the Divine likeness. It would surely have been easier for him to recognise that only through becoming acquainted with the human Christ could human beings ascend to the contemplation of the Divine Word if he had been prepared to admit that the human Christ Himself needed to exercise His own will in order to ascend to the state which He eventually attained — that of perfect fellowship with God. It was a matter of eventually recognising what He had been sent into the world to do, after exploring other avenues and finding them unprofitable.

In Chapter III, it is pointed out that Origen's uncertainty about the significance of the Incarnation appears in so far as he occasionally suggests that it brought about a full knowledge of Christ, and yet suggests elsewhere that a deeper acquaintance with Christ is needed.

There is a striking passage in which it seems to be suggested that the Son Himself is not fully acquainted with the Father. This seems to suggest that Origen himself had doubts about whether the human Jesus should be identified with the Divine Word, since to do so is to deprive Him of the limitations essential to human nature.

There are passages where Christ is said to pass judgement on those who fail to give to the Father the honour due to Him. This of course is consistent with His true humanity. And yet in other passages, referred to in Chapter IV, he speaks of the Son as inflicting chastisement on evil-doers, as was done in the case of Pharaoh; but this can only be attributed to Christ in His Divine nature. Once more, Origen can with some justice be accused of obscuring the true function of Christ by putting Him on a pedestal which He would never have wished to occupy. Supreme Revealer of the effects of God's Spirit at work in the lives of human beings — yes: the all-pervading and all-controlling Divine Word — no.

From the evidence cited in Chapter V, it would appear that Origen's conception of the human Christ and his conception of the fallen spirit of men are interlinked. According to him, the πνεῦμα having become lukewarm in its love of God is degraded to the material sphere; but in order that it may be linked therewith through the sensations conveyed through the body, the "animal soul" has to be added thereto. Once more, the underlying idea is that of something perfect degenerating into something imperfect. The same is true of his conception of the Incarnation. He cannot really conceive of the Word of God as Himself becoming incarnate. It is the soul which continually cleaved to Him in love which alone can enter the material sphere, although it did not deserve to do this; and to this soul the "animal soul" must likewise be added. On the other hand, the higher soul is incapable of yielding to temptation because its love for God is unalterable: there is therefore no possibility of moral progress, and it can thus scarcely be termed "human" in the ordinary sense.[1]

It would appear that Origen's conception of the original state of the human soul (a state in which it can be termed πνεῦμα) leads him into difficulties when he discusses the temptations to which human beings are liable and to which they often succumb. The animal soul has to be added to the higher soul in order that the latter may become incarnate, and it is this lower soul which is subject to the attraction of spirit and body respectively: but the question is never answered how it is that it succumbs to the attraction of one or the other, because according to Origen it has no will of its own. Logically, it is the fallen spirit which should be thought of as taking the higher or the lower course as the result of its moral choice; but Origen does not find it easy to take that view, because it does not belong to the essential nature of the "spirit", even if fallen, to be associated with the body and with the things which this world contains.

Origen in fact falls between two stools in his account of the soul of man in its incarnate state. If he says that it is the higher soul which yields to temptation, this is in contradiction to his idea of this soul as essentially independent of the material world; if he says that it is the

[1] A.M. Farrer skirts the problem of Christ's genuine humanity when he says ("Lord, I Believe", pp.43,44) that "being innocent of sin, (Christ) made all choices wholesomely in his mere infancy, and uprightly when he became the master of his acts." That is indeed a denial of Christ's true humanity. Everything was predetermined: his moral freedom was mortgaged.

lower or "animal" soul, that means that the higher soul is absolved from guilt, and therefore it is hard to see why it should be incarnate at all.

Once we are prepared to abandon the idea of the original perfection of mankind, room is left for suggesting that what Origen terms the πνεῦμα, the highest part of the individual soul, only gradually becomes aware of itself, and so only gradually directs the activities of the other elements of human nature. Moral lapses can thus ultimately be traced to spiritual immaturity. In the same way, the incarnate Christ Himself needed to advance to the state of greater self-knowledge so as to fulfil His mission to the world. Origen himself appears to recognise this when he suggests that Jesus Christ was not as fully aware as the Father that he was obliged to drink the cup of suffering to the dregs, and so needed to be enlightened by the Father.

In the sixth chapter, it is suggested that Origen's conception of the enlightenment imparted by Christ derives directly from his strict division between the human Jesus and the Divine Son of God. The Divine Word cannot directly enter the material world (although in certain passages Origen regards Him as immanent within it!), and so an intermediate agent is employed for carrying out God's purpose of redemption. The effects of the work of the human Christ correspond to the character of the persons for whose benefit the work is done; some are enabled to pass from the knowledge of the earthly Christ to that of the Divine Word; others remain hidebound by their initial knowledge.

The knowledge of the "simple-minded" is not of course confined to the mere contemplation of Christ's earthly deeds: they are able to discern the moral principles underlying them and so use them as a pattern for their own lives. But those who are more intellectually gifted can learn more from Christ's earthly life than this: the events occurring in that life become for them symbols of heavenly realities which are apparently quite distinct from spiritual qualities as normally understood. But because Origen conceives of the ultimate destiny of man as that of a disembodied spirit, he is unable to give a clear indication of what those heavenly realities are.

In fact he seems at times to have an uneasy feeling that his account of the aim of Christ's earthly work is really inadequate, as it posits a two-tier outlook on reality which cannot be regarded as justified. The most important item in Christ's life, the Crucifixion, is something about which Origen is uncertain. Does it contain within itself the key to the inner nature of Christ, or is it a mere introduction to a higher form of knowledge which, once obtained, entitles its possessor to forget about the means whereby it was obtained; rather as though one climbed a ladder to an upper storey and then knocked it down once one had attained one's goal? Nowhere does Origen give a final answer to this question; different passages contradict each other. In one passage he says that the Crucifixion was the most important event of our Lord's life, and the one most worth recording. Surely this implies that whatever Origen may say elsewhere, the key to the full understanding of our Lord's nature lies in this event. It is not a mere introduction to the knowledge of the Son of God; it is in itself inseparable from that knowledge.

Origen almost suggests in fact that the Son of God Himself only attained to complete self-knowledge as the result of undergoing the sufferings of the Cross, because although He always desired to carry out the Father's will, he only fully understood the reasons why it was necessary for him to suffer after his sufferings were over.

In the seventh chapter it is pointed out that so far as Origen's conception of the work of Christ is concerned, it would doubtless be universally agreed that it is to introduce human beings to God, in the sense that as the result of being acquainted with Christ we eventually gain a clearer insight into the Divine nature. But once again, Origen cannot emancipate himself from the three-tier notion of knowledge which he has brought over from the Platonic tradition. First comes knowledge obtained by the senses, then a perception of the concepts by which sense-data can be classified, and finally the contemplation of the Form of the Good which gives rise to everything else. So in the case of Christ, the knowledge of the principles underlying His acts must eventually be superseded by the knowledge of the Divine nature which is the origin of everything else. But is that contemplation an end in itself, or is it the starting-point of world-transformation? Origen nowhere gives a decisive answer to that question. His thought is uncertain. Or take the question whether the world has degenerated to the extent that a U-turn is required of which the incarnate Christ is the starting-point, or is the world in a state of progress to which the incarnate Christ gives a boost? Once more, no decisive answer is given.

In fairness to Origen, we must allow that his conception of reason is one which is a wholesome corrective to the logic-chopping conception of reason so prevalent nowadays, and in particular to logical positivism. Only the saint is a fully rational person, because the saint participates fully in the Word of God. It would seem to follow that reason only fully operates in the sphere of action; it is the pre-requisite of all action which is really fruitful. Unfortunately Origen is still under the sway of the idea that the body is an encumbrance, and that reason will eventually operate in what we should regard as a vacuum, because it will be employed in mere contemplation, in thinking God's thoughts after Him on a purely theoretical level.

So far as Origen's conception of Christ's surrender of His Kingdom to the Father is concerned, we would doubtless agree that he corrects any superficial understanding of this surrender by pointing out that Christ does not cease to influence those who have been brought to the knowledge of the Father through Him. Rather, it is through His complete indwelling that they arrive at that knowledge and continue in it. They become His brothers instead of His disciples. But this requires complete docility, complete abandonment of self-satisfaction, complete willingness to be led to higher levels of spiritual perception. Self-fulfilment is thus only reached by self-abnegation.

Origen is led by his distinction between the pre-incarnate and the incarnate Christ into an unreal distinction between the general providential care exercised by the Word of God and the special activity of Christ in His earthly life. It would be impossible to maintain that distinction, so the present writer feels, without dividing Christ into two persons, because Christ's providence is not exercised *ab extra,* but extends to the bringing into being of everything that occurs. If He uses compulsion to divert human beings from evil courses of action, that is simply one expression of His immanent activity: but so is the persuasion He also employs, whether in His pre-incarnate or in His incarnate state. It is the contention of the present writer that Origen elevates the human Christ to a far higher position than the evidence really warrants, and that it is sufficient to regard the human Christ as the supreme embodiment of the universal Spirit of God.

INDEX OF PASSAGES REFERRED TO IN ORIGEN'S WORKS

The letter 'n' after a page number indicates that reference is made to the passage in one or more of the notes on that page.

GCS 1.
Exhort ad Mart.
12: 134, 135, 181n.
29: 111 (twice), 138, 165n (twice), 183n.
34: 135, 181n.
35: 141, 185n.
38: 48, 63n.
43: 48, 63n.
47: 11, 28n.

Contra Cels.
Bk.I.
13: 206, 223n.
32: 129, 130, 178n.
46: 110, 163n.
56: 112, 167n.
57: 88, 96n.
60: 136, 182n.
61: 107, 162n.
66: 136, 182n.
68: 105, 159n.

Bk.II.
2: 157, 194n.
9: 11, 12, 27n, 29n, 124, 135, 137, 141, 173n, 181n, 182n, 185n.
16: 121, 170n.
24: 139, 184n.
25: 136, 142, 182n, 186n.
31: 12, 29n.
34: 139, 184n.
43: 138, 184n.
58: 112, 163n.
64: 125, 174n.
65: 125, 174n.
66: 126, 175n.
69: 210, 225n.
71: 12, 29n.
79: 252, 280n.

Bk.III.
28: 122, 171n.
29: 105, 159n.
32: 121, 170n.
34: 12, 29n, 69, 79n.
37: 46, 62n.
41: 106, 161n.
52: 214, 228n.
53: 214, 228n.
59: 214, 228n.
60: 214, 228n.
61: 260, 284n.
62: 207, 223n.

Bk.IV.
3: 11, 28n, 248, 276n.
5: 108, 162n.
15: 116, 119, 121, 122, 166n, 169n, 171n, 172n.
16: 125, 174n.
18: 141, 142, 185n, 214, 227n.
19: 123, 172n.
29: 46, 61n.
31: 46, 81n.
54-end: 152, 192n.
57: 11, 27n.
99: 91, 99n.

GCS 2.
Bk.V.
1: 3, 19n.
4: 46, 62n.
11: 69, 70, 80n.

11: 69, 70, 80n.
12: 11, 27n, 37, 53n, 123, 173n.
15: 90, 98n.
37: 13, 29n.
39: 12, 29n.
60: 157, 194n.
Bk.VI.
14: 238, 270n.
17: 8, 21n, 73, 81n.
45: 142, 186n.
47: 140, 184n.
48: 140, 184n.
60: 4, 19n.
64: 4, 19n, 88, 96n.
66: 130, 178n.
67: 122, 172n.
68: 122, 126, 127, 172n, 174n, 177n (twice).
69: 4, 19n.
71: 14, 30n.
77: 128, 178n.
78: 11, 27n, 88, 96n.
79: 47, 62n, 199, 221n.
Bk.VII.
16: 106, 136, 137, 139, 161n, 182n (twice), 184n.
17: 11, 27n, 123, 140, 173n, 185n.
35: 11, 27n, 141, 185n.
43: 142, 186n.
57: 217, 229n.
65: 7, 21n, 46, 61n.
68: 251, 279n.
Bk.VIII.
4: 234, 269n.
9: 75, 83n.
12: 110, 164n.
14: 6, 21n.
15: 250, 252, 279n (twice).

42: 142, 186n.
69: 39, 54n.
70: 251, 252, 279n.
72: 254, 281n.
De Orat.
Intro: 10, 26n, 27n.
II.4: 43, 58n, 132, 179n.
II.6: 17, 33n.
IX.2: 134, 180n.
X.2: 11, 27n.
XIII.1: 112, 165n.
XIV.5: 132, 133, 179n.
XV.4: 48, 63n.
XXII.1: 43, 58n.
XXII.4: 48, 64n.
XXIII.2: 235, 269n.
XXIII.4: 204, 222n, 245, 274n.
XXV.1: 245, 274n.
XXV.3: 245, 274n.
XXVI.4: 254, 255, 281n.
XXVII.5: 214, 227n.
XXXI.2: 149, 191n.
GCS 3.
Hom. in Jer.
I.7: 127, 176n.
V.8: 77, 84n.
VIII.8: 116, 166n.
VIII.9: 116, 166n.
IX.1: 37, 53n, 233, 267n.
X2: 210, 225n.
XIV.5: 138, 183n.
XIV.6: 138, 183n.
XIV.7: 119, 169n.
XIV.9: 116, 167n.
XIV.10: 127, 176n.
XV.4: 138, 183n.
XV.6: 48, 64n, 249, 250, 278n.
XVI.2: 51, 65n.
XIX.1: 44, 59n.

Frag. in Jer.
10: 145, 190n.
16: 90, 98n.
17: 74, 83n.
18: 12, 29n.
19: 246, 275n.
20: 213, 226n.
23: 246, 275n.
25: 243, 273n.
52: 90, 98n.
68: 112, 165n.
Frag. in Lam.
VII: 134, 180n.
VIII: 11, 28n.
XLVI: 5, 20n, 254, 281n.
LIII: 131, 179n.
CI: 39, 54n.
CIV: 254, 281n.
CXVI: 37, 43, 53n, 58n.
CXXV: 17, 33n.
Hom. in I Sam.xxviii.3-25.
7: 11, 28n, 132, 179n.
8: 108, 138, 162n, 184n.
9: 45, 60n.
Frag. in I Sam.
IV: 90, 91, 99n.
X: 208, 224n.
Frag. in II Sam.XVII.
6, 21n.
Frag. in II Reg.XXI.
48, 63n.
GCS 4.
Comm. in Joh.
Bk.I.
6: 5, 20n, 157, 194n.
7: 39, 55n, 118, 126, 168n, 175n, 205, 223n.
10: 50, 64n, 69, 79n, 88, 96n.
15: 17, 33n.
16: 205, 261, 269n, 284n.

17: 45, 47, 48, 60n, 63n.
18: 125, 175n.
19: 4 (twice), 9 (twice), 19n, 20n, 22n, 23n.
20: 131, 179n, 243, 272n. 273n.
25: 71, 81n.
27: 73, 82n, 244, 273n.
28: 134, 136, 181n, 182n, 200, 201, 205, 214. 215, 221n, 222n, 228n, 244, 258, 273n, 283n.
32: 105, 129, 145, 159n, 178n, 189n, 190n.
34: 9, 23n, 47, 62n, 89, 97n.
35: 4, 20n, 48, 63n, 89, 97n, 118, 168n.
36: 91, 100n (twice).
37: 14, 31n, 126, 176n, 240, 241, 271n.
38: 37, 53n.
Bk.II.
1: 37, 53n.
2: 7, 8, 14, 21n, 22n, 31n, 45, 47, 60n, 63n.
3: 6, 7, 14, 21n (twice), 31n, 47, 62n, 87, 95n, 236, 237, 269n, 270n (twice).
6: 76, 83n, 236, 269n.
8: 75, 83n, 107, 125, 162n, 175n, 210, 225n.
10: 4, 19n.
11: 108, 162n.
14: 5, 8, 20n, 21n.
16: 243, 272n.
17: 70, 80n, 89, 96n, 97n, 122, 157, 172n, 195n.
18: 44, 45, 60n, 75, 83n, 89, 96n, 236, 237, 270n.
23: 69, 79n (twice).

26: 69, 79n, 137, 183n.
28: 74, 75, 83n.
31: 142, 185n.
34: 39, 40, 41, 55n, 56n.
35: 14, 30n.
Bk.VI.
3: 38, 54n.
4: 42, 57n, 58n.
6: 37, 38, 47, 48, 53n, 54n, 62n, 64n, 76, 83n.
11: 148, 191n.
20: 148, 191n.
30: 11, 27n, 130, 179n.
35: 151, 192n.
38: 11, 27n, 28n, 127, 172n, 248, 277n.
39: 12, 29n, 50, 64n.
49: 120, 127, 170n, 177n.
53: 106, 107, 161n.
55: 216, 228n.
57: 105n, 159n.
Bk.X.
6: 106, 118, 160n, 168n.
10: 233, 267n (twice).
23: 216, 228n.
24: 214, 227n.
25: 77, 84n.
27: 116, 167n.
28: 157, 194n, 245, 274n.
32: 88, 96n.
37: 109, 163n.
46: 74, 83n, 116, 166n.
Bk. XIII.
1: 203, 222n.
3: 233, 267n.
20: 240, 247, 271n, 275n.
24: 147, 148, 149, 191 (twice).
25: 50, 64n, 65n.
34: 73, 81n.
36: 110, 163n.

37: 73, 98n, 247, 276n.
43: 215, 216, 228n.
44: 41, 42, 57n.
46: 42, 57n.
47: 43, 58n, 157, 194n.
48: 43, 58n (twice), 157, 195n.
Bk.XIX.
2: 107, 161n.
3: 41, 57n.
4: 264, 286n.
5: 42, 43, 58n.
6: 234, 249, 250, 268n, 278n (twice).
10: 116, 167n.
11: 238, 270n.
14: 234, 269n.
16: 121, 170n.
22: 9, 23 (twice), 142, 185n.
Bk.XX.
1: 3, 19n.
2: 214, 215, 228n.
5: 87, 95n.
7: 261, 284n.
11: 106, 107, 161n (twice), 162n.
12: 37, 39, 40, 53n, 55n.
18: 12, 29n, 108, 162n.
19: 136, 152, 182n, 186n.
20: 15, 32n.
22: 146, 190n.
27: 47, 62n.
29: 46, 62n.
30: 212, 226n.
36: 106, 160n.
37: 106, 160n.
38: 77, 84n (twice).
42: 37, 53n.
44: 75, 76, 83n, 109, 163n.
Bk.XXVIII.
6: 112, 165n.

12: 109, 116, 163n, 167n.
18: 107, 118, 161n, 168n.
19: 105, 106, 160n.
23: 120, 170n (twice).
24: 37, 53n.
  Bk.XXXII.
3: 105, 106, 160n, 251, 279n.
4: 237, 270n.
9: 205, 223n.
18: 47, 62n, 127, 144, 176n, 188n.
24: 72, 81n.
25: 107, 161n, 201, 202, 221n.
27: 71, 80n.
28: 7, 8, 21n, 73, 74, 81n, 82n (twice), 199, 221n.
29: 75, 83n.
30: 260, 284n.
  Frag. in Joh.
I: 4, 5, 9, 20n (twice), 23n, 105, 159n.
II: 13, 29n, 46, 62n.
VI: 70, 80n.
IX: 12, 29n, 39, 55n.
X: 5, 20n.
XI: 38, 54n.
XII: 38, 53n.
XIII: 73, 82n.
XVII: 70, 80n.
XVIII: 128, 175n.
XX: 108, 109, 163n.
XXVI: 77, 84n.
XXX: 10, 27n.
XXXIII: 119, 170n.
XXXIV: 71, 81n.
XL: 123, 173n.
XLIV: 88, 96n.
XLVI: 37, 39, 53n, 55n.
XLVIII: 46, 61n.
L: 88, 96n, 251, 279n.

LI: 91, 99n.
LII: 119, 120, 170n.
LIII: 116, 117, 167n.
LV: 214, 227n.
LIX: 120, 121, 170n.
LXIX: 4, 19n.
LXXI: 238, 271n.
LXXIII: 238, 270n, 271n.
LXXV: 120, 170n.
LXXXI: 119, 170n.
LXXXII: 124, 174n.
LXXXIII: 119, 170n.
LXXXIV: 132, 179n.
LXXXVII: 259, 260, 283n (twice).
LXXXVIII: 138, 184n.
XCIII: 240, 271n.
XCIV: 72, 81n.
CVIII: 14, 15, 31n.
CIX: 13, 29n.
CXI: 5, 20n.
CXII: 71, 81n.
CXVII: 70, 80n.
CXVIII: 87, 95n.
CXX: 112, 113, 165n.
CXXVII: 5, 20n, 88, 96n.
CXXXVII: 71, 81n.
CXXXIX: 259, 260, 283n.
  GCS 5.
  De Princ.
  Bk.I.
Pref.1: 39, 54n.
Pref.4: 4, 5, 20n.
1.1: 69, 80n.
2.1: 105, 159n.
2.3: 9, 22n, 37, 53n.
2.4: 69, 80n.
2.6: 47, 48, 63n, 74, 82n, 110, 164n.
2.7: 69, 80n, 118, 119, 169n.

2.8: 46, 62n, 117, 118, 119, 167n, 169n.
2.10: 6, 9, 21n, 23n (twice), 255, 256, 281n, 282n.
2.13: 50, 64n.
3.5: 14, 30n.
3.6: 3, 14, 19n, 31n (twice).
3.8: 92, 100n.
4.3-5: 9, 23n.
5.2: 242, 272n.
5.3: 88, 96n.
5.5: 88, 96n.
6.1: 255, 281n.
6.2: 88, 96n, 258, 283n.
7.1: 4, 20n.
7.5: 235, 263, 269n, 285n.
8.3: 88, 89, 96n (twice).

Bk.II.

1.3: 258, 283n.
1.5: 10, 11, 27n.
2.1: 8, 21n.
4.3: 51, 65n.
5.3: 89, 97n.
6.1: 119, 169n.
6.2: 137, 140, 141, 182n, 185n.
6.3: 48, 64n, 128, 131, 136, 141, 152, 178n, 179n, 182n, 185n, 192n.
6.4: 136, 182n, 199, 200, 221n (twice).
6.5: 106, 160n.
6.6: 118, 169n.
6.7: 117, 168n.
7.3: 48, 64n.
8.1: 131, 179n.
8.2: 131, 179n.
8.3: 131, 135, 179n, 181n.
8.4: 138, 139, 184n.
8.5: 12, 13, 29n, 139, 184n.
9.2: 49, 64n, 249, 277n.

9.4: 49, 64n, 248, 276n.
9.5: 49, 64n.
9.6: 49, 64n (thrice), 248, 277n.
9.7: 135, 142, 181n, 185n.
9.8: 49, 64n.
10.7: 133, 145, 180 (twice), 189n.
11.3: 247, 275n.
11.4: 156, 194n.
11.6: 123, 173n.
11.7: 263, 285n.

Bk.III.

3.1 92, 100n.
3.2: 106, 161n.
4: 143, 187n.
4.2: 134, 144, 180n (twice), 187n, 188n.
4.3: 134, 144, 180n, 188n.
4.5: 144, 187n.
5.4: 9, 23n, 142, 185n.
5.5: 142, 185n, 186n.
5.6: 76, 84n, 105, 106, 159n, 253, 280n.
5.7: 76, 84n, 253, 280n, 281n.
5.8: 255, 256, 281n, 282n.
6.1: 248, 249, 263, 277n, 285n.
6.2: 249, 277n.
6.3: 249, 277n (twice).
6.5: 255, 281n.
6.9: 257, 282n.

Bk.IV.

1.5: 137, 182n.
1.6: 157, 194n.
2.2: 157, 194n.
2.4: 157, 195n.
2.7: 37, 53n, 118, 168n.
3.7: 8, 22n.
3.12: 243, 273n.
3.13: 117, 118, 167n, 168n.

3.14: 74, 83n.
4.1: 11, 14, 15, 27n, 31n (twice).
4.2: 48, 64n.
4.3: 10, 26n, 124, 173n.
4.4: 48, 64n, 130, 138, 139, 178n, 184n, 200, 221n.
4.5: 48, 64n, 130, 178n.
4.8: 48, 64n, 74, 82n.
4.9: 48, 64n.
4.10: 89, 97n.
Jerome, *Ep. ad Avitum* 12: 118, 168n.
Justinian, *Ep. ad Mennam,* Mansi IX.489B, 525, 528: 10, 26n.
GCS 6.
Hom. in Exod.
I.5: 4, 19n.
III.1: 37, 53n.
VI.1: 117, 167n.
VI.2: 8, 22n, 45, 60n.
VI.5: 46, 62n.
VI.9: 8, 22n.
VI.12: 115, 165n.
VII.8: 214, 227n.
VIII.2: 46, 62n.
VIII.3: 12, 29n.
VIII.4: 8, 22n.
VIII.5: 8, 22n.
VIII.6: 48, 64n.
X.4: 8, 22n.
XI.2: 210, 225n.
XI.6: 76n, 83n.
XII.3: 51, 65n.
XII.4: 215, 228n.
Hom. In Lev.
I.1: 157, 194n.
I.3: 208, 224n.
II.2: 147, 190n.
III.1: 105, 159n.
III.3: 213, 226n.

IV.6: 206, 207, 223n.
V.12: 235, 269n.
VII.2: 115, 165n, 253, 280n.
VIII.1: 116, 166n.
IX.5: 123, 173n, 218, 229n.
IX.11: 148, 191n.
XII.2: 126, 127, 176n.
XII.3: 148, 191n.
XII.5: 123, 173n.
XIII.2: 70, 80n.
XIII.3: 213, 226n.
XVI.2: 214, 228n.
XVI.5: 92, 101n.
XVI.7: 245, 274n.
GCS 7.
Hom. in Num.
III.2: 11, 27n.
III.3: 48, 64n.
VI.3: 152, 192n.
VII.5: 51, 65n.
VIII.1: 77, 84n.
IX.4: 157, 194n.
IX.5: 116, 130, 138, 139, 167n, 178n, 184n.
IX.9: 91, 100n.
XI.2: 235, 269n.
XI.4: 235, 269n.
XI.5: 235, 269n.
XI.6: 246, 275n.
XI.8: 87, 95n.
XII.1: 44, 59n, 69, 79n.
XII.2: 4, 20n, 256, 282n.
XII.4: 4, 19n, 69, 79n, 200, 221n.
XIII.1: 200, 221n.
XIII.8: 122, 171n.
XIV.4: 73, 82n, 244, 273n.
XVI.6: 251, 260, 279n, 283n.
XVI.9: 214, 227n.
XVII.5: 203, 222n.

XVII.6: 91, 100n, 109, 110,
    163n, 234, 251, 269n,
    279n.
XVIII.2: 74, 83n.
XVIII.4: 152, 192n.
XIX.3: 51, 65n.
XX.2: 48, 51, 63n, 65n, 69,
    79n.
XX.3: 233, 267n.
XXIII.4: 12, 29n, 69, 79n.
XXIII.6: 246, 275n.
XXIV.1: 105, 113, 159n, 165n.
XXIV.2: 6, 21n.
XXV.6: 216, 229n.
XXVII.1: 214, 227n.
XXVII.2: 8, 22n.
XXVII.3: 105, 159n.
XXVII.5,6: 69, 79n, 80n.
XXVII.12: 117, 167n.
XXVIII.2: 260, 283n.
XXVIII.3: 260, 283n.
XXVIII.4: 256, 260, 282n, 283n.
  Hom. in Jos.
II.2: 105, 159n.
III.2: 44, 59n.
III.5: 51, 65n.
V.3: 122, 172n.
VI.1: 245, 246, 275n.
VI.2: 46, 47, 62n.
VII.7: 123, 173n.
VIII.2: 17, 32n.
VIII.4: 117, 167n, 255, 281n.
VIII.6: 255, 281n.
IX.2: 235, 269n.
IX.9: 214, 227n.
XI.3: 203, 222n.
XIII.1: 245, 246, 275n.
XIII.4: 245, 246, 275n.
XIV.2: 256, 282n.
XV.1: 245, 246, 275n.

XVI.3: 255, 281n.
XVII.1: 70, 80n.
XVII.2: 70, 80n, 260, 283n.
XVII.3: 17, 32n.
XXIV.3: 247, 275n.
XXVI.2: 115, 166n.
  Hom. in Jud.
I.1: 71, 81n.
II.4: 91, 99n.
III.2: 90, 99n.
IV.4: 145, 189n.
V.6: 214, 228n.
VI.2: 245, 274n.
VI.3: 245, 274n.
VI.4: 46, 62n.
  GCS 8.
  Hom. in I Reg.
I.5: 244, 273n.
I.11: 87, 88, 95n.
  Hom. in Cant.
I.2: 200, 221n.
I.3: 200, 221n.
I.4: 118, 169n.
II.3: 115, 116, 165n, 166n, 167n.
  Comm. in Cant.
  Prol.
70: 77, 84n.
71: 8, 21n.
74: 73, 82n.
83: 257, 282n.
85: 117, 118, 176n.
86: 257, 282n.
  Bk.1.
91: 87, 95n.
92: 3, 19n.
98, 99, 100: 200, 221n.
102: 107, 118, 162n, 168n.
103, 104: 214, 227n.
107, 108: 118, 169n.
111: 127, 176n.

Bk.II.
135: 244, 273n.
138: 244, 273n.
152: 121, 171n.
153: 106, 121, 161n, 171n.
157, 158: 41, 57n.
162: 109, 110, 163n.
164: 127, 176n.
165: 245, 247, 257, 258, 274n, 275n, 283n.
169: 115, 165n.
Bk.III.
175: 125, 174n.
180: 48, 63n, 64n.
193, 194: 214, 227n.
206: 115, 127, 165n, 176n.
208: 17, 32n.
215: 73, 82n.
222: 105, 159n.
227: 245, 274n.
231: 51, 65n.
Hom. in Is.
I.2: 203, 222n.
I.5: 37, 51, 53n, 65 n.
III.3: 73, 81n.
IV.2: 249, 250, 278n.
IV.4: 110, 164n.
V.1: 203, 204, 222n.
VI.1: 116, 166n.
Hom. in Ezek.
I.5: 138, 183n.
I.6: 108, 163n.
I.9: 48, 63n.
I.10: 140, 185n.
IV.5: 48, 63n.
VI.6: 142, 143, 186n, 187n.
IX.1: 48, 63n.
IX.3: 70, 80n.
XIII.2: 48, 63n.
XIV.2,3: 11, 164n.

GCS 9.
Hom. in Luc.
III: 27, 177n.
VIII: 47, 63n.
XI: 105, 159n.
XIV: 216, 229n.
XXV: 50, 64n.
XXIX: 108, 163n.
Frag. in Luc.
16: 45, 60n.
24: 11, 28n.
25: 203, 222n.
43: 4, 20n.
59: 108, 162n.
77: 107, 108, 162n.
92: 45, 60n.
96: 109, 117, 163n, 167n.
97: 74, 83n.
100: 71, 81n.
113: 234, 250, 269n, 278n.
121: 132, 179n.
122: 70, 80n.
123: 70, 80n.
127: 74, 83n.
139: 240, 271n.
140: 116, 128, 167n, 177n.
151: 105, 106, 160n.
155: 243, 273n.
162: 41, 42, 56n, 57n.
163: 3, 19n.
165: 40, 41, 44, 56n, 59n.
171: 157, 195n.
172: 45, 61n.
174: 48, 64n.
175: 45, 60n.
186: 132, 179n.
195: 132, 179n.
204: 158, 196n.
210: 105, 159n.
214: 254, 281n.

253: 121, 171n.
255: 125, 126, 175n.
257: 239, 271n.
   GCS 10.
   Comm. in Matt.
   Bk.X.
5,6: 205, 223n.
9: 70, 80n.
14: 119, 170n, 245, 274n.
23: 120, 170n.
   Bk.XI.
2: 211, 212, 226n (twice).
4: 260, 284n.
5: 212, 226n.
6: 113, 165n.
12: 157, 158, 196n.
17: 116, 167n, 214, 227n, 228n.
   Bk.XII.
2: 109, 163n.
4: 145, 157, 189n, 196n.
5: 157, 194n.
6: 116, 166n.
9: 233, 267n.
14: 92, 101n.
15: 210, 211, 225n (twice).
17: 237, 270n.
18: 237, 238, 270n (twice).
19: 208, 224n, 237, 270n.
20: 208, 224n.
24: 245, 273n.
29: 127, 277n.
30: 126, 176n.
31: 214, 228n.
32: 128, 177n.
36: 125, 174n.
37: 206, 223n.
39: 128, 177n.
41: 125, 174n.
42: 43, 58n.

43: 51, 65n.
   Bk.XIII.
8: 105, 106, 160n.
17: 142, 186n.
18: 8, 22n, 108, 163n.
26: 127, 176n.
   Bk.XIV.
3: 146, 147, 190n.
7: 129, 178n.
11: 11, 27n.
13: 8, 22n.
17: 45, 60n.
18: 157, 194n.
   Bk.XV.
6: 214, 228n.
10: 50, 65n.
11: 50, 64n, 90, 99n.
12: 157, 195n.
24: 130, 131, 179n.
   Bk.XVI.
3: 70, 80n.
5: 113, 165n.
8: 105, 151, 159n, 192n.
10: 42, 57n.
16: 244, 273n.
17: 211, 226n.
19: 129, 178n.
21: 90, 99n, 138, 184n.
29: 46, 62n.
   Bk.XVII.
2: 109, 163n.
5: 214, 215, 228n.
14: 44, 60n.
17: 91, 100n.
19: 47, 62n, 90, 99n.
20: 91, 100n.
32: 38, 47, 53n, 62n.
36: 40, 56n, 250, 278n.

GCS 11.
Matt. Comm. Series
8: 250, 257, 279n, 282n.
28: 3, 19n, 37, 53n.
32: 127, 128, 177n, 236, 250, 269n, 278n.
33: 75, 83n, 109, 163n.
35: 128, 178n, 239, 240, 271n.
45: 5, 20n.
50: 42, 57n, 116, 166n, 167n.
55: 123, 126, 127, 173n, 176n, 253, 281n.
62: 76, 83n.
65: 124, 174n, 236, 269n.
70: 116, 167n.
73: 137, 183n.
75: 105, 106, 160n.
83: 124, 174n.
85: 250, 278n.
87: 71, 81n.
90: 137, 138, 183n.
91: 138, 184n.
92: 138, 184n, 237, 270n.
93: 243, 272n.
95: 111, 165n.
99: 109, 163n.
100: 128, 178n.
102: 120, 170n.
111: 47, 62n.
112: 109, 163n.
113: 109, 163n.
118: 76, 84n.
121: 69, 79n.
126: 137, 182n.
130: 217, 229n.
132: 109, 163n.
135; 118, 168n.
GCS 12.
Frag. ex Tom. I Matt. Comm.
2: 120, 170n.

Frag. in Matt.
3: 40, 41, 56n.
5: 47, 62n.
8: 120, 170n.
11: 105, 116, 159n, 166n.
12: 4, 19n.
14: 116, 166n.
38: 88, 96n.
43: 70, 80n.
52: 105, 159n.
54: 125, 175n.
65: 120, 170n.
67: 5, 20n.
70: 119, 170n.
71: 234, 268n.
99: 157, 195n.
122: 246, 275n.
125: 132, 179n.
138: 240, 271n.
141: 89, 97n.
154: 109, 163n.
163: 9, 23n.
187: 125, 132, 174n, 179n.
188: 120, 170n.
191: 38, 53n.
192: 45, 60n.
193: 149, 191n.
202: 76, 83n.
214: 145, 189n.
218: 46, 62n.
227: 243, 272n.
230: 38, 53n.
235: 121, 122, 171n.
239: 112, 165n.
242: 5, 6, 20n.
243: 47, 62n.
265: 132, 179n.
274: 145, 189n.
288: 130, 178n.
321: 112, 165n.

338: 124, 174n.
339: 109, 163n.
344: 119, 170n.
357: 128, 177n, 178n.
365: 51, 65n.
396: 5, 6, 20n, 21n.
401: 40, 55n.
404: 10, 27n.
413: 5, 20n.
430: 214, 227n.
433: 214, 227n.
460: 38, 39, 54n.
464: 128, 176n.
504: 127, 128, 174n.
526: 39, 54n.
530: 126, 127, 165n.
531: 125, 126, 159n.
551: 204, 222n.
552: 204, 222n.
558: 138, 184n.
560: 149, 191n.
562: 151, 192n.
571: 204, 222n.
  Hom. in Matt.
I.239: 108, 162n.
I.240: 108, 116, 123, 162n, 166n, 173n.
I.242: 130, 178n.
I.243: 105, 159n.
II.247: 39, 54n.
II.248: 116, 166n.
II.251: 39, 54n, 119, 124, 170n, 174n.
II.257: 120, 170n.
III.258: 6, 21n.
III.259: 6, 21n, 120, 170n.
III.261: 116, 166n, 167n.
IV.268: 4, 20n.

PG XII.
  Comm. in Gen. Tom. I. Frag.
7, 21n.
  Ex Comm. in Ex.
89, 90, 97n.
  Sel. in Num.
XXIII.1: 244, 273n.
XXIV.8: 47, 62n.
  Sel. in Jos.
V.2: 115, 166n.
  Sel. in I Reg.
47, 62n.
  Hom. in Reg.
74, 82n.
  Frag. in Apol. of Pamph.
71, 81n.
  Sel. in Gen.
VI.7: 255, 281n.
XXII.6: 105, 159n.
XXXII.24, 28, 30: 39, 54n.
XLIX.9: 90, 98n.
  Sel. in Ps.
I.1: 129, 178n.
I.2: 8, 21n.
I.3: 108, 162n, 213, 226n.
II.1,2: 251, 279n.
II.8: 203, 222n.
II.9: 254, 281n.
III.2,3: 8, 22n.
III.8: 88, 96n, 109, 163n.
IV.1: 256, 282n.
IV.2: 88, 96n, 109, 163n.
IV.3: 47, 62n, 243, 272n.
IV.6: 245, 273n.
IV.9,10: 75, 83n, 116, 167n.
V.7: 47, 62n.
VII.7: 254, 281n.
IX.2,3: 74, 83n.
IX.5: 110, 164n.
XII.1: 47, 62n.

XV.3: 110, 164n.
XV.5: 204, 222n.
XVI.1: 88, 96n.
XVI.8: 5, 20n.
XVII.5,6: 138, 184n.
XVII.12: 45, 60n.
XVII.32: 45, 60n.
XVII.36: 5, 20n.
XVIII.6: 110, 164n.
XXI.2: 120, 170n.
XXI.10: 109, 163n, 132, 179n.
XXII.4: 254, 281n.
XXII.5: 243, 272 (thrice).
XXIII.6: 47, 62n.
XXIII.10: 6, 21n.
XXIV.16: 48, 63n.
XXVI.5: 110, 164n.
XXVII.2: 110, 164n.
XXIX.2: 240, 271n.
XXIX.5: 50, 64n.
XXIX.6: 3, 19n.
XXIX.7: 141, 142, 185n.
XXIX.8: 9, 23n, 115, 167n.
XXXIII.2: 6, 32n.
XXXV.10: 234, 268n.
XL.6: 134, 180n.
XLI.10: 142, 143, 187n.
XLII.3: 129, 178n.
XLIII.3: 5, 20n.
XLIV.5: 5, 20n.
XLIV.7: 254, 281n.
XLVI.9: 126, 127, 164n.
XLVII.2: 45, 61n.
XLVII.11: 5, 20n.
XLIX.1: 37, 53n.
XLIX.2: 5, 20n.
LIV.4: 128, 129, 184n.
LV.2: 127, 168n.
LXI.2: 138, 184n, 253, 254, 280n, 281n.

LXIV.3: 131, 179n.
LXIV.5: 110, 164n.
LXVII.5: 116, 167n.
LXVII.9: 241, 242, 271n.
LXVIII.3: 137, 183n.
LXX.1: 120, 170n.
LXX.18: 5, 20n.
LXXIII.7: 132, 179n.
LXXIV.3: 6, 21n.
LXXVI.11: 117, 168n.
LXXVI.14: 7, 21n.
LXXXVIII.32: 110, 164n.
XC.10: 91, 100n.
XCVIII.6: 203, 204, 222n.
CI.25: 70, 71, 80n.
CIV.15: 47, 62n.
CXVII.24: 70, 71, 80n, 81n.
CXVII.27: 126, 175n.
CXVIII.32: 245, 274n.
CXVIII.97: 71, 72, 81n.
CXVIII.117: 157, 196n.
CXVIII.164: 71, 81n.
CXIX.5: 71, 81n.
CXXVI.1: 237, 270n.
CXXXV.3: 45, 61n.
CXXXV.4: 6, 21n.
CXLIV.20: 242, 272n.
CXLV.10: 203, 222n.
Hom. in Ps.
XXXVI.I.2: 246, 275n.
XXXVI.I.4: 246, 275n.
XXXVI.II.1: 253, 280n.
XXXVI.II.4: 88, 96n.
XXXVI.II.5: 240, 271n.
XXXVI.III.3: 37, 53n.
XXXVI.III.9: 70, 71, 75, 80n, 83n.
XXXVI.IV.1: 51, 65n.
XXXVI.IV.3: 92, 101n.
XXXVI.V.4: 107, 162n.

XXXVI.V.5: 3, 4, 19n.
XXXVII.I.2: 105, 106, 160n.
XXXVIII.I.8: 70, 71, 80n.
XXXVIII.I.10: 3, 19n.
XXXVIII.II.2: 117, 168n.
    PG XIII.
    Excerpt. in Cant.
V.6: 211, 226n.
VI.1: 247, 275n.
VI.4: 128, 177n.
VI.7: 129, 178n.
    Comm. in Ezek.
I.3: 46, 62n.
III.12: 110, 164n.
IV.9: 246, 275n.
VII.3: 91, 100n.
VII.4: 90, 98n.
VII.10: 91, 100n.
VIII.18: 90, 98n.
XXX.4: 242, 272n.
    Sel. in Ezek.
VII.27: 142, 143, 187n.
XIV.4: 147, 190n.
    Frag. in Ezek.
XVI.8: 142, 143, 186n, 187n.
    PG XIV.
    Comm. in Rom.
    Bk.I.
1: 263, 285n.
4: 118, 151, 152, 168n, 192n.
6: 201, 221n.
10: 145, 189n.
13: 206, 223n.
16: 91, 99n.
17: 146, 190n.
    Bk.II.
5: 43, 48, 58n, 64n.
10: 146, 189n.
14: 46, 62n, 237, 238, 270n.

    Bk.III.
1: 47, 62n.
2: 87, 88, 95n, 96n.
4: 147, 148, 191n.
6: 88, 96n.
8: 106, 107, 160n, 161n.
    Bk.IV.
4: 40, 55n.
5: 4, 19n.
6: 41, 57n.
7: 41, 57n.
8: 117, 118, 168n.
9: 47, 62n.
    Bk.V.
2: 105, 159n.
3: 252, 253, 280n.
6: 145, 190n.
8: 72, 81n.
    Bk.VI.
1: 144, 145, 189n.
3: 117, 168n.
5: 259, 283n.
6: 145, 190n.
7: 39, 55n.
9: 145, 189n.
12: 108, 162n.
    Bk.VII.
1: 47, 62n.
3: 144, 189n.
4: 117, 168n.
5: 242, 253, 272n, 280n.
7: 106, 127, 161n, 177n.
9: 5, 20n, 105, 106, 160n.
12: 145, 147, 189n, 191n.
13: 5, 20n.
16: 90, 97n.
    Bk.VIII.
1: 211, 225n.
2: 11, 28n, 123, 173n.
5: 10, 14, 27n, 31n, 76, 83n,

     235, 269n.
9:   255, 281n.
12: 90, 99n.
     Bk.IX.
1:   91, 99n.
2:   3, 19n.
25: 145, 189n.
32: 71, 81n.
36: 214, 228n.
39: 251, 279n.
41: 259, 283n.
     Bk.X.
43: 42, 43, 58n (twice), 205, 223n.

Frag. in Gal.
45, 60n, 118, 168n.

Frag. in Eph.
149, 191n.

Frag. in Col.
38, 53n.

Frag. in I Thess.
42, 57n.

Frag. in Heb.
15, 32n.

JTS 3.
Frag. in Eph.
I.2-14: 4, 19n.
I.12-18: 39, 54n.
II.2-7: 4, 19n.
IX.90-95: 76, 84n.
IX.103-108: 252, 253, 280n.
IX.113-120: 204, 222n.
XV.15-22: 246, 275n.
XVII.5,6: 40, 56n.
XIX: 132, 133, 179n.
XXI.15-18: 145, 146, 190n.
XXII.9-14: 91, 99n.
XXVI.13-18: 147, 190n.
XXXIII.24, 25: 149, 191n.

JTS 9.
Frag. in I Cor.
IX.6-12: 205, 223n.
X.2-5: 90, 98n.
X.6-10: 149, 191n.
XII.2-18: 214, 227n.
XVII.4-6: 147, 191n.
XVIII.6-10: 205, 223n.
XXIV. 2, 3, 9, 11-13, 16-18: 146, 190n.
XXXV.12, 13: 149, 191n.
XXIX.57-59: 131, 179n.

JTS 13.
Frag. in Rom.
I.38-41: 128, 129, 178n.
XI.1-8: 38, 54n.
XV.3-5: 76, 83n.
XXV.56-58: 3, 4, 19n.
XXXI.5-11: 144, 188n.
XXXI.6-11: 146, 147, 190n.
XXXI.16-18: 144, 145, 146, 189n, 190n.
XXXI.19-28: 50, 55n.
XXXV.13: 157, 194n.
XXXVI.32, 33: 157, 194n.
XXXVI.63-67: 157, 194n.
XXXVI.75-80: 42, 58n.
LII.7-17: 147, 191n.

Philocal.JAR.
Hom. in Jer.XXXIX.
3, 19n, 45, 60n.

Comm. in Ps. I.
11, 28n.

Comm. in Ps. L.
157, 195n.

Comm. in Oseam.
262, 284n.

Ep. ad Greg.
234, 169n.

Comm. II in Gen.
50, 64n.
Comm. III in Gen.
7, 8, 21n, 22n.
Comm. I in Rom.
106, 161n, 199, 221n.
Convs. with Heracl.
2.11-13: 7, 21n.
2.26,27: 11, 27n.
3.12-20: 131, 132, 179n.
3.12-4.9: 7, 21n.
4.24-27: 7, 21n.
6.20-8.17: 150, 151, 192n.
6.20-7.7: 138, 139, 184n.
8.5-17: 216, 229n.
14.8-16: 244, 273n.
17.2-6: 157, 195n.
23.2-7: 149, 191n.
27.4-8: 118, 168n.
27.14-28.6: 157, 195n.
Cadiou, *Frag. in Ps.*
II.6a: 203, 222n.
II.8a: 203, 222n.
II.12c: 90, 98n.
XLII.2: 47, 62n.
XLIV.2: 74, 83n.
XLIV.7: 45, 61n.
C.8: 71, 81n.
CV.2: 37, 53n.
CV.4: 90, 98n.
CV.32, 33: 148, 191n.
CIX.2b: 254, 281n.
CXIII.21: 211, 226n.
CXVIII.29: 90, 98n.
CXVIII.44a: 157, 195n.
CXVIII.65: 90, 98n.
CXVIII.74: 47, 63n.
CXVIII.81: 134, 181n.
CXVIII.91a: 71, 81n.
CXVIII.160: 238, 239, 271n.

CXVIII.175a: 4, 19n.
CXXIV.2: 11, 28n.
CXLI.8: 146, 190n.
Pitra A.S.II.
354: 5, 20n.
356: 89, 90, 97n.
382: 71, 81n.
383: 74, 83n.
384: 6, 21n.
447: 203, 222n.
448: 157, 195n.
449: 90, 98n.
458: 145, 190n.
464: 254, 281n.
471: 203, 222n.
474: 157, 195n.
479: 147, 191n.
480: 243, 272n.
482: 6, 21n.
Pitra A.S.III.
13: 90, 98n.
14: 90, 98n.
32: 146, 190n.
34: 3, 4, 19n.
38: 89, 90, 97n.
40: 199, 221n.
41: 199, 221n.
46: 129, 178n.
52: 148, 191n.
62: 146, 190n.
79: 90, 99n.
86: 138, 184n.
99: 5, 20n.
104: 76, 84n.
108: 5, 20n.
117: 157, 195n.
119: 146, 190n.
126, 127: 146, 190n.
130: 91, 99n.
134: 5, 20n.

136: 146, 147, 190n.
140: 47, 62n.
141: 47, 62n.
160: 75, 83n.
167: 4, 20n.
169: 90, 98n.
173: 129, 178n.
181: 243, 272n.
195: 117, 167n.
199: 8, 22n.
210: 157, 194n.
215: 90, 91, 99n.
226: 108, 162n.
227: 202, 203, 222n.
228: 202, 203, 222n.
245: 127, 177n.

265: 90, 98n.
268: 76, 84n.
274: 90, 98n.
290: 157, 195n.
291: 157, 195n.
292: 72, 73, 81n.
301: 76, 84n.
302: 76, 84n.
330: 129, 178n.
336: 11, 28n.
344: 149, 191n.
348: 40, 41, 56n.
539: 246, 275n.
540: 70, 71, 81n.
545: 243, 273n.

INDEX OF AUTHORS REFERRED TO

Aeby G., 24n, 56, 63n, 82n (twice), 135, 163n, 174n (twice), 186n, 258, 274n, 283n (twice).
Armantage J., 153, 193n (6 times).
Balas D., 23n, 31n, 46, 61n (twice), 79n, 96n, 100n.
Balthasar H. von, 54n, 224n, 265, 286n.
Bardy G., 224n.
Barnes E.W., 49, 50, 64n.
Bertrand F., 223n, 227n, 238, 270n (twice).
Beskow P., 274n, 275n, 282n.
Boon R., 24n, 80n, 161n, 181n, 276n.
Burke G., 23n, 63n, 150, 192n (thrice), 276n.
Cadiou R., 96n, 179n, 186n, 208, 209 (twice), 221n, 224n (twice), 270n, 277n, 282n.
Cadoux C.J., 165n, 193n, 241, 271n.
Casel O., 93, 101n, 225n.
Cornelis H., 23n, 99n, 185n, 192n, 281n.
Crouzel H.
  L'Image, 19n, 27n, 53n, 60n, 61n, 62n (twice), 63n, 64n, 79n, 80n, 84n, 99n, 100n, 129, 132, 133, 160n, 161n (twice), 164n, 166n, 168n, 178n (twice), 179n, 180n (twice), 189n, 191n, 192n, 194n, 226n, 261, 262, 272n (twice), 273n, 276n, 284n.
  La Conn., 19n, 53n, 54n, 56n (twice), 58n (thrice), 59n, 60n, 63n, 79n, 80n (twice), 81n, 82n, 97n, 100n, 164n, 166n, 168n, 174n, 176n, 177n, 178n, 179n, 180n, 182n, 194n (twice), 195n, 207, 223n (twice), 226n, 227n, 228n, 261, 262, 269n, 270n, 275n, 278n, 284n.
  "O. devant l'Inc. et l'hist.", 125, 127, 176n (twice)., 187n, 225n, 284n.
D'Ales A., 61n, 107, 162n, 170n, 171n.
Danielou J., 167n, 194n (twice).
D'hôtel J.C., 95n, 154, 193n (thrice).
Dupuis J., 23n, 30n, 57n, 133 (twice), 150 (twice), 151, 160n, 161n, 163n, 168n, 179n (thrice), 180n (twice), 190n, 192n (thrice), 262, 284n.
Eichinger M., 162n, 171n, 172n, 177n, 179n, 181n, 185n (twice), 202, 207, 221n (twice), 223n, 226n, 284n.
Farrer A.M., 290n.
Faye, E. de, 28n (twice), 61n, 100n, 107, 162n, 170n, 171n, 176n, 209, 210, 223n, 225n, 283n, 284n, 286n.
Fitzgerald E., 27n, 37, 40, 53n (thrice), 55n (twice), 58n,

59n, 95n, 168n, 176n, 178n,
181n, 186n, 192n, 213,
221n, 223n, 226n (twice),
269n, 272n, 278n.
Franco R., 95n, 221, 233, 257,
258 (twice), 267n (twice),
274n (twice), 275n, 277n,
280n, 282n, 285n.
Gögler R., 175n, 195n.
Grillmeier A., 121, 125, 129,
170n, 171n (twice), 175n,
178n, 181n.
Gronau K., 98n, 277n.
Gross J., 270n, 284n.
Gruber G., 19n, 54n, 168n, 179n,
189n.
Hanson R.P.C., 126, 128, 172n,
177n, 178n, 212, 225n,
226n.
Harl M., 21n, 22n, 30n, 32, 53n
(twice), 54n, 56n, 58n, 65n,
66n, 79n, 81n, 95n (twice),
100n, 119, 122, 123, 124,
159n, 161n, 164n, 165n,
166n, 167n, 168n, 169n,
170n, 172n, 174n (thrice),
175n (twice), 176n (twice),
183n, 185n, 191n, 194n,
209, 212, 223n (twice),
224n, 226n, 228n (twice),
242, 262, 272n, 284n (twice).
Hirschberg M., 93, 98n, 101n,
174n, 175n, 188n, 215, 223n,
224n, 227n, 228n (twice),
273n.
Javierre A., 188n.
Kelber W., 30n, 95n, 96n, 161n,
173n, 174n, 177n, 185n,
202, 210, 221n, 222n, 225n,
226n, 274n, 278n, 284n.

Koch H., 24n, 49, 57n, 62n,
64n, 92, 98n, 100n (twice),
101n, 172n, 174n, 176n,
196n, 210, 223n, 250, 268n,
273n, 276n, 278n (twice),
283n, 285n.
Laeuchli S., 131 (twice), 169n,
179n.
Lebreton J., 57n, 175n, 176n,
209, 224n (thrice), 226n.
Lieske A., 23n, 24n, 28n, 31n,
47, 57n, 61n, 63n (twice),
129, 136, 160n, 164n
(twice), 178n, 179n, 180n,
182n, 183n, 201, 221n
(twice), 223n, 262, 271n
(twice), 274n, 276n, 284n
(twice).
Lomiento G., 165n, 212n, 226n,
227n, 273n.
Loofs F., 172n.
Lot-Borodine M., 65n, 66n,
188n, 224n, 225n, 228n.
Lowry C.W., 21n, 23n, 27n,
164n.
Lubac H. de, 39, 54n, 55n
(twice), 80n, 194n, 195n.
Macaulay W., 40, 55n, 152,
153, 161n, 193n.
Marcus W., 29n, 30n, 173n,
228n, 279n, 280n.
Maydieu J., 22n (twice), 24n,
47, 55n (twice), 59n, 60n
(twice), 63n, 66n, 73, 80n,
82n (thrice), 110, 164n,
269n.
Mersch E., 81n, 173n, 221n,
222n, 239, 271n, 280n.
Miura-Stange A., 125, 139, 174n
(thrice), 182n, 184n, 207,

223n.
Molland E., 56n, 57n, 58n, 167n, 168n (twice), 192n, 208, 224n, 225n, 239, 271n.
Mumm H.J., 83n, 174n, 188n, 192n.
Nemeshegyi P., 19n (thrice), 23n (twice), 31n, 58n, 61n, 62n (twice), 63n, 80n, 82n, 84n, 97n (twice), 135, 136 (twice), 139 (twice), 159n, 164n, 182n (4 times), 184n (twice), 227n, 262 (twice), 271n, 272n, 275n (twice), 280n, 284n (twice).
Nygren A., 27n, 28n, 92, 101n, 210, 224n, 225n, 228n.
Orbe A., 53n (twice), 54n (twice), 55n, 56n, 58n, 59n.
Pannenberg W., 26n, 143 (twice), 187n (twice), 199, 221n.
Pollard T.E., 155 (twice), 193n (twice).
Prat F., 31n, 82n, 122, 172n.
Primmer A., 98n, 99n (twice), 143, 159n, 162n, 185n, 187n (5 times), 210, 225n (twice).
Puech H., 224n, 282n.
Rahner H., 24n, 149, 159n, 180n (twice), 190n (twice), 192n, 274n, 275n, 276n, 277n, 284n.
Refoulé F., 136, 140, 175n, 182n (twice), 184n (twice), 193n, 199, 221n, 263, 285n (twice).
Rivière J., 159n.
Rossi G., 25n.
Rius-Camps J., 19n, 31n, 32n,

53n, 54n, 57n, 58n (twice), 59n, 60n (twice), 62n, 64n, 80n, 95n, 96n (twice), 97n (twice), 98n, 99n, 100n, 110, 133, 164n (twice), 168n, 175n, 180n, 193n, 194n (twice), 221n, 279n, 283n.
Rüsche F., 133n, 180n (twice), 188n.
Schendel E., 162n, 191n, 209, 221n (twice), 225n, 262, 273n, 278n, 280n, 281n, 285n (thrice).
Teichtweier G., 23n, 59n, 82n, 180n, 183n, 184n, 186n, 188n (thrice), 189n, 192n, 223n, 276n, 283n.
Temple W., 15, 27n, 69, 79n, 187n, 193n (twice).
Vagaggini C., 21n, 63n, 223n, 263, 264 (twice), 285n (twice), 286n (twice).
Vanstone W.H., 13, 14, 30n.
Verbeke G., 134, 180n (thrice), 195n.
Völker W., 60n, 62n, 97n, 111, 140, 161n, 165n (twice), 169n, 184n, 209, 224n (twice), 262, 271n, 276n, 277n, 278n, 282n, 283n, 285n.
Wiles M., 24n, 25n.
Wilken R.L., 155 (twice), 193n, 194n.
Wintersig A., 24n, 121, 171n, 177n, 182n, 192n, 210, 225n (twice).